The Caning of Senator Sumner

T. Lloyd Benson
Furman University

THOMSON

WADSWORTH

Australia • Canada • Mexico • Singapore • Spain • United Kingdom • United States

THOMSON

WADSWORTH

Publisher/Executive Editor: Clark Baxter
Assistant Editor: Julie Yardley
Editorial Assistant: Eno Sarris
Consulting Editor: John F. McClymer
Marketing Manager: Caroline Croley
Marketing Assistant: Mary Ho
Advertising Project Manager: Tami Strang
Project Manager, Editorial Production:
Catherine Morris

Print/Media Buyer: Rebecca Cross
Permissions Editor: Sarah Harkrader
Production Service: Shepherd, Inc.
Copy Editor: Francine Banwarth
Cover Designer: Preston Thomas
Cover Image: Library of Congress
Compositor: Shepherd, Inc.
Cover and Text Printer: Webcom

Printed in Canada
1 2 3 4 5 6 7 07 06 05 04 03

For more information about our products, contact us at:
Thomson Learning Academic Resource Center
1-800-423-0563

For permission to use material from this text, contact us by: **Phone: 1-800-730-2214**
Fax: 1-800-730-2215
Web: http://www.thomsonrights.com

Library of Congress Control Number:
ISBN: 0-15-506347-2

Wadsworth/Thomson Learning
10 Davis Drive
Belmont, CA 94002-3098
USA

Asia
Thomson Learning
5 Shenton Way #01-01
UIC Building
Singapore 068808

Australia/New Zealand
Thomson Learning
102 Dodds Street
Southbank, Victoria 3006
Australia

Canada
Nelson
1120 Birchmount Road
Toronto, Ontario M1K 5G4
Canada

Europe/Middle East/Africa
Thomson Learning
High Holborn House
50/51 Bedford Row
London WC1R 4LR
United Kingdom

Latin America
Thomson Learning
Seneca, 53
Colonia Polanco
11560 Mexico D.F.
Mexico

Spain/Portugal
Paraninfo
Calle/Magallanes, 25
28015 Madrid, Spain

For Vicki and Joshua

Contents

Preface   x

1   The Caning and Its Origins   1

Prologue: The Incident   1

    Majority Report on the Sumner Caning Incident   2

    Minority Report on the Summer Caning Incident   4

Senate Violence and the Transformation of Mid-century America   7

The Social Origins of an Abolitionist Senator   10

    The True Grandeur of Nations   13

The Personal World of Brooks and Butler   18

    Federal Writer's Project: Slave Narrative of Henry Ryan   19

    Runaway Slave Advertisement, Edgefield *Advertiser,* 4 May 1854   21

    Francis Wilkinson Pickens, General Directions as to the Treatment
        of Negroes (1839)   22

    Report of the South Carolina College Faculty on the Expulsion
        of Preston S. Brooks   26

    Speech by Preston Brooks on Nebraska and Kansas, March 15, 1854   28

The Personal Politics of the Nebraska Bill and Fugitive Slaves   33

    Appeal of the Independent Democrats   34

    Senator Douglas's Speech on the Nebraska Bill, 30 January 1854   36

    Nebraska in the Senate   41

    The Landmark of Freedom   42

    Senator Andrew Butler's Speech on the Nebraska Bill,
        24–25 February 1854   48

    Nebraska Bill Debates, 3 March 1854   54

    Sumner's Final Protest Against the Nebraska Bill and Remonstrances
        from the New England Clergy   56

    Senator Mason of Virginia Debates Sumner over Northern Religion
        and Politics   59

Sumner and Petitions for the Repeal of the Fugitive Slave Act   60

    The Fugitive Slave Case in Boston   60

    The Boston Riot—Charles Sumner   62

    Sumner's Speech on the Petition to Repeal the Fugitive Slave Act,
        26 June 1856   63

    Senator Butler's Reply to Sumner   65

Senator Mason's Reply to Sumner   67
Senator Clay Attacks Sumner   68
Sumner's Reply to Assailants and Oath to Support the Constitution 70
Senator Butler's Final Response   77
The Know-Nothing Interlude   84
Notes   87

2   The Crime and the Caning   94
Introduction: The Territorial Crisis   94
"The Crime Against Kansas:" Sumner's Introductory Remarks   96
    The Crime Against Kansas: The Apologies for the Crime:
    The True Remedy   97
The Crime Against Kansas, Section One   100
The Crime Against Kansas, Section Two: The Apologies
    (19–20 May 1856)   108
The Crime Against Kansas, Section Three: The Remedies
    (20 May 1856)   112
The Crime Against Kansas: Concluding Remarks (20 May 1856)   116
Reaction from the Senate   121
    Response from Democratic Senator Lewis Cass, of Michigan   122
    Response from Stephen A. Douglas   123
    Response from Democratic Senator James Mason, of Virginia   127
    Sumner's Response   129
The Attack: Firsthand Accounts   131
    Preston Brooks Describes the Incident to His Brother   131
    Apology of Preston Brooks to the Senate   135
    Testimony of Charles Sumner   136
    Testimony of New York Times Reporter James W. Simonton   138
    Testimony of Democratic Rep. Henry A. Edmundson of Virginia   139
    Speech of Hon. A. P. Butler, 12 June 1856   141
The Assault: Legislative Debate   146
    Speech of Massachusetts Senator Henry Wilson, 23 May 1856   147
    Massachusetts Legislative Resolves Concerning the Recent Assault
        upon the Honorable Charles Sumner at Washington   148
    Resignation Speech of Preston Brooks, 14 July 1856   149
Notes   154

3   Coming to Terms with the Caning   157
Editorial Reactions   157
Home Town Responses: Boston   158
    The Assault on Mr. Sumner   158

Attack on Mr. Sumner	161
Attack on Mr. Sumner	161
Home Town Responses: South Carolina	163
The Washington Difficulty	164
Capt. Brooks' Castigation of Senator Sumner	164
Violence in the Political Arena	165
The Attack on Mr. Sumner	166
The Right View of the Subject	167
Chivalry and Degradation	168
Freedom of Speech	170
The Ruffians in the Senate	171
Liberty of Speech, of the Press, and Freedom of Religion	172
The Progress of the Revolution	173
Editorial Implications	175
Public Rallies and Resolutions	175
Ralph Waldo Emerson Speaks at the Concord Indignation Meeting	176
Resolutions of the Citizens of Martin's Depot, South Carolina, 27 May 1856	178
Resolutions of the Students of Union College, Schenectady, New York, 27 May 1856	178
Proceedings of the New England Antislavery Convention Wednesday, 28 May and Thursday 29 May 1856	180
Resolutions of the Colored Citizens of Boston, 6 June 1856	183
Public Approval of Mr. Brooks	184
Letter from Congressman John McQueen	185
Private Letters of Praise, Consolation, and Condemnation	186
Letter of James W. Stone to Charles Sumner	189
Letter from "A Friend Indeed" to Charles Sumner, 22 May 1856	189
W. Richardson to Charles Sumner, 24 May 1856	190
"Cuffy" to Charles Sumner, 26 May 1856	191
Seaborn Jones to Preston S. Brooks, 1 June 1856	192
Mary Rosamond Dana to Charles Sumner, 1 June 1856	193
John Van Buren to Charles Sumner, 10 June 1856	193
W. F. Holmes to Preston Brooks, 27 May 1856	194
Images of the Caning	194
The Fate of Preston Brooks	197
Trial Remarks By Preston Brooks	198
Duels	199
Brooks's Canada Song	200
Remarks of Preston S. Brooks on Party Politics and Kansas	201

Epitaph	203
Sumner's Illness: Was He Shamming?	205
Possuming	205
Doctor Cornelius Boyle's Testimony (Tuesday 27 June)	206
Doctor Marshall Perry's Testimony (Wednesday 28 June)	208
Charles Sumner Reports on His Recuperation, 22 July 1856	210
The Libels on Senator Sumner; Testimony of His Physicians	211
Sumner's Letter to the People of Massachusetts, 22 May 1858	213
The State of Mr. Sumner's Health	215
The Latest Bulletin	216
Implications	217
Notes	219
Index	223

List of Illustrations

Figure 1.1: Winslow Homer, "Arguments of the Chivalry"   2

Figure 1.2: Charles Sumner   10

Figure 1.3: Andrew Pickens Butler   24

Figure 1.4: Preston S. Brooks   25

Figure 3.1: Origins of Letters Sent to Charles Sumner from Massachusetts   187

Figure 3.2: Origins of Letters Sent to Charles Sumner
from Massachusetts   188

Figure 3.3: Henry Magee, "Southern Chivalry: Argument Versus Clubs"   195

Figure 3.4: "The Assault in the Senate Chamber," from *Frank Leslie's
Illustrated Weekly*   196

Figure 3.5: Republican Party Campaign Print, "The Democratic
Platform Illustrated"   197

Figure 3.6: Preston S. Brooks Gravesite, Edgefield, South Carolina   204

The Caning of Senator Sumner

The caning of Massachusetts Senator Charles Sumner by South Carolina Representative Preston S. Brooks is one of the most dramatic moments in American history . The incident shattered the fragile truce that had existed between North and South. In the North, the newly formed Republican party used the caning to seize dominance from their Know-Nothing and Democratic rivals. In dozens of mass meetings Northerners condemned "Bully Brooks" for his assault on free speech. In the South, leading citizens showered Brooks with congratulatory letters and canes to replace the one he had broken in the assault. College students held campus rallies and passed resolutions lauding the chastisement. Editors praised the action and urged the Congressman to "hit him again!" The incident is justly treated by historians as one of the key turning points in the coming of the Civil War. Because the incident incorporated so many of the era's key issues, including slavery and abolition, personal liberty laws and state rights, "Bleeding Kansas" and territorial expansion, ideals of gender and manhood, competing visions of labor and the economic order, and the revolutionary shift between the Whig-based "second party system" and its Republican-dominated third party successor, it provides an excellent window into the mind of a nation on the brink of conflict. Americans used the incident to reflect on their most basic beliefs, to contrast their own views with the "corrupt and degrading" notions of opposing parties and sections, and to offer their aspirations for the nation's future. The incident's debates over candor, chivalry, and honor in a democracy highlight the profound cultural differences that existed between North and South as well as within each section. The incident's diversity of editorial commentary and political cartooning, and the outpouring of personal correspondence that followed the attack show political leaders actively seeking to manipulate popular outrage for partisan political purposes. That some of these attempts were ultimately more successful than others reveals the complex patterns of intellectual geography that affected the diffusion of ideas in nineteenth century America. Finally, outpouring of commentary and speechmaking offers many characteristic examples of nineteenth century rhetorical and argumentative style. To give the full nineteenth century flavor of these arguments this volume includes extensive selections from congressional speeches by Sumner, Stephen Douglas, and others along with shorter letters, editorials, and images.

ACKNOWLEDGMENTS

One of the great pleasures of the historical profession is listening to historians swap stories. This work has benefited immensely from these exchanges. Vernon Burton's generosity is legendary; he guided me on several memorable trips to Edgefield and has offered countless other moments of advice and assistance. Ed Ayers gave me an early interest in the caning. Our running conversations about community, geography, Southern culture, technology, and undergraduate teaching have improved every part of this work. Mark Shantz's encouragement and comments came at crucial moments, especially as I pondered how the incident reflected nineteenth century values about gender, class, religion, and the "culture of death." His reading of part one sparked a number of valuable revisions. Michael Holt and Lex Renda alerted me to valuable resources, provided insights into state-level politics and elections, and raised critical questions about the incident's ultimate significance. David Shi was similarly helpful in encouraging me to clarify my views on the role of nineteenth century intellectual movements in the incident. Matt Gallman shared his own unpublished essay on the caning and alerted me to some vital subtleties in Sumner's "Crime Against Kansas" speech. A. V. Huff's role as colleague, friend, critic has been instrumental. His support has extended not only to me but to my entire family. Donald Ritchie and Betty Koed at the Senate Historical Office led me to a number of interesting details surrounding the incident. Thanks also to the two anonymous readers whose positive words and helpful suggestions for revisions were first-rate. Sheila Farland helped trim the manuscript at a crucial moment. Series editor John McClymer has been an essential source of encouragement, guidance, and patience. None of these scholars would agree with every choice in this volume, but it has certainly been improved by their counsel. The editorial staff at Wadsworth, especially Sue Gleason and Julie Yardley, were unfailingly patient, encouraging, and constructive in their comments.

There are not enough kind words in the language to recompense the contributions of the librarians and archivists who helped with this project. Steve Richardson in the Furman University reference department has been essential collaborator and cheerleader for the project. I am awed by how much effort and skill he displayed in tracking down obscure facts, acquiring copies of manuscript materials, locating newspapers, and alerting me to new resources relevant to the incident. His knowledge of South Carolina history and his splendid network of connections with other librarians in the state have been invaluable. Lilli Ann Hall, James Harper, Brenda Custard, and dozens of anonymous student assistants in the interlibrary loan office went beyond the call of duty with my endless requests. Henry Fulmer at the South Carolinian Library and Nicholas Graham of the Massachusetts Historical Society were especially enthusiastic and insightful in locating primary source materials. Staff members at the American Antiquarian Society, the Harvard, Cornell, Princeton, Duke, Virginia, and Johns Hopkins University libraries, and the Greenville,

Edgefield, Greenwood, and Boston Public Libraries were equally prompt and friendly in providing materials. Bettis Rainsford of the Edgefield Historical Society treated me like family instead of the stranger that I was.

A number of colleagues who specialize in fields other than antebellum American history provided useful information, advice, and commentary. Ron Granieri's critical reading of part three and ongoing engagement with the project were of inestimable value. Linda Julian of Furman's English department also read parts of the manuscript and alerted me to important aspects of nineteenth century literary culture. David Morgan and Pat Pecoy in Furman's Languages department helped with several translations and attributions. Paul Rasmussen in Furman's Psychology department indulged my marathon-length questions about the temperament of the incident's protagonists. Alan Scarborough of Augusta College, Barbara Carson of Rollins College, Fred Ashe of Birmingham-Southern College, and Wade Berryhill of the University of Richmond saw the genesis of this project as a "teaching slice" at the Associated Colleges of the South microteaching workshop. Their positive and perceptive feedback encouraged me to expand the scope of students' encounter with the incident in my classes. Thanks to Hayden Porter of Furman's Computer Science department who provided funding for the project from a Mellon technology grant and to his colleague Kevin Treu who gave me the technical information needed to put the Sumner editorials on the Internet. Likewise, Arnold Murdock at the University of Southern Illinois-Carbondale provided essential technical advice and a willing critical ear for the story. Carolyn Sims helped with transcriptions, travel arrangements, and a thousand other administrative details. Jim Leavell has been omnipresent in his role as friend and mentor.

The ongoing contributions of Furman students to this project deserve special mention. Marcus Rozbitsky, Amber Anders, and Jenny Adamson located editorials and made transcriptions. Furman has generously provided a number of Furman Advantage undergraduate research fellows for the project since 1996, including Jeff Bollerman, Ryan Burgess, Ben Barnhill, and Nicole Pascoe. All of them provided valuable advice about the structure, topics, and document selections of this work, generated mountains of transcriptions, and raised valuable interpretive questions. Beatrice Burton's ardent claim that Brooks has been depicted too harshly by most academic scholars led me to revisit my own views. Our collaborative roll-call analysis of his voting record in the 33d and 34th congresses led to a better understanding of how his views evolved during the period. The history department's student assistants have helped with a thousand administrative and housekeeping details, including the helpful drudgery of ordering interlibrary loan materials and making photocopies of important articles and primary sources.

I have been fortunate that my family has been so supportive of the Sumner project. Ongoing conversations with my mother about how slavery intersected with religion, intellectual activities, culture, and social structure in the Atlantic world context have benefited my scholarship more than hers, which is, I suppose, as it should be. My brother Lauck shared his home, his close readings of Sumner editorials, and his computer expertise during frequent trips to Boston, along with healthy doses of antebellum banjo music. My brother Jake and his friend Joey applied their professional skills in book conservation and graphics to a number of items appearing in this collection. More than any others, though, Vicki and Joshua have endured and inspired the process of assembling *The Caning of Senator Sumner.*

I

The Caning and Its Origins

Prologue: The Incident

Few people disputed the facts of the case. In late May 1856 Abolitionist Senator Charles Sumner of Massachusetts had given a bitter two-day speech called "The Crime Against Kansas." He had been provoked by almost two years of sectional strife. In his address Sumner sought to show how President Franklin Pierce, in association with merciless pro-slavery "border ruffians," had outraged the rights of the new territory's innocent settlers. The speech included brief but acidic comments about how Senators Stephen A. Douglas of Illinois and Andrew P. Butler of South Carolina had assisted in this crime. Many Southerners in Congress resented the speech and detested its author, but none was more outraged than Preston S. Brooks, a Congressman from South Carolina and a kinsman of Senator Butler. Brooks vowed a thorough and humiliating revenge. He found his enemy at work in the Capitol. There, on the floor of the Senate, Brooks beat Sumner to unconsciousness with a gentleman's walking cane. Never before had a Senator been attacked like this, and certainly never by another member of Congress. The incident shocked the nation. Universal outrage, however, did not lead to universal agreement. This incident became a classic illustration of how partisan and sectional differences led to conflicting interpretations of the same historical moment.

The following descriptions of the incident, produced by opposing factions in the congressional committee responsible for its investigation, differ starkly in their emphasis. The committee, consisting of three Northern moderates and two Democrats from the South, began deliberations a few days after the caning. The committee voted to give Brooks the right to question witnesses for his own defense, though he chose not to participate. A string of hearings generated testimony from more than two-dozen eyewitnesses, all of whom agreed about the main outlines of what had happened. Eight days after the caning the two factions completed their summaries. The majority report, written by the committee's three non-Democrats, dramatized the details of the assault, the weapon used, and the wounds inflicted. Its terse treatment of Sumner's speech bears close comparison with the treatment of the same speech in the minority report.

FIGURE 1.1   Winslow Homer, "Arguments of the Chivalry"

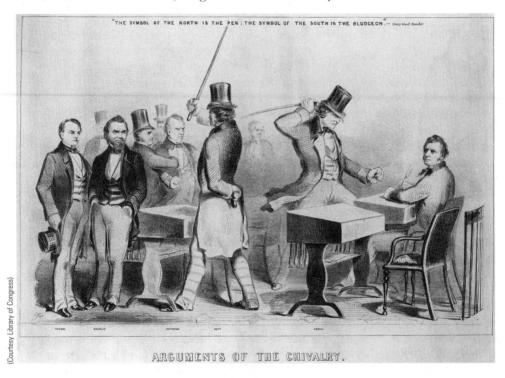

Majority Report on the Sumner Caning Incident[1]

On Monday and Tuesday, the 19th and 20th days of May, 1856, Mr. Sumner delivered a speech in the Senate, in reply to a Senator from South Carolina, (Mr. Butler,) and other senators. . . . It appears that, as early as Tuesday, before the speech was concluded, Mr. Brooks took exception to the remarks of the Senator; and that on Wednesday morning, after delivery of the speech, he declared to Mr. Edmundson, of the House, by whom he was casually met, in the Capitol grounds, a short time before the meeting of the two Houses, that he had determined to punish Mr. Sumner, unless he made an ample apology for the language he had uttered in his speech, and expressed a desire that Mr. Edmundson[2] should be present as a witness to the transaction; that they thereupon took a seat near the walk leading from Pennsylvania Avenue to the Capitol, and there remained some fifteen minutes, awaiting the approach of Mr. Sumner; and he not making his appearance, they then proceeded to the Capitol.

On Thursday morning he was again casually met by Mr. Edmundson at the western entrance of the Capitol grounds, on Pennsylvania Avenue, a point which commands a view of all the approaches to the Capitol from that portion of the city in which Mr. Sumner resides. Here Mr. Brooks informed Mr. Edmundson that he was on the lookout for Mr. Sumner, and again declared his purpose to resent the language of Mr. Sumner's speech; and after remaining for a short period, Mr. Sumner not approaching, the two again proceeded to the Capitol.

After the reading of the journal of the House on Thursday, the death of the honorable Mr. Miller,[3] of Missouri, was announced, addresses delivered, the customary resolutions adopted, and thereupon the House adjourned.

When the message was received by the Senate from the House, announcing the death of Mr. Miller, a tribute of respect was paid to the deceased by Senator Geyer,[4] in an address, and that body thereupon also adjourned. Most of the Senators left the Senate chamber, a few only remaining. Mr. Sumner continued in his seat engaged in writing. Mr. Brooks approached, and, addressing a few words to him, immediately commenced the attack by inflicting blows upon his bare head, whilst he was in a sitting posture, with a large and heavy cane. Stunned and blinded by the first blow, and confined by his chair and desk, Mr. Sumner made several ineffectual efforts to rise, and finally succeeded by wrenching his desk from its fastenings. The blows were repeated by Mr. Brooks with great rapidity and extreme violence, while Mr. Sumner, almost unconscious, made further efforts of self-defence, until he fell to the floor under the attack, bleeding and powerless.

The wounds were severe and calculated to endanger the life of the Senator who remained for several days in a critical condition. It appears that the blows were inflicted with a cane, the material of which was about the specific gravity of hickory or whalebone, one inch in diameter at the larger end, and tapering to the diameter of about five-eighths of an inch at the smaller end. It is not too much to say that the weapon used was of a deadly character, and that the blows were indiscriminately dealt, at the hazard of the life of the assailed.

The committee have extended to the parties implicated the fullest facilities for taking exculpatory testimony. There is no proof to show, nor has been in any way intimated, that Mr. Brooks at any time, in any manner, directly or indirectly, notified Mr. Sumner of his intention to make the assault. There is no evidence that Mr. Sumner ever carried weapons, either for the purpose of attack or defence; on the contrary, it appears that he did not anticipate personal violence until at the instant he received the first blow, and that he was not armed or otherwise prepared in any respect for self-defence.

There is no evidence beyond the character of the attack tending to show an intention on the part of Mr. Brooks to kill the Senator, his expressions being that he did not intend to kill, but to punish him; but the committee cannot but regard the assault as a most flagrant violation, not only of the privileges of the Senate and of the House, as co-ordinate branches of the legislative department of the government, and the personal rights and privileges of the Senator, but of the rights of his constituents and of our character as a nation. It was premeditated during a period of at least two days, without any other provocation than words lawfully spoken in debate in the Senate chamber, not ruled out of order by the President of the Senate, nor objected to by any Senator as violative of the rules established for the government and order of that body. The act cannot, therefore, be regarded by the committee otherwise than as an aggravated assault upon the inestimable right to freedom of speech guarantied by the Constitution. It asserts for physical force prerogative over governments, constitutions, and laws; and, if carried to its ultimate consequences, must result in anarchy and bring in its train all the evils of a "reign of terror . . ."

The minority report had a different focus. Rather than emphasizing the attack, report authors Howell Cobb of Georgia and Alfred Greenwood of Alabama (both Democrats) insisted on a technical legal argument about the constitutional privileges of House members. After reviewing the history of free speech protections in the English parliament, and criticizing its excesses, they explored the scope of American constitutional exemptions. Their core claim, summarized in the report's final resolutions, asserted that the House of Representatives had neither constitutional nor legal jurisdiction over the actions of Brooks and therefore could not discipline him for the caning. In the minority report's summary the relative weight of Sumner's speech versus Brooks's assault was almost exactly inverse of the majority's account. The report's frequent allusions to the proper rules of gentlemanly debate and combat deserve attention. The report's discussion of the danger to minority rights posed by a majority censure is similar to arguments made by preeminent South Carolina senator and political theorist John C. Calhoun, who believed that the rights of the South were endangered by the North's growing preponderance of population. The mere fact of being in a majority, he insisted, did not carry with it the authority to legislate away basic rights and liberties.[5]

Minority Report on the Sumner Caning Incident

House of Representatives, 34th Congress, 1st Session, Report No. 132

It appears, from the evidence before the committee, that, on the 19th and 20th of May, Mr. Sumner delivered in the Senate of the United States, and subsequently published in pamphlet form for circulation a speech from which we make the following extracts:

[The report here included extensive selections from the speech in which Sumner attacked Senators Butler and Douglas. These excerpts can be found in part two of this volume.]

These extracts contain language, which, in the opinion of Mr. Brooks, was insulting to the State of South Carolina, which he, in part, represented, and personally offensive to Senator Butler, of the same State, his relative and kinsman, and who was absent from the city at the time of the delivery of a speech. On the 22d day of May, two days after its delivery, Mr. Butler still being absent, Mr. Brooks approached Mr. Sumner in the Senate chamber, after adjournment of that body, and addressed to him the following language: "Mr. Sumner, I have read your speech carefully, and with as much calmness as I could be expected to read such a speech. You have libeled my State, and slandered my relation, who is aged and absent, and I feel it to be my duty to punish you for it."

He then struck Mr. Sumner with his walking cane, giving him repeated and severe blows.

It appears, also, from the testimony, that Mr. Edmundson, of Virginia, and Mr. Keitt, of South Carolina, both members of the House, had been told by Mr. Brooks that he intended to call Mr. Sumner to account for the offensive portion of the speech already alluded to, and did not communicate that fact to Mr. Sumner, or to any other person as far as the committee are informed; but neither of them knew when or where Mr. Brooks intended to execute his purpose, nor does it appear that Mr. Brooks had informed any other person of his intention. . . .

We now proceed to inquire, what privilege of the Senate, or of the House, or of any member, has been violated, for which this House has authority to punish, as disclosed in the facts which we have set forth in the commencement of this report?

The first allegation is, that the privilege of Mr. Sumner has been violated in this: that he has been questioned for the delivery of a speech in the Senate, in violation of that provision of the Constitution which declares that "for any speech or debate in either House they shall not be questioned in any other place." This provision of the Constitution was evidently intended to protect members of Congress from such legal liability as they might incur for words spoken in debate in their respective Houses. It can hardly be supposed that the Constitution was providing against a mode of questioning which, in itself, even without such provision, would have been, not only unauthorized by law, but in direct violation of the criminal law of the land. It is far from being well settled, that this immunity *from* responsibility goes to the extent claimed for it by those from whom we differ in this matter.

If members of Congress seek this shield and protection which the Constitution gives them, is it an onerous condition imposed upon them that their speech shall be proper and legitimate in the discharge of their constitutional duty? Ought they to be permitted to avail themselves of the position given them by a confiding constituency, to indulge in language and reflections in nowise necessary for the discharge of their official duty, nor promotive of the public good? And, even granting this right to its fullest extent, can they go beyond this exercise of speech or debate, and afterwards publish and circulate, in pamphlet form, libellous matter, under the pretext that it is, in this published form, privileged speech or debate in Congress? Even the British Parliament, with all its disposition to protect its members, and under the doctrine of privilege to extend to them powers and immunities, refused to extend the doctrine beyond the strict limits of debate upon the floor of Parliament. The language of our Constitution, in this respect, is drawn from the parliamentary law; and we suppose it will not be contended that our members of Congress have greater latitude, in this respect, than the members of the British Parliament. . . .

Each House must guard its own privileges and the privileges of its own members, except so far as both may unite in the passage of laws *or* joint rules for the declaration and protection of those privileges. Although we have been unable to acquiesce in the principles of all the precedents which are to be found in the history of Congress, yet we find it unnecessary, in the consideration of this branch of the subject, to assail any of those precedents, as none have gone to the extent now claimed—of one House assuming jurisdiction over the privileges of the other, for the purpose of affording protection to them.

The only provision of the Constitution under which the power can be exercised, on which the majority of our committee have relied, is the one already quoted, which declares that:

"Each House may determine the rules of its proceedings, punish its members for disorderly behavior, and, with the concurrence of two thirds, expel a member."

It is a question which has been much discussed, and one which it is important to decide correctly: To what extent is the power given to the two Houses, by this provision of the Constitution, to punish their members? Taking the whole paragraph in its connected sense, it seems to us that it has reference to the House while in session, in the actual discharge of its constitutional duties. The power of providing rules for its proceedings, it will be seen, is coupled in the same sentence with the power to punish its members for disorderly behavior, and the power, with the concurrence of two thirds, to expel a member. If it had been contemplated that the powers conferred in this provision were to be exercised to the extent now claimed for them, they would hardly have been placed in such intimate connexion with the simple power of providing rules for the proceedings of the two Houses. We entertain no doubt that the whole of this provision looks to the session of the House; to the providing of rules for its proceedings during its session; to punishing its members for such disorderly conduct as would interrupt its session; and, where that conduct amounted to such an outrage upon the rules and proprieties of the House as would justify it, to expel the member.

To place any other construction upon this provision would be to make the members of each House, and their moral conduct and deportment, subject to the whim, caprice, and discretion of a majority of the body. Extend it beyond the presence of the session of the House and it becomes an unlimited power, operative not only during the session of Congress, but during the recess; to be exercised not only in reference to the conduct of members when in Washington city or in the District of Columbia, but when they have returned to their respective homes, and even when they have gone beyond the limits of the country. When you have passed the limits which we have laid down, there is no other boundary short of congressional discretion. And we cannot believe that it was the intention of the framers of the Constitution to place the moral conduct and deportment of members of the two Houses of Congress under the control and discretion of a majority of either House. . . . Such unlimited power would not have been conferred by the wise men who framed our Constitution in such vague and indefinite language.

Entertaining these opinions, we hold that there has been no violation, in this case, of the privileges of either House of Congress, or any member thereof, over which this House has any jurisdiction. Whatever offence may have been committed is properly cognizable before the courts of the country, and we propose to dismiss the subject to that jurisdiction provided by the Constitution and laws of the country for its investigation. We hold it would be improper for the House to express any opinion upon the facts, and we have purposely avoided doing so. . . . Indeed, it would seem that the Constitution, in exempting this class of cases from the privileges which it grants to members of Congress, contemplated the impropriety of any action on our part in reference to them. The House ought not to desire to influence, by any expression of theirs, the judicial tribunal which is to pass upon the facts, and, having no jurisdiction over the matter, should, in our judgment, remain silent.

It will be seen, from the view which we have taken of the Constitution on this subject, that we do not differ from the majority of the committee upon the fact that the two Houses should have the power to protect themselves in their deliberations, and in the discharge of all their constitutional duties. We differ only as to the source from which that power is derived, and the mode in which it is to be exercised. Those who claim for Congress these peculiar privileges look to parliamentary law, British precedents, and the necessity of the case, for their authority. We, on the contrary, look to the Constitution of the country for the authority, and to the laws passed in pursuance thereof for the mode and manner of its enforcement; and it is for the House to say whether it will rest its claim to privileges upon the one or the other of these sources of power. Holding, as we do, that neither House has any privileges except those which are written and declared either in the Constitution or some law or rule passed in pursuance thereof, and that the facts developed by the evidence show no violation of any such written and recognized privileges, we recommend the adoption of the following resolution:

Resolved, That this House has no jurisdiction over the assault alleged to have been committed by the Hon. Preston S. Brooks, a member of this House from the State of South Carolina, upon the Hon. Charles Sumner, a senator from the State of Massachusetts; and therefore deem it improper to express any opinion on the subject.

SENATE VIOLENCE AND THE TRANSFORMATION OF MID-CENTURY AMERICA

It is not hard to see why the attack on Sumner escalated sectional tensions. Northerners saw in Brooks a vivid example of the Southern violence, intolerance, arrogance, and disregard for opponent's political rights that abolitionists had been warning of for decades. Southerners saw in Sumner an equally vivid example of the Northern boorishness, fanaticism, and weak sentimentality for an "inferior" race (meaning African-Americans) that radical Southern secessionists (men often called "fire-eaters") had been warning of for just as long. For all groups the incident served to prove the arguments they had developed during a generation of sectional tensions. During most of this period neither the abolitionists nor the fire-eaters had been able to generate widespread political support. In the caning incident both sides found an effective means of convincing moderates that the republic was in danger of subversion. By converting the abstract debates over slavery into something personal and by showing how sectional conflict could disrupt the nation's temple of democracy, the Sumner incident became a momentous symbolic landmark on the path to Civil War.[6]

A broad pattern of social upheavals of the 1850s provided a backdrop for the incident's drama and profoundly shaped how ordinary citizens would interpret its meaning. In the years immediately before the encounter almost every institution in the nation had changed. In the early 1850s the traditional two party system of Whigs and Democrats had dissolved, leaving remnants of the old parties to struggle for voter loyalty with the new Prohibitionist, Free-Soiler, Know-Nothing, Southern Rights, Unionist, and Republican factions. In this disarray voters chose to stay home almost as often as they voted for one party or another. The economy changed with equal rapidity and equal disruptiveness. Between 1850 and 1855 the nation's railroad mileage more than doubled, displacing local economic systems and relocating financial power to the major cities. Even the railroad's beneficial effects, including more rapid mail delivery, lower prices, and wider markets, contributed to the era's frenzied uncertainty. So too with the telegraph. The first message had been sent by Samuel F. B. Morse in the mid 1840s. In less than a dozen years more than forty thousand miles of line had been strung. Telegraph companies connected every major town, allowing news to spread across the nation in minutes rather than days. The nation's cities were the prime beneficiaries of these communications changes, and they too became sources of anxiety. Tens of thousands flocked to New York, Boston, Chicago, and other urban centers, overwhelming city resources and challenging traditional elites.[7]

With such upheaval it was not surprising to see an outburst of religious activism and cultural controversy. In the period between the 1780s and the 1840s Americans went from historic lows in church attendance to a wave of revivals historians call the "Second Great Awakening."[8] Whole new denominations were organized and became mainstream, including Methodists, Baptists, Disciples of Christ, and Unitarians. Other groups, most notably the Mormons, developed amidst a storm of controversy. Even some of the country's oldest denominations in this period fractured in quarrels over theology, ritual, and strategy. They had also struggled to cope with an influx of outsiders. European famine and revolution drove unparalleled numbers of immigrants to America, most of whom settled in Northern cities. Between 1848 and 1855 more than 2.6 million had arrived, the majority from Germany and Catholic Ireland. Native Protestants viewed immigrant customs as disruptive or even diabolical. Finally, there were unprecedented alterations in family structure and the status of women. Declining family sizes and the spread of companionate marriage customs marked by spousal cooperation and women's increased control over a "sacred household sphere" presaged the emergence of the women's rights movement in the North after 1848. These came at the expense of traditional patriarchal authority. Democrats and Southerners resisted these changes, associating them with abolitionism and the breakdown of society's God-ordained domestic order. Whigs and Republicans in the North proved more receptive to the new family models, and while only a small group of Northerners supported full legal and civil equality, the region's women's rights advocates attracted considerable attention. These transformations affected the North most, but Southern communities participated in enough of the changes to fear their consequences. Americans everywhere had a sense that things were changing more quickly than they could be controlled.[9]

Even in this context the incident was shocking and unprecedented. By 1856 Northerners and Southerners had been sparring over territorial slavery for more than two generations without Senate violence. Sumner had been a young boy and Brooks a toddler when the Missouri Compromise had passed. Since then legendary orators had attacked their sectional opponents using angry, insulting, and personal terms that rivaled anything said in Sumner's "Crime Against Kansas." Over a decade had passed since John C. Calhoun of South Carolina had publicly equated free society in Massachusetts with insanity, poverty, crime, and depravity, and even longer since Abolitionists had denounced the American Constitution as a document dripping with the blood of slaves.[10] Yet not once in tens of thousands of words of debate stretching over a quarter century had any man felt compelled to beat another legislator in the Senate chamber. The caning represented a new departure, and every participant realized the gravity of its consequences. In the context of this age of disorder it ended complacency and reinforced the sense that the old policies and institutions no longer sufficed to keep society from disintegrating. The result was one of the most important political restructurings in the nation's history. As news of the caning broke, newspapers also began reporting lurid stories of renewed conflicts in the territories. Together, "bleeding Sumner" and "bleeding Kansas" served to divide one political party, anesthetize a second, and bury a third. Party loyalties dissolved into sectional passions. The ascendency of the modern Republican party dates from this moment. The incident also gave new life to Southern Rights extremists, many of whom had gone into retirement after the triumphs of Southern Unionism in 1851 and 1852. The incident also legitimized violence as political remedy. In its wake, people in both sections concluded that physical force was the only language their opponents could comprehend. The caning was thus a crucial step in the psychological preparation for war.[11]

The incident also serves as an important example of the transformative ways Americans have used history to debate current events. We have already seen how the two congressional reports differed in their interpretations. Behind the caning lay a two-year running quarrel between Sumner and Butler over the future of the territories, a quarrel conducted using historical arguments. The American revolution became their favored interpretive battleground. In selecting a handful of events from the past and omitting others the two men contended for sharply differing visions of the nation's future. For Sumner the leaders of the revolution bequeathed a legacy of freedom and equality to their descendents. To Butler the founding fathers offered history's greatest example of heroic resistance to tyranny. By invoking the revolution both men sought to complement their own logic with the force and authority of history. Ironically, in doing so they converted the revolution into a merely partisan weapon and may have caused Americans to become less connected to the founding era. The 1850s represented a pinnacle of popular regard for revolutionary history. After the Civil War it would be the legacy of Lincoln rather than Washington that would be the subject of the fiercest debates. In using the revolution for sectional ends, Sumner and Butler hastened the conflict that undermined the founding era in American memory.[12]

THE SOCIAL ORIGINS OF AN ABOLITIONIST SENATOR

Sumner's didactic uses of history were rooted in his own origins. His home town of Boston, Massachusetts, had been founded as a model religious commonwealth. From the beginning the city was shaped by moral imperatives. The Puritans were reformers. As members of a dissenting sect they developed a vibrant tradition of criticism against established English society and the Anglican church. Through their dominance of Boston, however, the Puritans themselves became part of the established social order and the defenders of religious orthodoxy. Puritan leaders could be severe to their enemies, as popular preacher Anne Hutchinson, religious dissenter Roger Williams, and the neighboring Algonquian peoples so unhappily found out. From its beginnings Boston was also a city of merchants and craftsmen, individuals whose ambitions for gain or invention often conflicted with the community's religious purposes. Its fine harbor attracted business from Europe, China and most other world ports. Ship-owners merchants, and financiers crowded its wharves, elbow to elbow with immigrants, longshoremen, fishermen, and farmers, all eager for work and trade. Their competitive individualism both challenged and

FIGURE 1.2 Charles Sumner

sustained local authority, contributing, among other things, to the ideals and actions of the American revolution. Commerce and the revolution made the city at once transatlantic and insular. In such a crowded place people were hard to get to know and harder to judge for character. Elite families such as the Winthrops, Adamses, and Otises responded by emphasizing the stability and exclusiveness of their bloodlines and the superior quality of their educational refinement. Bostonians became justifiably proud of their schools, academies, and colleges.

In Sumner's own time the city was being transformed by technological improvements, including canals, railroads, and the nation's first modern factories. Population boomed. After a bitter debate between traditionalists who sought to preserve the informal communitarianism of an older era and the local commercial elites who sought the efficiency and professionalism of strong local government, Boston officially received its charter as a city in 1822. For all its growth, however, Boston was overshadowed by New York and Philadelphia. Critics (including Sumner) decried the community's somnolence and stodgy provincialism. The same era witnessed a religious revolution in the emergence of Unitarianism and Transcendentalism. Thus Sumner's Boston was a place of paradox. Here innovation and convention, orthodoxy and dissent, Europeanism and anti-Europeanism, refinement and egalitarianism, fatalistic Calvinism and new sense of self-improvement and upward mobility competed, coexisted, and reinforced each other.[13]

Sumner was born to a middle class family that exemplified self-improvement. His grandfather, Job Sumner, had fought in the American Revolution. Among his acquaintances had been an officer from South Carolina named Charles Pinckney. After the war Job renamed his son Charles Pinckney Sumner in the South Carolinian's honor. Job's son went to Harvard, was married, and became a lawyer. Charles P. Sumner's eldest son, Charles S. Sumner, was born in 1811. Evidence suggests that the elder Charles was a severe and exacting father and that Charles's mother, Relief Jacob Sumner, was scarcely more nurturing. Historians have attributed much of the Senator's punctiliousness, obsession with principle and social awkwardness to the formality of his parental relationships. Yet his letters to parents and siblings showed an intense combination of affection, enthusiasm, and mutual criticism. Family members could be stunningly direct to each other. They apparently believed that principled reproofs were just as valuable to family integrity as tender personal sentiment. In 1821 Charles began attending the prestigious Boston Latin Grammar School. In its curriculum he encountered the ancient classics that would be so important to his future oratory. Family connections and a stroke of fortune secured him admission to Harvard in 1826. A struggle with mathematics kept Sumner out of the school's first ranks but classmates remembered him as second to none in the subjects of language, history, and literature. None were surprised when Sumner went on to Harvard Law School. He flourished, becoming an obsessive student of legal and political texts. Joseph Story, a professor at the law school and also an associate justice of the United States Supreme Court, took a special liking to the young scholar. Sumner in turn became Story's adoring and devoted pupil. Sumner completed his degree in 1833 and opened a law practice in Boston. The following year he visited Washington for the first time. The visit gave Sumner his first sight of national politics and of slaves in bondage. He left the city disdainful of both.[14]

There was little in Sumner's career at this point to distinguish him from dozens of other young attorneys in Boston's establishment. His transformation to radical reformer happened gradually. Neither the publication of the *Liberator* by fellow Bostonian William Lloyd Garrison in 1831 nor the formation of the New England Antislavery Society in 1832 distracted the young man from his scholarship. In later years Sumner recalled that his activism had not begun until he became a member of the Boston Peace Society. Under the influence of the society Sumner came to believe that military conflicts between nations had no more justification than physical combat between individuals. Both were acts of barbarism unfitted to a rational and enlightened world. A conjunction of circumstances in the late 1830s pushed Sumner further toward community activism. In 1836 his father was indirectly involved in the escape of a pair of slaves. A storm of criticism against his father from the local elites contributed to the younger Sumner's doubts about the establishment's morality. It was at about this time that he began friendships with leading Unitarian thinker William Ellery Channing, educational reformer Horace Mann, prison reformer Samuel Gridley Howe, and poet Henry Wadsworth Longfellow. In an effort to complete his education Sumner departed in 1837 for an eighteen-month European tour. In visits to France, Germany, Italy, and England, Sumner encountered many of the leading intellectuals and politicians of the era, including William Wordsworth, Thomas Carlyle, Harriet Martineau, Lord John Russell, and Klemens von Metternich.[15] He devoted much of his attention to the legal and legislative affairs of Europe and to questions of international law, and even attempted to help the American diplomats in Paris and London as they struggled with several international trade disputes. He returned to Boston reluctantly, forced back home when his money ran out.

After his return Sumner began spending less time as a lawyer and more as an activist. He became especially absorbed by the *Creole* slave ship case of 1841–42. This involved a group of American slave captives who mutinied and sailed their ship to a British port where they were declared free by the British government. The efforts of then Secretary of State Daniel Webster to return the mutineers to their alleged owners in America led an outraged Sumner to publish an article on the case. Sumner argued that slavery existed strictly as a local institution with no legal validity outside of the slaveholding states. Any slave who came onto free soil was instantly and automatically emancipated. Because slavery had no standing in international law, he concluded, the *Creole* mutineers had become free the minute they left American territorial waters. The *Creole* case was followed within months by a national debate over Texas annexation. Texas had won independence from Mexico and become its own republic in 1836. Its political leaders began calling almost immediately for unification with the United States, but American President Martin Van Buren had resisted their efforts. It was not until 1843 that President John Tyler had renewed negotiations with the Texas government. Submission of an annexation treaty to the Senate in 1844 had generated a ferocious backlash, especially from antislavery forces who feared the subdivision of Texas into as many as five new slave states. The measure's opponents also worried that annexation would provoke war with Mexico. Prodded by these episodes, Sumner moved slavery and antislavery to the forefront of his interests.[16]

These events also set the context for Sumner's first controversial public incident, his keynote address for Boston's fourth of July celebration in 1845. His speech, "The True Grandeur of Nations," was a thinly veiled indictment of President Polk's belligerence toward Mexico and England. Democrats, soldiers and the city's Brahmin elite were visibly offended by the speech, though others praised his courage and thought he had made a persuasive case against administration policies. If nothing else the speech demonstrated Sumner's willingness to challenge the Massachusetts establishment. Sumner's attitudes about the Mexican war would contrast sharply with those of Preston Brooks.

The True Grandeur of Nations

Speech at Boston, 4 July 1845[17]

All hearts first turn to the Fathers of the Republic. Their venerable forms rise before us, and we seem to behold them in the procession of successive generations. They come from the frozen rock of Plymouth, from the wasted bands of Raleigh, from the heavenly companionship of William Penn, from the anxious councils of the Revolution, and from all those fields of sacrifice, on which, in obedience to the Spirit of their Age, they sealed their devotion to duty with their blood. . . .

It becomes us on this occasion, as patriots and citizens, to turn our thoughts inward, as the good man dedicates his birthday to the consideration of his character, and the mode in which its vices may be corrected and its virtues strengthened. Avoiding, then, all exultation in the prosperity that has enriched our land, and in the extending influence of the blessings of freedom, let us consider what we can do to elevate our character, to add to the happiness of all, and to attain to that righteousness which exalteth a nation. In this spirit, I propose to inquire *What, in our age, are the true objects of national ambition; what is truly national glory, national honor;* WHAT IS THE TRUE GRANDEUR OF NATIONS? I hope to rescue these terms, so powerful over the minds of men, from the mistaken objects to which they are applied,—from deeds of war and the extension of empire,—that henceforward they may be attached only to acts of Justice and Humanity. . . .

Far be from our country and our age the sin and shame of contests hateful in the sight of God and all good men, having their origin in no righteous though mistaken sentiment, in no true love of country, in no generous thirst for fame,—that last infirmity of noble minds,—but springing in both cases from an ignorant and ignoble passion for new territories; strengthened, in one case, by an unnatural desire in this land of boasted freedom to fasten by new links the chains which promise soon to fall from the limbs of the unhappy slave! In such contests, God has no attribute which can join with us. Who believes that the *national honor* will be promoted by a war with Mexico or England? What just man would sacrifice a single human life, to bring under our rule both Texas and Oregon? It was an ancient Roman—touched, perhaps, by a transient gleam of Christian truth—who said, when he turned aside from a career of Asiatic conquest, that he would rather save the life of a single citizen than become master of all the dominions of Mithridates.[18] A war with Mexico would be mean and cowardly; but with England it would be at least bold, though parricidal. . . .

In our age there can be no peace that is not honorable; there can be no war that is not dishonorable. The true honor of a nation is to be found only in deeds of justice and in the happiness of its people, all of which are inconsistent with war. In the clear eye of Christian judgment vain are its victories, infamous are its spoils. He is the true benefactor and alone worthy of honor who brings comfort where before was wretchedness; who dries the tear of sorrow; who pours oil into the wounds of the unfortunate; who feeds the hungry and clothes the naked; who unlooses the fetters of the slave; who does justice; who enlightens the ignorant; who enlivens and exalts, by his virtuous genius, in art, in literature, in science, the hours of life; who, by words or actions, inspires a love for God and for man. This is the Christian hero; this is the man of honor in a Christian land. He is no benefactor, nor deserving of honor, whatever may be his worldly renown, whose life is passed in acts of force; who renounces the great law of Christian brotherhood; whose vocation is blood; who triumphs in battle over his fellow-men. Well may old Sir Thomas Browne exclaim, 'The world does not know its greatest men;' for thus far it has chiefly discerned the violent brood of battle, the armed men springing up from the dragon's teeth sown by Hate, and cared little for the truly good men, children of Love, guiltless of their country's blood, whose steps on earth have been as noiseless as an angel's wing. . . .

But are we aware that this monstrous and impious usage [the trial by battle], which our enlightened reason so justly condemns in the cases of individuals, is openly avowed by our own country, and by the other countries of the earth, as a proper mode of determining justice between them? Be upon our heads and upon our age the judgment of barbarism, which we pronounce upon those that have gone before! At this moment, in this period of light, when the noon-day sun of civilization seems, to the contented souls of many, to be standing still in the heavens, as upon Gibeon, the relations between nations are governed by the same rules of barbarous, brutal force which once prevailed between individuals. The dark ages have not passed away; Erebus and black Night, born of Chaos, still brood over the earth; nor shall we hail the clear day, until the mighty hearts of the nations shall be touched as those of children, and the whole earth, individuals and nations alike, shall acknowledge *one and the same rule of Right.* . . .

Within a short distance of this city stands an institution of learning, which was one of the earliest cares of the early forefathers of the country, the conscientious Puritans. The University at Cambridge [Harvard] now invites our homage as the most ancient, the most interesting, and the most important seat of learning in the land,—possessing the oldest and most valuable library; one of the largest museums of mineralogy and natural history; a school of Law, which annually receives into its bosom more than one hundred and fifty sons from all parts of the Union, where they listen to instruction from professors whose names have become among the most valuable possessions of the land; a school of Divinity, the nurse of true learning and piety; one of the largest and most flourishing schools of Medicine in the country . . . It appears from the last Report of the Treasurer that the whole available property of the University, the various accumulations of more than two centuries of generosity, amounts to $703,175.

There now swings idly at her moorings in this harbor a ship-of-the-line, the 'Ohio,' carrying ninety guns, finished as late as 1836 for $547,888; repaired only two years afterwards, in 1838, for $223,012; with an armament which has cost $53,945; making an amount of $834,845 as the actual cost at this moment of that single ship,—more than $100,000 beyond all the available accumulations of the richest and most ancient seat of learning in the land! Choose ye, my fellow-citizens of a Christian State, between the two caskets,—that wherein is the loveliness of knowledge and truth, or that which contains the carrion death! . . . Let us abandon the system of preparation for war in time of peace as irrational, unchristian, vainly prodigal of expense, and having a direct tendency to excite the very evil against which it professes to guard.

And now, if it be asked why, on this National Anniversary, in the consideration of the TRUE GRANDEUR OF NATIONS, I have thus dwelt singly and exclusively on war, it is because war is utterly and irreconcilably inconsistent with true greatness. Thus far mankind has worshipped in military glory an idol, compared with which the colossal images of ancient Babylon or modern Hindostan are but toys; and we, in this blessed day of light, in this blessed land of freedom, are among the idolaters. . . .

The true greatness of a nation cannot be in triumphs of the intellect alone. Literature and art may widen the sphere of its influence; they may adorn it; but they are in their nature but accessories. *The true grandeur of humanity is in moral elevation, sustained, enlightened, and decorated by the intellect of man.* The truest tokens of this grandeur in a State are the diffusion of the greatest happiness among the greatest number, and that passionless godlike Justice which controls the relations of the State to other States, and to all the people who are committed to its charge. . . . But war crushes with bloody heel all justice, all happiness, all that is godlike in man. . . .

And peace has its own peculiar victories, in comparison with which Marathon and Bannockburn and Bunker Hill—fields held sacred in the history of human freedom—shall lose their lustre. Our own Washington rises to a truly heavenly stature, not when we follow him over the ice of the Delaware to the capture of Trenton, not when we behold him victorious over Cornwallis at Yorktown, but when we regard him, in noble deference to justice, refusing the kingly crown which a faithless soldiery proffered, and at a later day upholding the peaceful neutrality of the country, while he received unmoved the clamor of the people wickedly crying for war. What glory of battle in England's annals will not fade by the side of that great act of Justice, by which her Legislature, at a cost of one hundred million dollars, gave freedom to eight hundred thousand slaves! And when the day shall come (may these eyes be gladdened by its beams!) that shall witness an act of greater justice still,—the peaceful emancipation of three millions of our fellow-men, 'guilty of a skin not colored as our own,' now held in gloomy bondage under the Constitution of our country,—then shall there be a victory, in comparison with which that of Bunker Hill shall be as a farthing-candle held up to the sun. That victory shall need no monument of stone. It shall be written on the grateful hearts of uncounted multitudes, that shall proclaim it to the latest generation. It shall be one of the great land-marks of civilization; nay more, it shall be one of the links in the golden chain by which humanity shall connect itself with the throne of God. . . .

Far be from us, fellow-citizens, on this Anniversary, the illusions of national freedom in which we are too prone to indulge. We have but half done, when we have made ourselves free. Let not the scornful taunt be directed at us, 'They wish to be *free*, but know not how to be *just*. Freedom is not an end in itself, but a means only; a means of securing justice and happiness,—the real end and aim of States, as of every human heart. It becomes us to inquire earnestly if there is not much to be done by which these can be promoted. If I have succeeded in impressing on your minds the truths which I have upheld to-day, you will be ready to join in efforts for the abolition of war, and of all preparation for war, as indispensable to the true grandeur of our country . . . Let it not be said that the age does not demand this work. The mighty conquerors of the Past from their fiery sepulchres demand it; the blood of millions unjustly shed in war crying from the ground demands it; the voices of all good men demand it; the conscience even of the soldier whispers 'Peace. . . . ' War is known as the last reason of kings. Let it be no reason of our republic. Let us renounce and throw off for ever the yoke of a tyranny more oppressive than any in the annals of the world. As those standing on the mountain-tops first discern the coming beams of morning, let us, from the vantage ground of liberal institutions, first recognize the ascending sun of a new era! Lift high the gates, and let the King of Glory in: the King of true Glory—of Peace.

After the speech Sumner became identified with the so-called "Conscience Whigs" who challenged their party's collaboration with Whig slaveholders in the South. In Massachusetts their opponents, known as "Cotton Whigs," were led by Daniel Webster (now a Senator) and Congressman Robert Winthrop. Although both men disliked slavery, in the interests of sectional harmony they had downplayed opposition to the Mexican War and supported legislative compromises. Their Unionism attracted considerable support among Massachusetts voters. Disgusted with the compromises of Whiggery, Sumner and other leading Conscience Whigs bolted to the Free Soil Party in the late 1840s. Sumner reluctantly agreed to run for Congress against Winthrop but was soundly defeated in the 1848 elections.

Not until after the Compromise of 1850, which Webster had supported wholeheartedly, did popular currents begin to shift in favor of Sumner. In what turned out to be a crucial component of the Compromise, Congress had greatly strengthened the federal fugitive slave act. To invigorate the otherwise reluctant governments in Northern states, the new act forced all local officials to be deputized into Federal service and doubled their bounties if the alleged fugitives were returned South rather than set free. These slaves would then be returned without a jury trial. Although the compromise had the backing of Webster and received positive reactions in Massachusetts, the new fugitive component proved far less popular. None reacted more angrily than the Free-Soilers, who redoubled their efforts to overturn the pro-compromise establishment. By late 1850 Sumner and the other Free-Soilers began collaborating with their former enemies in the Democratic party to break the Whig monopoly over state government. Despite deep philosophical differences between the two factions this strange anti-Whig coalition managed to win the 1850 elections. Chief among the spoils from this victory was Daniel Webster's Senate seat, vacated when President Fillmore drafted him to once again become Secretary of State. As part of the complex power-sharing arrangements that followed, the legislature appointed Sumner to be Webster's replacement. Sumner took his seat in the Fall of 1851, one of only three Free-Soilers in the United States Senate. He would serve until his death in 1874.[19]

During this period Sumner maintained his interest in local humanitarian issues. In 1849 he joined with African-American lawyer Robert Morris to argue the famous Roberts case seeking an end to racial segregation in Boston's public schools. They lost, but their arguments would be used in 1855 to support the passage of a state school integration law, the first such law in American history. Sumner's rejection of the fugitive slave law led him to actively support Boston's runaways. In April 1851 he served as co-counsel in defense of Thomas Sims, an alleged runaway claimed by slaveholders from Georgia. (Sims lost. He was forced by the federal fugitive slave commissioner to be returned South.) Sumner's politics and philanthropy also led him in the early 1850s to strengthen his association with New England's leading Transcendentalists. Among these were his old friend Henry W. Longfellow, the poet John Greenleaf Whittier, and the movement's dominant figure, Ralph Waldo Emerson. All three shared Sumner's antislavery politics. They also shared a belief in the romantic ideals of personal courage and authenticity. These were most clearly expressed in Emerson's 1841 essay "Self Reliance," in which he celebrated the value of individual imagination and intuition along with the nobility of remaining true to one's principles even in the face of hostile public opinion. These ideas, rooted in the European Romanticism of Goethe, de Staël, and Carlyle, as well as Emerson's readings of Christian scriptures and the era's evolving notions of masculinity, strongly influenced Sumner's outlook and behavior. "There is one thing needful in our public men," Sumner wrote in condemnation of the Cotton Whigs, "—*backbone*. In this is comprised that moral firmness, without which they yield to the pressure of interests of party, of fashion, of public opinion."[20]

By 1854 the traits in Sumner's character that provoked the incident were clearly visible. Above all, he preferred principles over persons. His strongest friendships were with intellectuals who shared his love of ideas. He found intimate personal relationships, particularly with women, awkward to sustain. Sumner would remain a bachelor until after the war. A brief and miserable marriage in 1866 to the daughter of a Congressman would end in scandal and divorce. His true love was the rule of law. He believed that when law served the cause of justice it represented civilization itself. The practices of slavery, inequality, and physical violence betrayed these ideals. Ending them became his obsession. Other political matters received less of his attention. Although rightly considered by historians to be one of the founding figures of the modern Republican party, he had little taste for ordinary party politics. The trades, deals, and negotiations that were a necessary part of the democratic legislative process he avoided as unseemly. Even members of his own coalition found him difficult to work with. From the beginning of his term in office there was talk that he would be a one-term Senator.

THE PERSONAL WORLD OF BROOKS AND BUTLER

The Edgefield District of South Carolina, home of both Preston Brooks and Andrew P. Butler, was a place far removed from the frenzied traditionalism of Boston. By Massachusetts standards this community was very recent. The district's first European settlers had arrived more than a hundred years after the Puritans had first inhabited New England. The population grew slowly. As late as 1850 the largest village in the district had no more than a thousand residents. Throughout the era Edgefield remained rural and agricultural. From the smallest log cabins and plain frame farm houses to the biggest plantations, cotton, weather, and the season's tasks were the constant focus of activity and conversation. As the chief labor source for agriculture, slavery pervaded Edgefield. In the antebellum period almost half of the community's white families were slaveowners, and almost a quarter of these were planters who owned twenty or more slaves. Slaves increasingly outnumbered whites after 1830, a fact of some concern to the local white leadership. Although planters were quick to proclaim the docility of their slaves, the slave community's daily resistance to plantation rules and occasional habit of disappearing into the woods left owners perpetually insecure. As the slave population outstripped the free population these fears only increased. Local reformers worked hard to increase the variety of crops and of businesses in the community but with limited success. Although unpredictable, plantation agriculture's long-term profitability prevented economic diversification and led to increasing concentration of wealth in Edgefield as the decades passed. This in turn produced heavy out-migration from both the district and the state. It was not surprising that white South Carolinians took such an interest in territorial expansion; the district's transformations made it increasingly difficult for the community's middling sorts to advance without new territory for new farms.[21]

At the bottom of the social hierarchy but decisive in their influence on Edgefield's economy, culture, and politics, were Edgefield's African-Americans. By 1850, they comprised 59 percent of the district's total population. Because slaves in Edgefield and elsewhere were forbidden to read and write, the majority of them (with some important exceptions) were locked in illiteracy. Their voices in the historical record have been relatively silent in comparison to white political leaders such as Butler and Brooks. Yet scholars have been able to recover a surprisingly large body of evidence about conditions of slavery, the economic, cultural, and religious practices of slave communities, the complex nature of the relationships that existed between racial groups in the South, and even the role of slaves as political influences. Federal census returns, state and local tax rolls, plantation records, wills and deeds, church minutes, trial transcripts and other court proceedings, and autobiographical accounts by escaped slaves all provide clues, as do artifacts of material culture and slavery's archeological remains.

Among the most fruitful resources for understanding slavery is a series of interviews collected from ex-slaves in the late 1920s and 1930s, first as a project by Fisk

University in Tennessee, and later under the auspices of the Federal Writer's Project of the Works Progress Administration. As the following narrative from Henry Ryan illustrates, these narratives are not without their limitations. Any person still alive when the interviews were conducted was probably a child during slavery and therefore insulated from its worst aspects. Because decades had passed since emancipation, the interviewee's memories had faded, become simplified, or had been recast to fit classic (and more easily recallable) storytelling conventions and frameworks. In the following narrative, for example, Henry Ryan incorrectly reports his age at the time of Judge Butler's death. Moreover, the context of the interview itself proved significant. Slaves interviewed by white collectors tended to minimize the harshness of their own experiences in slavery, incorporating the most brutal details in camouflaged language and double-entendres. Ryan's narrative offers especially intriguing clues about how people in Edgefield reconciled the paradox of slaves as mere capital assets of a fixed status that were to be utilized maximally, versus slaves as human beings with basic needs for autonomy, self-improvement, and self-expression. The narrative shows both the coercive aspects of slavery and the ways in which slaves asserted (and masters conceded) "breathing space."[22]

Ryan's narrative also underscores how actively and decisively slaves contributed to the era's political debates. No issue more deeply divided Southern leaders such as Butler from Northern antagonists such as Sumner than the question of fugitive slaves. Indeed, the failure of Northern states to return escapees would be the single most important issue emphasized in South Carolina's 1860 declaration of the causes of secession. Ryan's stories about slaves resisting slave patrollers and his assertions about successful escapes (on other plantations, of course) suggests the ways in which slaves provoked a national political controversy by voting against slavery with their feet and their fists.[23]

Federal Writer's Project: Slave Narrative of Henry Ryan[24]

I was born in Edgefield county, S.C., about 1854. I was the son of Larkin and Cheny Ryan who was the slaves of Judge Pickens Butler who lived at Edgefield Courthouse. I has some brothers and sisters, but don't remember them all. We lived in a log house with but one room. We had good beds to sleep in, and always had plenty to eat. Old Judge Butler was a good man. I was 10 years old when he died. Before then I worked in and around the house, and freedom come I stayed with the Butler family two years, then went to Dr. Maxwell's.

In slavery time we had extra patches of ground to work for ourselves which we sometimes worked on Saturday afternoons as we had dat time off, Judge Butler used to give us a little money, too, before freedom come, for our work. We bought clothes and things we had to have. We had a big plantation garden dat the overseers planted for all on de place to eat out of. . . .

Old Marse Butler and his mistress was good, de best folks in de country. They lived in a big house, had a girl and a boy, and over 1000 or maybe 2,000 acres of land, on several farms. One was on Saluda River. His overseers some was no good, but master wouldn't let them treat slaves cruel, just light whipping. "We used to have to wake up at sun-up and work till sundown. We didn't learn to read and write; but we had a prayer house on de plantation where we could go to sometimes, until freedom come, then we went on to it just the same. Old man Bennefield, a nigger preacher, talked to us there. I can 'member one of de favorite songs we sung:

> Show pity, O Lord, forgive, Let e'er repentant sinner live;
> Are not thy mercies large and free, May not a sinner trust in Thee."
> My crimes are great, and can't surpass.

• • •

None of Major Pickens Butler's slaves ever went away from him, but some in de neighborhood did run away, and dey never heard of dem again.

The paderrollers would catch a nigger if he didn't have a pass. Some would pass and re-pass in the road, and maybe get catched and such scuffling would go on!

We worked on Saturday afternoons unless boss give time off to work our own little patches or do some other work we had to do. But some would frolic then and wash up for Sunday, or set around. On Sunday we went to church and talked to neighbors. On Christmas we celebrated by having a big dinner which the master give us. We had three days holiday or sometimes a week. We had New Year's Day as a special day for working, 'cause it was a sign if we worked good dat day, we would work good all de year. . . .

We didn't have schools; started them the second year after freedom. Old General Butler give us old slaves a home each and a small patch to work.

I married when I was 21 years old, the first time in Edgefield County, now called Saluda County. I have six children, nine grand-children, and four great-grand-children.

I think Abe Lincoln was good man and he was Providential arrangement. I think Jeff Davis was good man, same. Booker T. Washington is good man, done lots for young Niggers. I rather like it now, and not slavery time. I joined church when I was 18 to turn from evil way and to live a better life.

Contemporary evidence confirms Ryan's testimony concerning slave escapes. To prevent these, slaveholders established a regular, though clearly imperfect, network of slave patrols, required all slaves to have written passes from their owners, forbade slaves to gather or travel at night without white supervision, and punished captured escapees with public severity. Although the expense of newspaper fees and reward money made advertising for runaways a last resort for slaveholders, nearly every issue of the Edgefield *Advertiser* in the early 1850s contained at least one runaway slave advertisement. The following advertisement was representative of those published in newspapers across the South. This one is typical of such ads in that the escapee still remained in the area and was believed to be in the vicinity of a spouse or family member.

Runaway Slave Advertisement,
Edgefield *Advertiser,* 4 May 1854[25]

$20 Reward

Ranaway from the Subscriber on the 7th March past, a Negro man named MARCH. Said March is five feet ten inches high, of rather dark complexion and sharp features, and limps from having had a leg broken. He speaks rather slowly.

The Subscriber purchased him on Sale-day in March at Sheriff's sale. Before he reached his house with him, the Negro ran away, and has not been seen or heard of since. He is said to have a wife at Dr. Bradford's, Beech Island, and may be lurking about that vicinity.

The above reward will be given for his apprehension and delivery at the Jail at Edgefield District

W. B. Dorn

The largest planters in Edgefield typically owned several plantations in different places and held hundreds of slaves in their service. These circumstances necessitated that they turn daily management of those in bondage to spouses, adult children, business partners, and hired overseers. Planters provided careful guidelines to these supervisors, often in written form. The following rules, written by Francis W. Pickens, who was a neighbor, associate, and future political rival of Preston Brooks, were typical of such regulations. As with the slave narratives, the Pickens evidence can be read in several ways. Pickens clearly sought to avoid what he considered abusive overwork of his slaves. Yet the fact that he had to explicitly forbid the employment of sick women and children, especially in Winter, suggests that such labor practices would have been followed had he not ruled them out. In an age in which middle and upper class white women were strictly limited to work in the "domestic sphere" of the home, and when married women, even among the working classes, avoided working outside the house unless family finances required it, the employment of African-American women in gang and field labor, even when pregnant, became one of slavery's most distinctive features. Every slave, young or old, male or female, represented a capital investment of many hundreds of dollars, in an age when a typical free laborer earned about a dollar a day. Slaveholders had every incentive to work this capital as hard as it could be worked, even in the face of otherwise powerful cultural proscriptions against women's manual labor. The strict control that Pickens sought to exert over slave's private life, family and courtship is also striking. Under South Carolina law, slaves were merely personal property of the owner, with no substantive protections for their civil or personal rights. Neither the Federal Bill of Rights nor similar protections outlined in the South Carolina state constitution applied legally to slaves. As the Pickens rules illustrate, even the most basic acts of free expression, freedom of movement, and the right to control over one's personal and family life were subject to the whims of the owner. When emancipation came these rights were among the first asserted by emancipated slaves. Freedwomen ceased working in the fields for whites, former slaves took great delight in simply walking around without a pass, and there was a massive relocation as emancipated slaves sought out spouses and kinfolk who had been sold, auctioned, or inherited away to other plantations and other communities.[26]

Francis Wilkinson Pickens, General Directions as to the Treatment of Negroes (1839)[27]

1st. They must be well clothed and fed and attended to in sickness.

2d. The crop must never be too great. Rather lose too little planted than too much.

3d. The women and children must be particularly attended to in sickness, and the former never pushed when complaining.

4th. *The women are never to work out at all in cold wet weather in the Winter,* but must be kept in the house to spin, &c. They must not be exposed.

5th. There must be general rules adopted and always adhered to.

6th. No Negro must be allowed to go off the place without a pass and to a particular place and no where else.

7th. They must not be allowed to go off but very seldom, except to church every Sunday and must then be on the plantation before sun down.

8th. No strange Negroes must come on the plantation at all, except when on business.

9th. No Negro man is to have a wife off of the plantation, and no strange Negro is to have a wife on the plantation.

10th. There is to be no noise by any Negro on the place after 10 O'clock at night, but at that time the overseer must see that all go to bed, and no light allowed in any house after that time, except a fire to warm by.

11th. All must start to work at *light* in the morning.

12th. No torch to be allowed about the lots or plantation for fear of fire.

Economic concentration led to the emergence of a prosperous and cultured planter class, of which men like Butler, Brooks, and Pickens were leading figures. The community's elites were as proud of their kinship connections as any Boston Brahmin, and devotion to family was one of the district's most distinctive traits. Like Bostonians they took religion seriously. A number of important planter families belonged to the Episcopal Church, though many other planters and most of Edgefield's ordinary residents were Baptists or Methodists. Although as in Boston these churches occasionally incited their believers to criticize community customs as much as individual behavior, most Southern church leaders came to believe that churches and church leaders should avoid direct interference in politics or public policy issues. That Northern churchmen such as Emerson had fallen simultaneously into the horrors of theological innovation, abolition, and political activism provided further proof of the dangers this might bring. Yankee religion, like Yankee politics, should be avoided at all costs.

The young men of Edgefield's upper class often mixed their religious beliefs with adherence to uniquely Southern traditions of honor and deference. Rooted in the courtly customs of seventeenth and eighteenth century European aristocrats, shaped by the novels of Sir Walter Scott and other Romantic writers, sustained by a slave-based social hierarchy, and aided by patriarchal family structures, the concept of honor was of critical importance to men such as Brooks and Butler. To Brooks especially, honor meant unflinching courage and unswerving personal devotion. To live an honorable life required having such purity and refinement in behavior that no person could raise the slightest question about one's character. Like the Chevalier Bayard, hero of a popular 1847 novel by Charlestonian William Gilmore Simms, men should live lives "without fear and without reproach." For many Edgefield men the concept of honor also included adherence to the *code duello*. Expert guidance in dueling came from former South Carolina governor John Lyde Wilson, whose 1838 book *The Code of Honor, or Rules for the Government of Principals and Seconds in Duelling*, became the definitive volume on the subject. In a reversal of Sumner's argument against war, Wilson claimed that "if an oppressed nation has a right to appeal to arms in defence of its liberty and the happiness of its people, there can be no argument used in support of such appeal, which will not apply with equal force to individuals."[28]

To believe something sincerely, the code held, meant the willingness to fight or even to die for it. Any social equal who refused to back his words with manly courage was considered a coward. Because this act of violence could be provoked at any instant, duelists argued, society itself was improved. Men would measure their words and thus avoid coarse or disrespectful statements. The code made exceptions for inferiors and dependents since these by definition could not be gentlemanly or independent. Accordingly, women, children, slaves, and men of the lower classes could not be participants but were to be protected or disciplined as circumstances required. Cowards and scoundrels were also excluded from the duel because of their obviously inferior character. Such men should be caned or horse-whipped instead, much as one might punish an unruly dog. Implicit in the code was the fear of degradation into a lower status. To tolerate an insult would lead to the debasement of one's reputation in the community. Ultimately it might lead to the loss of independence itself since none would respect your courage or fear your commands. It was in this cultural environment that Andrew P. Butler and Preston Brooks were raised.

Andrew P. Butler's father, William Butler, was a junior officer in the Revolution who served for eight years in the South Carolina campaigns. His son, born in 1796, was named after Andrew Pickens, a distinguished leader in the war and one of Butler's commanding officers. The elder Butler was elected to the United States Congress in 1801 and served until 1813 when he returned to South Carolina to command the state's militia during renewed war with the British. Andrew Butler grew up in Edgefield on the family's plantation, attended Moses Waddell's famous academy in Abbeville, and then South Carolina College (now the University of South Carolina). Like Charles Sumner he developed a fondness for scholarship and the law. After passing the bar in 1818 he developed a busy practice. His reputation attracted clients from across the South Carolina upcountry and led to his election to the state

FIGURE 1.3   Andrew Pickens Butler

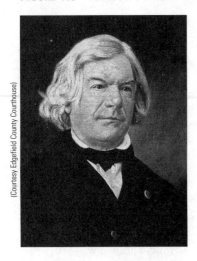

(Courtesy Edgefield County Courthouse)

legislature in 1824. His acquaintances considered him well-read and intelligent but not precise enough to be truly brilliant. He became associated with John C. Calhoun and the moderate state rights wing of the Democratic party. After nine years in the legislature he became a circuit court judge. In the 1835 post-nullification reorganization of the South Carolina judiciary he was placed on the state's highest body, the Court of Appeals. In 1846 he was appointed to South Carolina's vacant seat in the United States Senate. Butler remained a Senator until his death in 1857. As a judge and in the Senate he developed a reputation for good-natured but sharp-edged humor. He suffered from a minor facial deformity that gave him a speech impediment and caused him to spit while talking. While this sometimes led strangers to underestimate his abilities, it did not prevent him from advancing in the Senate. At the time of the caning he chaired the Senate judiciary committee.[29]

Preston Brooks had a similar story. His grandfather, Zachariah Brooks, had fought in the American Revolution. His father, Whitfield Brooks, attended college and received training as a lawyer before taking up a career as a planter. Their estate, "Roselands," located near the village of Ninety Six in the northern part of the district, was one of the community's largest plantations and was famous for its extensive flower gardens. The Brooks family's prominence in the community was reinforced by kinship ties with many of Edgefield's most powerful clans, including the Butlers, Bonhams, Birds, and Simkinses. Among the most important of these relatives was Butler, who was Whitfield Brooks's first cousin. In 1818 Whitfield Brooks married Mary Carroll, member of another prominent area family with ties to the Butlers. Preston Brooks was born in 1819. He was especially devoted to his mother, living within a few miles of her until his death in 1857. His early years were typical for a boy of his status and condition. In the elementary years he attended village schools in the community. Like Butler he attended Moses Waddell's academy.

He was barely seventeen when admitted to South Carolina College. After paying fifty dollars tuition Brooks entered the freshman class of 1836. He encountered

FIGURE 1.4 Preston S. Brooks

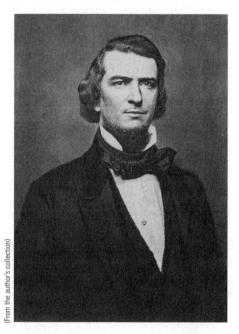

a faculty almost as new to the institution as he was. A scandal two years before had unhinged the college. The former president, secessionist Thomas Cooper, and several faculty members had been forced to resign because of their religious atheism. In an effort to restore the college's reputation, Andrew Pickens Butler (then serving on the board of trustees) convinced his associates to create a faculty chair in the evidences of Christianity and sacred literature. They selected Presbyterian minister James Henley Thornwell, who would later become famous for his religious contributions to the proslavery argument. They also appointed the noted scholar Francis Lieber to a vacant chair in history and political economy. Coincidentally, Lieber had recently become one of Charles Sumner's closest correspondents. To answer suspicions about his own radicalism Lieber felt compelled to declare in public that he was neither an atheist nor an abolitionist. In selecting Thornwell and confirming Leiber's reliability the trustees sought to guarantee that students would be insulated from philosophical extremes.[30]

Like Sumner, Brooks was a very good student who did well on examinations. Unlike Sumner, Brooks was less interested in books than in the other entertainments of college life. He became involved in several incidents which provide a snapshot of his character and foreshadow his later behavior. While still a freshman he was disciplined by the faculty for leaving campus without permission. As a sophomore he was suspended for skipping too many recitations. After being readmitted he spent so much time at local taverns that the faculty not only punished him but rewrote the disciplinary code to clarify its most ambiguous passages. The following January he accused fellow student Lewis Simons of being a "falsifier." Simons challenged Brooks to a duel. Brooks responded by claiming that since they were both still boys a duel was dishonorable and that at any rate the rules of the college prohibited it. The dispute ended in a fist-fight. Both were suspended. Brooks was readmitted as a senior and passed his final examinations with distinction. Between finals and graduation he got involved in a scuffle with the Columbia town marshal over an alleged insult to his brother. In November 1839 the faculty voted not to give Brooks his degree. The trustees sustained the faculty, and Brooks never officially graduated. Their report of the events is given here:[31]

Report of the South Carolina College Faculty on the Expulsion of Preston S. Brooks[32]

Mr. Preston Brooks of the senior class was summoned to account for riotous behavior on the preceding Sunday evening. He stated he had heard from a Negro an exaggerated report that his brother had been carried by the town Marshall in an ignominious manner to the guard house. That in his excitement he took a pair of pistols which had been some time ago been presented by a friend and had been lying at the bottom of his trunk without the intention or wish on his part to use them during the college course. That having no ammunition he went somewhere in Columbia, where he knew it was to be procured. That he loaded his pistols and proceeded to the Guard House with the design of rescuing his brother from his supposed ignominious treatment. He admitted that after he found his brother no longer in confinement he continued to display his pistols in a threatening manner and proclaimed his intention of shooting the aggressors. He urged in extenuation of his conduct that he had not considered himself subject to the discipline of the college, because his examinations were completed—and that his offence against the laws of morality and the land, which he did not wish to justify, was one which the natural excitement of the circumstances and the fervor of youth should render venial. The faculty resolved unanimously that Mr. Preston Brooks be suspended from college and reported to the Board of Trustees for expulsion.
William H. Ellet
Secretary of the Faculty
    Mr. Barnwell also submitted the petition of the students praying that Mr. Brooks may be restored to his former position in the college. Gen'l McDuffie moved that the prayer of the petitioners be granted which was decided in the negative.

The expulsion did not affect his career. After returning to Edgefield Brooks began working to become a lawyer. Within months, kinship, politics, and honor interfered, leaving Brooks entangled in another incident. The conflict involved fellow Edgefield resident and former South Carolina classmate Louis T. Wigfall, who would later become a Senator from Texas. The two men and their families supported rival candidates for governor in 1840. Inflammatory statements published by both families in the local newspaper led to a brawl between Brooks and Wigfall and a request by Wigfall for a duel. A board of reconciliation led both men to retract their challenges. Within days of the rapprochement Wigfall responded to rumors about his concessions in the agreement by publishing an attack on Preston Brooks. In defense of his son, Whitfield Brooks issued an inflammatory attack on Wigfall, who responded with a challenge to the father. The Elder Brooks refused the duel, leading Wigfall to "post" him as a coward. Preston Brooks defended his father by renewing the earlier challenge. After fighting and winning two duels with other Brooks relatives Wigfall accepted Preston Brooks's request. Because dueling was illegal in South Carolina the two men met on an island in the Savannah River, on the border with neighboring Georgia. An exchange of shots left both men severely injured. Wigfall left the field with a bullet through his hip. Brooks took a bullet through his thigh and lower abdomen. Wigfall was never able to recover his reputation in Edgefield. Six years later he departed for Texas. The duel seems to have done less damage to Brooks's fortunes.[33]

Brooks married Caroline Means of Columbia in 1841. She died in 1843. That same year he passed the bar exam, and was elected the following year to the state legislature. During the 1844 controversy over the imprisonment of free black sailors from Massachusetts it was Brooks who escorted Massachusetts Senator Hoar from the state, in what amounted to a combination of protective custody and forcible removal. In 1845 he married Caroline's sister Martha and settled on a small plantation near Edgefield. When the Mexican War broke out Brooks enlisted immediately, along with his brother and a hundred other men from the district. Calling themselves the "96 Boys," they became part of the Palmetto Regiment of South Carolina Volunteers. In those days soldiers selected their officers through a democratic vote. Brooks was elected captain of his company. After several months in Mexico he caught a severe fever which was aggravated by his old dueling injuries. Over Brooks's protest the medical officer returned him to Edgefield to serve as the local recruiting officer. A quick return to health led to rumors he was shirking duty. Mortified, Brooks begged superior officers for transfer back to the front. Approval for his return to Mexico was granted in late September, 1847. He arrived in time to discover that not only had most fighting ended but that his older brother had recently been killed in action. Brooks returned home with a promotion to colonel but saddened over his personal loss. Despite the costs, however, the war experience reinforced his belief that deeds outranked words.[34]

Brooks resumed his residence in the Edgefield District. He devoted most of his time to managing the affairs of his plantation and also looked after his mother's interests at Roselands. He gradually renewed his interest in politics. By 1852 he had allied himself with the faction in the state dominated by Congressman James Orr. These men believed that Southern interests could best be preserved by building ties with the national Democratic party. They were considered moderates, at least in the South Carolina context. This placed Brooks in opposition to the so-called "Irreconcilables," who believed South Carolina's interests lay outside the national Democratic party. The ultras in this group advocated immediate secession from the United States. Fortunately for Brooks, post-compromise Unionism in the state and the success of Northern Democrat Franklin Pierce in the presidential election gave the state's moderates a slim edge. When Congressman Armistead Burt retired in late 1852, Brooks and three other candidates (including erstwhile radical Francis W. Pickens) decided to run for the vacant seat. In an incident revealing of Brooks's temperament, he accused the local newspaper editor of relying on the dubious credibility of the pen, rather than the more legitimate qualification of military service, to make his claims. He also challenged one of the paper's anonymous contributors to a duel for writing statements that he said had scandalized the women of his family. No duel resulted, but Brooks's reputation must have been maintained. When the election was over he had received 32 percent of the total, defeating his nearest challenger by 601 votes out of 6502 cast. Like Sumner and Butler, Brooks would serve in Congress until his death.[35]

Brooks delivered his first speech to Congress during the Nebraska Bill debates. Although his comments did not directly speak to the issue that provoked the caning, they do give a good depiction of his political beliefs on the eve of the incident. In the address below he gives a concise restatement of the "proslavery argument." According to this theory, which was supported widely by Southern planters and intellectuals, slavery benefited both servant and master. Proslavery advocates claimed that slavery's bonds of mutual obligation produced a society far superior to any system available to workers in the North. Brooks's suspicion of social equality came naturally from this position. He showed no tolerance for ideas that might undermine the stability of the existing social order. And while he supported popular sovereignty as a solution to the territorial problem, his comments in favor of immigrant exclusion indicate strong distrust of mass democracy. He was equally hostile to Northern abolitionism, which he condemned as a "false" and "counterfeited" philanthropy. The speech vividly displays Brooks's fears about the fate of the South should these Northerners seize control of the nation. His harsh opinion of Northern society is almost exactly inverse of the position Sumner would take regarding South Carolina in his "Crime Against Kansas" speech.[36]

Speech by Preston Brooks on Nebraska and Kansas, March 15, 1854[37]

Mr. Brooks said:

Mr. Chairman: I desire to express my views upon the bill which is engrossing the thoughts of every member on this floor, and I wish to do so before the ground is altogether covered by the army of speakers who are holding themselves in reserve. Should aught of intemperance of language escape me in the remarks I am about to make, I trust that it may be regarded as directed towards principles and positions, and not to the persons from whom they proceed.

I have lived long enough to learn, that to do justice to the opinions and even prejudices of others, is the surest way to secure a just consideration of my own.

Nor, sir, does it jump with my humor or my appreciation of honor to assail those who, in obedience to a local sentiment, are averse to a resort but too common in a warmer latitude. It is a cheap display of chivalry to insult when no risk is incurred; and, for my own part, I would prefer the condition of him who bears the wound than of him by whom it is, under such circumstances, needlessly inflicted. . . .

[Here Brooks gave a summary of the historic compromises leading up to the Nebraska Bill and offered the doctrine of popular sovereignty as the best solution to the current crisis, and then voiced his support for a measure excluding foreign immigrants from entering the territories.]

Such is the infatuation of a portion of those who oppose this bill, that, with the history of the foreign population in America fresh in their memories—a history which, at the North, is but a succession of riots and of mobs, in which private houses have been invaded, public edifices demolished, railroads subverted, churches burned, and our citizens murdered—that they condescend to appeal even to those outcast from the purlieus of the cities of the Old World, to bring their influence to bear upon this Federal Legislature. . . . Will it be said by Free-Soilers, in support of their philanthropy, that they desired us to provide homes for the Negro as well as for the whites? Then the proposition amounts to this, that we of the South, after being robbed of our slaves, are asked by abolitionists and Free-Soilers to relieve them of a population which they have corrupted into nuisances, by setting apart a portion of territory, of which we are joint owners, for the benefit of these very runaways and free Negroes, while our slaves and ourselves are to be deliberately excluded. . . .

I know, sir, that the equality loving Free-Soilers of the North, "unless pressed by a hard and cruel necessity," refuse to work beside slaves. I know that, after seducing them from their homes of cheerfulness and comfort at the South, they are left to starve in the streets, while the "freedom-loving" immigrant from Europe monopolizes every avenue of thrift and of employment; and I also know, that hundreds who are now dragging out a miserable existence, in want and in crime, would joyfully return to their former owners could they by honest labor but secure the necessary means. Let Free-Soilers come to the South, sir, and we will show them the white and the black man in a relation of friendship never dreamed of in their philosophy. We will show them slaves, devoted to the family interests, family name, and family honor of their masters. And we will show them, in every gentleman, a man who will pour out his money, and peril his life, if needs be, to protect his bondsman from cruelty and injustice. A majority of our best men, and many of our ablest men have labored side by side with their slaves, through years of enjoyment, of usefulness, and respectability.

But, sir, the humanity of Free-Soilers would exclude the poor Negro, who owes his condition to the cupidity of their ancestors, from "the rich lands of this large Territory," and surrender it, without fear or reward, to the descendants of, possibly, the very Hessians—the minions of King George, who warred against our liberties, when the Negro, by his labor, fed the Continental Army of America.

Sir, the jealousy of the political power of slavery is not to be covered by so flimsy a veil; and let me tell those who are sincere in a morbid sympathy for the imaginary sufferings of slavery, and who, with incorrupt motives, indulge in schemes of restricting it, that a better knowledge of the workings of the institution would teach them that genuine philanthropy demands its extension.

The operations of a great system are to be learned by an observation of the operation of smaller systems. In every section where there is a scarcity of land its value is increased. The poor, who might desire to enter it, are unable to buy; and those who are there are generally tempted, by an extravagance of price, to seek their fortunes elsewhere. The men of wealth absorb the small farms into large estates, from which they are frequently absent, and the management of which is usually entrusted to agents who have no interest in them beyond their annual wages and a regard for their professional reputation. The character of this reputation is too often determined by no other consideration than the amount of the crops which are annually raised. Large gangs of Negroes are congregated upon large estates, with no social intercourse but with each other. They are thus denied the watchful providence of the master, and the elevating influences of his association with them. Loyal to their owner, and proud of their relation to him, they are jealous of a substitute. Wanting in mental resources, imitative by nature, and conscious of a natural inferiority and dependence upon a superior race, when left to themselves, they become the prey of the wildest superstitions, and, removed from the example of their superiors, they descend in the scale of creation.

But, on the other hand, where lands are abundant they are also cheap. The poor man, when provided with a home, next looks around for something upon which he shall expand his successive annual gains, and which will bring the greatest amount of comfort and convenience to his family and himself. Should his money be invested in a Negro, he introduces it into his family circle. The same hand that prepares the daily food of the master, prepares that also of the slave. They labor in the same field, drink from the same spring of water, and worship at the same altar. The Negro is enlightened and enobled by the association, and an experienced southern eye can tell a glance, by the shining face, the more athletic form, and jaunty air, that his home is upon a small farm, and that the white man is the companion of his daily toil.

Were Free-Soilers permitted to carry out their plans of restricting slavery to its present limits, the first effect in the South would be to expel our poor white population, who could not resist the temptation of high prices for their lands; and the second would be still lower to degrade the Negro, and more thoroughly to enslave them.

I will now proceed to the argument urged in opposition to this bill, which is drawn from the assumed immorality, tyranny, and inexpediency of slavery.

It may be convenient to attack a constitutional right by appeals to the passions, but so long as we are sustained at all points by the authority of law, we are not in very much danger from sentiment. It may be that slavery was originally morally wrong; but we know that it existed before the Christian era—that it was sanctioned by our Saviour, who enjoined upon servants obedience to their masters—that it was to be found in Greece and in Rome—that it has obtained in France, England, Spain, Holland, and Brazil, and other modern States, and that the responsibility of its introduction in these States is upon those who have gone before us. It may be that the sovereignty of these States should have been surrendered to the General Government, yet it was not done.

It may be that property in slaves should have been prohibited by the Constitution; yet the importation of slaves was authorized by it until the year 1808, and import duty of $10 per head was imposed, as on other species of imported property; and constitutional provision made whereby this property might be recovered, notwithstanding "any law or regulation" to the contrary existing in the State where it may be found. It may be that the equal rights of the States to the common territory of all should have been constitutionally denied. Yet it is constitutional law. It is too late to inquire what ought to have been done at the time this Government was established—our sole business is to know what was done. . . .

Mr. Chairman, this cant about the immorality and horrible tyranny of slavery may answer its purpose among the masses of the North, who have been systematically deceived, and for a purpose, but it is out of place here. If slavery be morally wrong, then those gentlemen who so regard it should have paused before they took the oath to support a Constitution which so thoroughly recognizes it as a right. The very grave question presents itself to them—whether it be the greater sin to violate a moral sentiment peculiar to themselves, or to violate an oath which they have taken in the face of the country, and which is recorded in Heaven. . . ?

It is, sir, a question of political power between the manufacturing and agricultural states. . . . When, sir, a northern man meets me with manly frankness, and tells me that slave and free labor cannot coexist, or that our three fifths representation is unequal or unjust, I can reason with him with patience, and, if proper, agree to disagree. I would say to him, sir, it is as impossible for you to judge correctly of the institution of slavery as for a blind man to judge of colors. Your prejudices were formed before your judgment had matured. They have been fostered through life by association, misrepresentation, and remoteness. You know nothing of the Negro character, or of his intimate and inseparable connection with the moral, social, and political condition of the South. If you wish either of us well let us alone. If you would not crowd a ship already full, give us our constitutional rights in the Territories.

The incompatibility of free and slave labor is only a northern notion. It is not so at the South. You object to having three fifths of our Negroes represented, because of the political power it gives us. If they were free the whole would be represented, as at the North, and the political power of the slave States would be increased to the extent of the remaining two fifths.

But, sir, when the positions assumed, and the drift of the argument deduced, is, by necessary implication, to charge my people with the blackest offenses in the catalog of crime, I meet it with scorn and detestation. The history of the African contains proof upon every page of his utter incapacity for self-government. His civilization depends upon his contact with and his control by the white man. Though elevated and educated by this association, taught by experience the blessings of law, and provided with all of the machinery of government ready to his hand, when he is left to his own government, he descends to the level of the brute. Let Free-Soilers read the history of the blacks on the Island of Jamaica since their emancipation, and if one drop of genuine philanthropy runs in their veins, they will guard a population, of which they are par excellence the champions, from the evils of such a liberty.

The institution of slavery, which it is so fashionable now to decry, has been the greatest of blessings to this entire country. At the North it has served as a vent for fanaticism, communism, and all those secretions of a morbid sentimentality, which, without this safety-valve, would long since have resulted in a social explosion; and which will be as cruel to the pure and the good, when it does come, as is certain in the future. From Maine to Texas the slaves have been the pioneers of civilization. The forest has bowed before their march, the earth yielded its rich harvests to their labor, and given us a commerce which excites the admiration and jealousy of the world. . . . Every section of this Confederacy is now in the enjoyment of the rich rewards of the labor of the slave. He gives employment to the shipping interest of the East, wealth to the manufacturer of the North, and a market for the hemp and live-stock of the West.

But, sir, I propose to show that other debts of gratitude are due from the North to the institution of slavery. . . . If there be any truth in the doctrine that the producer of exports pays in reality the duties upon the imports, although the imports be credited to northern ports, the account between the two sections will stand thus: That while the Southern States produce two thirds of the entire domestic productions of the country, we collect but one ninth of the duties on imports. Nor is this all; for, according to the record, it appears that four fifths of the public monies thus collected have been appropriated to the non-slaveholding States for Government purposes and internal improvements. . . .

Sir, I venture to declare the opinion that slavery has been the strongest bond of union between these States. Every section of the Confederacy has reaped its blessings, and the people of the North have been too long accustomed to levy blackmail upon it now to deny themselves so fruitful a source of thrift and of profit. The South has been the goose of the golden egg to the North, which Free-Soilers, in their mad cupidity and fanatical tamperings, are threatening to destroy.

If by some convulsion of nature the slave States could be sunken beneath the level of the waters, it would involve millions of the inhabitants of the North in bankruptcy, and ruin, and inutterable miseries.

Your lordly merchant and fattened manufacturer, your omnibus men and porters, mall, with truth, exclaim "Othello's occupation's gone!"[38]

Your cities, now your pride and strength, would dwindle into towns; your crowded harbors grow empty and wild; and thousands who now live in contentment and comfort would beg for bread.

Reverse the picture, and suppose the free States blotted from creation. Why, sir, the fact would be felt only by our railroad conductors, captains of steamboats, and a few politicians with national aspirations. Our harbors would be filled with foreign shipping; our marine towns grow into cities, rivaling in their magnificence and prosperity the present condition of those of the North. Every kind of manufactory would spring up over our streams; our revenue would be collected and expended among the people who now bear an unequal burden in supporting the Government, and who are unequally protected by it.

Mr. Chairman, the cry that the Union is in danger has been so often raised that men have ceased to regard it. But sir, disunion may come while we are sleeping in security. Before God, I believe that if this bill—which simply establishes the principle that the people, in their condition of sovereign States, should be permitted to decide for themselves upon all matters affecting their internal government—fails to pass this House, we will be in greater danger of disunion than at any time since the formation of this Government. I make no threat of disunion. The failure of the passage of this bill may not so result. But, sir, our young men are becoming familiar with the sound of a word which was breathed by their sires only in secrecy, or forced from their lips by the agony of accumulated wrong. The South is now united, and she is sustained by the intelligent and gallant spirits of the West. The Southern backsliders of 1850 have vanished before the breath of popular indignation like "clouds before a Biscay gale," and their seats have been filled by true men. . . .

We will continue to have a great country, a country continuing and increasing in greatness, if we are but true to the principles of the Constitution. It is distinct in letter and equitable in spirit. It is sanctified by the blood and the wisdom of patriots, and has stood the surest of all tests—the test of time. I call upon the good and the true men of every section to array themselves before it, and tell the assailants it is a sacred thing, and not to be polluted by their fanatical touch. The South asks for nothing more.

If the natural laws of climate and of soil exclude us from the territory of which we are the joint owners we should not and we will not complain. But, sir, when a coalition of tenants in common attempt a monopoly, and, by laws at once unconstitutional and unjust, endeavor to restrict us, and by a surveyors line, to a part of these United States, while they are permitted to walk the whole domain, we cannot and we will not submit to so odious a distinction.

THE PERSONAL POLITICS OF THE NEBRASKA BILL AND FUGITIVE SLAVES

The Nebraska Bill debates and their aftermath proved crucial to the caning. It was during this contest that the quarrel between Butler and Sumner erupted for the first time. Before the debate the two men had been friends. Their acquaintance was initiated by the accident of Sumner's place in the Senate chamber. Since the Massachusetts senator belonged to neither the Whigs nor the Democrats he had no predetermined seat. He took up a desk on the back row of the chamber, occupying the place held previously by Jefferson Davis. This was located in Democratic side of the chamber. In January 1853 he described the situation and its implications: "on the floor of the Senate I sit between Mr. Butler, of South Carolina, the early suggester of the Fugitive Slave bill, and Mr. Mason, of Virginia, its final author, with both of whom I have constant and cordial intercourse. This experience would teach me, if I needed the lesson, to shun harsh and personal criticism of those from whom I differ."[39] Despite differences with Sumner over slavery, Butler found a common interest with him in discussions of diplomatic issues, legal reform, history, and the literary classics. It would take six months of debate to destroy their relationship.

Neither man intentionally sought the collision. It arose as a by-product of Sumner's anger over the Nebraska bill. For over a decade Stephen A. Douglas had attempted to open Kansas and Nebraska for settlement. Each time his initiatives had been blocked by Southerners. Both territories lay above the Missouri Compromise line of 30 degrees 30 minutes latitude. Southerners rightly feared the addition of four free state senators to Congress without an equivalent number from slave states. They also recognized that a Missouri surrounded on three sides by free territory would soon give up slavery too, which would further tilt the sectional balance away from the South. By January 1854, however, settlement pressures could no longer be resisted. Southern Democrats agreed to support Douglas's measure in exchange for language allowing the new territorial legislatures to vote on slavery. This amounted to what historians have described as a "stealth repeal" of the Missouri Compromise. Because the compromise would ban slavery until the legislature organized, however, Southern Whigs attacked the stealth compromise as proof that Southern Democrats were soft on slavery. To gain credibility as slavery's best defenders Southern Whig Archibald Dixon introduced a measure on January 16 attacking Douglas's plan as unconstitutional and calling for the explicit repeal of the Missouri Compromise. Sumner, who until this moment had taken very little interest in territorial issues, was now goaded into action. The next day he introduced a resolution to reaffirm the Missouri compromise's express ban on slavery in the two territories. In doing so he established himself as the Nebraska bill's leading opponent and initiated the sequence of events that would bring Butler into the quarrel.[40]

Sumner's immediate concern was with the bill and its sponsor, Stephen Douglas. Two days after his resolution the Freesoil delegation in Congress produced a manifesto against the bill. Their document, the *Appeal of the Independent Democrats*, was a joint effort. Representative Joshua Giddings of Ohio developed the major points, Senator Salmon P. Chase of Ohio, wrote the text, and Sumner gave the document its final stylistic revisions. Their work appeared in major newspapers on Monday, January 24, just in time for the opening debates on the Nebraska bill. Because the *Appeal* led to a rupture between Northern and Southern Whigs it is considered one of the foundational documents leading to the creation of the modern Republican Party.[41]

Appeal of the Independent Democrats[42]

Washington, Thursday Jan. 19, 1854.

FELLOW-CITIZENS: As Senators and Representatives in Congress of the United States, it is our duty to warn our constituencies whenever imminent danger menaces the Freedom of our Institutions or the Permanency of our Union. . . .

At the present session, a new Nebraska bill has been reported by the Senate Committee on Territories, which, should it unhappily receive the sanction of Congress, will open all the unorganized territory of the Union to the ingress of slavery.

We arraign this bill as a gross violation of a sacred pledge; as a criminal betrayal of precious rights; as part and parcel of an atrocious plot to exclude from a vast unoccupied region, emigrants from the Old World and free laborers from our own States, and convert it into a dreary region of despotism, inhabited by masters and slaves. . . .

In 1820, the Slave States said to the Free States, "Admit Missouri with slavery, and refrain from positive exclusion south of 36 [degrees] 30 [minutes], and we will join you in perpetual prohibition north of that line." The Free States consented. In 1854, the Slave States say to the Free States, "Missouri is admitted; no prohibition of Slavery south of 36 [degrees] 30 [minutes] has been attempted; we have received the full consideration of our agreement; no more is to be gained by adherence to it on our part; we, therefore, propose to cancel the compact." If this be not Punic faith, what is it? Not without the deepest dishonor and crime can the Free States acquiesce in this demand.

We confess our total inability properly to delineate the character or describe the consequences of this measure. Language fails to express the sentiments of indignation and abhorrence which it inspires; and no vision, less penetrating and comprehensive than that of the All-Seeing, can reach its evil issues. . . .

From the rich lands of this large Territory, also, patriotic statesmen have anticipated that a free, industrious, and enlightened population will extract abundant treasures of individual and public wealth. There, it has been expected, freedom-loving emigrants from Europe, and energetic and intelligent laborers of our own land, will find homes of comfort and fields of useful enterprise. If this bill shall become a law, all such expectation will turn to grievous disappointment. The blight of Slavery will cover the land. The Homestead Law, should Congress enact one, would be worthless there. Freemen, unless pressed by a hard and cruel necessity, will not; and should not, work beside slaves. Labor cannot be respected where any class of laborers is held in abject bondage. It is the deplorable necessity of Slavery, that to make and keep a single slave, there must be slave law; and where slave law exists, labor must necessarily be degraded. . . .

Thus you see, fellow-citizens, that the first operation of the proposed permission of Slavery in Nebraska, will be to stay the progress of the Free States westward, and to cut off the Free States of the Pacific from the Free States of the Atlantic. It is hoped, doubtless, by compelling the whole commerce and the whole travel between the East and the West, to pass for hundreds of miles through a Slaveholding region, in the heart of the Continent, and by the influence of a Federal Government, controlled by the Slave Power, to extinguish Freedom and establish Slavery in the States and Territories of the Pacific, and thus permanently subjugate the whole country to the yoke of a Slaveholding despotism. . . .

We warn you that the dearest interests of Freedom and the Union are in imminent peril. Servile demagogues may tell you that the Union can be maintained only by submitting to the demands of Slavery. We tell you that the safety of the Union can only be insured by the full recognition of the just claims of Freedom and Man. The Union was formed to establish justice, and secure the blessings of liberty. When it fails to accomplish these ends it will be worthless and when it becomes worthless it can not long endure. We entreat you to be mindful of that fundamental maxim of Democracy, EQUAL RIGHTS AND JUSTICE for all men. Do not submit to become agents in extending Legalized Oppression and Systematized injustice over a vast Territory yet exempt from these terrible evils.

We implore Christians and Christian Ministers to interpose. Their Divine Religion requires them to behold in every man a brother, and to labor for the Advancement and Regeneration of the Human Race. . . .

For ourselves, we shall resist it by speech and vote, and with all the abilities which God has given us. Even if overcome in the impending struggle, we shall not submit. We shall go home to our constituents, erect anew the standard of Freedom, and call on the People to come to the rescue of the country from the domination of Slavery. We will not despair; for the cause of Human Freedom is the cause of God.

The *Appeal of the Independent Democrats* enraged Stephen Douglas. He considered it as much a personal attack as a political manifesto. His own speech on the Nebraska Bill, given less than a week after the publication of the *Appeal,* sought to defend his version of popular sovereignty against the charges raised by Sumner and his associates. It is a clear statement of Northern Democratic doctrine that the will of the people, as expressed in majority rule, should prevail. The speech also provides an interesting window into parliamentary procedure. According to Senate rules, anyone violating the prohibition against personal attacks could be "called to order" by the chair. Senator Chase's invocation of the rule in reaction to Douglas's language contrasts with the choice of Douglas and Sumner's other opponents to not call him to order in 1856.

Senator Douglas's Speech on the Nebraska Bill, in the United States Senate, January 30, 1854.[43]

MR. DOUGLAS: said—Mr. President: When I proposed, on Tuesday last, that the Senate should proceed to the consideration of the bill to organize the territories of Nebraska and Kansas, it was my purpose only to occupy ten or fifteen minutes in explanation of its provisions. . . . [In submitting the bill, The Committee on Territories] took the principles established by the compromise acts of 1850 as our guide, and intended to make each and every provision of the bill accord with those principles. Those measures established and rest upon the great principle of self-government—that the people should be allowed to decide the questions of their domestic institutions for themselves, subject only to such limitations and restrictions as are imposed by the Constitution of the United States, instead of having them determined by an arbitrary or geographical line. . . . Sir, this is all that I intended to say, if the question had been taken up for consideration on Tuesday last; but since that time occurrences have transpired which compel me to go more fully into the discussion. It will be borne in mind that the senator from Ohio [Mr. Chase] then objected to the consideration of the bill, and asked for its postponement until this day, on the ground that there had not been time to understand and consider its provisions; and the senator from Massachusetts, [Mr. Sumner] suggested that the postponement should be for one week for that purpose. These suggestions seeming to be reasonable to senators around me, I yielded to their request, and consented to the postponement of the bill until this day.

Sir, little did I suppose, at the time I granted that act of courtesy to those two senators, that they had draughted and published to the world a document, over their own signatures, in which they arraign me as having been guilty of a criminal betrayal of my trust, as having been guilty of an act of bad faith, and been engaged in an atrocious plot against the cause of free government. Little did I suppose that those two senators had been guilty of such conduct when they called upon me to grant that courtesy, to give them an opportunity of investigating the substitute reported from the committee. I have since discovered that on that very morning the *National Era,* the abolition organ in this city, contained an address, signed by certain abolition confederates, to the people, in which the bill is grossly misrepresented, in which the action of the members of the committee is grossly falsified, in which our motives are arraigned and our characters calumniated. And, sir, what is more, I find that there was a postscript added to the address, published that very morning, in which the principle amendment reported by the committee was set out, and then coarse epithets applied to me by name. Sir, had I known those facts at the time I granted that act of indulgence, I should have responded to the request of those senators in such terms as their conduct deserved, so far as the rules of the Senate and a respect for my own character would have permitted me to do. In order to show the character of this document—of which I shall have much to say in the course of my argument—I will read certain passages:

"We arraign this bill as a gross violation of a sacred pledge; as a criminal betrayal of precious rights; as part and parcel of an atrocious plot to exclude from a vast, unoccupied region emigrants from the Old World, and free laborers from our own states, and convert it into a dreary region of despotism, inhabited by masters and slaves."

A SENATOR: By whom is the address signed?

MR. DOUGLAS: It is signed 'S. P. Chase, senator from Ohio; Charles Sumner, senator from Massachusetts; J. R. Giddings and Edward Wade, representatives from Ohio; Gerrit Smith, representative from New York; Alexander De Witt, representative from Massachusetts,' including, as I understand, all the representatives from the abolition party in Congress.

Then, speaking of the committee on territories, these confederates use this language:

"The PRETENCES, therefore, that the territory, covered by the positive prohibition of 1820, sustains a similar relation to slavery with that acquired from Mexico, covered by no prohibition except that of disputed constitutional or Mexican law, and that the compromises of 1850 require the incorporation of the pro-slavery clauses of the Utah and New Mexico bill in the Nebraska act, are MERE INVENTIONS, DESIGNED TO COVER UP FROM PUBLIC REPREHENSION MEDITATED BAD FAITH."

"Mere inventions to cover up bad faith." Again:

"Servile demagogues may tell you that the Union can be maintained only by submitting to the demands of slavery."

Then there is a postscript added equally offensive to myself, in which I am mentioned by name. That address goes on to make an appeal to the legislatures of the different states, to public meetings, and to ministers of the gospel in their pulpits, to interpose and arrest the vile conduct which is about to be consummated by the senators who are thus denounced. That address, sir, bears the date Sunday, January 22d, 1854—Thus, it appears, that on the holy Sabbath, while other senators were engaged in attending divine worship, these abolitionists were assembled in secret conclave, plotting by what means they should deceive the people of the United States and prostrate the character of brother senators. This was done on the Sabbath day, and by a set of politicians, to advance their own political and ambitious purposes, in the name of our holy religion.

But this is not all. It was understood from the newspapers that resolutions were pending before the Legislature of Ohio, proposing to express their opinions upon this subject. It was necessary for these confederates to get up some exposition of the question, by which they might facilitate the passage of the resolutions through that Legislature. Hence, you find that on the same morning that this document appears over the names of these confederates in the Abolition organ of this city, the same document appears in the New York papers—certainly in the *Tribune, Times,* and *Evening Post*—in which it is stated, by authority, that it is "signed by the Senators and a majority of the Representatives from the State of Ohio;" a statement which I have every reason to believe was utterly false, and known to be so at the time that these confederates appended it to the address. It was necessary, in order to carry out this work of deception, and to hasten the action of the Ohio Legislature, under a misapprehension, to state that it was signed, not only by the Abolition confederates, but by the whole Whig representation and a portion of the Democratic representation in the other House from the State of Ohio.

MR. CHASE: Mr. President—

MR. DOUGLAS: Mr. President, I do not yield the floor. A Senator who has violated all the rules of courtesy and propriety—who showed a consciousness of the character of the act he was doing by concealing from me all knowledge of the fact—who came to me with a smiling face, and the appearance of friendship, even after that document had been uttered, who could get up in the Senate and appeal to my courtesy in order to get time to give the document a wider circulation before its infamy could be exposed—such a senator has no right to my courtesy upon this floor.

MR. CHASE: Mr. President, the Senator misrepresents the facts—

MR. DOUGLAS: Mr. President, I decline to yield the floor.

MR. CHASE: And I shall make my denial pertinent when the time comes.

MR. DOUGLAS: Sir, if the Senator does interpose, in violation of the rules of the Senate, to a denial of the fact, it may be that I shall be able to nail that denial, as I shall the statements here which are over his own signature, as a base falsehood, and prove it by the solemn legislation of this country.

MR. CHASE: I call the Senator to order.

THE PRESIDENT: The Senator from Illinois is certainly out of order.

MR. DOUGLAS: Then I will only say that I shall confine myself to this document, and prove its statements to be false by the legislation of the country. Certainly that is in order.

MR. CHASE: You cannot do it.

MR. DOUGLAS: The argument of this manifesto is predicated upon the assumption that the policy of the fathers of the Republic was to prohibit slavery in all the territory ceded by the old States to the Union and made United States territory, for the purpose of being organized into new States. I take issue upon that statement. . . .

   Sir, in 1848 we acquired from Mexico the country between the Rio Del Norte and the Pacific ocean. Immediately after that acquisition, the Senate, on my own motion, voted into a bill a provision to extend the Missouri compromise indefinitely westward to the Pacific ocean, in the same sense, and with the same understanding with which it was originally adopted. That provision passed this body by a decided majority—I think by ten at least—and went to the House of Representatives, and was there defeated by northern votes.

Now, sir, let us pause and consider for a moment. The first time that the principles of the Missouri compromise were ever abandoned, the first time they were ever rejected by Congress, was by the defeat of that provision in the House of Representatives in 1848. By whom was that defeat effected? By northern votes, with Free-Soil proclivities. It was the defeat of that Missouri compromise that created the tremendous struggle of 1850. It was the defeat of that Missouri compromise that created the necessity for making a new compromise in 1850. Had we been faithful to the principles of the Missouri compromise in 1848, this question would not have arisen. Who was it that was faithless? I undertake to say it was the very men who now insist that the Missouri compromise was a solemn compact, and should never be violated or departed from. Every man who is now assailing the principle of the bill under consideration, so far as I am advised, was opposed to the Missouri compromise in 1848 . . .

I am now dealing with the truth and veracity of a combination of men who have assembled in secret caucus upon the Sabbath day, to arraign my conduct and belie my character. I say, therefore, that their manifesto is a slander either way; for it says that the Missouri compromise was not superseded by the measures of 1850, and then it says that the same words in my bill do repeal and annul it. They must be adjudged guilty of one falsehood in order to sustain the other assertion. . . . I submit to the Senate if I have not convicted this manifesto, issued by the Abolition confederates, of being a gross falsification of the laws of the land, and by that falsification that an erroneous and injurious impression has been created upon the public mind? I am sorry to be compelled to indulge in language of this severity; but there is no other language that is adequate to express the indignation with which I see this attempt, not only to mislead the public, but to malign my character by deliberate falsification of the public statutes and public records. . . .

Mr. President, I repeat, that so far as the question of slavery is concerned, there is nothing in the bill under consideration which does not carry out the principle of the compromise measures of 1850, by leaving the people to do as they please, subject only to the provisions of the Constitution of the United States. If that principle is wrong, the bill is wrong. If that principle is right, the bill is right. It is unnecessary to quibble about phraseology or words; it is not the mere words, the mere phraseology, that our constituents wish to judge by. . . .

Sir, I do not recognize the right of the Abolitionists of this country to arraign me for being false to sacred pledges, as they have done in their proclamation. Let them show when and where I have ever proposed to violate a compact. I have proved that I stood by the compact of 1820 and 1845, and proposed its continuance and observance in 1848. I have proved that the Free-Soilers and Abolitionists were the guilty parties who violated that compromise then. I should like to compare notes with these Abolition confederates about adherence to compromises. When did they stand by or approve of any one that was ever made?

Did not every Abolitionist and Free-Soiler in America denounce the Missouri compromise in 1820? Did they not for years hunt down ravenously for his blood every man who assisted in making that compromise? Did they not in 1845, when Texas was annexed, denounce all of us who went for the annexation of Texas, and for the continuation of the Missouri compromise line through it? Did they not in 1848 denounce me as a slavery propagandist for standing by the principles of the Missouri compromise, and proposing to continue the Missouri compromise line to the Pacific ocean? Did they not themselves violate and repudiate it then? Is not the charge of bad faith true as to every Abolitionist in America, instead of being true as to me and the committee, and those who advocate this bill. . . ?

This tornado has been raised by Abolitionists, and Abolitionists alone. They have made an impression upon the public mind in the way in which I have mentioned, by a falsification of the law and the facts; and this whole organization against the compromise measures of 1850 is an Abolition movement. I presume they had some hope of getting a few tender-footed Democrats into their plot; and, acting on what they supposed they might do, they sent forth publicly to the world the falsehood that their address was signed by the Senators and a majority of the Representatives from the State of Ohio; but when we come to examine signatures, we find no one Whig there, no one Democrat there; none but pure, unmitigated, unadulterated Abolitionists. . . .

When you propose to give them a territorial government, do you not acknowledge that they ought to be erected into a political organization; and when you give them a Legislature do you not acknowledge that they are capable of self-government? Having made that acknowledgement, why should you not allow them to exercise the rights of legislation? Oh, these Abolitionists say they are entirely willing to concede all this, with one exception. They say they are willing to trust the Territorial Legislature, under the limitations of the Constitution, to legislate upon the rights of inheritance, to legislate in regard to religion, education, and morals, to legislate in regard to the relations of husband and wife, of parent and child, of guardian and ward, upon everything pertaining to the dearest rights and interests of white men, but they are not willing to trust them to legislate in regard to a few miserable Negroes. That is their single exception. They acknowledge that the people of the Territories are capable of deciding for themselves concerning white men, but not in relation to Negroes. The real gist of the matter is this: Does it require any higher degree of civilization, and intelligence, and learning, and sagacity, to legislate for Negroes than for white men? If it does, we ought to adopt the abolition doctrine, and go with them against this bill. If it does not—if we are willing to trust the people with the great, sacred, fundamental right of prescribing their own institutions, consistent with the Constitution of the country, we must vote for this bill as reported by the Committee on Territories. That is the only question involved in the bill. I hope I have been able to strip it of all the misrepresentation, to wipe away all of that mist and obscurity with which it has been surrounded by this Abolitionist address. . . .

I am in favor of giving every enemy of the bill the most ample time. Let us hear them all patiently, and then take the vote and pass the bill. We who are in favor of it know that the principle on which it is based is right. Why then should we gratify the Abolition party in their effort to get up another political tornado of fanaticism, and put the country again in peril, merely for the purpose of electing a few senators to the Congress of the United States?

The following editorial was typical of the commentaries published by Whig papers in response to Douglas's speech. The *Gazette*'s condemnation of personal attacks launched by Douglas contrasts pointedly with the paper's vocal support two years later for Sumner's right to make personal comments. Its claim that Democrats, Southerners, and Catholics opposed free speech would become a standard element of Know-Nothing and Republican party rhetoric on the eve of the Civil War.

Nebraska in the Senate

Pittsburgh, Pennsylvania, *Gazette*, 2 February 1854.

The debate on the Nebraska bill was opened in the Senate by Mr. Douglas, on Monday last. The speech is reported in full in the Eastern papers. It was insolent and bullying in its tone, coarse in its invective, and contemptible in its argument. It was probably the best that its author could do, under the circumstances; but that only shows how weak is the cause of which he undertakes the championship. Men who have a good measure to advocate do not usually open their advocacy of it by lavishing coarse abuse and insulting epithets on its opponents; and in thus distinguishing his leadership on this question, Mr. Douglas betrays his own sense of its inherent wickedness. His ill-humor, moreover, would seem to indicate a consciousness of its failing prospects.

The Eastern and Southern papers, in the interest of this new inroad upon the rights of the North, betray their appreciation of fair dealing, by publishing Mr. Douglas' speech in full, and withholding all notice of the replies of Messrs. Chase and Sumner. This is Slavery fairly developed. Like Catholicism, it cannot bear discussion. It shrinks from the light with as strong a disrelish for it as owls and bats. The very bitterness of intolerance is concentrated in this act of suppressing the arguments of those to whom the Slavery party is opposed.

The replies of Messrs. Chase and Sumner to Mr. Douglas had reference only to the personal attacks made on them by the puny Senator from Illinois. Their answers were firm and determined, but dignified. They could not sink the gentleman in the controversialist, as Mr. Douglas did. Respect for themselves and their constituency, as well as their own inherent sense of propriety, restrained them from bandying fish-market epithets with one who seemed to lack all such requisites.

Sumner's response to Douglas focused less on the Illinois senator's personal challenges than on the legal technicalities of the bill. Sumner intended it as a point by point rebuttal. The speech closely follows the positions taken by William H. Seward in his famous "Higher Law" speech of 1850. Sumner's argument about the "primal truth of the Equality of men" showed his opposition to the social views of Preston Brooks and other proslavery Southerners. His legal interpretation of the local and municipal nature of slave law dates back to his reflections on the *Creole* incident in the 1840s. The most controversial part of the speech was his historical argument. Sumner asserted that the current generation of Southerners had betrayed the antislavery beliefs of earlier Southerners. This accusation of Southern declension from the ideals of the revolutionary generation would greatly irritate Butler.

The Landmark of Freedom[44]

Speech in Congress by Charles Sumner, 21 February 1854.

Mr. President,—I approach this discussion with awe. The mighty question, with untold issues, oppresses me. Like a portentous cloud surcharged with irresistible storm and ruin, it seems to fill the whole heavens, making me painfully conscious how unequal to the occasion I am,—how unequal, also, is all that I can say to all that I feel.

In delivering my sentiments to-day I shall speak frankly, according to my convictions, without concealment or reserve. If anything fell from the Senator from Illinois [Mr. DOUGLAS], in opening this discussion, which might seem to challenge a personal contest, I desire to say that I shall not enter upon it. Let not a word or a tone pass my lips to divert attention for a moment from the surpassing theme, by the side of which Senators and Presidents are but dwarfs. I would not forget those amenities which belong to this place, and are so well calculated to temper the antagonism of debate. . . .

The question for your consideration is not exceeded in grandeur by any which has occurred in our national history since the Declaration of Independence. In every aspect it assumes gigantic proportions, whether we consider simply the extent of territory it affects, or the public faith and national policy which it assails, or that higher question—that *Question of Questions*, as far above others as Liberty is above the common things of life—which it opens anew for judgment. . . .

The bill now before us proposes to organize and equip two new territorial establishments, with Governors, Secretaries, Legislative Councils, Legislators, Judges, Marshals, and the whole machinery of civil society. Such a measure at any time would deserve the most careful attention. But at the present moment it justly excites peculiar interest, from the effort made—on pretences unsustained by facts, in violation of solemn covenant, and in disregard of the early principles of our fathers—to open this immense region to Slavery.

According to existing law, this territory is now guarded against Slavery by a positive Prohibition, embodied in the Act of Congress approved March 6th, 1820, preparatory to the admission of Missouri into the Union as a sister State . . . It is now proposed to set aside this Prohibition. . . . All this is to be done on pretences founded upon the Slavery enactments of 1850. . . . I desire to say, that, such as they are, [the measures of 1850] cannot, by any rule of interpretation, by any charming rod of power, by any magic alchemy, be transmuted into a repeal of that original Prohibition. . . . It is clear, beyond contradiction, that the Prohibition of Slavery in this Territory was not superseded, or in any way contravened, by the Slavery Acts of 1850. The proposition before you is, therefore, original in character, without sanction from any former legislation, and it must, accordingly, be judged by its merits, as an original proposition.

Here, Sir, let it be remembered that the friends of Freedom are not open to any charge of aggression. They are now standing on the defensive, guarding the early intrenchments thrown up by our fathers. No proposition to abolish Slavery anywhere is now before you, but, on the contrary, a proposition to abolish Freedom. The term Abolitionist, so often applied in reproach, justly belongs, on this occasion, to him who would overthrow this well-established landmark. He is, indeed, no Abolitionist of Slavery; let him be called, Sir, Abolitionist of Freedom. For myself, whether with many or few, my place is taken. Even if alone, my feeble arm should not be wanting as a bar against this outrage.

On two distinct grounds, "strong both against the deed," I arraign it: *First*, in the name of Public Faith, as an infraction of solemn obligations, assumed beyond recall by the South, on the admission of Missouri into the Union as a Slave State. *Secondly*, I arraign it in the name of Freedom, as an unjustifiable departure from the original Antislavery policy of our fathers. . . . And now, Sir, when the conscience of mankind is at last aroused to these things, when, throughout the civilised world, a slave-dealer is a by-word and a reproach, we, as a nation, are about to open a new market to the traffickers in flesh that haunt the shambles of the South. Such an act, at this time, is removed from all reach of that palliation often vouchsafed to Slavery. This wrong, we are speciously told by those who seek to defend it, is not our original sin. It was entailed upon us, so we are instructed, by our ancestors; and the responsibility is often thrown, with exultation, upon the mother country.

Now, without stopping to inquire into the value of this apology, which is never adduced in behalf of other abuses, and which availed nothing against that kingly power imposed by the mother country, but overthrown by our fathers, it is sufficient for the present purpose to know that it is now proposed to make Slavery our own original act. Here is a fresh case of actual transgression, which we cannot cast upon the shoulders of any progenitors, nor upon any mother country, distant in time or place. The Congress of the United States, the people of the United States, at this day, in this vaunted period of light, will be responsible for it, so that it shall be said hereafter, so long as the dismal history of Slavery is read, that in the year of Christ 1854 a new and deliberate act was passed by which a vast territory was opened to its incursions. . . .

As the effort now making is extraordinary in character, so no assumption seems too extraordinary to be advanced in its support. The primal truth of the Equality of Men, proclaimed in our Declaration of Independence, is assailed, and this Great Charter of our country discredited. Sir, you and I will soon pass away, but that charter will continue to stand above impeachment or question. The Declaration of Independence was a Declaration of Rights, and the language employed, though general in character, must obviously be confined within the design and sphere of a Declaration of Rights, involving no such pitiful absurdity as was attributed to it yesterday by the Senator from Indiana [MR. PETTIT]. Sir, who has pretended that all men are born equal in physical strength or in mental capacities, in beauty of form or health of body? Certainly not the signers of the Declaration of Independence, who could have been guilty of no such self-stultification. Diversity is the law of creation, unrestricted to race or color. But as God is no respecter of persons, and as all are equal in his sight, both Dives and Lazarus, master and slave, so are all equal in natural inborn rights; and pardon me, if I say it is a mere quibble to adduce, in argument against this vital axiom of Liberty, the physical or mental inequalities by which men are characterized, or the unhappy degradation to which, in violation of a common brotherhood, they are doomed. To deny the Declaration of Independence is to rush on the bosses of the shield of the Almighty,—which, in all respects, the supporters of this measure seem to do. . . .

It is clear, beyond dispute, that by the overthrow of this Prohibition Slavery will be quickened, and slaves themselves will be multiplied, while new room and verge will be secured for the gloomy operations of Slave Law, under which free labor will droop, and a vast territory be smitten with sterility. Sir, a blade of grass would not grow where the horse of Attila had trod; nor can any true prosperity spring up in the footprints of a slave. . . .

And now, Sir, in the name of that Public Faith which is the very ligament of civil society, and which the great Roman orator tells us it is detestable to break even with an enemy, I arraign this scheme, and hold it up to the judgment of the country. . . . Sir, the proposition before you involves not merely the repeal of existing law, but the infraction of solemn obligations, originally proposed and assumed by the South, after protracted and embittered contest, as a covenant of peace. . . . This arrangement between different sections of the Union, the Slave States of the first part and the Free States of the second part, though usually known as the Missouri Compromise, was at the time styled a compact. In its stipulations for Slavery, it was justly repugnant to the conscience of the North, and ought never to have been made; but on that side it has been performed. And now the unperformed outstanding obligations to Freedom, originally proposed and assumed by the South, are resisted. . . .

The Compromise took its life from the South, so, in the judgment of its own statesmen at the time, and according to unquestionable facts, the South was the conquering party. It gained forthwith its darling desire, the first and essential stage in the admission of Missouri as a Slave State, successfully consummated at the next session,—and subsequently the admission of Arkansas, also as a Slave State. From the crushed and humbled North it received more than the full consideration stipulated in its favor. On the side of the North the contract has been more than executed. And now the South refuses to perform the part which it originally proposed and assumed in this transaction. With the consideration in its pocket, it repudiates the bargain which it forced upon the country. This, Sir, is a simple statement of the present question.

A subtile German has declared that he could find heresies in the Lord's Prayer; and I believe it is only in this spirit that any flaw can be found in the existing obligations of this compact. As late as 1848, in the discussions of this body, the Senator from Virginia [Mr. MASON], who usually sits behind me, but who is not now in his seat, while condemning it in many aspects, says: "Yet, as it was agreed to, as a Compromise, by the *South*, for the sake of the Union, *I would be the last to disturb it.*"

Even this determined Senator recognized it as an obligation which he would not disturb. And, though disbelieving the original constitutionality of the arrangement, he was clearly right. I know, Sir, that it is in form simply a Legislative Act; but as the Act of Settlement in England, declaring the rights and liberties of the subject and settling the succession of the Crown, has become a permanent part of the British Constitution, irrepealable by any common legislation, so this Act, under all the circumstances attending its passage, also by long acquiescence, and the complete performance of its conditions by one party, has become part of our fundamental law, irrepealable by any common legislation. As well might Congress at this moment undertake to overhaul the original purchase of Louisiana as unconstitutional, and now, on this account, thrust away that magnificent heritage, with all its cities, States, and Territories, teeming with civilization. The Missouri Compact, in its unperformed obligations to Freedom, stands at this day as impregnable as the Louisiana purchase. I appeal to Senators about me not to disturb it. . . .

Sir, Congress may now set aside this obligation, repudiate this plighted faith, annul this compact; and some of you, forgetful of the *majesty of honest dealing,* in order to support Slavery, may consider it advantageous to use this power. . . . You are asked to destroy a safeguard of Freedom, consecrated by solemn compact, under which the country is reposing in the security of peace, and thus confirm the supremacy of Slavery. To this institution and its partisans the proposition may seem advantageous; but nothing can be more unjust. Let the judgment of the Athenian democracy be yours.

This is what I have to say upon this head. I now pass to the second branch of the argument.

MR. PRESIDENT: —It is not only as an infraction of solemn compact, embodied in ancient law, that I oppose this bill; I arraign it as a flagrant and extravagant departure from the original policy of our fathers, consecrated by their lives, opinions, and acts. . . .

Sir, the original policy of the country, begun under the Confederation, and recognized at the initiation of the new Government, is clear and unmistakable. Compendiously expressed, it was *non-intervention by Congress with Slavery in the States, and its prohibition in all the national domain.* In this way discordant feelings on this subject were reconciled. Slave-masters were left at home in their respective States, under the protection of local laws, to hug Slavery without interference from Congress, while all opposed to it were exempted from any responsibility therefor in the national domain. . . .

Our Republic has swollen in population and power, but it has shrunk in character. It is not now what it was in the beginning, a Republic merely permitting, while it regretted Slavery,—tolerating it only where it could not be removed, and interdicting it where it did not exist,—but a mighty Propagandist, openly favoring and vindicating it,—visiting, also, with displeasure all who oppose it.

Sir, our country early reached heights which it could not keep. Its fall was gentle, but complete. . . . Without tracing this downward course through its successive stages, let me refer to facts which too palpably reveal the abyss that has been reached. Early in our history no man was disqualified for public office by reason of his opinions on this subject; and this condition continued for a long period. . . . It is needless to add, that no determined supporter of the prohibition of Slavery in the Territories at this day could expect that eminent trust. . . .

These things prepare us to comprehend the true character of the change with regard to the Territories. In 1787 all existing national domain was promptly and unanimously dedicated to Freedom, without opposition or criticism. . . . But now, Sir, here in 1854, Freedom is suddenly summoned to surrender even her hard-won moiety. Here are the three stages: at the first, all consecrated to Freedom; at the second, only half; at the third, all grasped by Slavery. The original policy of the Government is absolutely reversed. Slavery, which at the beginning was a sectional institution, with no foothold anywhere on the National Territory, is now exalted as national, and all our broad domain is threatened by its blighting shadow.

Thus much for what I have to say, at this time, of the original policy, conse-crated by the lives, opinions, and acts of our fathers. Certain reasons are adduced for the proposed departure from their great example, which, though of little valid-ity, I would not pass in silence.

The Prohibition of Slavery in the Territories is assailed, as beyond the power of Congress, and an infringement of local sovereignty. On this account, at this late day, it is pronounced unconstitutional. Now, without considering minutely the sources from which the power of Congress over the national domain is derived . . . it seems to me impossible to deny its existence, without invalidating a large portion of the legislation of the country, from the adoption of the Constitu-tion down to the present day. . . . I call upon Senators to remark, that this sacred right, reputed so essential to the very existence of Government, is abridged in the bill before us. . . .

I am unwilling to admit, Sir, that the Prohibition of Slavery in the Territories is in any just sense an infringement of local sovereignty. Slavery is an infraction of the immutable Law of Nature, and as such cannot be considered a natural incident to any sovereignty, especially in a country which has solemnly declared, in its Dec-laration of Independence, the unalienable right of all men to life, *liberty*, and the pursuit of happiness. In an age of civilization, and in a land of rights, Slavery may still be tolerated *in fact;* but its prohibition within a municipal jurisdiction by the government thereof—as by one of the States of the Union,—cannot be considered an infraction of natural rights; nor can its prohibition by Congress in the Territories be regarded as an infringement of local sovereignty, founded, as it must be, on nat-ural rights. . . .

This argument proceeds on an assumption which cannot stand. It assumes that Slavery is a National Institution, and that property in slaves is recognized by the Constitution of the United States. Nothing can be more false. By the judgment of the Supreme Court of the United States, and also by the principles of the Common Law, Slavery is a local municipal institution, deriving its support exclusively from local municipal laws, and beyond the sphere of these laws it ceases to exist, except so far as it may be preserved by the uncertain clause for the rendition of fugitives from service. Madison thought it wrong to admit in the Constitution the idea that there can be property in men; and I rejoice to believe that no such idea can be found there. The Constitution regards slaves always as "persons," with the rights of "persons,"—never as property. When it is said, therefore, that every citizen may enter the national domain with his property, it does not follow, by any rule of logic or of law, that he may carry his slaves. . . .

It will be in vain, that, while doing this thing, you plead in apology the principle of *self-government*, which you profess to recognize in the Territories. Sir, this very principle, when truly administered, secures equal rights to all, without distinction of race or color, and makes Slavery impossible. By no rule of justice, and by no subtlety of political metaphysics, can the right to hold a fellow-man in bondage be regarded as essential to self-government. The inconsistency is too flagrant. It is apparent on the bare statement. It is like saying *two* and *two* make *three*. In the name of Liberty you open the door to Slavery. With professions of Equal Rights on the lips, you trample on the rights of Human Nature. With a kiss upon the brow of that fair Territory, you betray it to wretchedness and shame. Well did the patriot soul exclaim, in bitter words, wrung out by bitter experience, "O Liberty, what crimes are committed in thy name !"

In vain, Sir, you will plead that this measure proceeds from the North. . . . As yet, there is no evidence that this attempt, though espoused by Northern politicians, proceeds from that Northern sentiment which throbs and glows, strong and fresh, in the schools, the churches, and the homes of the people. . . . And could the abomination which you seek to perpetrate be now submitted to the awakened millions whose souls are truly ripened under Northern skies, it would be flouted at once, with indignant and undying scorn.

But the race of men, "white slaves of the North," described and despised by a Southern statesman, is not yet extinct there, Sir. It is one of the melancholy tokens of the power of Slavery, under our political system, and especially through the operations of the National Government, that it loosens and destroys the character of Northern men, exerting its subtle influence even at a distance,—like the black magnetic mountain in the Arabian story, under whose irresistible attraction, the iron bolts which held together the strong timbers of a stately ship, floating securely on the distant wave, were drawn out, till the whole fell apart, and became a disjointed wreck. Alas! too often those principles which give consistency, individuality, and form to the Northern character, which render it stanch, strong, and seaworthy, which bind it together as with iron, are sucked out, one by one, like the bolts of the ill-fated vessel, and from the miserable loosened fragments is formed that human anomaly, *a Northern man with Southern principles*. Sir, no such man can speak for the North.

[Here there was an interruption of prolonged applause in the galleries.]

THE PRESIDENT (MR. STUART in the chair):   The Chair will be obliged to direct the galleries to be cleared, if order is not preserved. No applause will be allowed.

SEVERAL VOICES: Let them be cleared now.

MR. SUMNER: Mr. President, this bill is proposed as a measure of peace. In this way you vainly think to withdraw the subject of Slavery from National Politics. This is a mistake. Peace depends on mutual confidence. It can never rest secure on broken faith and injustice. Permit me to say, frankly, sincerely, and earnestly, that the subject of Slavery can never be withdrawn from the National Politics until we return once more to the original policy of our fathers, at the first organization of the Government under Washington, when the national ensign nowhere on the National Territory covered a single slave. . . .

The North and the South, Sir, as I fondly trust, amidst all differences, will ever have hand and heart for each other; and believing in the sure prevalence of Almighty Truth, I confidently look forward to the good time, when "both will unite, according to the sentiments of the Fathers and the true spirit of the Constitution, in declaring Freedom, and not Slavery, NATIONAL, to the end that the Flag of the Republic, wherever it floats, on sea or land, within the National jurisdiction, may cover none but freemen. Then will be achieved that Union contemplated at the beginning, against which the storms of faction and the assaults of foreign power shall beat in vain, as upon the Rock of Ages,—and LIBERTY, seeking a firm foothold, WILL HAVE AT LAST WHEREON TO STAND AND MOVE THE WORLD.

Butler would respond to Sumner's oration a few days later in his own Nebraska bill speech. His language shows both the respect that still existed between the two men and signs of their impending breach. By claiming that emancipation had produced Northern decline he gave a mirror opposite of Sumner's Southern declension argument. Like Preston Brooks he argued that the "pseudo-philanthropy" of abolition had caused effeminate weakness in Northern society. He made repeated allusions in the speech to the Roman author Juvenal, a writer who had contrasted the sexual excesses and gender role reversals of decadent imperial Rome with the crude but virile era of the early Roman republic. Butler's horror that women had "unsexed themselves" through the abolitionist movement found confirmation in these historical parallels. Likewise, in making reference to English emancipationist Samuel Wilberforce, Butler sought to remind his audience of the supposedly devastating consequences of British emancipation on the West Indies. The claim that freedom had turned these once prosperous colonies into outposts of shame and destitution was a standard part of the proslavery argument. Butler's attack on Massachusetts may be the most interesting part of the speech. His criticisms of that state were as zealous as anything offered by Sumner against South Carolina in the "Crime Against Kansas" speech.

Senator Andrew Butler's Speech on the Nebraska Bill, 24–25 February 1854[45]

MR. BUTLER: The state of my voice is such that I may not be able to speak with articulate clearness; but I will say one thing before I go further—if I had the tongue of Juvenal, I would not use it as a rasp to exasperate sectional differences; I certainly would not use it to irritate, or in any manner to wound the feelings of those from the North, who in good faith are inclined to do the South justice. But, sir, the honorable Senator from Massachusetts, [MR. SUMNER,] the honorable Senator from New York, [MR. SEWARD,] and the honorable Senators from Ohio [MESSRS. CHASE and WADE,] have said some hard things. They have uttered language which might well call from me that of retaliation and hostility. Sir, I shall not, however, draw from my quiver any poisoned arrows; and if I give them aim, they will only strike where, I think, they should strike. For the honorable Senator from Massachusetts, who sits near me, as a neighbor, as a gentleman of classic taste, as one with whom I frequently converse upon subjects of that kind, I have a respect which such attainments may well inspire. It has always given me pain when I have seen him, under the influence of feelings, rather than of principles—I do not allude to principles in a moral point of view, but to those principles which should guide a statesman—rising and speaking in the style and temper in which he spoke the other day. I must be permitted to say, that whilst I award to him the merit of having spoken with the taste and fervor and eloquence of an accomplished orator, he has not, in my deliberate judgment, spoken with the wisdom, the judgment, and the responsibility of a statesman. . . .

I might begin by adopting the remark quoted by the honorable Senator from Massachusetts, [MR. SUMNER:]

"Oh, Liberty! what crimes have been committed in thy name!"

The blood that lay in pools around the posts of the guillotine would make a historical response; but there may have been, with the French people, some excuse, at least, for their excesses. If, however, the efforts of fanatical organization shall result as that honorable Senator has indicated they must result, in breaking down the distinction between the black and the white man, and elevating one, or degrading the other to an equality, the horrors of the French Revolution, in all their frantic ferocity and cruelty, will be nothing compared to the consequences which must flow from such a state of things. None but an incendiary can look upon the picture but with horror. The effort to confound castes between whom God has made an indelible distinction, would but result in the destruction of one, or the base degradation of the higher class. It is presumptuous, arrogant, and criminal to deal with such elements in the spirit which has manifested itself in the speeches of the gentlemen to whom I have referred. Liberty! Sir, liberty is like fire, which may be used either to warm and preserve the temple in which it is kindled, or to be the means of its destruction. . . . How can this Union be preserved? By requiring all to observe the obligations of good faith; by dispensing with those temporary expedients, and by doing justice one to another. "Therefore all things whatsoever ye would that men should do to you, do ye even so to them."

The temper and judgment of the public mind underwent a great change after the adoption of the compromise. The press and statutes will verify this.

Now, sir, I shall quote a statute, with no purpose . . . to assail Massachusetts or her legislation, but as a commentary upon the state of public opinion before and after the Missouri compromise. My object is to show, that from the time the Missouri compromise was first introduced here as a topic of discussion, agitation has gone on; and it is under the influence of discussions which then took place, and not before, that we find one section in hostile array against the other. I make this statement broadly, and I challenge denial—that the Missouri compromise, in making a geographical line, made one of odious distinction and sectional alienation.

The honorable Senator from Massachusetts [MR. SUMNER,] said that southern statesmen, distinguished men from Virginia, North Carolina, South Carolina, and Georgia, at one time were free to give their opinions upon this subject, and they were generally against the institution of slavery. He is entirely true. I can remember the time when it was regarded, even in South Carolina, as a moral evil; but, sir, from the time when the North, or a portion of the North, undertook to make an issue upon the subject, you have never heard a single southern man, of any reputation, on this floor or anywhere else, undertake to give up that question. I have said that before the adoption of the Missouri compromise even the northern States were not so very kind and philanthropic towards this race, which is now under the peculiar care of the Senator from Massachusetts, as he would represent. I have before me a statute of that State, which I ask my friend from Alabama, who sits beside me, to read.

MR. CLAY read it, as follows:

"Sec. 6. *Be it further enacted by the authority aforesaid,* That no person, being an African or negro, other than . . . a citizen of some one of the United States . . . shall tarry within this Commonwealth for a longer time than two months; and, upon complaint made to any justice of the peace within this Commonwealth, that any such person has been within the same more than two months, the said justice shall order the said person to depart out of this Commonwealth; and in case that the said African or Negro shall not depart as aforesaid, any justice of the peace within this Commonwealth . . . shall commit the said person to any house of correction within the county, there to be kept to hard labor . . . until the sessions of the peace next to beholden within and for the said county . . . ; If, upon trial at the said court, it shall be made to appear that the said person has thus continued within the Commonwealth contrary to the tenor of this act, he or she shall be whipped not exceeding ten stripes, and ordered to depart out of this Commonwealth within ten days; and if he or she shall not so depart, the same process shall be had and punishment inflicted, and so *toties quoties.*"

MR. BROADHEAD: What is the date of that statute?

MR. BUTLER: Seventeen hundred and eighty-eight; and it remained on the statute-book in full force until 1823, until after the adoption of the Missouri compromise. I will call it the *toties quoties* act. [Laughter.] The Negroes were to be whipped every time they happened to get to Boston, or any other place in Massachusetts. That is a specimen of statutory philanthropy at least. I do not quote it to reproach Massachusetts, for it has become a common principle of legislation in many of the non-slaveholding States. The truth is, that a black population was regarded by Massachusetts as a nuisance.

MR. SUMNER and MR. EVERETT both rose.

MR. SUMNER: The Senator from South Carolina is so jealous of the honor of his own State, that he will pardon me if I interrupt him for one moment merely to explain the offensive statute to which he has referred. I have nothing to say in vindication of it; I simply desire that it should be understood. This statute, which bears date 1788, anterior to the Federal Government, was applicable only to Africans or Negroes not citizens of some one of the United States; and, according to contemporary evidence, it was intended to protect the Commonwealth against the vagabondage of fugitive slaves. But I do not vindicate the statute; I only explain it; and I add, that it has long since been banished from the statute-book.

MR. BUTLER: I say that the Missouri compromise produced this; and to prove it, I refer to the fact that this *toties quoties* act was repealed almost immediately after the adoption of the Missouri compromise. Take it as the gentleman would have us construe it, and what is it? He says it was passed to prevent fugitive slaves going there. I suppose, therefore, that since they have repealed it, it was to let the fugitive slaves go to Boston, and that has become a common ground for runaways. The gentleman cannot escape the dilemma—that before its repeal, fugitive Negroes were banished, and that after its repeal, under the sentiment of the Missouri compromise, they were invited to come to Massachusetts.

Sir, the fact is, my habitual reverence for Massachusetts as a historical entity is very great; but I believe she is no better than any other Commonwealth—not a whit. I think there are other Commonwealths besides her; but I respect her for her real history, when hardy morality, when wisdom, when brave justice, instead of sickly sentimentality, governed her counsels, and made her a Commonwealth; when her great men were Senators of Rome, when Rome survived. The historian has written another thing of Massachusetts. I have forgotten the book in which it is written, but I can produce it if need be. I refer to it only to show how Negroes were once regarded there, not, to show how the gentleman regards them now; because it seems to me that if he wished to write poetry, he would get a Negro to sit for him. [Laughter.] Sir, it is just as notorious as that I am stating it—and a historian has gravely said so—that at the time of the passage of the law in Massachusetts abolishing slavery, pretty nearly all the grown Negroes disappeared somewhere; and, as the historian expresses it, the little Negroes who were left there, without father or mother, and with hardly a God, were sent about as puppies, to be taken by those who would feed them. That is in the book. If any gentleman wishes it, I can find the book; it is in the library. This is the truth; and I suppose nobody can complain of me for speaking the truth. Grown and working slaves disappeared in Massachusetts with slavery; but it is too true—not to be freemen, but slaves of southern owners, with their proceeds in northern pockets. Yes, sir, we are taking care of the descendents of those who were committed to bondage when they could have been free. . . .

This was all before the Missouri compromise; and now, what has been the state of feeling since that compromise has been adopted. . . ? Since its adoption, the Missouri line has been that in which have been drilled the seeds of agitation, and they have brought forth the fruits of bitterness, of strife, and contention. . . . I may say that the Missouri controversy gave rise to a discussion which for the first time opened to the North the certainty that it had power to interfere with slavery. Until then it never did interfere upon this floor as an antagonistic power; but when it found that it had the power it did interfere, has interfered, and will continue to interfere with the institution, unless statesmen and patriots shall come forward to arrest the billows of criminal agitation. . . .

[The Senate adjourned. Senator Butler concluded his speech the following day.]

The branch of the subject which I was discussing at the time of the adjournment yesterday, was that not only the terms, obligations, and implications of the Missouri compromise had been disregarded in fact, but that the remarks of the Senator from Massachusetts [MR. SUMNER] showed that it was disregarded and violated in spirit. I was making some remarks, also, not by way of reprimand, certainly, because I have no right to reprimand him, but such as I thought ought to have refuted and rebuked him, when he undertook to say that education in the South was neglected, and that the name of a slaveholder was a by-word and a reproach to the civilized world. I am a slaveholder, and I have a right to take exception to such remarks.

MR. SUMNER: Slave-dealer, not slave-owner, was the word I used. I said that I understood that, even in the slave States, the name of slave-dealer was a by-word and a reproach. I have understood so from slaveholders themselves.

MR. SHIELDS: That was the Senator's language.

MR. BUTLER: I thought he used the remark in relation to a slaveholder.

MR. SUMNER: No, sir, but in relation to a slave dealer.

MR. SHIELDS: I recollect distinctly that such was the Senator's expression.

MR. BUTLER: Mr. President, in the remarks which I have made in reference to such suggestions as were advanced by the Senator from Massachusetts, I have endeavored to confine myself within the province of parliamentary courtesy and propriety, and I certainly have no disposition to go further. It is but fair now that I should distinctly state that, notwithstanding the effort which has been made to throw into the shade of the contrast the civilization and the morality of the South in comparison with that of the North, I think the census will show, and fairness would suggest, that, in many respects, at least, the North has no right to court such a comparison. . . .

[Senator Butler produced statistics showing that the per capita rates of insanity, poverty, and alcohol production were higher and church attendance lower in the New England states of Connecticut and Massachusetts than in the Southern states of Kentucky and Tennessee.]

MR. BUTLER: Mr. President, I have resorted to facts, and "facts are stubborn things" in argument. I have drawn no contrast in all that I have said. I have not claimed for the South any superiority; and I have not detracted from the North any of her merits, nor do I intend to do so now. The pauperism, the lunacy, and the drunkenness in those States may be attributable to a very different cause, [than] from the fact that they are a non-slaveholding population. It may arise from the fact that there is a more dense population than that which exists in the States with which they have been brought into comparison; or it may arise from the fact that—

MR. EVERETT: Will my friend from South Carolina yield me the floor for a moment?

MR. BUTLER: Certainly.

MR. EVERETT: I simply rise to say that Massachusetts relieves annually from eleven to twelve thousand foreign paupers, who are thrown in upon us in consequence of the great tide of immigration from Europe.

MR. BUTLER: I was about to suggest that as one of the causes. I do not mention these things as a matter of reproach to the North at all; but I was going to show that I, who represent the South, will not take advantage of matters of this kind to throw either the one or the other section into the shades of contrast. It might not be fair to do so. The Senator from Massachusetts has anticipated me as to one point, which I would otherwise have mentioned. I think it very probable that some of these results are attributable to the cause which he has named. In regard to the spirits which, it is mentioned in these statistics, go out from the North, I may say that I think abolitionism is one of the tributary streams inflaming, maddening, and distracting the public mind of the country, and may lead to results more baneful than those that follow the vice of intemperance. These results will be sectional alienation, local division, injustice, civil strife, and, perhaps, servile insurrection. I think the best antidote for the latter would be to send the slaves to the North, where they would find hunger and contumacious neglect strong inducements to go back home. . . .

It was said of Rome, Mr. President, that when her morals were most corrupt her legislation was most sentimental. Juvenal,[46] who describes in such vivid colors the degeneracy, the debauchery, and the corruption which prevailed in the days of the emperors of the Roman people . . . has drawn the contrast between the simple virtues of the time when Cato lived and when Tiberius reigned. . . .

I will say what is the truth, that this pseudo-philanthropy which is now, to some extent, pervading the public mind of the North, was unknown to the hardy morality of our forefathers. They were practical statesmen that could deal with all the elements of a different society with justice, and not rhetorical dialecticians, who would make such elements themes, for their *mere* eloquence and professions of philanthropy—such as would free the slave, and afterwards subject him to starvation—a philanthropy that is heated into a *flame* more to *hate* the *white race* than to preserve the black—a philanthropy of adoption more than affection—one that professes much and does nothing—with a *long* advertisement and *short* performance. . . .

Those best acquainted with the institutions, civilization, and social habits of the people of the southern States, are better reconciled to them than are those who stand aloof and hold up an ideal standard of morality, emblazoned by imagination and sustained in ignorance, or, perhaps, more often planted by a criminal ambition and heartless hypocrisy.

I appeal to those who hear me, if gentlemen who have gone to the South, who have lived amidst slaveholders, who have partaken of their hospitality, and have seen the administration of justice and all the graver forms of civilization there, are not better reconciled to the institution of slavery than that class and school of persons who read and take in their notions from "Uncle Tom's Cabin"?[47]

Sir, there are various *isms* at the North. . . . When we come to Abolitionism, to Maine-liquor-lawism, to Strong-minded-womanism, Bloomerism, and all the *isms* which now pervade some portions of the North, I am far from supposing that they do infuse into the social system anything like a healthful action. No, sir; they are the cankers of theoretical conceit, of impudent intrusion, and cheerless infidelity. They are the fungi of self-constituted societies, or the organization of Church and State. They are impudent usurpers. The most extraordinary development of that class of persons and that temper of society that gives rise to such *isms*, is to be found in conventions of women, who step from the sphere prescribed to them by God, to enter into the political arena, and claim the rights of men. . . .

Sir, I am now speaking on a subject, which, as I think, is intimately connected with the sentiments which the honorable Senator from Massachusetts [MR. SUMNER] has put forth; and with some of the sentimentality which he has expressed. If I were to say any one thing more true than another on this point, it is, that when woman violates the law which God has given her, she has no law, and is the creature of hateful anarchy. . . . These are sentiments which are likely to prevail, if these women in men's clothes are to take upon themselves the jurisdiction which they claim. These are part of the *isms* which have resulted, I may say, from abolitionism. They are, at least, the symptoms of a dangerous revolution in the social organization. . . .

Having shown yesterday that the Missouri compromise was not only disregarded and violated, but that the whole spirit of it, that should inculcate harmony, has been offensively abused in the Senate and House, I go to the next proposition, which I propose to discuss, that there was no constitutional competency in Congress to adopt such an arbitrary line as that indicated in what is called the Missouri compromise line. . . .

Why should gentlemen insist so strenuously upon the right to impose or retain this restriction? The North is in the majority, and if Nebraska and Kansas tomorrow were to become slaveholding Territories, the North would still be in a majority. Whenever they think proper to use their power they can do it. If they do not acknowledge the counsels of magnanimity, and are disposed to follow the dictates of power, they are always able to do so; and if they claim such a jurisdiction, by the exercise of a majority, there is no limit to this Government, and this Confederacy will be resolved into a confederacy in which an unlimited and uncontrollable majority shall rule. I know, sir, that it may be regarded as the result of what are called Democratic institutions. I have no more regard for the despotism of a democracy than I have for any other form of government. The very name may give it the power to do injustice. I want a Government that rests upon some *veto* power against an irresponsible will. . . .

Having expressed my views freely, Mr. President, I am willing to take this bill as it is. I am willing to take it, even upon the assumption that no slaves will go into Nebraska or Kansas. I am willing to take it upon the ground that, if you adopt it, it will take a festering thorn from the side of the South. I am willing to take it upon the ground that by it the sentiments of honor are regarded. . . . With the convictions on my mind that the Missouri compromise is unconstitutional, I should be bound to vote for the bill. I never will compromise with a measure of transient expediency. . . . The South has no bigotry, no disposition to make war upon, or to assume an adversary position to the northern portion of this Confederacy, if she can receive constitutional justice. They never have had any but the interests of equality. Insinuations are frequently made against those who assume the attitude of secessionists. They occupy a different position from those who call themselves abolitionists. The former are defending their rights, the latter are aggressors. Sir, if the South, at any time were united, they could stand on the threshold and say, "Thus far thou shalt go, and no further." If, however, they mean to go on with this agitation, I give notice, as far as I can speak for the South, that if they keep it up, they must do so at the peril of this Union.

Douglas continued to fume over Sumner's position. The following debate excerpt contains a strikingly personal exchange between the two men. Douglas's claim of consistency between 1850 and 1854 was true to a point. During the compromise debates he had contended that states, rather than the federal government, had been responsible for establishing or prohibiting slavery. In 1850, however, he had not called for an explicit legislative repeal of the Missouri compromise, and did not do so until pressured by Southern Democrats in 1854. Likewise, Sumner's protestations of not seeking a position in the Senate significantly understate how much during the senatorial selection process he had restrained his opinions on issues such as the return of fugitive slaves to remain acceptable to the Democrats. It is reflective of the two men's shared sense of decorum that despite their harsh words neither in this debate nor in their later conflicts did either man feel the need for violence.[48]

Nebraska Bill Debates, 3 March 1854

MR. DOUGLAS: Mr. President, the Senators from Ohio and Massachusetts, [MR. CHASE and MR. SUMNER,] have taken the liberty to impeach my motives in bringing forward this measure. I desire to know by what right they arraign me, or by what authority they impute to me other and different motives than those which I have assigned. I have shown from the record that I advocated and voted for the same principles and provisions in the compromise acts of 1850, which are embraced in this bill. I have proven that I put the same construction upon those measures immediately after their adoption that is given in the report which I submitted this session from the Committee on Territories. I have shown that the Legislature of Illinois at its first sessions, after those measures were enacted, passed resolutions approving them, and declaring that the same great principle of self-government should be incorporated into all territorial organizations. Yet, sir, in the face of these facts, these Senators have the hardihood to declare that this was all an "after-thought" on my part, conceived for the first time during the present session; and that the measure is offered as a bid for presidential votes! Are they incapable of conceiving that an honest man can do a right thing from worthy motives? I must be permitted to tell those Senators that their experience in seeking political preferment does not furnish a safe rule by which to judge the character and principles of other Senators. . . . ! I must be permitted to remind the Senator from Massachusetts that I did not enter into any combinations or arrangements by which my character, my principles, and my honor, were set up at public auction or private sale in order to procure a seat in the Senate of the United States! I did not come into the Senate by any such means. . . . !

MR. SUMNER: Mr. President, I shrink always instinctively from any effort to repel a personal assault. I do not recognize the jurisdiction of this body, at this time, to try my election to the Senate; but I do state, in reply to the Senator from Illinois, that if he means to suggest that I came into this body by any waiver of principles; by any abandonment of my principles of any kind; by any effort or activity of my own, in any degree—he states that which cannot be sustained by the facts. I never sought, in any way, the office which I now hold; nor was I a party, in any way, directly or indirectly, to those efforts which placed me here. . . .

MR. DOUGLAS: Sir, the Senator from Massachusetts comes up with a very bold front, and denies the right of any man to put him on defense for the manner of his election. He says it is contrary to his principles to engage in personal assaults. If he expects to avail himself of the benefit of such a plea, he should act in accordance with his professed principles, and refrain from assaulting the character and impugning the motives of better men than himself. Everybody knows that he came here by a coalition or combination between political parties holding opposite and hostile opinions. But it is not my purpose to go into the morality of the matters involved in his election. The public know the history of that notorious election, and have formed its judgment upon it. It will not do for the Senator to say that he was not a party to it, for he thereby betrays a consciousness of the immorality of the transaction, without acquitting himself of the responsibilities which justly attach to him. As well might the receiver of stolen goods deny any responsibility for the larceny, while luxuriating in the proceeds of the crime, as the Senator to avoid the consequences resulting from the mode of his election, while he clings to the office. I must be permitted to remind him of what he certainly can never forget, that when he arrived here to take his seat for the first time, so firmly were Senators impressed with the conviction that he had been elected by dishonorable and corrupt means, there were very few who, for a long time, could deem it consistent with personal honor to hold private intercourse with him. So general was that impression, that for a long time he was avoided and shunned as a person unworthy of the association of gentlemen. Gradually, however, these injurious impressions were worn away by his bland manners and amiable deportment; and I regret that the Senator should now, by a violation of all the rules of courtesy and propriety, compel me to refresh his mind upon these unwelcome reminiscences.

The Senate passed the Nebraska bill on 4 March, 1854. The bill was forwarded to the House of Representatives where it passed on 22 May. President Pierce's pressure on Northern Democrats to support the bill as a party measure proved decisive. After a conference committee the bill was returned to the Senate for final passage. Sumner was one of the last speakers against the bill. He used the moment to present petitions from Northern religious leaders calling for the repeal of the fugitive slave law. The original version of the petition had been sponsored by Harriet Beecher Stowe, who used money from sales of *Uncle Tom's Cabin* to fund the collection of signatures. This petition had been presented to Congress in March by the Conservative Massachusetts Whig Edward Everett, where it was roundly denounced by both Northern and Southern Democrats. Physically ill and demoralized by these attacks, Everett resigned in mid-May. This left Sumner as the state's only Senator. He seized on the final debate as his opportunity to present additional signatures to Congress and reopen debate on the fugitive slave bill. His use of religious authority to support his position on a political issue would generate hot responses from Democratic delegates and lead to the first threats on his life.[49]

Sumner's Final Protest Against the Nebraska Bill and Remonstrances from the New England Clergy[50]

Speech in the Senate, 25 May 1854.

MR. PRESIDENT,—It is now midnight. At this late hour of a session drawn out to unaccustomed length, I shall not fatigue the Senate by argument. . . . I now present the remonstrance of a large number of citizens of New York against the repeal of the Missouri Compromise.

I also present the memorial of the religious Society of Friends in Michigan against the passage of the Nebraska Bill, or any other bill annulling the Missouri Compromise Act of 1820.

I also present the remonstrance of the clergy and laity of the Baptist denomination in Michigan and Indiana against the wrong and bad faith contemplated in the Nebraska Bill.

But this is not all. I hold in my hand, and now present to the Senate, one hundred and twenty-five separate remonstrances, from clergymen of every Protestant denomination in Maine, New Hampshire, Vermont, Massachusetts, Rhode Island, and Connecticut, constituting the six New England States. These remonstrances are identical in character with the larger one presented by my distinguished colleague [MR. EVERETT],—whose term of service here ends in a few days by voluntary resignation, and who is now detained at home by illness,—and were originally intended as part of it, but did not arrive in season for annexation to that interesting and weighty document. They are independent in form, though supplementary in nature, helping to swell the protest of the pulpits of New England. . . .

"In the name of Almighty God, and in his presence," these remonstrants protest against the Nebraska Bill. In this solemn language, most strangely pronounced blasphemous on this floor, there is obviously no assumption of ecclesiastical power, as is perversely charged, but simply a devout observance of the Scriptural injunction, "Whatsoever ye do, in word or deed, do all in the name of the Lord." Let me add, also, that these remonstrants, in this very language, have followed the example of the Senate, which, at our present session, has ratified at least one important treaty beginning with these precise words, "In the name of Almighty God." Surely, if the Senate may thus assume to speak, the clergy may do likewise, without imputation of blasphemy, or any just criticism, at least in this body.

I am unwilling, particularly at this time, to be betrayed into anything like a defence of the clergy. . . . Sir, from the first settlement of these shores, from those early days of struggle and privation, through the trials of the Revolution, the clergy are associated not only with the piety and the learning, but with the liberties of the country. New England for a long time was governed by their prayers more than by any acts of the Legislature; and at a later day their voices aided even the Declaration of Independence. The clergy of our time speak, then, not only from their own virtues, but from echoes yet surviving in the pulpits of their fathers.

For myself, I desire to thank them for their generous interposition. Already they have done much good in moving the country. They will not be idle. In the days of the Revolution, John Adams, yearning for Independence, said, "Let the pulpits thunder against oppression!" And the pulpits thundered. The time has come for them to thunder again. So famous was John Knox for power in prayer, that Queen Mary used to say she feared his prayers more than all the armies of Europe. But our clergy have prayers to be feared by the upholders of wrong. . . .

The clergy of New England, some of whom, forgetful of the traditions of other days, once made their pulpits vocal for the Fugitive Slave Bill, now, by the voices of learned divines, eminent bishops, accomplished professors, and faithful pastors, uttered in solemn remonstrance, unite at last in putting a permanent brand upon this hateful wrong. Surely, from this time forward, they can never more render it any support. Thank God for this! Here is a sign full of promise for Freedom. These remonstrances have especial significance, when it is urged, as has been often done in this debate, that the proposition still pending proceeds from the North. Yes, Sir, proceeds from the North: for that is its excuse and apology. The ostrich is reputed to hide its head in the sand, and then vainly imagine its coward body beyond the reach of pursuers. In similar spirit, honorable Senators seem to shelter themselves behind scanty Northern votes, and then vainly imagine that they are protected from the judgment of the country. The pulpits of New England, representing in unprecedented extent the popular voice there, now proclaim that six States, with all the fervor of religious conviction, protest against your outrage. To this extent, at least, I maintain it does not come from the North. . . .

From the depths of my soul, as loyal citizen and as Senator, I plead, remonstrate, protest, against the passage of this bill. I struggle against it as against death; but, as in death itself corruption puts on incorruption, and this mortal body puts on immortality, so from the sting of this hour I find assurance of that triumph by which Freedom will be restored to her immortal birthright in the Republic.

Sir, the bill you are about to pass is at once the worst and the best on which Congress ever acted. *Yes, Sir, WORST and BEST at the same time.*

It is the worst bill, inasmuch as it is a present victory of Slavery. In a Christian land, and in an age of civilization, a time-honored statute of Freedom is struck down, opening the way to all the countless woes and wrongs of human bondage. Among the crimes of history, another is soon to be recorded, which no tears can blot out, and which in better days will be read with universal shame. Do not start. The Tea Tax and Stamp Act, which aroused the patriot rage of our fathers, were virtues by the side of your transgression; nor would it be easy to imagine, at this day, any measure which more openly and wantonly defied every sentiment of justice, humanity, and Christianity. Am I not right, then, in calling it the worst bill on which Congress ever acted?

There is another side, to which I gladly turn. Sir, it is the best bill on which Congress ever acted; *for it annuls all past compromises with Slavery, and makes any future compromises impossible.* Thus it puts Freedom and Slavery face to face, and bids them grapple. Who can doubt the result? It opens wide the door of the Future, when, at last, there will really be a North, and the Slave Power will be broken,— when this wretched Despotism will cease to dominate over our Government, no longer impressing itself upon everything at home and abroad,—when the National Government will be divorced in every way from Slavery, and, according to the true intention of our fathers. Freedom will be established by Congress everywhere, at least beyond the local limits of the States. Slavery will then be driven from usurped foothold here in the District of Columbia, in the National Territories, and elsewhere beneath the national flag; the Fugitive Slave Bill, as vile as it is unconstitutional, will become a dead letter; and the domestic Slave-Trade, so far as it can be reached, but especially on the high seas, will be blasted by Congressional Prohibition. Everywhere within the sphere of Congress, the great *Northern Hammer* will descend to smite the wrong; and the irresistible cry will break forth, "No more Slave States. . . !"

Virginia Senator James Mason reacted with an impassioned defense of separation between church and state. As the slavery issue had intensified, Southern churchmen had increasingly condemned Northern evangelicals for interfering with the South's civil, political, and domestic affairs. Since political parties demanded that their followers be willing to sacrifice their own principles in favor of the party line, Southerners thought, the compromises inevitable in partisan politics would force clergymen to give up their moral credibility. The marriage between church and state would lead to the corruption of both. The mixture of politics and abolition was especially frightening. Pro-slavery defenders believed that because emancipation would lead inevitably to race war, the murder of families, and the economic desolation of the South, anyone espousing emancipation could not be a true Christian. In the late 1830s and early 1840s this caused the nation's major Protestant churches to split into separate Northern and Southern denominations. Southerners received support from Democrats in the North, many of whom were Catholics who resented Protestant evangelical attacks on private Catholic schools, convents, prison ministries, and alchohol consumption. Democratic advocacy of "liberty of conscience" and church-state separation became one of the party's hallmarks.[51]

Senator Mason of Virginia Debates Sumner over Northern Religion and Politics[52]

On the subject of this bill. I object to its reception; and I object to it because I understand that Senator to say that it is *verbatim* the petition that was presented by his honorable colleague, who is not now with us, in which the clergy presented themselves in this Senate and to the country as a third estate, speaking not as American citizens, but as clergymen, and in that character only. I object to its reception. I object to it, that I may not in any manner minister to the unchristian purposes of the clergy of New England, as the Senator has just announced them. I object to it, that I may be in no manner responsible for the prostitution of their office (once called holy and sacred, with them no longer so) in the face of the Senate and of the American people. I object to it, that the clergymen of my own honored State, and of the South, may, as holding a common office in the ministry of the Gospel, be in no manner confounded with or contaminated by these clergymen of New England, if the Senator represents them correctly. . . .

Sir, it is the first time in the history of this country that a Church of any denomination has asserted a right to be heard, as a Church, upon the floors of legislation; and if the Senator represents that body correctly, they have profaned their office, and I predict now a total separation between the Church North and the Church South, if I understand the sentiments of the Church South. . . .

If the Senator who has just taken his seat has correctly expounded the clergymen of New England, I object to that petition. If he has correctly stated that it is *verbatim,* copied from the petition presented by his colleague, I say it is a prostitution of their office to the embrace of political party; and the Senate shall not, by my assent, be made the medium of so unholy an alliance. I do not mean to go further into this debate; but I object to the reception of the petition.

MR. SUMNER: Sir, in refusing to receive these remonstrances, or in neglecting them in any way, on reasons assigned in this chamber, you treat them with an indignity which becomes more marked, because it is the constant habit of the Senate to welcome remonstrances from members of the Society of Friends in their religious character, and from all other persons, by any designation which they may adopt. Booksellers remonstrate against the international copyright treaty; lastmakers against a proposed change in the patent laws; and only lately the tobacconists have remonstrated against certain regulations touching tobacco: and all these remonstrances are received with respect, and referred to appropriate committees in the Senate. But the clergy of New England, when protesting against a wicked measure, which, with singular unanimity, they believe full of peril and shame to our country, are told to stay at home. Almost the jeer is heard, "Go up, thou bald head!"

SUMNER AND PETITIONS FOR THE REPEAL OF THE FUGITIVE SLAVE ACT

One day after the passage of the Nebraska Bill, the Anthony Burns slave incident erupted in Boston. Burns had escaped from his Virginia owners in March 1854. He had gone to Boston to find work and protection but was arrested on 26 May. Since the fugitive slave act of 1850 had federalized the legal process of returning escaped slaves, he was imprisoned at the Federal Courthouse in Boston. Abolitionists unsuccessfully attempted to rush the courthouse and free Burns. In the process a guard named James Batchelder was killed. Burns was escorted back to his owners. It required the protection of Federal soldiers authorized by President Pierce to bring Burns through the crowds between the courthouse and the docks. Southern political leaders immediately connected Sumner's Nebraska speech and the Burns riots, even though the speech had not reached Boston when the incident occurred.[53] Like Butler, the following editorialists called into question the manliness of Sumner and other Northerners. Despite the writer's denials, approval of physical violence against Sumner is implicit in these editorials. Sumner's response anticipated future events. "The howl of the press here against me has been the best homage I ever received," he wrote to abolitionist clergyman Theodore Parker. "The threats to put a bullet through my head and hang me—and mob me—have been frequent. I have always said: 'let them come: they will find me at my post.' "[54]

The Fugitive Slave Case in Boston

Washington, D. C., *Evening Star,* 30 May 1854

Advices have been received by letter in this city to-day, from Boston, which represent everything safe and quiet inside the court-house in Boston. The United States Troops are still on duty in the building to prevent a rescue of the fugitive, and to protect the federal officers in the execution of the law. Outside of the building there is still a large crowd, many of them worthy citizens attracted by curiosity, but most of them rioters and assassins, collected and summoned by Parker and Philips, acting under the suggestions of Charles Sumner, and his satellite in congress, Mr. Banks. Circulars have been addressed by the Abolition Vigilance Committee of Boston, to the surrounding towns, urging the "faithful" to come to the city by the early trains. The following is a copy of the document. *It bears the earmarks of being the offspring of Sumner and Chase:*

"Boston, May 27, 1854.—To the Yeomanry of New England! Countrymen and Brothers! the vigilance committee of Boston have to inform you that the mock trial of the poor fugitive slave has been further postponed to Monday next, at 11 o'clock, A.M. You are requested, therefore, to come down and lend the moral weight of your presence and the aid of your council to the friends of justice and humanity in the city. Come down, then, sons of the Puritans, for even if the poor victim is to be carried off by the brute force of arms, and delivered over to slavery, you should at least be present to witness the sacrifice, and you should follow him in sad procession, with your tears and your prayers, and then go home and take such action as your manhood and patriotism may suggest. Come, then, by the early trains on Monday, and rally in Court Square. Come with courage and resolution in your hearts, but, this time, with only such arms as God gave to you."

Notwithstanding all this preparation and effort, we are satisfied that the forms of law will be carried out, and that the slave will be returned to his owner. The troops of the United States are sufficient thereto, even without the aid of the citizen soldiery, or of the city government, which, with the exception of the Common Council, is in the hands of the Free Soilers. . . . We understand that Giddings of Ohio left this city last evening for Boston. He is undoubtedly the bearer of dispatches from Sumner and Chase and Banks. Why does not Sumner take the field in person, and lead the mob, whose passions he has inflamed by his recent speeches and letters? Why does he not expose himself to danger along side of the deluded men whom he has designedly led astray? Is he not deficient in courage and common manhood? Men everywhere draw that conclusion. He prefers to affect the airs and grimaces of a Broadway fop upon the avenue, and in the Senate Chamber, to leading his fanatical confederates to the accomplishment of the ends, for the attainment of which he has so often pronounced himself ready to sacrifice everything.

Public sentiment in Alexandria, we learn, is intensely excited in condemnation of Sumner and his allies. We know that it increases in this city every hour. The masses look upon Sumner as responsible for the death of Batchelder. They attribute, and justly, the action of the murderers to the counsel of Sumner. We hope that public sentiment against these abolition miscreants who infest Congress, and our fair city, and fill the atmosphere in which they move with the odor of a brothel, will not descend to acts of personal violence. Such conduct can find no justification. But let public opinion condemn these men every where, in the street, in the Capitol, in every place where men meet. Let Sumner and his infamous gang feel that he cannot outrage the fame of his country—counsel treason to the laws—incite the ignorant to bloodshed and murder—and still receive the countenance and support of the society of this city, which he has done so much to vilify.

The Boston Riot—Charles Sumner

Washington, D. C., *Evening Star,* 30 May 1856.

The Boston riot, with its attendant outrage and bloodshed, has not only called forth the sentiments of the deepest indignation in this city, but it has also satisfactorily demonstrated to the world that, in all questions affecting the honor of the country, or the stability or sacredness of its laws, the American people are united as one man. The press of nearly every political shade have, with unexampled unanimity of purpose and sentiment, denounced the authors of the cowardly, bloody outrage in Boston in terms of unmitigated scorn, contempt, and loathing. The insane idiots who composed that frenzied mob should have been treated as mad men or mad dogs are usually treated—caught and caged, if possible; but shot down if they persisted in their course of death and danger. But what punishment is meet for such men as Sumner, Giddings & Co.? If it had not been for the incendiary, traitorous appeals of these creeping, crawling, cowardly enemies of the Republic, the Abolition mob of Boston would have let off their excess of steam in the customary shrieks, stamps and scoldings. In the place of murdering Batchelder, they would have been content with stigmatising Washington as a slave breeder, or wreaking their vengeance on the president in an effigy demonstration.

It may be that before this excitement passes away, when men's minds are in too inflammable a state to permit the cool exercise of the reasoning faculties the crazed abolitionists of New England will discover that if madmen will resort to the argument of brute force, that "there are blows to receive as well as to take." If Southern gentleman are to be threatened and assaulted, while legally seeking to obtain possession of property, for the use of which they have a solemn constitutional guarantee—if legal rights can only be sought for and established at the bayonet's point—certain Northern men, now in our midst, will have to evince a little more circumspection than they have ever evinced in their walk, talk and acts. While the person of a Virginia citizen is only safe from rudeness and outrage behind the serried ranks of armed men, Chas. Sumner is permitted to walk among the "slave catchers" and "fire eaters" of the South in peace and security. While he invites his constituents to resist the federal laws, even to the shedding of blood, concocts his traitorous plots, and sends forth his incendiary appeals under the broad, protecting panoply of the laws he denounces, he retains his seat in the Senate, and yet daily violates the official oath which he took to support the Constitution of the United States. If we contrast the treatment which a Southern slaveholder receives at the hands of a Northern abolitionist, with the treatment which the latter receives at the hands of the former, we may proudly assert that, among the many virtues which adorn the Southern character, *forbearance* is not the least conspicuous.

The Nebraska bill's supposed repeal of previous compromises and the Burns case produced an outcry in Massachusetts against the fugitive slave act. By mid-June nearly three thousand people had signed a new petition for its repeal. These were submitted to the Senate by Julius Rockwell, who had been temporarily appointed to the Senate as a replacement for Everett. Sumner's initial speech was a response to Senator James Jones of Tennessee, who had attacked both Rockwell and Sumner for supporting treason against federal officers in the Burns case. Sumner, as he had done several times before in the Senate, challenged the constitutionality of the Fugitive Slave Act's details and enforcement. This would be construed by his political opponents as a refusal to uphold the Constitution. Sumner's defense of state rights against federal encroachments would be echoed in the "Crime Against Kansas" address two years later. The outburst that came in response to this speech caused the destruction of his friendships with Butler and other Southerners in Congress. They viewed his historical analogy between resistance to the Stamp Act and Boston's obstructions of the fugitive slave act in the Burns case as especially obnoxious, since (in their judgment) the acts of King George III had been created undemocratically, while the Fugitive Slave Act had been a lawful act of Congress in full harmony with key mandates of the United States Constitution.

Sumner's Speech on the Petition to Repeal the Fugitive Slave Act, 26 June 1856[55]

MR. PRESIDENT: —I begin by answering the interrogatory. . . : "Can any one suppose, that, if the Fugitive Slave Act be repealed, this Union can exist?" To which I reply at once, that, if the Union be in any way dependent on an act—I cannot call it a *law*—so revolting in every aspect as that to which he refers, then it ought not to exist. . . . Its violation of the Constitution is manifold; and here I repeat but what I have often said. Too often it cannot be set forth, so long as the infamous statute blackens the land.

It commits the great question of human freedom,—than which none is more sacred in the law,—not to a solemn trial, but to summary proceedings.

It commits this great question, not to one of the high tribunals of the land, but to the unaided judgment of a single petty magistrate. . . .

It authorizes judgment on *ex parte* evidence, by affidavit, without the sanction of cross-examination.

It denies the writ of *habeas corpus*, ever known as the palladium of the citizen.

Contrary to the declared purposes of the framers of the Constitution, it sends the fugitive back "at the public expense."

Adding meanness to the violation of the Constitution, it bribes the Commissioner by a double fee to pronounce against Freedom. If he dooms a man to Slavery, the reward is ten dollars; but saving him to Freedom, his dole is five dollars.

This is enough, but not all. On two other capital grounds do I oppose the Act as unconstitutional: first, as it is an assumption by Congress of powers not delegated by the Constitution, and in derogation of the rights of the States; and, secondly, as it takes away that essential birthright of the citizen, trial by jury, in a question of personal liberty and a suit at Common Law. Thus obnoxious, I have always regarded it as an enactment totally devoid of all constitutional, as it is clearly devoid of all moral, obligation. . . .

In response for Massachusetts, there are other things. Something surely must be pardoned to her history. In Massachusetts stands Boston. In Boston stands Faneuil

Hall, where, throughout the perils which preceded the Revolution, our patriot fathers assembled to vow themselves to Freedom. Here, in those days, spoke James Otis, full of the thought that "the people's safety is the law of God." Here, also, spoke Joseph Warren, inspired by the sentiment that "death with all its tortures is preferable to Slavery." And here, also, thundered John Adams, fervid with the conviction that "consenting to Slavery is a sacrilegious breach of trust." Not far from this venerable hall . . . is the street where, in 1770, the first blood was spilt in conflict between British troops and American citizens, and among the victims was one of that African race which you so much despise. Almost within sight is Bunker Hill; further off, Lexington and Concord. Amidst these scenes a Slave-Hunter from Virginia appears, and the disgusting rites begin by which a fellow-man is sacrificed. Sir, can you wonder that our people are moved?

"Who can be wise, amazed, temperate and furious, loyal and neutral, in a moment? *No man.*"[56]

It is true that the Slave Act was with difficulty executed, and that one of its servants perished in the madness. On these grounds the Senator from Tennessee [Mr. Jones] charges Boston with fanaticism. I express no opinion on the conduct of individuals; but I do say, that the fanaticism which the Senator condemns is not new in Boston. It is the same which opposed the execution of the Stamp Act, and finally secured its repeal. It is the same which opposed the Tea Tax. It is the fanaticism which finally triumphed on Bunker Hill. The Senator says that Boston is filled with traitors. That charge is not new. Boston of old was the home of Hancock and Adams. Her traitors now are those who are truly animated by the spirit of the American Revolution. In condemning them, in condemning Massachusetts, in condemning these remonstrants, you simply give proper conclusion to the utterance on this floor, that the Declaration of Independence is "a self-evident lie."

Here I might leave the imputations on Massachusetts. But the case is stronger yet. I have referred to the Stamp Act. The parallel is of such aptness and importance, that, though on a former occasion I presented it to the Senate, I cannot forbear from pressing it again. . . . This Act was denounced in the Colonies at its passage, as contrary to the British Constitution, on two principal grounds, identical in character with the two chief grounds on which the Slave Act is now declared to be unconstitutional: first, as an assumption by Parliament of powers not belonging to it, and an infraction of rights secured to the Colonies; and, secondly, as a denial of trial by jury in certain cases of property. On these grounds the Stamp Act was held to be an outrage. . . .

The Stamp Act was welcomed in the Colonies by the Tories of that day, precisely as the unconstitutional Slave Act has been welcomed by an imperious class among us. . . . The elaborate answer of Massachusetts—the work of Samuel Adams, one of the pillars of our history—was pronounced " the ravings of a parcel of wild enthusiasts," even as recent proceedings in Boston, resulting in the memorial before you, have been characterized on this floor. Am I not right in this parallel?

The country was aroused against the execution of the Act. . . . The opposition spread and deepened, with a natural tendency to outbreak and violence. On one occasion in Boston, it showed itself in the lawlessness of a mob most formidable in character, even as is now charged. Liberty, in her struggles, is too often driven to force.

Thus was the Stamp Act annulled, even before its actual repeal, which was pressed with assiduity by petition and remonstrance, at the next meeting of Parliament. . . .

Within less than a year from its original passage, the Stamp Act—assailed as unconstitutional on the precise grounds which I now occupy in assailing the Slave Act—was driven from the statute-book.

Sir, the Stamp Act was, at most, an infringement of *civil* liberty only, not of *personal* liberty. How often must I say this? It touched questions of property only, and not the personal liberty of any man. Under it, no freeman could be seized as a slave. There was an unjust tax of a few pence, with the chance of amercement by a single judge without jury; but by this statute no person could be deprived of that vital right of all which is to other rights as soul to body,—*the right of a man to himself.* Who can fail to see the difference between the two cases, and how far the tyranny of the Slave Act is beyond the tyranny of the Stamp Act? The difference is immeasurable. And this will yet be pronounced by history. . . .

The petition asks simply the repeal of an obnoxious statute, which is entirely within the competency of Congress. It proceeds from a large number of respectable citizens, whose autograph signatures are attached. It is brief and respectful, and, in its very brevity, shows that spirit of freedom which should awaken a generous response. In refusing to receive it or refer it, according to the usage of the Senate, or in treating it with any indignity, you offer an affront not only to these numerous petitioners, but also to the great Right of Petition, which is never more sacred than when exercised in behalf of Freedom against an odious enactment. Permit me to add, that by this course you provoke the very spirit which you would repress.

Butler, who came into the chamber as the speech was being delivered, responded with spontaneous anger. His reaction is marked by a struggle to maintain civility, a palpable sense of personal betrayal, and a growing frustration with Sumner's principled inflexibility. The exchange between the two men over enforcement of the fugitive slave law would shape Southern impressions of Sumner and of Northern character for years.

Senator Butler's Reply to Sumner[57]

Speech in Congress, 25 June 1854.

MR. BUTLER . . . . There is one thing which I wish to say in reply to the honorable gentleman who sits near me, [MR. SUMNER.] When Faneuil Hall was illustrated by eloquence, and immortalized by patriotism; when Otis spoke, and John Hancock acted, and John Adams made the declarations which have been so much applauded by the gentleman, they were the representatives of slaveholding States. They represented Massachusetts as she *was*—hardy, slaveholding Massachusetts. Sir, when blood was shed upon the plains of Lexington and Concord, in an issue made by Boston, to whom was an appeal made, and from whom was it answered? The answer is found in the acts of slaveholding States—*animus opibusque parati*.[58] Yes, sir, the independence of America, to maintain republican liberty, was won by the arms and treasure, by the patriotism and *good faith* of slaveholding communities.

Sir the Senator has chosen to exhibit a good deal of sensibility upon abstract questions of liberty; but he knows that this Confederacy could not have been formed without a Constitution made by practical statesmen, in which New England entered into a compact with slaveholders. If the sentiments which he entertains now be the general sentiments of Boston and Massachusetts, it is a Commonwealth which ought not to belong to a Confederacy of slaveholders. That ought to be their feeling. If they cannot associate with us, under a common Constitution, let them say so. Sir, the gentleman has made his declarations with much pomp, and, I must say, not with his usual taste; with a species of rhetoric which is intended, I suppose, to feed the fires of fanaticism which he has helped to kindle in his own State—a species of rhetoric which is not becoming the gravity of this body. Let me tell him that when all those distinguished acts took place, to which he has alluded, they came from the organs of a public opinion representing peaceful wisdom—those who made compacts to observe them—those who could have their own, but could respect and conform to the opinions of others. They were gentlemen.

Perhaps, sir, I have said more than I ought to have said on this subject; but when gentlemen rise and flagrantly misrepresent history, as that gentleman has done, by a fourth of July oration, by vapid rhetoric, by a species of rhetoric which, I am sorry to say, ought not to come from a scholar—a rhetoric with more fine color than real strength—I become impatient under it. . . .

I have never made a threat on this floor; but I will tell him that if these agitations go on, the consequence will be that an issue will be made between the North and the South. Each section will become united—maintaining the position of units. I do not undertake to indicate these things; but will say, if sectional agitation is to be fed by such sentiments, such displays, and such things as come from the honorable gentleman near me, [MR. SUMNER,] I say we ought not to be in a common Confederacy, and we should be better off without it. In such a state of things, I might well entertain feelings of respect for the gentleman—as representing a different confederacy; but even if such should be its character—if I do not mistake the gentleman—he would extend to me the protection of an honorable and respected flag. My condition is different when I am assailed by a confederate, making war upon me under the covering of a common camp. In one, and a plain word, if the proceedings of this Senate are to be made the vehicle of denunciation or assault, the thing cannot be tolerated. Sir, I am understood to be somewhat an excitable man, but I have never here, on any occasion, made any remark which I am not willing to qualify, and make conformable to the judgment which my responsible position would require of me. I can, as I do, entertain strong feelings, but they shall not find expression in violent threats. Such, I may well appeal to the Senate, has not been my habit. I have been betrayed into remarks not intended. . . .

If we repeal the fugitive slave law, will the honorable Senator tell me that Massachusetts will execute the provision of the Constitution without any law of Congress? Suppose we should take away all laws, and devolve upon the different States the duties that properly belong to them, I would ask that Senator whether, under the prevalence of public opinion there, Massachusetts would execute that provision as one of the constitutional members of this Union? Would they send fugitives back to us after trial by jury, or any other mode? Will this honorable Senator [MR. SUMNER] tell me he will do it?

MR. SUMNER: Does the honorable Senator ask me if I would personally join in sending a fellow-man into bondage?

"Is thy servant a dog, that he should do this thing?"[59]

MR. BUTLER: These are the prettiest speeches that I ever heard. [Laughter.] He has them turned down in a book by him, I believe, and he has them so elegantly fixed that I cannot reply to them. [Laughter.] They are too delicate for my use. [Renewed laughter.] They are beautiful things; made in a factory of rhetoric somewhat *of a peculiar shape.* But, I must be permitted to say, not of a definite texture. Now, what does he mean by talking about his not being a dog? [Continued laughter.] What has that to do with the Constitution, or the constitutional obligations of a State? [Laughter.] Well, sir, it was a beautiful sentiment, no doubt, as he thought, and perhaps he imagined he expressed it with Demosthenian abruptness and eloquence. [Laughter.] I asked him whether he would execute the Constitution of the United States without any fugitive slave law, and he answered me, is he a dog—

MR. SUMNER: The Senator asked me if I would help to induce a fellow-man to bondage? I answered him.

MR. BUTLER: Then you would not obey the Constitution. Sir, [turning to MR. SUMNER,] standing here before this tribunal, where you swore to support it, you rise and tell me that you regard it the office of a dog to enforce it. You stand in my presence, as a coequal Senator, and tell me that it is a dog's office to execute the Constitution of the United States?

MR. PRATT: Which he has sworn to support.

MR. SUMNER: I recognized no such obligation.

MR. BUTLER: I know you do not. But nobody cares about your recognition as an individual; but as a Senator, and a constitutional representative, you stand differently related to this body. But enough of this. . . .

Senator Mason, as the principle author of the fugitive slave bill, also responded vigorously to Sumner's speech. This act had been the most important concession given to Southern political leaders in the compromise of 1850. Mason's accusations that Sumner was a liar and was insane matched in harshness anything Sumner would say in the "Crime Against Kansas" speech.

Senator Mason's Reply to Sumner[60]

Speech in Congress, 25 June 1854.

MR. MASON: I say, sir, the dignity of the American Senate has been rudely, wantonly, grossly assailed by a Senator from Massachusetts, and not only the dignity of the Senate, but of the whole people, trifled with in the presence of the American Senate, either ignorantly or corruptly—I do not know which, nor do I care. . . .

I do not know whether the Senator claims to be a jurist; I know not his position at home; but I know something of his associations there from his language here. Sir, he has denounced a gentleman from Virginia who goes under the protection of the Constitution, and the sanction of the law into his State, to reclaim his property. He has the boldness to speak here of such a man as "a slave-hunter from Virginia." Sir, my constituents need no vindication from me from such a charge, coming from such a quarter. The Senator from Massachusetts, in the use of such vulgar language here, betrays the vulgarity of his associations at home; and shall it be tolerated in the American Senate. . . ?

But, sir, I may say neither that law nor any other law could require vindication from attacks made by one mad enough to announce to the American Senate and the American people, that although the Constitution provides that fugitives from service shall be surrendered up, he would recognize himself as a dog were he to execute that provision. . . . Why, sir, am I speaking of a fanatic, one whose reason is dethroned! Can such a one expect to make impressions upon the American people from his vapid, vulgar declamation here, accompanied by a declaration that he would violate his oath now recently taken? . . . Let the honorable Senator remember that he says he would be a dog to surrender a fugitive slave, although the Constitution imposes the duty on his State, and he has sworn to obey it. . . .

Mason's attacks were followed by additional comments from Senator Clement C. Clay of Alabama. Clay's call for all honorable men to shun Sumner was adopted by all Southern members of Congress. It was one of the clearest examples of how Clay and other Southerners viewed the importance of community reputation as a judge of individual character. The refusal of Southern senators to acknowledge Sumner's presence was probably the reason they did not call him to order during the 'Crime Against Kansas' speech two years later.

Senator Clay Attacks Sumner[61]

Speech in Congress, 28 June 1854.

MR. CLAY: The Senator from South Carolina asked the Senator from Massachusetts whether, if the fugitive slave act were repealed, he would fulfill the obligation of his oath, and maintain and support the Constitution by returning, in conformity to its requirements, a fugitive slave. Here is the real answer, and I shall show what is the pretended answer. He said, "Does the Senator ask me what I would do?" And then answered, "Is thy servant a dog that he should do this thing. . . ?" What was the inference, the universal inference of the Senate, from this denial? Why, that he would violate the Constitution; that he was willing to prove his desecration of this Senate Chamber with his tread and his pollution of the Holy Evangelists, with his lips, by violating a solemn oath; that he was willing to commit moral perjury—a crime in the eyes of God and honorable men, as odious and as infamous as that legal perjury which would be visited with the penitentiary, or with the branding of the letter "P" upon the hand or forehead. That was the inference, the legitimate inference. How does he endeavor to shirk it? How does he endeavor to avoid the just and condign sentence of condemnation visited upon him by every honorable mind in this Senate? Why, sir, by going to that reporter, and foisting into the report, words which he never uttered, materially qualifying his denial. . . . I appeal to those honorable men, who sat near him, to say whether they were uttered. I do not believe he can find anybody here to sustain him, unless it be his *confrere* and uniform supporter, [MR. CHASE,] who was suggesting to him responses, and who sits near him. If he said it; he spoke it *sub rosa*—in a whisper. I would rather believe, to make the best of it, that it was one of those mental reservations with which he took his oath; but I do not even believe that there was any mental reservation. He did utter, and he did mean what was charged by the Senators from South Carolina,

[MR. BUTLER,] from Virginia, [MR. MASON,] and from Indiana, [MR. PETTIT;] but after he found the indignation it invoked upon his head, and heard the denunciations hurled at him from every quarter, and saw the smiles of scorn that played upon every face, he shrunk from the words he uttered, and endeavored to make an instrument of the reporter of this body to shield him from the infamy which he deserved. . . .

Why, sir, that notwithstanding this qualified denial, the Senator from South Carolina treated it as a positive denial of the Senator from Massachusetts, that he would support the Constitution of the United States. Now, I ask, does any intelligent man believe, if the Senator had qualified that denial in the manner in which it appears now, that the Senator from South Carolina would still have maintained that he refused to obey his oath, that he had refused to sustain the Constitution. . . ?

Let me ask, suppose a private citizen, however wealthy and well born, however highly cultivated his mind, however great his talents, however rich his acquirements, should openly avow a readiness to commit moral perjury; should day by day evince a disposition to instigate other men to crime, which, from want of personal courage he did not dare perpetrate himself; should daily encourage other men to violate the rights of his neighbors, to steal their property, to kidnap their slaves, and to refuse to return them; should daily assail the feelings of his neighbors by wanton, rude, and uncalled for assaults upon their characters, and, when rebuked for it in the harshest, most offensive, and opprobrious language, like the spaniel, should quietly submit or beg for quarter, but never repair the wrong or resent the insult—a sneaking, sinuous, snake-like poltroon, who would violate all the rights of associates or friends, and never make reparation or acknowledge his error, and who held himself irresponsible to all law, feeling the obligation neither of the Divine law, nor the law of the land, nor of the law of honor. I ask you, how would such a miscreant be treated? Why, if you could not reach him with the arm of the municipal law, if you could not send him to the penitentiary, you would *send him to Coventry.* You would exclude him from the pale of society; you would neither extend him the courtesies that are shown gentlemen, nor permit him to offer such to you. You would make him feel that he was shunned like a leper, and loathed like a filthy reptile. . . . If we cannot restrain or prevent this eternal warfare upon the feelings and rights of Southern gentleman, we may rob the serpent of his fangs. We can paralyze his influence by placing him in that nadir of social degradation which he merits. I am surprised, I repeat, I am surprised, that honorable men, but especially Southern men, should so far forget their rights, and those of their constituents, and their duties to them, as well as to themselves, as to lend any countenance to such a character as I have portrayed.

Sumner replied by giving an address he had prepared in response to Butler's initial challenge. His opponents would have a long memory of this speech. His attack on the "imbecility" of South Carolina during the American Revolution would still be a festering sore for Butler and Brooks in 1856. As with Sumner's "Petition" speech earlier, its arguments were derived from Sumner's interpretation of history. Sumner's description of Democratic president Andrew Jackson's constitutional views during the "Bank War" of 1832 was intended as an especially pointed barb at his "Assailants," nearly all of whom were Democrats and admirers of Jackson. Sumner's references to Butler's "gurgling speech" would anticipate his ridicule of Butler's speech impediment in the 1856 "Crime Against Kansas" speech.

Sumner's Reply to Assailants and Oath to Support the Constitution[62]

Speech in Congress, 28 June 1854.

MR. PRESIDENT: - Since I had the honor of addressing the Senate two days ago, various Senators have spoken. . . If to them it seems fit, courteous, parliamentary, let them

"unpack the heart with words,
And fall a-cursing, like a very drab,
A scullion. . ."[63]

I think, Sir, that I am not the only person on this floor, who, listening to these two self-confident champions of that peculiar fanaticism of the South, was reminded of the striking words of Jefferson, picturing the influence of Slavery, where he says: "The whole commerce between master and slave is a perpetual exercise of the most boisterous passions, the most unremitting despotism, on the one part, and degrading submission on the other. Our children see this, and learn to imitate it, for man is an imitative animal. . . . . The parent storms. The child looks on, catches the lineaments of wrath, puts on the same airs in the circle of smaller slaves, gives a loose to the worst of passions, and, thus nursed, educated, and daily exercised in tyranny, cannot but be stamped by it with odious peculiarities. The man must be a prodigy, who can retain his manners and morals undepraved by such circumstances."[64] Nobody, who witnessed the Senator from South Carolina or the Senator from Virginia in this debate, will place either of them among the "prodigies" described by Jefferson. As they spoke, the Senate Chamber must have seemed to them, in the characteristic fantasy of the moment, a plantation well-stocked with slaves, over which the lash of the overseer had free swing. . . . I desire to warn certain Senators, that, if, by any ardor of menace, or by any tyrannical frown, they expect to shake my fixed resolve, they expect a vain thing . . . .

Where a person degrades himself to the work of chasing a fellow-man, who, under the inspiration of Freedom and the guidance of the North Star, has sought a freeman's home far away from coffle and chain,—that person, whosoever he may be, I call Slave-Hunter. If the Senator from Virginia, who professes nicety of speech, will give me any term more precisely describing such an individual, I will use it. Until then, I must continue to use the language which seems to me so apt. But this very sensibility of the veteran Senator at a just term, truly depicting an odious character, shows a shame which pleases me. It was said by a philosopher of Antiquity that a blush is the sign of virtue; and permit me to add, that, in this violent sensibility, I recognize a blush mantling the cheek of the honorable Senator, which even his plantation manners cannot conceal.

And the venerable Senator from South Carolina, too, [MR. BUTLER,]—he has betrayed his sensibility. Here let me say that this Senator knows well that I always listen with peculiar pleasure to his racy and exuberant speech, as it gurgles forth,—sometimes tinctured by generous ideas,—except when, forgetful of history, and in defiance of reason, he undertakes to defend what is obviously indefensible. This Senator was disturbed, when, to his inquiry, personally, pointedly, and vehemently addressed to me, whether I would join in returning a fellow-man to Slavery, I exclaimed: "Is thy servant a dog, that he should do this thing?" In fitful phrase, which seemed to come from unconscious excitement, so common with the Senator, he shot forth various cries about "dogs," and, among other things, asked if there was any "dog" in the Constitution? The Senator did not seem to bear in mind, through the heady currents of that moment, that, by the false interpretation he fastens upon the Constitution, he has helped to nurture there a whole kennel of Carolina bloodhounds, trained, with savage jaw and insatiable scent, for the hunt of flying bondmen. No, Sir, I do not believe that there is any "kennel of bloodhounds," or even any "dog," in the Constitution. . . .

I have been charged with openly declaring a purpose to violate the Constitution, and to break the oath which I have taken at that desk, I shall be pardoned for showing simply how a few plain words will put all this down. The authentic report in the "Globe" shows what was actually said. The report in the "Sentinel" is substantially the same. And one of the New York papers, which has been put into my hands since I entered the Senate Chamber to-day, under its telegraphic head, states the incident with substantial accuracy,—though it omits the personal, individual appeal addressed to me by the Senator, and preserved in the "Globe." Here is the New York report.

MR. BUTLER: I would like to ask the Senator, if Congress repealed the Fugitive Slave Law, would Massachusetts execute the Constitutional requirements, and send back to the South the absconding slaves?

MR. SUMNER: Do you ask me if I would send back a slave?

MR. BUTLER: Why, yes.

MR. SUMNER: "Is thy servant a dog, that he should do this thing?' "

To any candid mind, either of these reports renders anything further superfluous. The answer is explicit and above impeachment. Indignantly it spurns a service from which the soul recoils, while it denies no constitutional obligation. But Senators who are so swift in misrepresentation, and in assault upon me as disloyal to the Constitution, deserve to be exposed, and it shall be done. Now, Sir, I begin by adopting as my guide the authoritative words of Andrew Jackson, in 1832, in his memorable veto of the Bank of the United States. To his course at that critical time were opposed the authority of the Supreme Court and his oath to support the Constitution. Here is his triumphant reply.

"If the opinion of the Supreme Court covered the whole ground of this Act, it ought not to control the coordinate authorities of this Government. The Congress, the Executive, and the Court must, each for itself, be guided by its own opinion of the Constitution. Each public officer, who takes an oath to support the Constitution, swears that he will support it as he understands it, and not as it is understood by others. It is as much the duty of the House of Representatives, of the Senate, and of the President, to decide upon the constitutionality of any bill or resolution which may be presented to them for passage or approval, as it is of the Supreme Judges, when it may be brought before them for judicial decision. . . . The authority of the Supreme Court must not, therefore, be permitted to control the Congress or the Executive, when acting in their legislative capacities, but to have only such influence as the force of their reasoning may deserve."[65]

Mark these words: "Each public officer, who takes an oath to support the Constitution, swears that he will support it as he understands it, and not as it is understood by others." Yes, Sir, AS HE UNDERSTANDS IT, and not as it is understood by others. Does any Senator here dissent from this rule? Does the Senator from Virginia? Does the Senator from South Carolina. . . ? [Here Mr. Sumner paused, but there was no reply.] In swearing to support the Constitution at your desk, Mr. President, I did not swear to support it as you understand it,—oh, no. Sir!—or as the Senator from Virginia understands it,—by no means!—or as the Senator from South Carolina understands it, with a kennel of bloodhounds, or at least a "dog" in it, "pawing to get free his hinder parts," in pursuit of a slave. No such thing. Sir, I swore to support the Constitution as I understand it,—nor more, nor less. . . .

This is precisely what I intend to do on the proposition to hunt slaves. . . .

Sir, as Senator, I have taken at your desk the oath to support the Constitution, as I understand it. And understanding it as I do, I am bound by that oath, Mr. President, to oppose all enactments by Congress on the subject of fugitive slaves, as a flagrant violation of the Constitution; especially must I oppose the last act, as a tyrannical usurpation, kindred in character to the Stamp Act, which our fathers indignantly refused to obey. Here my duties, under the oath which I have taken as Senator, end. There is nothing beyond. They are all absorbed in the constant, inflexible, righteous obligation to oppose every exercise by Congress of any power over the subject. In no respect by that oath can I be compelled to duties in other capacities, or as a simple citizen, especially when revolting to my conscience. Now in this interpretation of the Constitution I may be wrong; others may differ from me; the Senator from Virginia may be otherwise minded, and the Senator from South Carolina also; and they will, each and all, act according to their respective understanding. For myself, I shall act according to mine. On this explicit statement of my constitutional obligations I stand, as upon a living rock; and to the inquiry, in whatever form addressed to my personal responsibility, whether I would aid, directly or indirectly, in reducing or surrendering a fellow-man to bondage, I reply again, "Is thy servant a dog, that he should do this thing. . . ?"

And, Sir, looking round upon this Senate, I might ask fearlessly, how many there are, even in this body,—if, indeed, there be a single Senator,—who would stoop to any such service? Until some one rises and openly confesses his willingness to become a Slave-Hunter, I will not believe there can be one. [Here Mr. Sumner paused, but nobody rose.] And yet honorable and chivalrous Senators have rushed headlong to denounce me because I openly declared my repudiation of a service at which every manly bosom must revolt. . . .

Surely the Senator from South Carolina, with his silver-white locks, would have hesitated to lead this assault upon me, had he not for the moment been entirely oblivious of the history of the State which he represents. Not many years have passed since an incident occurred at Charleston, in South Carolina,—not at Boston, in Massachusetts,—which ought to be remembered. The postmaster of that place, acting under a controlling Public Opinion there, informed the head of his Department at Washington that he had determined to suppress all Antislavery publications, and requested instructions for the future. Thus, in violation of the laws of the land, the very mails were rifled, and South Carolina smiled approbation. . . .[66] And yet the venerable Senator from South Carolina now presumes to denounce me, when, for the sake of Freedom, and in the honest interpretation of my constitutional obligations, I decline an offensive service.

There is another incident in the history of South Carolina, which, as a loyal son of Massachusetts, I cannot forget, and which rises now in judgment against the venerable Senator. Massachusetts ventured to commission a distinguished gentleman, of blameless life and eminent professional qualities, who had served with honor in the other House [Hon. SAMUEL HOAR], to reside at Charleston for a brief period, in order to guard the rights of her free colored citizens, assailed on arrival there by an inhospitable statute, so gross in its provisions that an eminent character of South Carolina, a Judge of the Supreme Court of the United States [Hon. WILLIAM JOHNSON], had condemned it as "trampling on the Constitution," and "a direct attack upon the sovereignty of the United States."[67] Massachusetts had read in the Constitution a clause closely associated with that touching fugitives from service, to the following effect: "The citizens of each State shall be entitled to all privileges and immunities of citizens in the several States," and supposed that this would yet be recognized by South Carolina. But she was mistaken. Her venerable representative, an unarmed old man, with hair as silver-white almost as that of the Senator before me, was beset in Charleston by a "respectable" mob, prevented from entering upon his duties, and driven from the State,—while the Legislature stepped forward to sanction this shameless, lawless act, by placing on the statute-book an order for his expulsion.[68] And yet, Sir, the excitable Senator from South Carolina is fired by the fancied delinquencies of Massachusetts towards Slave-Hunters, and also by my own refusal to render them any aid or comfort. . . .

But enough for the present on the extent of my constitutional obligations to become Slave-Hunter. There are, however, yet other things in the assault of the venerable Senator, which, for the sake of truth, in just defence of Massachusetts, and in honor of Freedom, shall not be left unanswered. Alluding to those days when Massachusetts was illustrated by Otis, Hancock, and "the brace of Adamses," when Faneuil Hall sent forth notes of Liberty which resounded even to South Carolina, and the very stones in the streets of Boston rose in mutiny—against tyranny, the Senator with the silver-white locks, in the very ecstasy of Slavery, broke forth in exclamation that Massachusetts was then "slaveholding," and he presumed to hail these patriots representatives of "hardy, slaveholding Massachusetts. . . ."

The Senator opens a page on which I willingly dwell. Sir, Slavery never nourished in Massachusetts; nor did it ever prevail there at any time, even in early colonial days, in such measure as to be a distinctive feature of her progressive civilization. Her few slaves were for a term of years or for life. If, in fact, their issue was sometimes held in bondage, it was never by sanction of any statute or law of Colony or Commonwealth. Such has been the solemn and repeated judgment of her Supreme Court. . . . In all her annals, no person was ever born a slave on the soil of Massachusetts. This, of itself, is an answer to the imputation of the Senator. . . . And let me add, that, when this Senator presumes to say that American Independence "was won by the arms and treasure of slaveholding communities," he speaks either in irony or in ignorance.

The question which the venerable Senator from South Carolina opens by his vaunt I have no desire to discuss; but since it is presented, I confront it at once. This is not the first time, during my brief service here, that this Senator has sought on this floor to provoke comparison between slaveholding communities and the Free States.

MR. BUTLER [from his seat]: You cannot quote a single instance in which I have done it. I have always said I thought it was in bad taste, and I have never attempted it.

MR. SUMNER: I beg the Senator's pardon. I always listen to him, and I know whereof I affirm. He has profusely dealt in it. I allude now only to a single occasion. In his speech on the Nebraska Bill, running through two days, it was one of his commonplaces. There he openly presented a contrast between the Free States and "slaveholding communities" in certain essential features of civilization, and directed shafts at Massachusetts which called to his feet my distinguished colleague at that time [MR. EVERETT], and more than once compelled me to take the floor. And now, Sir, the venerable Senator, now rising from his seat and standing openly before the Senate, undertakes to deny that he has dealt in such comparisons.

MR. BUTLER: Will the Senator allow me?

MR. SUMNER: Certainly. I yield the floor to the Senator.

MR. BUTLER: Whenever that speech is read,—and I wish the Senator had read it before he commented on it with a good deal of rhetorical enthusiasm,—it will be found that I was particular not to wound the feelings of the Northern people who were sympathizing with us in the great movement to remove odious distinctions. I was careful to say nothing that would provoke invidious comparisons; and when that speech is read, notwithstanding the vehement assertion of the honorable Senator, he will find, that, when I quoted the laws of Massachusetts, particularly one Act which I termed the *Toties Quoties* Act, by which every Negro was whipped every time he came into Massachusetts, I quoted them with a view to show, not a contrast between South Carolina and Massachusetts, but to show that in the whole of this country, from the beginning to this time,—even in my own State,—I made no exception,—public opinion had undergone a change, and that it had undergone the same change in Massachusetts; for at one time they did not regard this institution of Slavery with the same odium that they do at this time. That was the purpose; and I challenge the Senator, as an orator of fairness, to look at it and see if it is not so.

MR. SUMNER: Has the Senator done?

MR. BUTLER: I may not be done presently; but that is the purport of that speech.

MR. SUMNER: Will the Senator refer to his own speech? He now admits, that, under the guise of an argument, he did draw attention to what he evidently regarded an odious law of Massachusetts. And, Sir, I did not forget, that, in doing this, there was, at the time, an apology which ill concealed the sting. . . . [See Senator Butler's speech, above.] I have avoided the contrasts founded on detail of figures and facts which are so obvious between the Free States and "slaveholding communities"; especially have I shunned all allusion to South Carolina. But the venerable Senator to whose discretion that State has intrusted its interests here will not allow me to be still.

God forbid that I should do injustice to South Carolina. . . ! I have no pleasure in dwelling on the humiliations of South Carolina; I have little desire to expose her sores; I would not lay bare even her nakedness. But the Senator, in his vaunt for "slaveholding communities," has made a claim for Slavery so derogatory to Freedom, and so inconsistent with history, that I cannot allow it to pass unanswered. . . .

The question of the comparative contributions of men by different States and sections of the country in the war of the Revolution was brought forward as early as 1790, in the first Congress under the Constitution, in the animated and protracted debate on the assumption of State debts by the Union. On that occasion, Fisher Ames, a Representative from Massachusetts, famous for classic eloquence, moved a call upon the War Department for the number of men furnished by each State to the Revolutionary armies. The motion, though vehemently opposed, was carried by a small majority. Shortly afterwards an answer to the call was received from the Department, at that time under the charge of General Knox. This answer, which is one of the documents of our history, places beyond cavil or criticism the exact contributions in arms made by each State. . . .

Looking . . . at the sum-total of continental troops, authenticated militia, and "conjectural" militia, we have 146,675 from the Southern States, while 249,463 were from the Northern: making upwards of 100,000 men contributed to the war by the Northern more than by the Southern. . . . [Sumner then quoted various histories of the American Rebellion showing moments when military preparedness was affected by fear of slave revolt or slave treason.]

The military weakness of this "slaveholding community" is but too apparent. As I show its occasion, you will join with me in amazement that a Senator from South Carolina should attribute Independence to anything "slaveholding." The records of the country, and various voices, all disown his vaunt for Slavery. The State of South Carolina itself, by authentic history, disowns it. . . .

It was during the war, and in the confessional of the Continental Congress, that, on bended knees, she shrived herself. But the same ignominious confession was made, some time after the war, in open debate, on the floor of Congress, by Mr. Burke, a Representative from South Carolina. "There is not a gentleman on the floor who is a stranger to the feeble situation of our State, when we entered into the war to oppose the British power. We were not only without money, without an army or military stores, but we were few in number, and likely to be entangled with our domestics, in case the enemy invaded us. . . ."[69]

And yet, in the face of this combined and authoritative testimony, we are called to listen, in the American Senate, to the arrogant boast, from a venerable Senator, that American Independence was achieved by the arms and treasure of "slaveholding communities. . . ."

But, while thus repelling insinuations against Massachusetts, and assumptions for Slavery, I would not unnecessarily touch the sensibilities of that Senator, or of the State which he represents. I cannot forget, that, amidst all diversities of opinion, we are bound together by ties of a common country, that Massachusetts and South Carolina are sister States, and that the concord of sisters ought to prevail between them; but I am constrained to declare, that, throughout this debate, I have sought in vain any token of that just spirit which within the sphere of its influence is calculated to promote the concord whether of State or of individuals.

And now, for the present, I part with the venerable Senator from South Carolina. Pursuing his inconsistencies, and exposing them to judgment, I had almost forgotten his associate leader in the wanton personal assault upon me in this long debate,—I mean the veteran Senator from Virginia [MR. MASON], who is now directly in my eye. With imperious look, and in the style of Sir Forcible Feeble, that Senator undertakes to call in question my statement, that the Fugitive Slave Act denies the writ of Habeas Corpus. . . . To his peremptory assertion, that the Fugitive Slave Act does not deny the Habeas Corpus, I oppose my assertion, peremptory as his own, that it does,—and there I leave that issue.

Mr. President, I welcome the sensibility which the Senator from Virginia manifests at the exposure of the Fugitive Slave Act. He is the author of that enormity. From his brain came forth the soulless monster. He is, therefore, its natural guardian. . . .

Let him now indicate, if he can, any article, clause, phrase, or word in the Constitution which gives to Congress any power to establish a "uniform law throughout the United States" on the subject of fugitive slaves. Let him now show, if he can, from the records of the National Convention, one jot of evidence inclining to any such power. Whatever its interpretation in other respects, the clause on which this bill purports to be founded gives no such power. Sir, nothing can come out of nothing; and the Fugitive Slave Act is, therefore, without any source or origin in the Constitution. It is an open and unmitigated usurpation. . . .

The Constitution has secured the inestimable right of Trial by Jury "in suits at Common Law, where the value in controversy shall exceed twenty dollars." Of course Freedom is not susceptible of pecuniary valuation; therefore there can be no question that the claim for a fugitive slave is within this condition. In determining what is meant by "suits at Common Law," recourse must be had to the Common Law itself, precisely as we resort to that law in order to determine what is meant by "Trial by Jury." Let the Senator, if he be a lawyer, undertake to show that a claim for a fugitive slave is not, according to early precedents and writs,—well known to the framers of the Constitution, especially to Charles Cotesworth Pinckney and John Rutledge, of South Carolina, both of whom had studied law at the Temple,—a suit at Common Law, to which, under the solemn guaranty of the Constitution, is attached the Trial by Jury, as an inseparable incident. Let the Senator show this, if he can.

And, Sir, when the veteran Senator has found a power in the Constitution where none exists, and has set aside the right of Trial by Jury in a suit at Common Law, then let him answer yet another objection. By the judgment of the Supreme Court of the United States, a claim for a fugitive slave is declared to be a case under the Constitution[70] within the judicial power; and this judgment of the Court is confirmed by common sense and Common Law. Let the Senator show, if he can, how such exalted exercise of judicial power can be confided to a single petty magistrate, appointed, not by the President, with the advice and consent of the Senate, but by the Court,—holding his office, not during good behavior, but merely during the will of the Court,—and receiving, not a regular salary, but fees according to each individual case. . . .

Such, Mr. President, is my response to all that has been said in this debate, so far as I deem it in any way worthy of attention. To the two associate chieftains in this personal assault, the veteran Senator from Virginia, and the Senator from South Carolina with the silver-white locks, I have replied completely. It is true that others have joined in the cry which these associates first started; but I shall not be tempted further. Some there are best answered by silence, best answered by withholding the words which leap impulsively to the lips. [Here Mr. Sumner turned to Mr. Mallory and Mr. Clay.]

And now, giving to oblivion all these things, let me, as I close, dwell on a single aspect of this discussion, which will render it memorable. On former occasions like this, the right of petition has been vehemently assailed or practically denied. Only two years ago, memorials for the repeal of the Fugitive Slave Act, presented by me, were laid on your table, Mr. President, without reference to any Committee. All is changed now. Senators have condemned the memorial, and sounded in our ears the cry of "Treason! treason!"—but thus far, throughout this excited debate, no person has so completely outraged the spirit of our institutions, or forgotten himself, as to persevere in objecting to the reception of the memorial, and its proper reference. It is true, the remonstrants and their representatives here are treated with indignity; but the great right of petition, the sword and buckler of the citizen, though thus dishonored, is not denied. Here, Sir, is a triumph for Freedom.

In Butler's reply he eagerly took up Sumner's historical challenge. His argument that Massachusetts was a slaveholding state at the time of the Revolution was technically true, though slavery would end in that state in the 1780s. More striking is Butler's charge that Sumner was lying. This attack on Sumner's honesty would parallel Sumner's language against Butler two years later. An indication of how angry Butler was during this speech is shown in his rejection of North Carolina Senator George Badger's adjournment call. Butler's sincere belief that he had not insulted Massachusetts deserves critical evaluation in light of his characterizations of the state and its representatives.

Senator Butler's Final Response

Speech in the Senate, 28 June 1854.

MR. BUTLER: Mr. President, if it be supposed by the Senate, or by the Senator from Massachusetts, that I shall indulge in any excited remarks, it will be a very great mistake. I think I never had a heart that could use a pen to write a libel, especially in matters involving truth and justice. . . .

Sir, I will say gravely, in the beginning of my remarks—and the Senator will have to take it as I assert it—that every thing which he has said for effect in Massachusetts has been upon a false issue made by himself, and not authorized by the facts. I do not know but that I might make the proposition more unqualified, and say that, in every issue upon which he has chosen to go to the country in regard to the topics involved in this debate, he has made an issue for his own purposes, without the authority of facts, and in perversion of them. But, sir, as the Senator assumes somewhat to speak as the organ of history, I will refute him in the estimation of every Senator here, and every page, and every individual who hears me.

MR. BADGER: I will ask my friend from South Carolina whether it would not be better for him to allow us now to adjourn?

MR. BUTLER: No sir; I would not subject myself to the temptation of preparing a reply that might have something in it that, like a hyena, I was scratching at the graves in Massachusetts to take revenge for the elaborate and vindictive assault that has been made by the gentleman who has just spoken. I prefer to go on now, trusting to recognized truth, rather than to consult musty records, for the purpose of producing effects that might be inconsistent with justice. I say, sir, that every issue upon which the Senator has chosen to go to the country by the remarks which he has submitted to the Senate, is not founded on the facts assumed by him. The facts assumed by himself are, as I shall show, unfair in statement; and his denials of the statement made by myself, in the speech to which he has alluded, are palpably against the truth of history. In what he has said he has aimed a shaft more to offend than it can hurt. He has been guilty of historical perversion. Sir, I made a remark the other day, and I thought truly, as a matter of history, that the independence of America was won by the arms and treasure of slaveholding

States. This remark is historically true. The sectional separation indicated by the gentleman was not in my mind—his own has made it. When the Declaration of Independence was made, was not Connecticut a slaveholding State?

MR. SUMNER: Not in any just sense.

MR. BUTLER: Sir, you are not the judge of that. Was not New York a slaveholding State?

MR. SUMNER: Let the Senator from New York answer.

MR. BUTLER: Sir, if he answers, he will answer the truth, and perhaps it will not be exactly agreeable to you. Was not New Jersey a slaveholding State? Was not Rhode Island, that sent Greene to South Carolina, a slaveholding State?

MR. SEWARD: It is due to the honorable Senator from South Carolina that I should answer his question in reference to New York, since it has been referred to me. At the time of the revolution every sixteenth man in the state of New York was a slave.

MR. BUTLER: The Senator from New York is right.

MR. SEWARD: I am sorry for it.

MR. BUTLER: Sir, I shall put the interrogatory in such a way that the Senator from Massachusetts will be ashamed of his historical proposition. I intend to make it so palpable that he cannot undertake to throw derision on me for the statement which I have made. I continue: was not New Hampshire a slaveholding State? Was not Pennsylvania a slaveholding State? Was not Delaware a slaveholding State? Was not Maryland a slaveholding State? Was not Virginia a slaveholding State? Was not North Carolina a slaveholding State? Was not Georgia a slaveholding State? So far as it regards the relation of *master* and slave, were they not as much so as South Carolina, the State selected for the gentleman's prepared attack.

MR. SEWARD: I am requested to make my answer a little more accurate, according to the truth. I understand that, at the time of the revolution, every twelfth man in New York was a slave.

MR. BUTLER: I do not care about the proportion; I do not think that at all important. But were not the States which I have named slaveholding States at the time of the Declaration of Independence? History can recognize no distinction between them. In the progress of events changes have taken place; this progress may go on, and greater changes may take place. These will afford no excuse for denying the irrevocable certainty of the past. They can afford no refuge for historical falsehood such as the gentleman has committed in the fallacy of his sectional vision. I have shown that twelve of the original States were slaveholding communities. Now, sir, I prove that the thirteenth, Massachusetts, was a slaveholding State before, and at the commencement of, the Revolution. But why talk of proving what no one can deny? The gentleman cannot deny the *fact*. As to the character of slavery in that State, that may be somewhat a different thing, which cannot contradict the facts stated in the newspapers of the day, that Negroes were held, were advertised for sale, with another truth, that many were sent to other slaveholding States in the way of traffic. When slavery was abolished, many that had been slaves, and might have been freemen, were sold into bondage, with the consideration in the pocket to afford a supply to the philanthropy of the vendor. I have said that the independence of America was achieved by the arms and treasure of slaveholding States. I will never, in a parliamentary sense, be personal; but I say that I convict him of historical falsehood. Dare you, sir, look me in the face and deny it?

MR. SUMNER: Deny what?

MR. BUTLER: That independence was won by the arms and treasure of slaveholding States? The presiding officer, [MR. STUART in the chair.] The Senator must address the Chair.

MR. BUTLER: He cannot and dare not deny it.

MR. SUMNER: Will the Senator yield the floor?

MR. BUTLER: Yes, sir, because I want to hear what you can say on that subject.

MR. SUMNER: What I can say is very easily said, and, I think, is very decisive. When, in our history, we speak of slaveholding States, we mean those in which slavery has been an established policy, and professedly an essential element in their civilization. This, I believe, is common, if not universal. Of such I spoke when I spoke of slaveholding States—such as were regarded as slaveholding States at the adoption of the Constitution—which, in those days, were called southern States, in contrast to the northern States, sometimes called the non-slaveholding States. By slaveholding States, of course I mean States which were peculiarly, distinctively, essentially slaveholding, and not States in which the holding of slaves seems to have been rather the accident of the hour, and in which all the people, or the greater part of the people, were ready to welcome emancipation.

MR. BUTLER: Mr. President, I think the remarks of the Senator verify exactly what I said, that when he chooses to be rhetorical it is upon an assumption of facts, upon his own construction, and by an accumulation of adjectives. I quit that part of the subject, For it is too palpable to need argument, and leave it to the country to say what shadow of truth has the gentleman to cover him in saying that I had made a remark betraying ignorance of the subject, or one made in irony? Upon this remark of mine, thus characterized by him, the gentleman has poured out what he would have us regard as rebuking invective.

I again repeat, that the independence of America was won *by the arms and treasure of slaveholding States.*

Sir, he made the assertion with a view to assail South Carolina. That was his object. He did it with a view to assail a State in which, I may say, whatever have been her distractions and difficulties, there is scarcely a stream or a path that was not sprinkled with the blood of men contending for the liberties of the country. Does he suppose that I can be required to defend South Carolina, or can be provoked into an attack on Massachusetts by anything that he—he—can say of South Carolina? No, sir; I never made the attack on Massachusetts imputed to me; but he has assumed that I did so, with a view to make his speech, exactly as he assumed the other day that I asked him a question which I never asked. . . .

But, sir, do you suppose I shall be provoked into assault upon Massachusetts? No, sir; Massachusetts and Boston, so far as I can see, have done their duty, and stand vindicated before the Confederacy, in spite of their misrepresenting advocate. Sir, what I said to the gentleman was not to him as the Representative of the people of Massachusetts, either as they were or as they are. I did not magnify him into the Representative of Massachusetts. In assailing the small target at which I shot, I never assumed that I was going to make an assault upon the gravity, the dignity, and the historical reputation of Massachusetts. He has thought proper, however, to turn round, and, by his miserable shifts, to dig up, in the last night, I suppose, by the aid of jackals and hunters—worse than slave-hunters, men whose malice would lead them to do anything—musty records, in order to distort and misrepresent history; and he expects me to-day, in a moment, to answer his libel. I can refute, and might denounce it, I shall trust to transient indignation.

Sir, in what I said the other day, and in what I have said at all times, I never instituted the comparison which the Senator has chosen to make. In the rather playful remarks which I made in reference to Massachusetts some time ago, to which the Senator has referred, I said that Massachusetts, like South Carolina, and all the other States, had undergone a material change of opinion on the subject of slavery; for at one time, as I showed, there was a statute in Massachusetts—illustrating opinion, I did not mention it by way of reproach—providing for whipping every Negro who returned there. Now, in their philanthropy, they are so much better off that, instead of their whipping Negroes, they invite them there, with a view, I suppose, to exhibit this wonderful spirit of liberty called "a spirit of resistance to *the Stamp Act!*"—for the purpose that I referred to the *toties quoties* statute, as I termed it, under which a colored man going into Massachusetts was liable to be whipped as often as he did go there from another State—I had a right to do so. It was to show that Massachusetts had very little sympathy then for the Negro race. It was to show the state of opinion that existed then. The truth is, Massachusetts at one time had the same opinions as other States in relation to the colored race. When she owned them, she used them as slaves.

Well, sir, the Senator has said that Massachusetts was not a slaveholding State at the time her distinguished heroes, statesmen, and poets illustrated her history. I might say now of the Senator and his *confreres*, that, like some of the degenerate poets of Rome and Greece, they could not praise Marathon, Thermopylae, and Salamis, but they never lived in a period when they were capable of the achievements of those whom they attempted to praise. I distinguish between the ripe orator, who is proud of the reputation of his State, and the vapid rhetorician. The gentleman has indulged himself in a tone of indignation in response to me, for saying that Massachusetts was once a slaveholding community. Nay, more; he has denounced me for my ignorance on the subject; and he seems specially to think that the laurels and honors of Hancock, Warren, and the Adamses, will be tarnished by anything that can be said of them, even by attribution, in connection with the character or relation of a slaveholding people. Why, sir, if he had made true that these great man did not live in slaveholding Massachusetts, would he have it supposed that, on *that account*, they would have claimed a superiority to their equally illustrious compeers? But let the gentleman take the truth, that these great men, with names illustrating a common history, were born and bred, in a slaveholding community, and that they were as good as others born since. Is it not now apparent that the gentleman has selected his own positions, and has erected his batteries for the discharge of his sectional cannon on grounds denied to him by truth? Has he not falsified history to make his production the vehicle of his designs? Has he not denied what I stated, and what all must admit is true? And for what purpose?—to take aim at South Carolina, from a rest. It is like the conceited archer, who shot at the star because he had his arrow aimed at it. . . .

Sir; it is a sore thing to the gentleman that I will not attack Massachusetts. It is what he wanted. It is what he has asserted. I have never assailed her. She is doing her duty now, as far as I know. All that I did say was, if the exaggerated feelings of which the Senator was, I thought, the vapid rhetorical advocate, did prevail generally, it would make up an issue, which we had to meet, of the separation of these States. . . .

I have now gone over the two issues upon which the Senator has spoken, and they are both false.

Now, sir, a few words in reference to the affair of Mr. Hoar, in Charleston; and I am sorry that it has been brought up again. Mr. Hoar did go to Charleston, with a view to interfere with the law which had been passed by South Carolina in reference to colored seamen. Here let me say that that law would never have been passed by South Carolina, but for the excited fanatical feeling of some portion of the northern States; I will not say Massachusetts particularly; I will guard myself in that respect. But, sir, I say that the law, to which the Senator has referred, and which he has reprobated with so much violence, was passed to guard against the very feelings which he would excite; to guard against the incendiary who would come and burn your dwelling in the night, and not act like the man in a fair fight, who would advertise you that he would meet you in on open field. . . .

The gentleman has spoken of Mr. Hoar being expelled by a mob. Sir, there was no mob. Mr. Hoar was informed by a committee of gentleman that it was desirable he should not continue in Charleston, with an intimation that he would have to leave, but with a declaration that any portion of his family with him would be treated even as guests, if they chose to remain.

But, sir, these are matters apart from the subject. I am very sorry that I have been provoked into this discussion. It is against my feelings that I partake in it at all, but I now will come to the most specific charge in the indictment against me.

It is not my wish or purpose, while I am a member of the body, to charge intentional falsehood made on any issue by a gentleman who represents a sovereign State, but so far as regards the remarks made the other day, I am bound to make a statement which I think justice demands, and let it go for what it is worth. The Senator will have to take it as I make it. I should not say a word about it if he had not gone back into the graves of South Carolina. He deserves no quarter, and perhaps I should give him none. The other Senator from Massachusetts will perhaps have to listen to what I am to say, and I think the Senator will have, in some measure, by its opinion at least, to hear testimony to the truth of what I do say. How far it may effect the Senator I know not. I was speaking the other day in regard to the petition praying for the repeal of the fugitive slave law which had been introduced, and had given rise to so much excitement. I said that originally I was rather opposed to such a law, believing that, if the Constitution, with its self-sufficing energy and powers was left to execute itself, the States themselves as parties to the compact ought to perform under that compact, the duty of returning to the master a fugitive slave, or of delivering him up, to use the language of the Constitution. Such was my belief, and believing that, I thought it was inadvisable for Congress to do anything until we saw that the States themselves would not act. We found in many instances that the States not only refused, but threw obstructions in the way. They not only did not afford the usual assistance in apprehending a runaway slave, they in many instances not only refused assistance, but interposed actual statutory opposition to the law. In doing so they took apology from the case of *Prigg vs. the Commonwealth of Pennsylvania*,[71] and to that extent they had some excuse.

I said that this memorial was likely to be referred to the committee of which I was chairman, and it was a subject upon which I had great difficulties. . . .I turned to the Senator near me, [MR. SUMNER,] and said, "What say you on the subject? What would you do?" I did not ask the Senator whether personally he would assist to reduce a human being to bondage, or return him to bondage?—as he has put it. I did not ask him any such question as that. I did not approach anything like it. I asked him a question of exactly the same import which I had put to the other Senator from that State: "What would you do?" I meant, what would you do as a public representative, on that subject? Would you advise the abrogation of the present fugitive slave law, with the understanding, on your part, that when you go home you will advise your constituents to do their duty in relation to this matter? I turned to him and asked him what he would do? Well, sir, what you think he said? I have no doubt he had his reply in his drawer fixed, ready for me. It is a pretty thing, no doubt. He did not, however, answer my question, nor did he answer the question which he made for himself.

MR. SUMNER: Will the Senator allow me to correct him?

MR. BUTLER: You may correct me, if you can.

MR. SUMNER: I am very reluctant to interrupt the Senator.

MR. BUTLER: I would rather you would not interrupt me. I do not think you can correct me.

MR. SUMNER: I wish to call the Senator's attention to a report to which I alluded before.

THE PRESIDING OFFICER, (MR. STUART.)   Does the Senator from South Carolina yield the floor to the Senator from Massachusetts?

MR. BUTLER: I think the Senator had better let me finish.

MR. SUMNER: I wish to show this now.

MR. BUTLER: Very well.

MR. SUMNER: The New York papers, which came to-day, under the telegraph head, give a report of what passed, which is necessarily more brief than that in the *Globe*. The statement here is as follows:

"He [MR. BUTLER] would like to ask the Senator, if Congress repealed the fugitive slave law, would Massachusetts execute the constitutional requirements, and send back to the South the absconding slaves?"

That is the statement of the Senator's interrogatory in the New York papers, as addressed to my colleague. Then the report in the *Globe*, which, I presume, has been revised by himself—

MR. BUTLER: No, sir, not that part; I never will touch personal matters; I give you to understand that.

MR. SUMNER: The report in the *Globe* goes on, "Will the honorable Senator [MR. SUMNER] tell me that he will do it?"

MR. BUTLER: That was my inquiry.

MR. SUMNER: Then the New York papers represent me as saying, "That you ask me if I would send back a slave?" Then they go on to say, that the Senator from South Carolina answered, "Why, yes." That is to say, the question was, would I send back a fugitive? to which I replied as you know.

MR. BUTLER: I will not undertake to say here what was the Senator's exact interrogatory. I know what mine was. Of that I have a right to speak.

MR. SUMNER: Unquestionably.

MR. BUTLER: Though I have been asked frequently by others, I will not say what his interrogatory was; for I never will do injustice.

MR. SUMNER: I cheerfully concede the Senator that right. I know he could not misstate on this floor; but what I concede to him I claim for myself; and I believe it is reasonable to suppose that what I said is better within my memory than within his. . . . I wish to say to the Senator from South Carolina—and I do say it most unfeignedly—that, in answering him at the time, I answered him honestly and frankly, according to my position. He addressed me, and I regarded the appeal as addressed to me individually—as, if I may say so, an *argumentum ad hominem*. Will you join in doing this? I still understood it; I so declared, and then I answered the Senator, understanding him to ask me if I would individually, personally, join in sending back a slave. That was my interpretation, and accordingly I answered, and by that answer I stand. I state this with all frankness and simplicity before the Senate. I think the controversy does not justly arise on the facts. . . .

MR. BUTLER: I do not think this matter very important. . . . I make now the qualified remark—for upon personal matters I wish always to be correct—that whatever may have been the Senator's assumptions, in nothing that I did say, in no interpretation that could be given of what I did say, ought he to have supposed that I would have asked the question, whether he, as a Senator of Massachusetts, was bound to join with the police and apprehend a slave. He may have been expecting such a question, and was prepared for it. Sir, I asked a graver question, whether he, in his place, as a Senator from Massachusetts, would say here that Massachusetts would execute the Constitution of the United States, and whether he would concur in carrying out that Constitution? That was the interrogatory I proposed to him; and he evaded it by saying, "If the gentleman says so and so, then I answer by this quotation." I made one issue by my interrogatory and he made another. I do not say that it may not have been a misconception. I will be qualified on the subject; but when he made that remark, I assumed that he regarded himself absolved from the obligation taken by his oath here to maintain that provision of the Constitution which required every State in this Union to perform its duty in returning a fugitive slave. . . .

Why, sir, did not that Senator rise and say in the Senate of the United States—not speaking in an adversary Commonwealth, whose flag had been erected by the voice of his own State, not as standing upon Bunker Hill and inspired by the spirit of liberty— he was willing to run the hazards and risks of battle; not that he was willing to encounter the pains and penalties of a separate movement against the Federal Government? But what I was excited at was that, in this Senate he should say that the provision of the Constitution of the United States, a compact into which Massachusetts entered, recognizing the existence of slavery and the obligations of the non-slaveholding States to perform their duties in returning a fugitive, *imposed no obligation upon him!* When I saw him rise upon this floor, and heard him say that clause, and all laws intended to carry it out, were worse than the Stamp Act, and that before God he would be as much justified in resisting them as our forefathers were in resisting the Stamp Act, I was excited. When a coequal Senator stood on this floor, and said it would be as lawful, as heroic, as glorious, to resist this provision of the Constitution, as to resist the Stamp act, I was indignant. As I understood him, he justified combined communities, mobs, in resisting the fugitive slave law, or that provision of the Constitution. Sir, he identified with the glorious resistance to the Stamp Act, as exhibited in Boston and elsewhere, resistance which he was willing to make to the Constitution of his own country!

Did he suppose that I, as a southern man, interested in the institution of slavery, representing a slaveholding Commonwealth, could stand here and hear myself denounced, and my community denounced, for maintaining an institution of that kind, and for insisting upon the constitutional obligations of others, to conform to the terms of the

Confederacy? When he said, that before God—I do not know whether he used those words, but he used some solemn asserveration—the enormities of the Stamp Act sunk into insignificance, compared with the enormities of this provision of the Constitution, or any act intended to carry it out, it was enough to excite me. It was, however, but a temporary excitement; and if the Senator had not this morning come here, and indited a libel against South Carolina—not in the name of Massachusetts, for she would not do it—if he had not come here this morning, with concocted malice, poured out a prepared speech, on the assumption that I had said a thing which I never said; if he had not come here deliberately prepared to take materials brought together in a fell spirit, with a view to make a distinction between the North and the South, and against South Carolina, I should have said nothing. God knows South Carolina has had her difficulties throughout the whole period of her existence. Her history is written in blood and trial. . . .

Sir, when he speaks of my honored state by culling history which I have not had an opportunity of examining, I admit we had our difficulties. The truth is, it is a wonder that South Carolina ever went to the rescue of Boston. Boston made the war with Great Britain. She was the first. She made it in the spirit of hearty Massachusetts, of slaveholding Massachusetts. I do not say, however, that the fact of her being or not being slaveholding had anything to do with it. I do not say that a State is better or worse for being slaveholding or non-slaveholding. But, sir, when Massachusetts made the declaration and involved the country in the issues of war, we came to her rescue, and our history will illustrate the annals of that day. I will not say more, for more would not become me or him on that point. . . .

I will now conclude by saying that what I have said has been the effusion of the moment, and not the effusion of the drawer; but what the Senator has said this morning has been the deliberate preparation of two or three nights' lucubrations, collecting the materials of history, and making them subservient to the maintenance of false issues. With that proposition I leave the subject. Upon false issues he has made the speech.

THE KNOW-NOTHING INTERLUDE

Free-soilers hoped that the furor over Nebraska and fugitive slaves would attract a host of new participants to their movement. During the summer of 1854 they organized rallies across the North to capitalize on indignation over these events. They extended invitations to all individuals "regardless of party," with the belief that the old political organizations had compromised themselves too much to meet the new needs of the era. Out of these meetings came the nucleus of the modern Republican party. In Massachusetts the first gatherings took place in late June and early July. Vigorous opposition from the state's Whigs nearly killed these initiatives, but the new party managed to hold a statewide rally in late August, followed by a formal Republican nominating convention at Worcester in September 1854. Sumner spoke at the rally for almost two hours, in what was his first public address since returning from Washington. He reiterated his claim that citizens of Massachusetts had no obligation to enforce the fugitive slave law, and argued that the old parties were dead. Calling for unity behind the new organization, he exclaimed that "as Republicans we go forth to encounter the *Oligarchs of Slavery*."[72]

Despite Sumner's exhortations his party benefited little from Whig and Democratic breakdown. For most of the state's voters the dangers he warned of were merely abstractions. The "oligarchs of slavery" lived hundreds of miles away. Most white people in the state had never seen a fugitive slave, much less witnessed a runaway being pursued by government agents. The Republicans also suffered from their image as backers of racial equality. Although Sumner himself was optimistic on the eve of the election the Republicans fared dismally at the ballot-box.

It was the dramatic social changes *within* Massachusetts rather than the external threat of the "Slave Power" that galvanized voters in the November elections. Especially troubling for the state's native-born Protestants was the recent mass immigration of Irish Catholics. This played into the state's long history of opposition to the Pope. Anti-Catholicism in Massachusetts dated from its founding. It was, after all, because they sought to purify the English church from all Roman Catholic influences that the colony's first settlers had been dubbed "Puritans." Likewise, fears that King George III might extend the laws and church of Catholic Quebec to New England had been a key motive for the Massachusetts revolutionaries of 1776. Although legal prohibitions against Catholics were weakened after the Revolution, Boston witnessed numerous anti-Catholic and anti-Irish riots in the 1830s, the most notorious of which was the burning of the city's Ursuline Convent in 1834. The 1840s were relatively quiet, but a sequence of events after 1848 reawakened nativism into a political force. Dramatic growth in the number of Irish voters, condemnation of the public school system by American Catholic leaders, President Pierce's selection of a Catholic postmaster and the vigorous anti-liberalism of Pope Pius IX increased concern among American Protestants. A visit to Boston by the Pope's representative, Cardinal Bedini, in early 1854, coupled with Irish opposition to a proposed alcohol prohibition law, led to a potent counter-reaction in Massachusetts.[73]

The result was the creation in 1854 of a second organization, the "Know-Nothings" or "American Party." The Know-Nothings had their origins in a New York secret society whose members claimed to "know nothing" about their association and its activities. The movement eventually went public, expanding its lodges across the North during 1854. The goal of this group was to block Catholic influence over American politics. They called for lengthened naturalization requirements, extended residency periods for voting eligibility, and attendance of Catholic children in public schools. Many Know-Nothings were also strong supporters of alcohol prohibition who saw "Rum and Romanism" as related forms of dependency. Know-Nothing attitudes toward slavery were more complex. The movement's conservatives viewed antislavery as an obstacle to a national party. On the other side, many abolitionists condemned the movement as just another form of bigotry. Most Massachusetts Know-Nothings fit between these extremes, opposing the Nebraska bill and the Federal Fugitive Slave Act as tyrannies similar to the assaults against rights and liberties they associated with the Pope. The

Know-Nothings were a new party, and not tainted by the Freesoiler's reputation for radicalism. They could therefore adopt the popular aspects of the Freesoiler program without taking on its liabilities. They could escape, in particular, any association with radical abolitionism's "holier than thou" moralism and the Garrisonians' call for racial and sexual equality. Nor did they suffer from the Massachusetts Freesoilers' reputation for questionable political maneuverings that arose from the 1851 "Coalition" that had put Sumner in the Senate. Indeed, demands for political reform and an end to corruption were a central part of the Know-Nothing campaign.[74]

Know-Nothing ideology resonated with Massachusetts voters. The party dominated the Fall elections, winning all nine of the state's seats in Congress and all but four seats in the legislature. The party's candidate for governor, Henry J. Gardner, received 63 percent of all votes cast. He was helped by his Republican opponent, Henry Wilson, who agreed to halt his own campaign if the Know-Nothings would support his election to the United States Senate the following year. Ordinary voters abandoned the Whig and Democratic parties in droves. A majority of Free-Soilers also followed Wilson into the new organization, though one in five chose to stay home on election day rather than support the Know-Nothing program. Voter apathy and disaffection grew from previous years but only contributed to the new party's success by keeping its opponents away from the ballot box.[75]

For Sumner the election was a reversal of fortune. In October he had boasted of his popularity, saying that if he were up for re-election he would be "returned without any opposition."[76] A month later he described himself as a man without a party. Despite his past willingness to ally with opponents on the antislavery issue he refused to join the new organization. In a letter to outgoing Senator Julius Rockwell he distanced himself from the victors. "I am ignorant enough," he wrote, "but I am not a Know Nothing."[77] His hostility was returned in equal measure. By late 1855 Governor Gardner and his associates had hatched a scheme to oust Sumner from his seat. Their idea was to shorten the end of Sumner's term to 1856 instead of 1857. According to the plan Gardner himself would take Sumner's place. Although the plot failed, the fact that such a bold attempt to tinker with constitutional precedents received consideration underscores the fragility of Sumner's political position.[78]

The instability of the political situation in Massachusetts shows clearly in the period's election returns. Both Whigs and Know-Nothings witnessed dramatic shifts from election to election. The Whig transformation from dominance to irrelevance is especially striking. More surprising is the relative stability of the other two parties. With the notable exception of 1854, neither the Democrats nor their Free-soiler and Republican competitors changed their turnout by more than a few percentage points over the entire five year period. Whereas the Whigs had scattered into the other parties, a Democrat in 1852 was likely to be a Democrat in 1855. Likewise, the majority of those who began the decade as Free-soilers had moved into the Republican party five years later. Despite the setback of 1854 both Democrats and Republicans were able to restore their base constituencies in the

TABLE 1.1 Massachusetts State Election Results, 1850–1855

Percentage of Eligible Electorate Voting for Gubernatorial Candidates, 1850–1855

PARTY/YEAR	1850	1851	1852	1853	1854	1855
Whig	34%	34	32	31	14	7
Democratic*	21	23	20	18	7	17
Free-Soil/Republican	16	15	19	15	3	18
Know-Nothing/American	0	0	0	0	42	25
Eligible but not voting	28	28	29	32	34	33

Number of Delegates to the Massachusetts House of Representatives

PARTY/YEAR	1850	1851	1852	1853	1854	1855
Whig	174	196	149	193	1	58
Democratic	0	0	18	0	1	30
"Coalition"	210	202	122	108	0	0
Free-Soil/Republican	0	0	0	0	1	80
Know-Nothing/American	0	0	0	0	377	152

*Includes totals for a separate "Hunker" Democratic candidate in 1853. Percentages calculated from *Tribune Almanac;* Dale Baum, *The Civil War Party System;* United States Population Censuses of 1850 and 1860.
Source: *Tribune Almanac.*

following election. Yet neither party was strong enough by itself to defeat the Know-Nothings, who kept Gardner in the governor's office and maintained a predominance in the legislature that seems small only in comparison to the previous year. Sumner believed that most people in Massachusetts shared his loathing of the "Slave Oligarchs," but knew it would take a tremendous effort to pull them from Know-Nothingism into the Republican party. Events in Kansas would give him the rallying point he needed to bring clarity to Massachusetts politics.[79]

NOTES

1. House of Representatives, 34th Congress, 1st Session, Report No. 132.
2. Henry A. Edmundson (1814–1890) was a Democratic Representative from Virginia.
3. John Gaines Miller, Democratic Representative from Missouri, died 11 May 1856.
4. Henry Geyer, Democratic Senator from Missouri.
5. For this argument see John C. Calhoun, *A Disquisition on Government and Selections from the Discourse*, C. Gordon Post, ed. (Indianapolis: Bobbs-Merrill Educational Publishing, 1953), esp. 7–16, 23–27.

6. The incident and its implications receive full discussion in William E. Gienapp, "The Crime Against Sumner: The Caning of Charles Sumner and the Rise of the Republican Party" *Civil War History* 25 (1979): 218–245; David H. Donald, *Charles Sumner and the Coming of the Civil War* (New York: Knopf, 1960); Harlan Joel Gradin, "Losing Control: The Caning of Charles Sumner and the Breakdown of Antebellum Political Culture" (Ph.D.: University of North Carolina, 1991); and Michael D. Pierson, " 'All Southern Society Is Assailed by the Foulest Charges:' Charles Sumner's 'The Crime Against Kansas' and the Escalation of Republican Anti-slavery Rhetoric" *New England Quarterly* 68 (December 1995): 531–557.

7. These changes are documented in the United States census reports of 1840, 1850, and 1860. See also Michael F. Holt, *The Rise and Fall of the American Whig Party: Jacksonian Politics and the Onset of the Civil War* (New York: Oxford University Press, 1999); George Rogers Taylor, *The Transportation Revolution, 1815–1860* (Armonk, New York: M. E. Sharpe, Inc., 1951).

8. The first Great Awakening had swept the American colonies from the 1720s to the 1750s.

9. See Charles Sellers, *The Market Revolution: Jacksonian America, 1815–1846* (New York: Oxford University Press, 1994); Leonard Dinnerstein and David M. Reimer, *Ethnic Americans: A History of Immigration and Assimilation* (New York: Columbia University Press, 1999); Rebecca M. Edwards, *Angels in the Machinery: Gender in American Party Politics from the Civil War to the Progressive Era* (New York: Oxford University Press, 1997); and Anne C. Rose, *Voices of the Marketplace: American Thought and Culture, 1830–1860* (New York: Twayne Publishers, 1995).

10. John C. Calhoun's remarks can be found in the famous "Southern Address" of 1849, of which he was the principal author. Garrisonian abolitionists had rejected the existing political order and participation in electoral politics since the 1830s. See James Brewer Stewart, *Holy Warriors: The Abolitionists and American Slavery* (rev. ed., New York: Hill and Wang, 1997).

11. These implications are fully discussed in the Geinapp, Gradin, and Pierson works. See note 1 above.

12. Uses of the Revolution and its heroes in antebellum America are discussed in Michael Kammen, *A Season of Youth: The American Revolution and the Historical Imagination* (New York: Alfred A. Knopf, 1978), and Barry Schwartz, *George Washington: The Making of an American Symbol* (New York: The Free Press, 1987).

13. Unitarians believed in the goodness of both humans and the Deity, and the practice of rational and benevolent religion rather than elaborate ritual or scriptural literalism. Transcendentalism stressed the value of an authentic intuition that transcended the ordinary limits of rational thought. The broader transformations of Boston and Massachusetts have been subjects of extensive scholarship. See, for example, Walter Muir Whitehill and Lawrence M. Kennedy, *Boston: A Topographical History* (Cambridge: Harvard University Press, 2000); Edmund Morgan, *The Puritan Dilemma: The Story of John Winthrop* (New York: Addison-Wesley Publishers, 1962); Stephen Innes, *Creating the Commonwealth: The Economic Culture of Puritan New England* (New York: W. W. Norton & Company, 1995); and Ronald P. Formisano and Constance K. Burns, eds., *Boston, 1700–1980: The Evolution of Urban Politics* (Westport, Connecticut: Greenwood Press, 1984).

14. Sumner's early life is detailed in Donald, *Charles Sumner and the Coming of the Civil War;* and Frederick J. Blue, *Charles Sumner and the Conscience of the North* (Arlington Heights, Illinois, Harlan Davidson, Inc., 1994). Additional biographical material and Sumner's personal correspondence can be found in Edward L. Pierce, ed., *Memoir and Letters of Charles Sumner,* (Boston: Roberts Brothers, 1894); and Beverly Wilson Palmer, ed., *The Selected Letters of Charles Sumner* (Boston, Northeastern University Press, 1990).

15. Wordsworth, Carlyle, and Martineau were prominent literary figures associated with the Romantic movement. Lord John Russell was a leading political figure in English Liberalism and a future Prime Minister. Austrian minister Klemens von Metternich was a defender of Conservatism and the European continent's most powerful political leader.

16. Pierce, *Memoir and Letters*, II, 193–196, 199–205.

17. Text from Pierce, ed., *Memoir and Letters*, II:347–355.

18. Mithridates of Pontus fought against Roman expansion until defeated by Pompey the Great.

19. Sumner's political evolution in this period is detailed in Donald, *Charles Sumner and the Coming of the Civil War,* 130–206.

20. Pierce, *Memoir and Letters*, III, 214. Sumner's integration efforts are described in Blue, *Charles Sumner,* 51–53. His relationship with Boston's intellectuals is discussed in Bill Ledbetter, "Charles Sumner: Political Activist for the New England Transcendentalists" *The Historian*, LVIV (1982), 347–363.

21. Three treatments of Edgefield's history are Orville Vernon Burton, *In My Father's House are Many Mansions: Family and Community in Edgefield, South Carolina* (Chapel Hill: University of North Carolina Press, 1985); and Judith N. McArthur and Orville Vernon Burton, *A Gentleman and an Officer: A Military and Social History of James B. Griffin's Civil War* (New York: Oxford University Press, 1996), 15–47. J. William Harris, *Planters and Plain Folk and Gentry in Slave Society* (Middletown, Conn.: Wesleyan University Press, 1985).

22. For discussion of the conditions of slavery in Edgefield and the American South in general, see Burton, *In My Father's House*, 148–190; Robert William Fogel, *Without Consent or Contract: The Rise and Fall of American Slavery* (New York: W. W. Norton & Company, 1989), esp. 41–198; William Freehling, *Road to Disunion: Secessionists at Bay, 1776–1854* (New York: Oxford University Press, 1990); and Peter Kolchin, *American Slavery, 1619–1877* (New York: Hill and Wang, 1994). The use of slave narratives as evidence is carefully explored in Paul D. Escott, *Slavery Remembered: A Record of Twentieth Century Slave Narratives* (Chapel Hill: University of North Carolina Press, 1979); and Donna J. Spindel, "Assessing Memory: Twentieth-Century Slave Narratives Reconsidered," *Journal of Interdisciplinary History* XXVII (Autumn 1996), 247–261.

23. For the South Carolina declaration see State of South Carolina, *Journal of the Convention of the People of South Carolina, Held in 1860, 1861, and 1862. Together with the Ordinances, Reports, Resolutions, etc.* (Columbia, S.C.: R. W. Gibbes, Printer to the Convention, 1862), 461–466. It is also available online at James Epperson, ed., "Declarations of Causes of Seceding States: South Carolina," *Causes of the Civil War* [http://members.aol.com/jfepperson/reasons.html#SouthCarolina] 2002. Similar discussion of the fugitive slave issue is found in Charles B. Dew, *Apostles of Disunion:*

Southern Secession Commissioners and the Causes of the Civil War (Charlottesville: University Press of Virginia, 2001.) See also John Hope Franklin and Loren Schweninger, *Runaway Slaves: Rebels on the Plantation* (New York: Oxford University Press, 1999), esp. 262–296. They estimate that at least 50,000 slaves a year in the South ran away during the 1850s.

24. Narrative of Henry Ryan (83), Newberry, S. C., G. Leland Summer, Newberry, S. C., interviewer, in Works Progress Administration, Federal Writers' Project, *Slave Narratives: South Carolina Narratives* (St. Clair Shores, Michigan: Scholarly Press, Inc., 1976), Part 4, 71–73.

25. Edgefield, South Carolina, *Advertiser,* 4 May 1854.

26. On slave women's work, the economic incentives for harsher treatment, and the transformation of work for freedmen, see Fogel, *Without Consent or Contract,* 72–80; Eric Foner, *Reconstruction: America's Unfinished Revolution, 1863–1877* (New York, Oxford University Press, 1986), 77–123; and Robert L. Ransom and Richard Sutch, *One Kind of Freedom: The Economic Consequences of Emancipation* (Cambridge: Cambridge University Press, 1977).

27. Francis W. Pickens, "General Directions as to the Treatment of Negroes (1839)" in Pickens Papers, Plantation Record Book, Duke University Archives.

28. For the intellectual context of honorific culture, see Bertram Wyatt-Brown, *Southern Honor: Ethics and Behavior in the Old South* (New York: Oxford University Press, 1982), and Rollin G. Osterweis, *Romanticism and Nationalism in the Old South* (New Haven: Yale University Press, 1949). Quote from John Lyde Wilson, *The Code of Honor: or, Rules for the Government of Principals and Seconds in Dueling* (Charleston, 1838); facsimile in Jack K. Williams, *Dueling in the Old South: Vignettes of Social History* (College Station: Texas A&M University Press, 1980), 88.

29. "Butler, Andrew Pickens," *Biographical Directory of the American Congress;* "Butler, Andrew Pickens," in *American National Biography;* "Andrew Pickens Butler," in *Biographical Directory of the S.C. Senate;* John Belton O'Neall, *Biographical Sketches of the Bench and Bar of South Carolina* (Charleston, S. C., S. G. Courtnay & Co., Publishers, 1859), I:198–205.

30. Biographical treatments of Preston Brooks during his early days can be found in "The Honorable Preston S. Brooks," *Southern Quarterly Review,* II (February 1857): 348–349; Robert Neil Mathis, "Preston Smith Brooks: The Man and His Image," *South Carolina Historical Magazine* 79: (1978), 296–310; Daniel Walker Hollis, *The University of South Carolina: Volume One: South Carolina College* (Columbia: University of South Carolina Press, 1951), 122–123.

31. Hollis, *South Carolina College,* 138–139; South Carolina College Trustee's Minutes, 27 November 1839).

32. *Ibid.*

33. Alvy L. King, *Louis T. Wigfall: Southern Fire-Eater* (Baton Rouge: Louisiana State University Press, 1970): 25–36; Burton, *In My Father's House,* 72–73; Whitfield Brooks Diary, 11 November 1840.

34. Brooks's life during the 1840s is outlined in the Martha Caroline Means Brooks Diary (transcribed in the *Edgefield Advertiser, Sesquicentennial Edition*); Burton, *In My Father's House,* 95–99; and "Preston S. Brooks," *Southern Quarterly Review,* 349.

35. 1853 election returns from *Congressional Quarterly Guide to U.S. Elections* (12th ed.): 755. Brooks received 2,098 votes, Sullivan 1,497, Francis W. Pickens 1,492, and Marshall 1,415. For the contest between the Irreconcilables and moderate or "National" Democrats, and Brooks's support of the latter, see Mathis, "Preston Smith Brooks," Harold S. Schulte, *Nationalism and Sectionalism in South Carolina, 1852–1860* (Durham: Duke University Press, 1950), 52–57; John B. Edmunds, *Francis Pickens and the Politics of Destruction* (Chapel Hill: University of North Carolina Press, 1986), 125–127; and Lacy K. Ford, Jr., *Origins of Southern Radicalism: The South Carolina Upcountry, 1800–1860* (New York: Oxford University Press, 1988), 338–348.

36. For the development of these social theories, see Larry Tise, *Proslavery: A History of the Defense of Slavery in America, 1701–1840* (Athens: University of Georgia Press, 1987).

37. *Congressional Globe*, 33d Congress, 1st Session, Appendix, 371–375.

38. Shakespeare, *Othello*, Act III, Scene III.

39. Sumner to Lydia Maria Child, 14 January 1853, quoted in Pierce, *Memoir*, I: 322. When he wrote to Child he had served in the Senate for slightly more than a year.

40. The political maneuvers surrounding the Nebraska bill are detailed in Freehling, *Road to Disunion*, 536–560; and Michael F. Holt, *The Rise and Fall of the American Whig Party: Jacksonian Politics and the Onset of the Civil War* (New York: Oxford University Press, 1999), 804–821. The Whig resolutions and Sumner's rejoinder are in the *Congressional Globe*, 33d. Congress, 1st. Session, 175, 186.

41. Donald, *Charles Sumner*, Part 1: 252.

42. Text from the *New York Times*, 24 January 1854.

43. *Congressional Globe*, 33d Congress, 1st Session, 275–280.

44. From Sumner's *Complete Works*, vol. IV.

45. *Congressional Globe*, 33d Congress, 1st Session, *Appendix*, 232–240.

46. Juvenal's works were written during the second century A.D.

47. Harriet Beecher Stowe's *Uncle Tom's Cabin*, painted a harsh portrait of the structural evils of slave society from the perspective of a Northern female evangelical. Intended to awaken sentiment against the fugitive slave law, the novel had originally appeared in serial form in the pages of the abolitionist newspaper *The National Era*, starting in 1851. First published as a book in early 1852, it became one of the most popular and widely read antislavery works of all time. See Elizabeth Ammons, ed., *Uncle Tom's Cabin: Authoritative Text, Backgrounds and Contents Criticism* (New York: W. W. Norton, 1994), and Stephen Railton, *Uncle Tom's Cabin and American Literature: A Multimedia Archive*, University of Virginia, [http://www.iath.virginia.edu/utc/], accessed 2002.

48. Robert W. Johahnsen, *Stephen A. Douglas* (New York: Oxford University Press, 1973), 271–297, 405–418; Donald, *Charles Sumner*, Part 1: 186–204.

49. Donald, *Charles Sumner*, Part 1: 259–261.

50. Text from Sumner's *Complete Works*, vol. IV.

51. For fine discussions of Democratic support for "liberty of conscience" and suspicion of ministerial "meddling" in politics, see Mitchell Snay, *Gospel of Disunion: Religion and Separatism in the Antebellum South* (Cambridge: Cambridge University Press, 1993); Richard J. Carwardine, *Evangelicals and Politics in Antebellum America* (Knoxville, University of Tennessee Press, 1997); and Joel Silbey, *The Partisan*

Imperative: The Dynamics of American Politics Before the Civil War (New York: Oxford University Press, 1985).

52. Congressional Globe, 33d Congress, 1st session, Appendix, 785–786.

53. The best recent account of this incident is Albert J. Von Frank, *The Trials of Anthony Burns: Freedom and Slavery in Emerson's Boston* (Cambridge: Harvard University Press, 1998). Burns was returned to Virginia.

54. Charles Sumner to Theodore Parker, 12 June 1854, in Palmer, ed., *Selected Letters*, I, 413–414.

55. Text from Sumner's *Complete Works*, vol. IV, 160–171.

56. Shakespeare, *Macbeth*, Act 2, Scene 3.

57. *Congressional Globe*, 33d Congress, 1st Session, 1516–1518.

58. "From far and near they drew, *their hearts prepared.*" from Virgil, *Aeneid*, Book 2.

59. 2 Kings, 7:13. Sumner quoted the King James Version of this passage.

60. *Congressional Globe*, 33d Congress, 1st Session, 1516–1518.

61. Text from *Congressional Globe*, 33d Congress, 1st Session, 1553–1554.

62. Text from Sumner's *Complete Works*, vol. IV.

63. Shakespeare, *Hamlet*, Act 2, Scene 2.

64. Sumner's note: *Notes on Virginia*, Query XVIII.

65. Sumner's note: Senate Journal, 22d Congress 1st Session, pp. 438, 439.

66. Sumner's note: Letter of Postmaster-General to Postmaster at Charleston, S.C., August 4, 1835: *Nile's Weekly Register*, 4th Ser. Vol. XII p. 448.

67. Sumner's note: Letter to John Quincy Adams, July 3, 1824; Opinion in *Ex parte Henry Elkison*, August 7, 1823: Report No. 80, Com. H. of R., 27th Congress 1st Session, Jan. 20, 1843, Appendix, pp. 14, 29.

68. Preston Brooks led the militia unit that escorted Hoar from the state.

69. Sumner's note: *Annals of Congress*, 1st Congress 2d Session, II. 1484, March 30, 1790.

70. Sumner's note: *Prigg v. Pennsylvania*, 16 Peters, 616.

71. *Prigg v. Commonwealth of Pennsylvania*, 41 U.S. 539 (1842), upheld the constitutionality of the federal fugitive slave law but ruled that *state* governments did not have to enforce it.

72. William Geinapp, *The Origins of the Republican Party: 1852–1856* (New York: Oxford University Press, 1987), esp. 87–91, 133–139; Dale Baum, *The Civil War Party System: The Case of Massachusetts, 1848–1876* (Chapel Hill: University of North Carolina Press, 1984), 24–35; Pierce, ed., *Memoir and Letters* III, 395–406; Blue, *Charles Sumner*, 83–85.

73. On anti-Catholicism, see John Highlon, Strangers in the Land: Patterns of American Nativism, 1860–1925 (N.Y.: Atheneum, 1981), esp. 4–7; On the influx of Irish immigrants to Boston and the social conflicts that erupted see Oscar Handlin, *Boston's Immigrants: A Study in Acculturation* (Cambridge: Belknap Press, 1779), 184–201.

74. Tyler Anbinder, *Nativism and Slavery: The Northern Know-Nothings & the Politics of the 1850s* (New York, Oxford University Press, 1992); John R. Mulkern, *The Know-Nothing Party in Massachusetts: The Rise and Fall of a People's Movement* (Boston: Northeastern University Press, 1990).

75. Baum, *Civil War Party System*, 33–34.

76. Charles Sumner to the Earl of Carlisle, 26 October 1854, in Pierce, ed., *Memoir and Letters*, III, 406.

77. Charles Sumner to Julius Rockwell, 26 November 1854, in Palmer, ed., *Selected Letters*.

78. Donald, *Charles Sumner*, Part I, 275–277.

79. For estimates of vote composition see Baum, *Civil War Party System*, Tables 2.2 through 2.6; Geinapp, *Origins of the Republican Party*, Tables 5.3, 7.12, and 7.13. On Sumner's strategy in late 1855 and early 1856 see Donald, *Charles Sumner*, Part I, 277–281, and Palmer, ed., *Selected Letters*, I, 432–450.

2

The Crime and the Caning

Introduction: The Territorial Crisis

Southerners knew they must make haste. The North's larger population and proximity to Kansas gave it a decisive edge in settlement. Moreover, Northerners controlled most of the publishing houses and newspapers that told emigrants how to get to Kansas, as well as the steamboats and railroads that transported them west. From the start of the territorial crisis a manifest sense of disadvantage had guided Southern strategy. The chief reason for repealing the Missouri Compromise had been to help slaveholders settle in Kansas before its territorial government was organized. A quick influx from the neighboring slave state of Missouri would be able to pack the government with pro-slavery legislators. Their dominance would advertise Kansas to all future emigrants as a slavery-friendly territory. By scaring away Free-Soilers in the territory's first days pro-slavery men would thwart the North's other advantages and keep Kansas safe for the South. In their rush to execute this plan, however, Southern pro-slavery activists engaged in a series of acts that provoked a national crisis. Sumner's "Crime Against Kansas" address would give a full report of these events from his decidedly antislavery perspective.

Both sides initiated settlement plans before the Nebraska bill passed. In April 1854 a group in Massachusetts received a charter for an emigrant aid association to help Free-state settlers migrate to the territories. Meanwhile, pro-slavery settlers from Missouri crossed the state line to scout for prime homesteads. They did so in advance of the legally required Federal surveys or even the completion of formal treaties with the Shawnee, Delaware, Osage, Fox, Sac, and other nations. Because these nations had already been relocated from homelands as far east as the Atlantic coast these encroachments represented a familiar betrayal, though neither Southerners nor Sumner worried excessively about this tragedy. By July 1854, self-described "Border Ruffians" in Kansas had formed the Platte County Self Defense Association. This association sought to defend slavery while intimidating free blacks and abolitionists from settling in the region. Other Borderers formed secret societies known as "blue lodges" with similar goals. When territorial governor Andrew Reeder arrived in October he found opposing camps of Free-Staters and pro-slavery Border Ruffians who were angry and armed.[1]

The first election for the territorial legislature took place in November 1854. Free-Staters contested seats in six districts where they had lost despite being a clear majority in the population. The governor ordered new elections for May 1855, which Free-Staters dominated and Borderers boycotted. The pro-slavery strategy was to ignore these elections and use their majority in the new legislature to nullify the credentials of any new Free-state delegates. When this pro-slavery legislature met in the summer of 1855 it created a law code for the territory that was deliberately hostile to the Free-Staters. The new code applied the death penalty for anyone who engaged in the "treason" of helping runaway slaves, declared it a felony for anyone to criticize slavery, and required all territorial officers to swear an oath to enforce the fugitive slave law. They also relocated the seat of government to Shawnee Mission, Kansas. This led to a fight with Governor Reeder. Pro-slavery Democrats accused Reeder of inciting treason against the territory and persuaded President Pierce to appoint a new governor in his place. Free-Staters responded by declaring the pro-slavery government a fraud and began organizing their own state government. In October 1855 the two rival camps held competing elections. By December a dubiously elected official government faced off against a popular but unauthorized (or "spurious") Free Soil government.

During this period of disintegration in Kansas Sumner focused on Massachusetts state politics. The fall elections of 1855 had important implications for the state's nascent Republican party and for his Senate seat. It was not until Free-Staters in Kansas petitioned Congress for statehood in early 1856 that he again took up the territorial issue. He did this, some historians have argued, to convince Massachusetts voters that the national slavery crisis represented a more serious problem for the state than local problems related to immigration.[2] A steady stream of correspondence from Free-Staters in the territories and from friends in the Emigrant Aid Association confirmed to Sumner the latest outrages of the "Slave Power." President Pierce compounded Sumner's anger by declaring in his annual address and in a message to Congress that territory's troubles were caused entirely by politically ambitious Northern extremists. Although he did not name names, Pierce's attack was aimed squarely at Sumner and his associates in the Republican coalition. "If the passionate rage of fanaticism and partisan spirit did not force the fact upon our attention," said the President, "it would be difficult to believe that any considerable portion of the people of this enlightened country could have so surrendered themselves to a fanatical devotion to the supposed interests of the relatively few Africans in the United States, as totally to abandon and disregard the interests of the twenty-five millions of Americans."[3] Sumner wrote in a letter to Salmon Chase that "the course of the Administration towards Kansas seems diabolic."[4] When Stephen Douglas presented a report in March accusing the Emigrant Aid Company of illegally invading Kansas, Sumner remarked that "Douglas has appeared at last on the scene & with him that vulgar swagger which ushered in the Nebraska debate. Truly—truly—this is a godless place."[5]

Debate on Kansas lasted through the Spring. Sumner began planning his own address in late March. The speech he produced was part history lesson, part prosecutorial indictment, and part rhetorical showmanship. Above all it was an attack on President Pierce's submissiveness to the Slave Power. Next in line for Sumner's wrath were Stephen A. Douglas and former Missouri Democratic Senator David Atchison, the two men who had sponsored the laws and the implementation of pro-slavery settlement. To illustrate the outrageousness of their conduct Sumner filled the speech with historical analogies. He relied most heavily on the works of Roman statesman Marcus Tullius Cicero (106–43 B.C.E.), who had been one of the most vocal defenders of political virtue and rule of law in the last days of the Roman Republic. Cicero's essay *On Verres* accused Rome's Sicilian territorial governor of bribery, intimidation through violence, desecration of religion, and sexual misconduct. Cicero's *Orations Against Catiline* were an attempt to awaken Rome's leadership to a conspiracy against the Republic and its freedoms which Cicero blamed on his arch-rival Catiline. Both of these orations were standard texts in antebellum American high schools and colleges. They were familiar to most members of Sumner's audience. Sumner also incorporated materials from Demosthenes' *On the Crown* as well as passages from the Bible, Shakespeare, Vergil, Milton, Dante, and antislavery poet James Russell Lowell.[6]

The speech also follows the arguments of earlier Kansas speeches made by Republican Senators Henry Wilson of Massachusetts, John P. Hale of New Hampshire, Jacob Collamer of Vermont, Lyman Trumbull of Illinois, and William Henry Seward of New York. Most of the examples of misconduct that he cites had been mentioned before by the previous speakers, though neither with the detail nor the richness of historical context presented by Sumner. In contrast to these other speeches and to his own behavior in the Nebraska debates, Sumner devoted little space in "The Crime Against Kansas" to a rebuttal of specific points raised in debate by his Southern and Democratic opponents. Ironically, it was the few personal remarks that he did make that caused the most controversy afterwards. These, however, were merely supporting arguments in his attack on what he saw as a more serious debasement of political virtue and core American liberties. It was less Senator Butler he meant to attack than a Pierce-dominated Slave Power conspiracy of which Butler was only a small part. "My heart is wrung by this outrage, & I shall pour it forth," he wrote to Salmon Chase a few days before the speech, "How small was all that our fathers endured compared with the wrongs of Kansas?"[7]

"THE CRIME AGAINST KANSAS:" SUMNER'S INTRODUCTORY REMARKS

When Sumner took the floor on May 19 it was a stiflingly hot day and the galleries were crowded beyond capacity. The audience had been attracted by his reputation for grand eloquence and by his prominence in the Free Soil wing of the Republican party. As he began speaking, Senators from Southern states made a show of shuffling papers, whispering with each other, and moving about the chamber. This was an effort to illustrate through actions their rejection of a man who had "refused to uphold the Constitution." It is likely that this response was pre-arranged. Such an action would explain their failure to call Sumner to order when he began personal attacks on Butler and Douglas, and was entirely consistent with Southern demands in 1854 that Sumner be shunned.[8]

Sumner's strategy was to claim that the Slave Power's deeds in Kansas could be counted as among the worst in recorded history. Throughout his career Sumner had condemned physical force as a relic of earlier and more primitive ages.[9] The doings in Kansas, he argued, were inconceivable in an age of progress. Implicit in the speech is the accusation that the Free-Soilers (who to him represented modern rule of law) were being victimized by uncivilized barbarians who were incapable of self-control. To make this point more vivid he filled the introduction with explicit sexual references. Not just any crime, the doings in Kansas were like those worst and most primitive of violations, prostitution and rape. His frequent invocation of Protestant heroes who resisted religious and political oppression played on widespread anti-Catholic sentiments. The episodes he mentioned would have been familiar and disturbing to his predominantly Protestant audience.

The Crime Against Kansas: The Apologies for the Crime: The True Remedy

Speech of Charles Sumner, of Massachusetts, In the Senate of the United States, May 18–19, 1856.[10]

You are now called to redress a great transgression. Seldom in the history of nations has such a question been presented. Tariffs, army bills, navy bills, land bills, are important, and justly occupy your care; but these all belong to the course of ordinary legislation. As means and instruments only, they are necessarily subordinate to the conservation of Government itself. Grant them or deny them, in greater or less degree, and you will inflict no shock. The machinery of Government will continue to move. The State will not cease to exist. Far otherwise is it with the eminent question now before you, involving, as it does, Liberty in a broad Territory, and also involving the peace of the whole country with our good name in our history for evermore. . . .

Against this Territory [Kansas], thus fortunate in position and population, a crime has been committed, which is without example in the records of the Past. . . . The wickedness which I now begin to expose is immeasurably aggravated by the motive which prompted it. Not in any common lust for power did this uncommon tragedy have its origin. It is the rape of a virgin Territory, compelling it to the hateful embrace of Slavery; and it may be clearly traced to a depraved longing for a new slave State, the hideous offspring of such a crime, in the hope of adding to the power of slavery in the National Government. Yes, sir, when the whole world, alike Christian and Turk, is rising up to condemn this wrong, and to make it a hissing to the nations, here in our Republic, force—aye, Sir, FORCE,—has been openly employed in compelling Kansas to this pollution, and all for the sake of political power. There is the simple fact, which you will vainly attempt to deny, but which in itself presents an essential wickedness that makes other public crimes seem like public virtues. . . .

But this enormity, vast beyond comparison, swells to dimensions of wickedness which the imagination toils in vain to grasp, when it is understood, that for this purpose are hazarded the horrors of intestine feud, not only in this distant Territory, but everywhere throughout the country. Already the muster has begun. The strife is no longer local, but national. Even now, while I speak, portents hang on all the arches of the horizon, threatening to darken the broad land, which already yawns with the musterings of civil war. The fury of the propagandists of slavery, and the calm determination of their opponents, are now diffused from the distant Territory over wide-spread communities, and the whole country, in all its extent—marshalling hostile divisions, and foreshadowing a strife, which, unless happily averted by the triumph of Freedom, will become war—fratricidal, parricidal war—with an accumulated wickedness beyond the wickedness of any war in human annals; justly provoking the avenging judgment of Providence and the avenging pen of history, and constituting a strife, in the language of the ancient writer, more than foreign, more than social, more than civil; but something compounded of all these strifes, and in itself more than war; *sed potius commune quoddam ex omnibus, et plus quam bellum.*[11]

Such is the crime which you are to judge. But the criminal also must be dragged into day, that you may see and measure the power by which all this wrong is sustained. From no common source could it proceed. In its perpetration was needed a spirit of vaulting ambition which would hesitate at nothing; a hardihood of purpose which was insensible to the judgment of mankind; a madness for slavery which should disregard the Constitution, the laws, and all the great examples of our history; also a consciousness of power such as comes from the habit of power; a combination of energies found only in a hundred arms directed by a hundred eyes; a control of public opinion, through venal pens and a prostituted press; an ability to subsidize crowds in every vocation of life—the politician with his local importance, the lawyer with his subtile tongue, and even the authority of the judge on the bench, and a familiar use of men in places high and low, so that none, from the President to the lowest border postmaster, should decline to be its tool; all these things and more were needed; and they were found in the slave power of our Republic. There, sir, stands the criminal—all unmasked before you—heartless, grasping, and tyrannical—with an audacity beyond that of Verres, a subtlity beyond that of Machiavel, a meanness beyond that of Bacon, and an ability beyond that of Hastings. Justice to Kansas can be secured only by the prostration of this influence; for this is the power behind,—greater than any President—which succors and sustains the Crime. Nay, the proceedings I now arraign derive their fearful consequence only from this connection. . . .

Such is the Crime, and such the criminal which it is my duty in this debate to expose; and, by the blessing of God, this duty shall be done completely to the end. . . .

My task will be divided under three different heads: first, THE CRIME AGAINST KANSAS, in its origin and extent; secondly, THE APOLOGIES FOR THE CRIME; and thirdly, the TRUE REMEDY. But, before entering upon the argument, I must say something of a general character, particularly in response to what has fallen from senators who have raised themselves to eminence on this floor in championship of human wrongs. I mean the senator from South Carolina, (MR. BUTLER,) and the senator from Illinois, (MR. DOUGLAS,) who, though unlike as Don Quixote and Sancho Panza, yet, like this couple, sally forth together in the same adventure. I regret much to miss the elder senator from his seat; but the cause, against which he has run a tilt with such activity of animosity, demands that the opportunity of exposing him should not be lost; and it is for the cause that I speak. The senator from South Carolina has read many books of chivalry, and believes himself a chivalrous knight with sentiments of honor and courage. Of course he has chosen a mistress to whom he has made his vows, and who, though ugly to others, is always lovely to him; though polluted in the sight of the world, is chaste in his sight—I mean the harlot, slavery. For her his tongue is always profuse in words. Let her be impeached in character, or any proposition made to shut her out from the extension of her wantonness, and no extravagance of manner or hardihood of assertion is then too great for this senator. The phrenzy of Don Quixote in behalf of his wench Dulcinea del Toboso is all surpassed. The asserted rights of slavery, which shock equality of all kinds, are cloaked by a fantastic claim of equality. If the slave States cannot enjoy what in mockery of the great fathers of the Republic, he misnames equality under the Constitution—in other words, the full power in the national Territories to compel fellow men to unpaid toil, to separate husband and wife, and to sell little children at the auction block—then, sir, the chivalric senator will conduct the State of South Carolina out of the Union! Heroic knight! Exalted senator! A Second Moses come for a second exodus!

But not content with this poor menace, which we have been twice told was "measured," the senator, in the unrestrained chivalry of his nature, has undertaken to apply opprobrious words to those who differ from him on this floor. He calls them "sectional and fanatical;" and opposition to the usurpation in Kansas, he denounces as "an uncalculating fanaticism." To be sure, these charges lack all grace of originality, all sentiment of truth; but the adventurous senator does not hesitate. He is the uncompromising, unblushing representative on this floor of a flagrant sectionalism, which now domineers over the Republic, and yet with a ludicrous ignorance of his own position—unable to see himself as others see him—or with an effrontery which even his white head ought not protect from rebuke, he applies to those here who resist his sectionalism, the very epithet which designates himself. The men who strive to bring back the government to its original policy, when freedom and not slavery was national, while slavery and not freedom was sectional, he arraigns as sectional. This will not do. It involves too great a perversion of terms. I tell that senator, that it is to himself, and to the "organization" of which he is the "committed advocate," that this epithet belongs. I now fasten it upon him. For myself, I care little for names; but since the question has been raised here, I affirm that the Republican party of the Union is in no just sense sectional, but, more than any other party, national; and that it now goes forth to dislodge from the high places of the government the tyrannical sectionalism of which the senator from South Carolina is one of the maddest zealots. . . .

[Here Sumner reiterated the arguments made in his "Landmark of Freedom" speech of 1854.]

As the senator from South Carolina is the Don Quixote, the senator from Illinois (MR. DOUGLAS) is the squire of slavery, its very Sancho Panza, ready to do all its humiliating offices. This senator, in his labored address, vindicating his labored report—piling one mass of elaborate error upon another mass—constrained himself, as you will remember, to unfamiliar, decencies of speech. Of that address I have nothing to say at this moment, though before I sit down I shall show something of its fallacies. But I go back now to an earlier occasion, when, true to his native impulses, he threw into this discussion, "for a charm of powerful trouble," personalities most discreditable to this body. I will not stop to repel the imputations which he cast upon myself; but I mention them to remind you of the "sweltered venom sleeping got," which, with other poisoned ingredients, he cast into the caldron of this debate. Of other things I speak. Standing on this floor, the senator issued his rescript, requiring submission to the usurped power of Kansas; and this was accompanied by a manner—all his own—such as befits the tyrannical threat. Very well. Let the senator try. I tell him now that he cannot enforce any such submission. The senator, with the slave power at his back, is strong; but he is not strong enough for this purpose. He is bold. He shrinks from nothing. Like Danton, he may cry, *"l'audace, l'audace, toujours l'audace!"* but even his audacity cannot compass this work. The senator copies the British officer, who, with boastful swagger, said that with the hilt of his sword he would cram the "stamps" down the throats of the American people, and he will meet a similar failure. He may convulse this country with civil feud. Like the ancient madman, he may set fire to this temple of constitutional liberty, grander than Ephesian dome, but he cannot enforce obedience to that tyrannical usurpation.

The senator dreams that he can subdue the North. He disclaims the open threat, but his conduct still implies it. How little that senator knows himself, or the strength of the cause which he persecutes! He is but a mortal man; against him is an immortal principle. With finite power he wrestles with the infinite, and he must fall. Against him are stronger battalions than any marshaled by mortal man—the inborn, ineradicable, invincible sentiments of the human heart; against him is nature in all her subtle forces; against him is God. Let him try to subdue these.

THE CRIME AGAINST KANSAS, SECTION ONE

In this first formal section of the speech Sumner revisited the history of the Nebraska Bill. His words here seem less like an effort to persuade his opponents in Congress to change their views than to discredit them in the eyes of the public. Some of his harshest attacks in this section were leveled against Democrats from the North, which lends credibility to the theory that the speech was intended as a campaign document for the upcoming November 1856 elections. His emphasis on the contradictions between Southern Democratic demands for "equal rights in the territories" (meaning the right to emigrate with slaves), and Northern Democratic insistence on popular sovereignty (meaning territories could choose to prohibit slavery) was an effort to drive a wedge between the Democratic party's Northern and Southern factions. In doing so Sumner clearly intended to convince Southerners that Northern Democrats were closet abolitionists. Likewise, he hoped to depict his Northern Democratic rivals as secretly allied with the forces of slavery and barbarism. It is also consistent with the electioneering potential of the speech that Sumner emphasized threats to existing white liberties rather than the horrors of slavery. His vivid image of the rape of the ballot box connects this "danger to white liberties" strategy to the sexual themes he developed in his introductory remarks.

It belongs to me now, in the first place, to expose the Crime Against Kansas, in its origin and extent. Logically, this is the beginning of the argument. I say crime, and deliberately adopt this strongest term, as better than any other denoting the consummate transgression. I would go further, if language could further go. It is the crime of crimes. . . .

[Here Sumner gave a summary of the Missouri Compromise and its subsequent repeal under the Nebraska Bill, accusing President Pierce and Senator Douglas of using corruption, intimidation, and legislative trickery to get it passed.]

Mr. President, I mean to keep absolutely within the limits of parliamentary propriety. I make no personal imputations; but only with frankness, such as belongs to the occasion and my own character, describe a great historical act, which is now enrolled in the Capitol. Sir, the Nebraska bill was in every respect a swindle. It was a swindle by the South of the North. It was, one the part of those who had already completely enjoyed their share of the Missouri Compromise, a swindle of these whose share was yet absolutely untouched; and the plea of unconstitutionality set up—like the plea of usury after the borrowed money has been enjoyed—did not make it less a swindle. Urged as a bill of peace, it was a swindle of the whole country. Urged as opening the doors to slave-masters with their slaves, it was a swindle of the asserted doctrine of popular sovereignty. Urged as sanctioning popular sovereignty, it was a swindle of the asserted rights of slave-masters. It was a swindle of a broad territory, thus cheated of protection against slavery. It was a swindle of a great cause, early espoused by Washington, Franklin, and Jefferson, surrounded by the best fathers of the republic. Sir, it was a swindle of God-given inalienable rights. Turn it over; look at it on all sides, and it is everywhere a swindle; and, if the word I now employ has not the authority of classical usage, it has, on this occasion, the indubitable authority of fitness. No other word will adequately express the mingled meanness and wickedness of the cheat. . . .

The offensive provision in the bill was, in its form, a legislative anomaly, utterly wanting the natural directness and simplicity of an honest transaction. It did not undertake openly to repeal the old prohibition of slavery, but seemed to mince the matter, as if conscious of the swindle. . . . Men are wisely presumed to intend the natural consequences of their conduct, and to seek what their acts seem to promote. Now, the Nebraska bill, on its very face, openly cleared the way for slavery,

and it is not wrong to presume that its originators intended the natural consequences of such an act, and sought in this way to extend slavery. Of course, they
did. And this is the first stage in the Crime against Kansas.

But this was speedily followed by other developments. The bare-faced
scheme was soon whispered that Kansas must be slave State. In conformity with
this idea was the Government of this unhappy Territory organized in all its depart-
ments; and thus did the President, by whose complicity the prohibition of slavery
had been overthrown, lend himself to a new complicity—giving to the conspirators
a lease of connivance, amounting even to copartnership. The governor, secretary,
chief justice, associate justices, attorney, and marshal, with a whole caucus of other
stipendaries, nominated by the President and confirmed by the Senate, were all
commended as friendly to Slavery. . . .

But the conspiracy was unexpectedly balked. The debate, which convulsed
Congress, had stirred the whole country. Attention from all sides was directed upon
Kansas, which at once became the favorite goal of emigration. The bill had loudly
declared that its object was "to leave the people perfectly [free] to form and regulate their domestic institutions in their own way;" and its supporters everywhere
challenged the determination of [the] question between freedom and slavery by a
competition of emigration. Thus, while opening the Territory to slavery, the bill
also opened it to emigrants from every quarter, who might by their votes redress
the wrong. The populous North, stung by a sharp sense of outrage, and inspired by
a noble cause, poured into the debatable land, and promised soon to establish a
supremacy of numbers there, involving, of course, a just supremacy of freedom.

Then was conceived the consummation of the crime against Kansas. What
could not be accomplished peaceably was to be accomplished forcibly. The reptile
monster, that could not be quietly and securely hatched there, was to be pushed
full-grown into the Territory. All efforts were now given to the dismal work of forc-
ing slavery on free soil. In flagrant derogation of the very popular sovereignty,
whose name helped to impose this bill upon the country, the atrocious object was
now distinctly avowed. And the avowal has been followed by the act. Slavery has
been forcibly introduced into Kansas, and placed under the formal safeguards of
pretended law. How this was done, belongs to the argument. . . .

A plain statement of facts will be a picture of fearful truth, which faithful history will preserve in its darkest gallery. In the foreground all will recognise a
familiar character, in himself a connecting link between the President and the border ruffian—less conspicuous for ability than for the exalted place he has
occupied—who once sat in the seat where you now sit, sir; where once sat John
Adams and Thomas Jefferson; also, where once sat Aaron Burr. I need not add the
name of David R. Atchison. You have not forgotten that, at the session of Congress
immediately succeeding the Nebraska bill, he came tardily to his duty here, and
then, after a short time, disappeared. The secret has been long since disclosed.
Like Cataline, he stalked into this Chamber, reeking with conspiracy—*immo in sen-
atum venit*—and then like Catiline he skulked away—*abiit, excessit, evasit, erupit* [He
is gone, he has departed, he has disappeared, he has rushed out][12]—to join and provoke the conspirators, who at a distance awaited their congenial chief. Under the
influence of his malign presence the crime ripened to its fatal fruits, while the

similitude with Catiline was again renewed in the sympathy, not even concealed, which he found in the very Senate itself, where, beyond even the Roman example, a senator has not hesitated to appear as his open compurgator. . . .

I begin with an admission from the President himself, in whose sight the people of Kansas have little favor. And yet, after arraigning the innocent emigrants from the North, he was constrained to declare that their conduct was "far from justifying the illegal and reprehensible counter-movement which ensued." Then, by the reluctant admission of the Chief Magistrate, there was a counter-movement, at once illegal and reprehensible. I thank thee, President, for teaching me these words; and I now put them in the front of this exposition, as in themselves a confession. Sir, this "illegal and reprehensible counter-movement" is none other than the dreadful crime—under an apologetic alias—by which, through successive invasions, slavery has been forcibly planted in this Territory. Next to this Presidential admission must be placed the details of the invasions, which I now present as not only "illegal and reprehensible," but also unquestionable evidence of the resulting crime. . . .

[Sumner then described the elections of 1854 and 1855, the formation of rival governments, and the intimidation of Free-Soilers by the Border Ruffians.]

At last, in the latter days of November, 1855, a storm, long brewing, burst upon the heads of the devoted people. The ballot boxes had been violated, and a legislature installed, which had proceeded to carry out the conspiracy of the invaders; but the good people of the Territory, born to freedom, and educated as American citizens, showed no signs of submission. Slavery, though recognized by pretended law, was in many places practically an outlaw. To the lawless borderers, this was hard to bear; and, like the Heathen of old, they raged, particularly against the town of Lawrence, already known by the firmness of its principles and the character of its citizens, as the citadel of the good cause. On this account they threatened, in their peculiar language, "to wipe it out." Soon the hostile power was gathered for this purpose.—The wickedness of this invasion was enhanced by the way in which it began. A citizen of Kansas, by the name of Dow, was murdered by one of the partisans of slavery, under the name of "law and order." Such an outrage naturally aroused indignation and provoked threats. The professors of "law and order" allowed the murderer to escape; and, still further to illustrate the irony of the name they assumed, seized the friend of the murdered man, whose few neighbors soon rallied for his rescue. This transaction, though totally disregarded in its chief front of wickedness, became the excuse for unprecedented excitement. The weak governor, with no faculty higher than servility to slavery—whom the President, in his official delinquency, had appointed to a trust worthy only of a well-balanced character—was frightened from his propriety. By proclamation he invoked the Territory. By telegraph he invoked the President. The Territory would not respond to his senseless appeal. The President was dumb; but the proclamation was circulated throughout the border counties of Missouri; and Platte, Clay, Carlisle, Sabine, Howard, and Jefferson, each of them contributed a volunteer company, recruited from the road sides, and armed with weapons which chance afforded—known as the "shot gun militia,"—with a Missouri officer as commissary general; dispensing rations, and another Missouri officer as general-in-chief; with two wagon loads of rifles, belonging to Missouri, drawn by six mules, from its arsenal at Jefferson City; with seven pieces of cannon belonging to the United States, from its arsenal at Liberty; and this formidable force, amounting to at least 1,800, terrible with threats, with oaths, and with whisky, crossed the borders, and encamped in larger part at Washerusa [sic], over against the doomed town of Lawrence, which was now threatened with destruction. With these invaders was the governor, who by this act levied war upon the people he was sent to protect. In camp with him was the original Catiline of the conspiracy, while by his side was the docile chief justice and the docile judges. . . .

Five several times and more have these invaders entered Kansas in armed array, and thus five several times and more have they trampled upon the organic law of the Territory. But these extraordinary expeditions are simply the extraordinary witnesses to successive uninterrupted violence. They stand out conspicuous, but not alone. . . . Thus was all security of person, of property, and of labor, overthrown; and when I urge this incontrovertible fact, I set forth a wrong which is small only by the side of the giant wrong, for the consummation of which all this was done. Sir, what is man—what is government—without security; in the absence of which, nor man nor government can proceed in development or enjoy the fruits of existence! Without security, civilization is cramped and dwarfed. Without security, there can be no freedom. Nor shall I say too much, when I declare that security, guarded of course by its offspring, freedom, is the true end and aim of government. Of this indispensable boon the people of Kansas have thus far been despoiled—absolutely, totally. . . . Scenes from which civilization averts her countenance, have been a part of their daily life. . . .

Private griefs mingle their poignancy with public wrongs. I do not dwell on the anxieties which families have undergone, exposed to sudden assault, and obliged to lie down to rest with the alarms of war ringing in their ears, not knowing that another day might be spared to them. Throughout this bitter winter, with the thermometer at 30 degrees below zero, the citizens of Lawrence have been constrained to sleep under arms, with sentinels treading their constant watch against surprise. . . . Murder has stalked—assassination has skulked in the tall grass of the prairie, and the vindictiveness of man has assumed unwonted forms. A preacher of the Gospel of the Saviour has been ridden on a rail, and then thrown into the Missouri, fastened to a log, and left to drift down its muddy, tortuous current. And lately we have had the tidings of that enormity without precedent—a deed without a name—where a candidate for the Legislature was most brutally gashed with knives and hatchets and then after weltering in blood on the snow-clad earth, was trundled along with gaping wounds, to fall dead in the face of his wife. . . . Now the tear must be dropped over the trembling solicitude of fellow-citizens, seeking to build a new State in Kansas, and exposed to the perpetual assault of murderous robbers from Missouri. Hirelings, picked from the drunken spew and vomit of an uneasy civilization—in the form of men. . . . In these invasions, attended by the entire subversion of all Security in this Territory, with the plunder of the ballot-box, and the pollution of the electoral franchise, I show simply the process in unprecedented crime. If that be the best Government, where an injury to a single citizen is resented as an injury to the whole State, then must our Government forfeit all claim to any such eminence, while it leaves its citizens thus exposed. In the outrage upon the ballot box, even without the illicit fruits which I shall soon exhibit, there is a peculiar crime of the deepest dye, though subordinate to the final crime, which should be promptly avenged. In countries where royalty is upheld, it is a special offence to rob the crown jewels, which are the emblems of that sovereignty before which the loyal subject bows, and it is treason to be found in adultery with the Queen, for in this way may a false heir be imposed upon the State; but in our Republic, the ballot-box is the single priceless jewel of that sovereignty which we respect, and the electoral franchise, out of which are born the rulers of a free people, is the Queen whom we are to guard against pollution. In this plain presentment, whether as regards Security, or regards Elections, there is enough, surely, without proceeding further, to justify the intervention of Congress, most promptly and completely, to throw over this oppressed people the impenetrable shield of the Constitution and laws. But the half is not yet told.

As every point in a wide-spread horizon radiates from a common centre, so everything said or done in this vast circle of crime radiated from the One Idea, that Kansas, at all hazards, must be made a slave State. In all the manifold wickednesses that have occurred, and in every successive invasion, the One Idea has been ever present, as the Satanic tempter—the motive power—the causing cause.

To accomplish this result, three things were attempted: first, by outrages of all kinds to drive the friends of freedom already there out of the Territory, secondly, to deter others from coming; and thirdly, to obtain the complete control of the Government. The process of driving out, and also of deterring, has failed. On the contrary, the friends of freedom there became more fixed in their resolves to stay and fight the battle, which they had never sought, but from which they disdained to retreat; while the friends of freedom elsewhere were more aroused to the duty of timely succors, by men and munitions of just self-defence.

But while defeated in the first two processes proposed, the conspirators succeeded in the last. By the violence already portrayed at the election, of the 30th March, when the polls were occupied by the armed hordes of Missouri, they imposed a Legislature upon the Territory, and thus under the mask of law, established a Usurpation not less complete than any in history. This was done, I proceed to prove. . . .

[Sumner then gave a series of examples showing how David Atchison and his lieutenants had invaded the territory and consciously used fraud and intimidation to "usurp" Free-soiler's rights.]

On this cumulative, irresistible evidence, in concurrence with the antecedent history, I rest. And yet senators here have argued that this cannot be so—precisely as the conspiracy of Catiline was doubted in the Roman Senate. . . . But confirmation comes almost while I speak. The columns of the public press are now almost daily filled with testimony, solemnly taken before the Committee of Congress in Kansas, which shows, in awful light, the violence ending in the Usurpation. Of this I may speak on some other occasion. Meanwhile, I proceed with the development of the crime. The usurping Legislature assembled at the appointed place in the interior, and then at once, in opposition to the veto of the Governor, by a majority of two-thirds, removed to the Shawnee Mission, a place in most convenient proximity to the Missouri borderers, by whom it had been constituted, and whose tyrannical agent it was. The statutes of Missouri, in all their text, with their divisions and subdivisions, were adopted bodily; and with such little local adaptation, that the word "State" in the original is not even changed to "Territory," but is left to be corrected by an explanatory act. But, all this general legislation was entirely subordinate to the special act, entitled "An act to punish offences against Slave Property," in which the One Idea, that provoked this whole conspiracy, is at last embodied in legislative form, and Human slavery openly recognised on Free Soil, under the sanction of pretended law. This act of thirteen sections is in itself a *Dance of Death*. But its complex completeness of wickedness without a parallel, may be partially conceived when it is understood, that in three sections only of it is the penalty of death denounced no less than forty-eight different times, by as many changes of language, against the heinous offence, described in forty-eight ways, of interfering with what does not exist in the Territory—and under the Constitution cannot exist there—I mean property in human flesh. Thus is liberty sacrificed to Slavery, and Death summoned to sit at the gates as guardian of the Wrong.

But the work of Usurpation was not perfected even yet. It had already cost too much to be left at any hazard.

————————————To be thus was nothing;
But to be safely thus![13]

Such was the object. And this could not be, except by the entire prostration of all the safeguards of Human Rights. The liberty of speech, which is the very breath of a Republic; the press, which is the terror of wrong-doers; the bar, through which the oppressed beards the arrogance of law; the jury, by which right is vindicated; all these must be struck down, while officers are provided, in all places, ready to be the tools of this tyranny; and then to obtain final assurance that their crime was secure, the whole Usurpation, stretching over the Territory, must be fastened and riveted by legislative bolts, spikes, and screws, so as to defy all effort at change through the ordinary forms of law. To this work, in its various parts, were bent the subtlest energies; and never, from Tubal Cain to this hour, was any fabric forged with more desperate skill and completeness.

Mark, sir, three different legislative enactments, which constitute part of this work. First, according to one act, all who deny, by spoken or written word, "the right of persons to hold slaves in this Territory," are denounced as felons, to be punished by imprisonment at hard labor for a term not less than two years—it may for life. And to show the extravagance of this injustice, it had been well put by the senator from Vermont, [MR. COLLAMER,] that should the senator from Michigan, [MR. CASS,] who believes that slavery cannot exist in a Territory, unless introduced by express legislative acts, venture there with his moderate opinions, his doom must be that of a felon! To this extent are the great liberties of speech and of the press subverted. Secondly, by another act, entitled "An Act concerning Attorneys at Law," no person can practice as an attorney unless he shall obtain a license from the Territorial courts.—Which, of course, a tyrannical discretion will be free to deny; and after obtaining such license, he is constricted to take an oath not only "to support" the Constitution of the United States, but also "to support and sustain"—mark here the reduplication—the Territorial act and the Fugitive

Slave bill, thus erecting a test for the function of the bar, calculated to exclude citizens who honestly regard that latter legislative enormity as unfit to be obeyed. And thirdly, by another act, entitled "An act concerning Jurors," all persons "conscientiously opposed to holding slaves," or "not admitting the right to hold slaves in the Territory," are excluded from the jury on every question, civil or criminal, arising out of asserted slave property. . . .

For the ready enforcement of all statutes against Human freedom, the President had already furnished a powerful quota of officers, in the Governor, Chief Justice, Judges, Secretary, Attorney, and Marshal. The Legislature completed this part of the work, by constituting, in each county, a Board of Commissioners, composed of two persons, associated with the Probate Judge, whose duty it is "to appoint a county treasurer, coroner, justices of the peace, constables, and all other officers provided for by law;" and then proceeded to the choice of this very Board; thus delegating and diffusing their usurped power, and tyrannically imposing upon the Territory a crowd of officers, in whose appointment the people have had no voice, directly or indirectly.

And still the final inexorable work remained. A Legislature, renovated in both branches, could not assemble in 1855; so that, during this long intermediate period, this whole system must continue in the likeness of law, unless overturned by the Federal Government, or, in default of such interposition, by a generous uprising of an oppressed people. But it was necessary to guard against the possibility of change, even tardily, at a future election; and this was done by two different acts, under the first of which, all who will not take the oath to support the Fugitive Slave bill are excluded from the elective franchise; and under the second of which, all others are entitled to vote who shall tender a tax of one dollar to the Sheriff on the day of election; thus, by provision of Territorial law, disfranchising all opposed to slavery, and at the same time opening the door to the votes of the invaders; by an unconstitutional shibboleth, excluding from the polls the mass of actual settlers, and by making the franchise depend upon a petty tax only, admitting to the polls the mass of borderers from Missouri. Thus, by tyrannical forethought, the Usurpation not only fortified all that it did, but assumed a self-perpetuating energy.

Thus was the crime consummated. Slavery now stands erect, clanking its chains on the Territory of Kansas, surrounded by a code of death, and trampling upon all cherished liberties, whether of speech, the press, the bar, the trial by jury, or the electoral franchise. And, sir, all this has been done, not merely to introduce a wrong which in itself is a denial of all rights, and in dread of which a mother has lately taken the life of her offspring; not merely, as has been sometimes said, to protect slavery in Missouri, since it is futile for this State to complain of freedom on the side of Kansas, when freedom exists without complaint on the side of Iowa and also on the side of Illinois; but it has been done for the sake of political power, in order to bring two new slaveholding senators upon this floor, and thus to fortify in the National Government the desperate chances of a waning Oligarchy. . . .

Sir, all this was done in the name of Popular Sovereignty. And this is the close of the tragedy. Popular sovereignty, which, when truly understood, is a fountain of just power, has ended in Popular slavery; not merely in the subjection of the unhappy African race, but of this proud Caucasian blood, which you boast. The profession with which you began, of All by the People, has been lost in the wretched reality of Nothing for the People. Popular sovereignty, in whose deceitful name plighted faith was broken, and an ancient Landmark of freedom was overturned. . . . The image is complete at all points; and, with this exposure, I take my leave of the crime against Kansas.

THE CRIME AGAINST KANSAS, SECTION TWO: THE APOLOGIES (19–20 MAY 1856)

In the second section of the speech Sumner sought to rebut the arguments offered by his opponents in justification of the Kansas pro-slavery forces. Sumner used the term "apology" in the old-fashioned sense of an ardent defense of a cause rather than in our familiar definition of an apology as an expression of regret over misdeeds. Sumner deliberately equated these apologies to the religious defenses offered up by Catholic defenders of the faith during the Protestant Reformation. His reference to the Anthony Burns fugitive slave case shows how much the events of 1854 remained a factor in his anger against Northern Democrats. Sumner's implied message to Massachusetts voters and the rest of the nation was that the Slave Power could neither be trusted to tell the truth nor defend justice. To underline this point he made additional attacks on the honesty of Senators Butler and Douglas. Sumner's celebration of his state's dominant contribution in the Revolution he intended as proof of the progress he believed possible in an enlightened age.

Emerging from all the blackness of this crime, in which we seem to have been lost, as in a savage wood, and turning our backs upon it, as upon desolation and death, from which, while others have suffered, we have escaped, I come now to The Apologies which the crime has found. Sir, well may you start at the suggestion that such a series of wrongs, so clearly proved by various testimony, so openly confessed by the wrong-doers, and so widely recognised throughout the country, should find Apologies. But the partisan spirit, now, as in other days, hesitates at nothing. The great crimes of history have never been without Apologies. The massacre of St. Bartholomew,[14] which you now instinctively condemn, was, at the time, applauded in high quarters, and even commemorated by a Papal medal, which may still be procured at Rome; as the crime against Kansas, which is hardly less conspicuous in dreadful eminence, has been shielded of this floor by extenuating words and even by a Presidential message, which, like the Papal medal, can never be forgotten in considering the madness and perversity of men.

Sir, the crime cannot be denied. The President himself has admitted "illegal and reprehensible" conduct. To such conclusion he was compelled by irresistible evidence; but what he mildly describes I openly arraign. Senators may affect to put it aside by a sneer; or to reason it away by figures; or to explain it by a theory, such as desperate invention has produced on this floor, that the Assassins and Thugs of Missouri were in reality citizens of Kansas; but all these efforts, so far as made, are only tokens of the weakness of the cause, while to the original crime they add another offence of false testimony against innocent and suffering men. But the Apologies for the crime are worse than the efforts at denial. In cruelty and heartlessness they identify their authors with the great transgression.

They are four in number, and four-fold in character. The first is the Apology tyrannical; the second, the Apology imbecile; the third, the Apology absurd; and the fourth, the Apology infamous. This is all. Tyranny, imbecility, absurdity, and infamy, all unite to dance, like the weird sisters, about this crime.

The Apology tyrannical; is founded on the mistaken act of Governor Reeder, in authenticating the Usurping Legislature, by which it is asserted that, whatever may have been the actual force or fraud in its election, the people of Kansas are effectually concluded, and the whole proceeding is placed under the formal sanction of law. According to this assumption, complaint is now in vain, and it only remains that Congress should sit and hearken to it, without correcting the wrong, as the ancient tyrant listened and granted no redress to the human moans that issued from the heated brazen bull, which subtle cruelty had devised. This I call the Apology of technicality inspired by tyranny. . . .

Next comes the Apology imbecile, which is founded on the alleged want of power in the President to arrest this crime. It is openly asserted that, under the existing laws of the United States, the Chief Magistrate had no authority to interfere in Kansas for this purpose. Such is the broad statement, which, even if correct, furnishes no Apology for any proposed ratification of the crime, but which is in reality untrue; and this I call the Apology of Imbecility. . . .

Where the Slave Power is indifferent, the President will see that the laws are faithfully executed; but, in other cases, where the interests of slavery are at stake, he is controlled absolutely by this tyranny, ready at all times to do, or not to do, precisely as it dictates. Therefore it is, that Kansas is left a prey to the Propagandists of slavery, while the whole Treasury, the Army and Navy of the United States, are lavished to hunt a single slave through the streets of Boston. You have not forgotten the latter instance; but I choose to refresh it in your minds. . . .

[Here Sumner gave a brief history of the Anthony Burns incident, including documents from President Pierce ordering Federal troops to assist in the case because "the law must be executed."]

This is the precise exigency that has arisen in Kansas—precisely this; nor more, nor less. The Act of Congress, constituting the very organic law of the Territory, which in peculiar phrase, as to avoid ambiguity, declares, "its true intent and meaning," that the people thereof "shall be left perfectly free to form and regulate their domestic institutions in their own way," has been from the beginning opposed and obstructed in its execution. If the President had power to employ the Federal forces in Boston, when he supposed the Fugitive Slave bill was obstructed, and merely in anticipation of such obstruction, it is absurd to say that he had not power in Kansas, when, in the face of the whole country, the very organic law of the Territory was trampled under foot by successive invasions, and the freedom of the people there overthrown. To assert ignorance of this obstruction—premeditated, long-continued, and stretching through months—attributes to him not merely imbecility, but idiocy. And thus do I dispose of this Apology.

Next comes the Apology absurd, which is, indeed, in the nature of a pretext. It is alleged that a small printed pamphlet, containing the "Constitution and Ritual of the Grand Encampment and Regiments of the Kansas Legion" was taken from the person of one George F. Warren, who attempted to avoid detection by chewing it. The oaths and grandiose titles of the pretended Legion have all been set forth, and this poor mummery of a secret society, which existed only on paper, has been gravely introduced on this floor, in order to extenuate the crime against Kansas. It has been paraded in more than one speech, and even stuffed into the report of the committee. . . .

It only remains, under this head that I should speak of the Apology infamous; founded on false testimony against the Emigrant Aid Company, and assumptions of duty more false than the testimony. Defying Truth and mocking Decency, this Apology excels all others in futility and audacity, while, from its utter hollowness, it proves the utter impotence of the conspirators to defend their crime. Falsehood, always infamous, in this case arouses peculiar scorn. An association of sincere benevolence, faithful to the Constitution and laws, whose only fortifications are hotels, school-houses and churches; whose only weapons are saw-mills, tools and books; whose mission is peace and good will, has been falsely assailed on this floor, and an errand of blameless virtue has been made the pretext for an unpardonable crime. Nay, more, the innocent are sacrificed, and the guilty set at liberty. They who seek to do the mission of the Saviour are scourged and crucified, while the murderer, Barabbas, with the sympathy of the chief priests, goes at large.

Were I to take counsel of my own feelings, I should dismiss this whole Apology to the ineffable contempt which it deserves; but it has been made to play such a part in this conspiracy that I feel it a duty to expose it completely. . . .

[Here Sumner described the founding of the New England Emigrant Aid Society, an organization Douglas had attacked as being a criminal conspiracy.]

A new charter [for the company was] received in February, 1855, in which the objects of the Society are thus declared:—

For the purposes of directing emigration Westward, and aiding in providing accommodations for the emigrants after arriving at their places of destination.

At any other moment an association for these purposes would have taken its place, by general consent, among the philanthropic experiments of the age; but crime is always suspicious, and shakes, like a sick man, merely at the pointing of a finger. The conspirators against freedom in Kansas now shook with tremor, real or affected. Their wicked plot was about to fail. To help themselves, they denounced the Emigrant Aid Company, and their denunciations, after finding an echo in the President, have been repeated with much particularity on this floor in the formal report of your committee. . . .

Sir, this Company has violated in no respect the Constitution or laws of the land, not in the severest letter or the slightest spirit. But every other imputation is equally baseless. . . .

The acts of the Company have been such as might be expected from auspices thus severely careful at all points. The secret through which, with small means, it has been able to accomplish so much is, that, as an inducement to emigration, it has gone forward and planted capital in advance of population. According to the old immethodical system, this rule is reversed; and population has been left to grope blindly, without the advantage of fixed centres, with mills, schools, and churches, all calculated to soften the hardships of pioneer life, such as have been established beforehand in Kansas. Here, sir, is the secret of the Emigrant Aid Company. By this single principle, which is now practically applied for the first time in history, and which has the simplicity of genius, a business association at a distance, without a large capital, has become a beneficent instrument of civilization, exercising the functions of various Societies, and in itself being a Missionary Society, a Bible Society, a Tract Society, an Education Society and a Society for the Diffusion of the Mechanic Arts.

I would not claim too much for this Company; but I doubt if, at this moment, there is any Society which is so completely philanthropic; and since its leading idea, like the light of a candle from which other candles are lighted without number, may be applied indefinitely, it promises to be an important aid to Human Progress. . . .

Such is the simple tale of the Emigrant Aid Company. Sir, not even suspicion can justly touch it. But it must be made a scapegoat. This is the decree which has gone forth. I was hardly surprised at this outrage, when it proceeded from the President, for, like Macbeth, he is stepped so far in, that returning were as tedious as go on; but I did not expect it from the senator from Missouri (MR. GEYER,) whom I had learned to respect for the general moderation of his views, and the name he has won in an honorable profession. Listening to him, I was saddened by the spectacle of the extent to which the Slave Power will sway a candid mind to do injustice. . . .

To cloak the overthrow of all law in Kansas, an assumption is now set up which utterly denies one of the plainest rights of the people everywhere. Sir, I beg senators to understand that this is a Government of laws; and that, under these laws, the people have an incontestable right to settle any portion of our broad territory, and, if they choose, to propagate any opinions there not openly forbidden by the laws. If this were not so, pray, sir, by what title is the senator from Illinois, who is an emigrant from Vermont, propagating his disastrous opinions on another State? Surely he has no monopoly of this right. Others may do what he is doing, nor can the right be in any way restrained. It is as broad as the people; and it matters not whether they go in numbers small or great, with assistance or without assistance, under the auspices of societies or not under such auspices. If this were not so, then by what title are so many foreigners annually naturalized, under Democratic auspices, in order to secure their votes for misnamed Democratic principles? And if capital as well as combination cannot be employed, by what title do venerable associations exist, of ampler means and longer duration than any Emigrant Aid Company, around which cluster the regard and confidence of the country—the Tract Society, a powerful corporation, which scatters its publications freely in every corner of the land—the Bible Society, an incorporated body, with large resources, which seeks to carry the Book of Life alike into Territories and States—the Missionary Society, also an incorporated body, with large resources, which sends its agents everywhere, at home and in foreign lands? By what title do all these exist. . . ?

God be praised! Massachusetts, honored Commonwealth that gives me the privilege to plead for Kansas on this floor, knows her rights, and will maintain them firmly to the end. This is not the first time in history that her public acts have been arraigned, and that her public men have been exposed to contumely. Thus was it when, in olden time, she began the great battle whose fruits you all enjoy. But never yet has she occupied a position so lofty as at this moment. By the intelligence of her population—by the resources of her industry—by her commerce, cleaving every wave—by her manufactures, various as human skill—by her institutions of benevolence, various as human suffering—by the pages of her scholars and historians—by the voices of her poets and orators, she is now exerting an influence more subtle and commanding than ever before—shooting her far-darting rays wherever ignorance, wretchedness, or wrong prevail, and flashing light even upon those who travel to persecute her. Such is Massachusetts; and I am proud to believe that you may as well attempt, with puny arm, to topple down the earth rooted, heaven-kissing granite which crowns the historic sod of Bunker Hill, as to change her fixed resolves for freedom everywhere, and especially now for freedom in Kansas. I exult, too, that in this battle, which surpasses far in moral grandeur the whole war of the Revolution, she is able to preserve her just eminence. To the first she contributed a larger number of troops than any other State in the Union, and larger than all the Slave States together; and now to the second, which is not of contending armies, but of contending opinions, on whose issue hangs trembling the advancing civilization of the country, she contributes, through the manifold and endless intellectual activity of her children, more of that divine spark by which opinions are quickened into life, than is contributed by any other State, or by all the Slave States together, while her annual productive industry excels in value three times the whole vaunted cotton crop of the whole South.

Sir, to men on earth it belongs only to deserve success, not to secure it; and I know not how soon the efforts of Massachusetts will wear the crown of triumph. But it cannot be that she acts wrong for herself or children when in this cause she thus encounters reproach. No; by the generous souls who were exposed at Lexington; by those who stood arrayed at Bunker Hill; by the many from her bosom who, on all the fields of the first great struggle, lent their vigorous arms to the cause of all; by the children she has borne, whose names alone are national trophies, is Massachusetts now vowed irrevocably to this work. What belongs to the faithful servant she will do in all things, and Providence shall determine the result.

And here ends what I have to say of the four Apologies for the crime against Kansas.

THE CRIME AGAINST KANSAS, SECTION THREE: THE REMEDIES (20 MAY 1856)

In part three Sumner sought to defend the legitimacy of Kansas's "spurious" Free Soil government and to prove the necessity for admitting the state without the normally required population. To overcome the most serious objections he drew examples from several states (especially Michigan and Florida) that had been admitted with insufficient population and that were currently represented in the

Senate by powerful Democrats. Nearly all of the authorities he would quote in defense of irregular admission were Democratic. He complemented this subtle partisan maneuver with a blunt comparison between President Pierce and English King George III. His most acidic charge in this section of the speech was a claim against Senator Butler, whom he accused of denying to Kansas settlers their most basic freedoms through the constitutional right to bear arms. As in the earlier sections, Sumner's emphasis on Kansas as a threat to white liberties rather than on the horrors of slavery itself is central to the speech.

From this simple survey, where one obstruction after another has been removed, I now pass, in the third place, to the consideration of the *various remedies proposed*, ending with the True Remedy. . . .

As the Apologies were four-fold, so are the Remedies proposed four-fold, and they range themselves in natural order, under designations which so truly disclose their character as even to supersede argument. First, we have the Remedy of Tyranny; next, the Remedy of Folly; next, the Remedy of Injustice and Civil War; and fourthly, the Remedy of Justice and Peace. There are four caskets; and you are to determine which shall be opened by senatorial votes.

There is the Remedy of Tyranny, which, like its complement, the Apology of Tyranny, though espoused on this floor, especially by the senator from Illinois— proceeds from the President, and is embodied in a special message. It proposes to enforce obedience to the existing laws of Kansas, "whether Federal or local," when, in fact, Kansas has no "local" laws except those imposed by the usurpation from Missouri, and it calls for additional appropriations to complete this work of tyranny. . . .

I expose simply the Tyranny which upholds the existing Usurpation; and asks for additional appropriations. Let it be judged by an example, from which in this country there can be no appeal. . . . George III . . . complained of a "daring spirit of resistance and disobedience to the law;" so also does the President. The King adds, that it has "broke forth in fresh violences of a very criminal nature;" so also does the President. The King declares that these proceedings have been "countenanced and encouraged in other of my Colonies;" even so the President declares that Kansas has found sympathy in "remote States. . . ." It is not money or troops that you need there; but simply the good will of the President. That is all, absolutely. Let his complicity with the crime cease, and peace will be restored. For myself, I will not consent to wad the National artillery with fresh appropriation bills, when its murderous hail is to be directed against the constitutional rights of my fellow-citizens.

Next comes the Remedy of Folly, which, indeed, is also a Remedy of Tyranny; but its Folly is so surpassing as to eclipse even its Tyranny. It does not proceed from the President. With this proposition he is not in any way chargeable. It comes from the senator from South Carolina, who, at the close of a long speech, offered it as a single contribution to the adjustment of this question, and who, thus far, stands alone in its support. It might, therefore, fitly bear his name; but that which I now give to it is a more suggestive synonym.

This proposition, nakedly expressed, is that the people of Kansas should be deprived of their arms. . . .

Really, sir, has it come to this? The rifle has ever been the companion of the pioneer, and, under God, his tutelary protector against the red man and the beast of the forest. Never was this efficient weapon more needed in just self-defence, than now in Kansas, and at least one article in our National Constitution must be blotted out; before the complete right to it can in any way be impeached. And yet such is the madness of the hour, that, in defiance of the solemn guarantee, embodied in the Amendments to the Constitution, that "the right of the people to keep and bear arms shall not be infringed." The people of Kansas have been arraigned for keeping and bearing them, and the senator from South Carolina has had the face to say openly, on this floor, that they should be disarmed—of course, that the fanatics of slavery, his allies and constituents, may meet no impediment. Sir, the senator is venerable with years; he is reputed also to have worn at home, in the State which he represents, judicial honors; and he is placed here at the head of an important Committee occupied particularly with questions of law; but neither his years, nor his position, past or present, can give respectability to the demand he has made, or save him from indignant condemnation, when, to compass the wretched purposes of a wretched cause, he thus proposes to trample on one of the plainest provisions of constitutional liberty.

Next comes the Remedy of Injustice and Civil War—organized by Act of Congress. This proposition, which is also an offshoot of the original Remedy of Tyranny, proceeds from the senator from Illinois, [MR. DOUGLAS,] with the sanction of the Committee on Territories, and is embodied in the bill which is now pressed to a vote. . . .

[Here Sumner argued that Kansas could be admitted with less than the minimum population required by statute, and that such a remedy was necessary to bypass the current territorial legislature, which he accused of being a fraudulent tool of the Slave Power.]

In characterizing this bill as the Remedy of Injustice and Civil War, I give it a plain, self-evident title. It is a continuation of the crime against Kansas, and as such deserves the same condemnation. It can only be defended by those who defend the crime. Sir, you cannot expect that the people of Kansas will submit to the usurpation which this bill sets up, and bids them bow before—as the Austrian tyrant set up his cap in the Swiss market place. If you madly persevere, Kansas will not be without her William Tell, who will refuse at all hazards to recognize the tyrannical edict; and this will be the beginning of civil war.

Next, and lastly, comes the Remedy of Justice and Peace, proposed by the senator from New York, [MR. SEWARD,] and embodied in his bill for the immediate admission of Kansas as a State of this Union, now pending as a substitute for the bill of the senator from Illinois. This is sustained by the prayer of the people of the Territory, setting forth a Constitution formed by a spontaneous movement, in which all there had opportunity to participate, without distinction of party. Rarely has any proposition, so simple in character, so entirely practicable, so absolutely within your power, been presented, which promised at once such beneficent results. In its adoption, the crime against Kansas will be all happily absolved, the Usurpation which it established will be peacefully suppressed, and order will be permanently secured. By a joyful metamorphosis this fair Territory may be saved from outrage.

"Oh help," she cries, "in this extremest need,
If you who bear are Deities indeed;
Gape earth, and make for this dread foe a tomb,
Or change my form, whence all my sorrows come."[15]

In offering this proposition, the senator from New York has entitled himself to the gratitude of the country. He has, throughout a life of unsurpassed industry, and of eminent ability, done much for freedom, which the world will not let die; but he has done nothing more opportune than this, and he has uttered no words more effective than the Speech, so masterly and ingenious, by which he has vindicated it.

Kansas now presents herself for admission with a Constitution republican in form. And, independent of the great necessity of the case, three considerations of fact concur in commending her. First. She thus testifies her willingness to relieve the Federal Government of the considerable pecuniary responsibility to which it is now exposed on account of the pretended Territorial Government. Secondly. She has by her recent conduct, particularly in repelling the invasion at Wakarusa, evinced an ability to defend her Government. And, thirdly, by the pecuniary credit which she now enjoys, she shows an undoubted ability to support it. What now can stand in her way?

The power of Congress to admit Kansas at once is explicit. It is found in a single clause of the Constitution, which, standing by itself, without any qualification applicable to the present case, and without doubtful words, requires no commentary. . . .

[Here Sumner gave an extensive discussion of the logic and precedents for admission of states before they had reached minimum population requirements.]

But there is a memorable instance, which contains in itself every element of irregularity which you denounce in the proceedings of Kansas. Michigan, now cherished with such pride as a sister State, achieved admission into the Union in persistent defiance of all rule. Do you ask for precedents? Here is a precedent for the largest latitude, which you who profess a deference to precedent, cannot disown. Mark now the stages of this case. The first proceedings of Michigan were without any previous enabling Act of Congress; and she presented herself at your door with a Constitution thus formed, and with senators chosen under that Constitution, precisely as Kansas now. This was in December 1835, while Andrew Jackson was President. By the leaders of the Democracy at that time, all objection for alleged defects of form was scouted, and language was employed which is strictly applicable to Kansas. . . .

[Sumner then quoted defenses of the "irregular" admission of Michigan by Democratic Senators Thomas Hart Benton and James Buchanan, and described the unusual legislative process by which Michigan achieved statehood.]

Thus . . . did the cause of Kansas prevail in the name of Michigan. A popular Convention—called absolutely without authority, and containing delegates from a portion only of the population—called, too, in opposition to constituted authorities, and in derogation of another Convention assembled under the forms of law, stigmatized as a caucus and a criminal meeting, whose authors were liable to indictment, trial, and punishment, was, after ample debate, recognized by Congress as valid, and Michigan now holds her place in the Union, and her senators sit on this floor, by virtue of that act. Sir, if Michigan is legitimate, Kansas cannot be illegitimate. You bastardize Michigan when you refuse to recognize Kansas.

Again, I say, do you require a precedent? I give it to you. But I will not stake this cause on any precedent. I plant it firmly on the fundamental principle of American Institutions, as embodied in the Declaration of Independence, by which Government is recognized as deriving its just powers only from the consent of the governed, who may alter or abolish it when it becomes destructive of their rights. In the debate on the Nebraska bill, at the overthrow of the Prohibition of slavery, the Declaration of Independence was denounced as a "self-evident lie." It is only by a similar audacity that the fundamental principle, which sustains the proceedings in Kansas, can be assailed. Nay, more, you must disown the Declaration of Independence, and adopt the circular of the Holy Alliance, which declares that "useful and necessary changes in legislation and in the administration of States ought only to emanate from the free will and the intelligent and well-weighed conviction of those whom God has rendered responsible for power." Face to face, I put the principle of the Declaration of Independence and the principle of the Holy Alliance, and bid them grapple! "The one places the remedy in the hands which feel the disorder; the other places the remedy in the hands which cause the disorder;" and when I thus truthfully characterize them, I but adopt a sententious phrase from the Debates in the Virginia Convention on the adoption of the Federal Constitution.[16] And now these two principles, embodied in the rival propositions of the senator from New York and the senator from Illinois, must grapple on this floor. . . .

Thus, on every ground of precedent, whether as regards population or forms of proceeding; also, on the vital principle of American Institutions; and, lastly, on the absolute law of self-defence, do I now invoke the power of Congress to admit Kansas at once, and without hesitation into the Union. "New States may be admitted by the Congress into the Union;" such are the words of the Constitution. If you hesitate for want of precedent, then I do appeal to the great principle of American Institutions. If, forgetting the origin of the Republic, you turn away from this principle, then, in the name of human-nature, trampled down and oppressed, but aroused to a just self-defence, do I plead for the exercise of this power. Do not hearken, I pray you, to the propositions of Tyranny and Folly; do not be ensnared by that other proposition of the senator from Illinois [Mr. Douglas,] in which is the horrid root of Injustice and Civil War. But apply gladly, and at once, the True Remedy, wherein are Justice and Peace.

THE CRIME AGAINST KANSAS: CONCLUDING REMARKS (20 MAY 1856)

In Sumner's closing remarks he reiterated most of the themes and historical analogies he had introduced before. His association between President Pierce and King George III was one of the most searing insults in the document. Sumner then attacked Butler's honesty by lampooning the South Carolinian's deformed lip and speech impediment.[17] He finished his list of responsible parties by denouncing

Stephen A. Douglas and James Mason. The speech ended with a series of contrasts between freedom and the Slave Power. In carefully gender-laden images Sumner contrasted a society of virginal, matronly, and progressive Christian virtue against a debauched, ignorant, and retrograde society lacking in decency and morality. Recalling the point of his "Landmark of Freedom" speech from two years before, Sumner accused the Slave Power of seeking to roll back history. This effort, though, would fail. Virtue and freedom would triumph, because, he said, "the great spirits of History combat by the side of the people of Kansas." The friends of slavery would be as "scattered ashes into History's golden urn." Time and Providence would triumph. Sumner's attacks in this section would be widely reprinted and discussed in the weeks following the speech.

Mr. President, . . . the people of Kansas, bone of your bone and flesh of your flesh, with the education of freemen and the rights of American citizens, now stand at your door. Will you send them away, or bid them enter? Will you push them back to renew their struggles with a deadly foe, or will you preserve them in security and peace? Will you cast them again into the den of Tyranny, or will you help their despairing efforts to escape. . . ?

At every stage the similitude between the wrongs of Kansas and those other wrongs against which our fathers rose becomes more apparent. Read the Declaration of Independence, and there is hardly an accusation which is there directed against the British Monarch, which may not now be directed with increased force against the American President. . . . And surely a President who has done all these things, cannot be less unfit than a Prince. At every stage the responsibility is brought directly to him. His offence has been both of commission and omission. He has done that which he ought not to have done, and he has left undone that which he ought to have done. By his activity the Prohibition of slavery was overturned. By his failure to act the honest emigrants in Kansas have been left a prey to wrong of all kinds. *Nullum flagitium exstitit nisi per te; nullum flagitium sine te* [There has now for many years been no crime committed but by you; no atrocity has taken place without you.].[18] And now he stands forth the most conspicuous enemy of that unhappy Territory. . . .

With regret, I come again upon the senator from South Carolina, [MR. BUTLER,] who, omnipresent in this debate, overflowed with rage at the simple suggestion that Kansas had applied for admission as a State; and, with incoherent phrases discharged the loose expectoration of his speech, now upon her representative, and then upon her people. There was no extravagance of the ancient Parliamentary debate which he did not repeat; nor was there any possible deviation from truth which he did not make, with so much of passion, I am glad to add, as to save him from the suspicion of intentional aberration. But the senator touches nothing which he does not disfigure—with error, sometimes of principles, sometimes of fact. He shows an incapacity of accuracy, whether in stating the Constitution or in stating the law, whether in the details of statistics or the diversions of scholarship. He cannot open his mouth, but out there flies a blunder. Surely he ought to be familiar with the life of Franklin; and yet he referred to this household character, while acting as agent of our fathers in England, as above suspicion; and this was done that he might give point to a false contrast with the agent of Kansas—not knowing, that, however they may differ in genius and fame, in this experience they are alike, that Franklin, when intrusted with the petition of Massachusetts Bay, was assaulted by a foul-mouthed speaker, where he could not be heard in defence, and denounced as a "thief" even as the agent of Kansas has been assaulted in this floor, and denounced as a "forger." And let not the vanity of the senator be inspired by the parallel with the British statesmen of that day; for it is only in hostility to freedom that any parallel can be recognized.

But it is against the people of Kansas that the sensibilities of the senator are particularly aroused. Coming, as he announces, "from a State"—ay, sir, from South Carolina—he turns with lordly disgust from this newly-formed community, which he will not recognize even as "a body politic." Pray, sir, by what title does he indulge in this egotism? Has he read the history of "the State" which he represents? He cannot surely have forgotten its shameful imbecility from slavery, confessed throughout the revolution, followed by its most shameful assumptions for slavery since. He cannot have forgotten its wretched persistence in the slave trade as the very apple of its eye, and the condition of its participation in the Union. He cannot have forgotten its constitution, which is republican only in name, confirming power in the hands of the few, and founding the qualifications of its legislature on a "settled freehold estate and ten Negroes." And yet the senator, to whom that "State" has in part committed the guardianship of its good name, instead of moving, with backward treading steps, to cover its nakedness, rushes forward, in the very ecstasy of madness, to expose it by provoking a comparison with Kansas. South Carolina is old; Kansas is young. South Carolina counts by centuries; where Kansas counts by years. But a beneficent example may be born in a day; and I venture to say, that against the two centuries of the older "State" may be already set the two years of trial, evolving corresponding virtue, in the younger community. In the one, is the long wail of slavery; in the other, the hymns of freedom. And if we glance at special achievements, it will be difficult to find anything in the history of South Carolina which presents so much of heroic spirit in an heroic cause as appears in that repulse of the Missouri invaders by the beleaguered town of Lawrence, where even the women gave their effective efforts to freedom. The matrons of Rome, who poured their jewels into the treasury for the public defence—the wives of Prussia, who with delicate fingers, clothed their defenders against French invasion—the mothers of our own revolution, who sent forth their sons, covered over with prayers and blessings, to combat for human rights, did nothing of self-sacrifice truer than did these women on this occasion. Were the whole history of South Carolina blotted out of existence, from its very beginning down to the day of the last election of the senator to his present seat on this floor, civilization might lose—I do not say how little, but surely less than it has already gained by the example of Kansas, in its valiant struggle against oppression, and in the development of a new science of emigration. Already in Lawrence alone there are newspapers and schools, including a high school, and throughout this infant Territory there is more academic mature scholarship in proportion to its inhabitants, than in all South Carolina. Ah, sir, I tell the senator that Kansas, welcomed as a free State, will be a "ministering angel" to the republic, when South Carolina, in the cloak of darkness which she hugs, "lies howling."

The senator from Illinois [MR. DOUGLAS] naturally joins the senator from South Carolina in this warfare, and gives to it the superior intensity of his nature.

He thinks that the national government has not completely proved its power, as it has never hanged a traitor; but, if the occasion requires, he hopes there will be no hesitation; and this threat is directed at Kansas, and even at the friends of Kansas throughout the country. Again occurs the parallel with the struggles of our fathers, and I borrow the language of Patrick Henry, when to the cry from the senator, of "treason," "treason," I reply, "if this be treason, make the most of it." Sir, it is easy to call names; but I beg to tell the senator that if the word "traitor" is in any way applicable to those who refuse submission to a tyrannical usurpation, whether in Kansas or elsewhere, then must some new word, of deeper color, be invented, to designate those mad spirits who would endanger and degrade the republic, while they betray all the cherished sentiments of the fathers and the spirit of the Constitution, in order to give new spread to slavery. Let the senator proceed. It will not be the first time in history, that a scaffold erected for punishment has become a pedestal of honor. Out of death comes life, and the "traitor" whom he blindly executes will live immortal in the cause.

> "For Humanity sweeps onward; where to-day the martyr stands,
> On the morrow crouches Judas, with the silver in his hands;
> While the hooting mob of yesterday in silent awe return,
> To glean up the scattered ashes into History's golden urn."[19]

Among these hostile senators, there is yet another, with all the prejudices of the senator from South Carolina, but without his generous impulses, who, on account of his character before the country, and the rancor of his opposition, deserves to be named. I mean the senator from Virginia, [MR. MASON,] who, as author of the fugitive slave bill, has associated himself with a special act of humanity and tyranny. Of him I shall say little, for he has said little in this debate, though within that little was compressed the bitterness of a life absorbed in the support of slavery. He holds the commission of Virginia; but he does not represent that early Virginia, so dear to our hearts, which gave to us the pen of Jefferson, by which the equality of men was declared, and the sword of Washington, by which independence was secured; but he represents that other Virginia, from which Washington and Jefferson now avert their faces, where human beings are bred as cattle for the shambles, and where a dungeon rewards the pious matron who teaches little children to relieve their bondage by reading the Book of Life. It is proper that such a senator, representing such a State, should rail against Free Kansas. . . .

Senators such as these are the natural enemies of Kansas, and I introduce them with reluctance, simply that the country may understand the character of the hostility which must be overcome. Arrayed with them, of course, are all who unite, under any pretext or apology, in the propagandism of human slavery. To such, indeed, the time-honored safeguards of popular rights can be a name only and nothing more. What are trial by jury, habeas corpus, the ballot-box, the right of petition, the liberty of Kansas, your liberty, sir, or mine, to one who lends himself, not merely to the support at home, but to the propagandism abroad, of that preposterous wrong, which denies even the right of a man to himself! Such a cause can be maintained only by a practical subversion of all rights. It is, therefore, merely according to reason that its partisans should uphold the usurpation in Kansas.

To overthrow this usurpation is now the special, importunate duty of Congress, admitting of no hesitation or postponement. To this end it must lift itself from the cabals of candidates, the machinations of party, and the low level of vulgar strife. It must turn from that slave oligarchy which now controls the republic, and refuse to be its tool. Let its power be stretched forth towards this distant Territory, not to bind, but to unbind; not for the oppression of the weak, but for the subversion of the tyrannical; not for the pomp and maintenance of a revolting usurpation, but for the confirmation of liberty.

"These are imperial arts, and worthy thee!"[20]

Let it now take its stand between the living and dead, and cause this plague to be stayed. All this it can do; and if the interests of slavery did not oppose, all this it would do at once, in reverent regard for justice, law, and order, driving far away all the alarms of war; nor would it dare to brave the shame and punishment of this Great Refusal. But the Slave Power dares anything, and it can be conquered only by the united masses of the People. From Congress to the people I appeal. . . .

It was said of old, "Cursed be he that removeth his neighbor's Landmark. And all the people shall say Amen."[21] Cursed, it is said, in the city and in the field; cursed in basket and store; cursed when thou comest in, and cursed when thou goest out. These are terrible imprecations; but if ever any Landmark were sacred, it was that by which an immense territory was guarded forever against slavery; and if ever such imprecations could justly descend upon any one, they must descend now upon all who, not content with the removal of this sacred Landmark, have since, with criminal complicity, fostered the incursions of the great Wrong against which it was intended to guard. But I utter no imprecations. These are not my words; nor is it my part to add to or subtract from them. But thanks be to God! they find a response in the hearts of an aroused People, making them turn from every man, whether President, or Senator, or Representative, who has been engaged, in this crime—especially from those who, cradled in free institutions, are without the apology of education or social prejudice—until of all such those other words of the prophet shall be fulfilled "I will set my face against that man, and make him a sign and a proverb, and I will cut him off from the midst of my people."[22] Turning thus from the authors of this crime, the People will unite once more with the Fathers of the Republic, in a just condemnation of slavery—determined especially that it shall find no home in the National Territories—while the Slave Power, in which the crime had its beginning, and by which it is now sustained, will be swept into the charnel house of defunct Tyrannies.

In this contest Kansas bravely stands forth—the stripling leader, clad in the panoply of American Institutions. In calmly meeting and adopting a frame of Government, her people have with intuitive promptitude performed the duties of freemen; and when I consider the difficulties by which she was beset, I find dignity in her attitude. In offering herself for admission into the Union as a FREE STATE, she presents a single issue for the people to decide. And since the Slave Power now stakes on this issue all its ill-gotten supremacy, the People, while vindicating Kansas, will at the same time overthrow this Tyranny. Thus does the contest which now begins involve not only Liberty for herself, but for the whole country. God be praised, that she did not bend ignobly beneath the yoke! Far away on the prairies, she is now battling for the Liberty of all, against the President, who misrepresents all. . . .

In all this sympathy there is strength. But in the cause itself, there is angelic power. Unseen of men, the great spirits of History combat by the side of the people of Kansas, breathing a divine courage. Above all towers the majestic form of Washington once more, as on the bloody field, bidding them to remember those rights of Human Nature for which the War of Independence was waged. Such a cause, thus sustained, is invincible.

The contest, which, beginning in Kansas, has reached us, will soon be transferred from Congress to a broader stage, where every citizen will be not only spectator, but actor; and to their judgment I confidently appeal. To the People, now on the eve of exercising the electoral franchise, in choosing a Chief Magistrate of the Republic, I appeal, to vindicate the electoral franchise in Kansas. Let the ballot-box of the Union, with multitudinous might, protect the ballot-box in that Territory. Let the voters everywhere, while rejoicing in their own rights, help to guard the equal rights of distant fellow citizens; that the shrines of popular institutions, now desecrated, may be sanctified anew; that the ballot-box, now plundered, may be restored; and that the cry, "I am an American citizen," may not be sent forth in vain against outrage of every kind. In just regard for free labor in that Territory, which it is sought to blast by unwelcome association with slave labor; in Christian sympathy with the slave, whom it is proposed to task and to sell there; in stern condemnation of the crime which has been consummated on that beautiful soil; in rescue of fellow-citizens, now subjugated to a tyrannical Usurpation; in dutiful respect for the early Fathers, whose aspirations are now ignobly thwarted; in the name of the Constitution, which has been outraged—of the Laws trampled down—of Justice banished—of Humanity degraded—of Peace destroyed—of freedom crushed to earth; and, in the name of the Heavenly Father, whose service is freedom, I make this last appeal.

REACTION FROM THE SENATE

Although Sumner was not once called to order during the speech, when he sat down the Senate erupted. His words provoked three formal responses from his colleagues. Michigan Democratic Senator Lewis Cass spoke first. Sumner and Cass had been acquainted for at least two decades. They met when Sumner was touring Europe and Cass was on a diplomatic mission. Cass was also famous as the originator of the concept of "popular sovereignty" later adopted by Stephen A. Douglas. It was Cass also who had been the Democratic party's presidential candidate in 1848. The Michigan Senator's assessment of the speech was frequently quoted by Sumner's enemies. Since much of Sumner's speech had been an attack on the immorality of Democrats from the North, it was perhaps appropriate that a Northern Democrat gave the first retort.

Response from Democratic Senator Lewis Cass, of Michigan[23]

MR. CASS: I have listened with equal regret and surprise to the speech of the honorable
Senator from Massachusetts. Such a speech—the most un-American and unpatriotic
that ever grated on the ears of the members of this high body—as I hope never to hear
again here or elsewhere. But, sir, I did not rise to make any comments on the speech of
the honorable Senator, open as it is to the highest censure and disapprobation. I rise for
another purpose. The honorable Senator has so misunderstood and misapplied the case
of Michigan, which he brings forward as a justification of the proceedings in Kansas,
that, as I know the facts connected with it, I feel bound to say a few words—and but
very few they will be—to the Senate upon the subject.

The honorable Senator has spoken of the right of the people to form conventions
with a view to obstruct the authorized laws of the country. I deny such a right. I do not
deny the right of any portion of the American people to form conventions; but conventions formed to obstruct the existing laws of the country, unless they succeed, are
rebellion. . . . Michigan was guilty of no such crime as that, I am proud to say. The
proceedings in that State have no analogy with the proceedings in Kansas. The convention in Michigan was not for the purpose of opposing the law. . . .

Michigan had a population of sixty thousand, and came forward for admission into the
Union. A convention was called, not by the act of the people—that is, not by the act of
individuals—but by a law passed by the Territorial Legislature. Their convention assembled and formed a State constitution, and came forward claiming their boundary to the
line established by the ordinance of Congress, and not acknowledging the Ohio line. My
honorable friend from California, who was then a citizen of Ohio, I presume was in the
State at the time. He knows there was almost civil war. He must remember that the militia of Ohio and of Michigan were called out. I was here in the Cabinet of General
Jackson. I knew his anxiety. We were all apprehensive lest a war might break out.

MR. WELLER: It came very near it.

MR. CASS: If my friend was in Ohio at the time he would have been engaged in it, in
defense of the rights of that State.

Under these circumstances, it must be obvious to every Senator that there was, here
and elsewhere, much anxiety to close the matter. The people of Michigan were exceedingly warm and tenacious about their rights; for they were in the right. What was the
proposition of Congress agreed to admit her into the Union, provided a convention of
the people—that is all the provision—not called in this way, or that way, or the other,
but a convention of the people, should signify their assent to this change of the boundary line, so as to give to Ohio the whole country south of the north cape of the Maumee
Bay. A convention was called, and refused its consent to the proposition. Affairs then
looked worse and worse. Civil war seemed to be almost imminent.

MR. SEWARD: How was that first convention called?

MR. CASS: By the Governor and Legislature I think; at any rate it was called by legal authority. The sole object of it—and it was so declared by the act of Congress—was to assent to
the change of the line. The first convention refused its assent. By a spontaneous act of the

people, a second convention was called—not to oppose the laws, like the Kansas convention—not to establish another government—not to get up and oppose the acts of Congress, or of the Territorial Legislature—not to make a revolution, but to escape from a civil war, to get out of a difficulty merely by saying that the people of the State were willing to accept the proposition of Congress. That convention did so; the people of the State unanimously acquiesced in it; the State came here to Congress, and was admitted into the Union.

I did not hear distinctly what the Senator said in relation to the grounds taken by Mr. Buchanan. He referred to his views, and I thought incorrectly. I venture to say here, that every word which Mr. Buchanan uttered on the subject of conventions will be found in accordance with the sentiments I have expressed. Mr. Buchanan does not lay down the right of any portion of the people in our country to form a convention and institute unlawful proceedings to destroy the existing Government. Whenever you examine what Mr. Buchanan said upon that subject, you will find it to be what I have stated. I shall not detain the Senate longer.

Stephen Douglas had been one of Sumner's chief targets. He responded by bringing up many of the old charges he had made during the Nebraska bill and Fugitive Slave repeal debates. Douglas's anger over Sumner's premeditated personal attacks reflects the notion that insults hurled spontaneously in the heat of debate could be more easily excused than those that had been preplanned. Douglas's response is consistent with the long history of conflict between the two men. Despite their animosity, however, it is worth noting that neither Douglas nor his associates felt the need to defend his honor by using violence.

Response from Stephen A. Douglas[24]

MR. DOUGLAS: I shall not detain the Senate by a detailed reply to the speech of the Senator from Massachusetts. Indeed, I should not deem it necessary to say one word, but for the personalities in which he has indulged, evincing a depth of malignity that issued from every sentence, making it a matter of self-respect with me to repel the assaults which have been made.

As to the argument, we have heard it all before. Not a position, not a fact, not an argument has he used, which has not been employed on the same side of the Chamber this year, and replied to by me twice. I shall not follow him, therefore, because it would only be repeating the same answer which I have twice before given to each of his positions. He seems to get up a speech, as in Yankee land they get up a bed quilt. They take all the old calico dresses of various colors that have been in the house from the days of their grandmothers, and invite the young ladies of the neighborhood in the afternoon, and the young men to meet them at a dance in the evening. They cut up these pieces of old dresses and make pretty figures, and boast of what beautiful ornamental work they have made, although there was not a new piece of material in the whole quilt.

[Laughter.] Thus it is with the speech which we have had rehashed here to-day in regard to matters of fact, matters of law, and matters of argument—everything but the personal assaults and the malignity.

I beg pardon; there is another point. We have had another dish of the classics served up—classic allusions, each one only distinguished for its lasciviousness and obscenity—

each one drawn from those portions of the classics which all decent professors in respectable colleges cause to be suppressed, as unfit for decent young men to read. Sir, I cannot repeat the words. I should be condemned as unworthy of entering decent society, if I repeated those obscene, vulgar terms which have been used at least a hundred times in that speech. It seems that his studies of the classics have all been in those haunts where ladies cannot go, and where gentlemen never read Latin. [Laughter.] I have no disposition to follow him in that part of his speech.

His endeavor seems to be an attempt to whistle to keep up his courage by defiant assaults upon us all. I am in doubt as to what can be his object. He has not hesitated to charge three fourths of the Senate with fraud, with swindling, with crime, with infamy, at least one hundred times over in his speech. Is it his object to provoke some of us to kick him as we would a dog in the street, that he may get sympathy upon the just chastisement? What is the object of this denunciation against the body of which we are members? A hundred times he has called the Nebraska bill a "swindle," an act of crime, an act of infamy, and each time went on to illustrate the complicity of each man who voted for it in perpetrating the crime. He has brought it home as a personal charge to those who passed the Nebraska bill, that they were guilty of a crime which deserved the just indignation of Heaven, and should make them infamous among men.

Who are the Senators thus arraigned? He does me the honor to make me the chief. It was my good luck to have such a position in this body as to enable me to be the author of a great, wise measure, which the Senate has approved, and the country will indorse. That measure was sustained by about three fourths of all the members of the Senate. It was sustained by a majority of the Democrats and a majority of the Whigs in this body. It was sustained by a majority of Senators from the slaveholding States, and a majority of Senators from the free States. The Senator by his charge of crime, then, stultifies three fourths of the whole body, a majority of the North, nearly the whole South, a majority of Whigs, and a majority of Democrats here. He says they are infamous. If he so believed, who could suppose that he would ever show his face among such a body of men? How dare he approach one of those gentlemen to give him his hand after that act? If he felt the courtesies between men he would not do it. He would deserve to have himself spit in the face for doing so.

This charge is made against the body of which we are members. It is not a charge made in the heat of debate. It is not made as a retort growing out of an excited controversy. If it were of that nature, I could make much allowance for it. I can pay great deference to the frailties and the impulses of an honorable man, when indignant at what he considers to be a wrong. If the Senator, betraying that he was susceptible of just indignation, had been goaded, provoked, and aggravated, on the spur of the moment, into the utterance of harsh things, and then apologized for them in his cooler hours, I could respect him much more than if he had never made such a departure from the rules of the Senate; because it would show that he had a heart to appreciate what is due among brother Senators and gentlemen. But, sir, it happens to be well known, it has been the subject of conversation for weeks, that the Senator from Massachusetts had his speech written, printed, committed to memory, practiced every night before the glass with a Negro boy to hold the candle and watch the gestures, and annoying the boarders in the adjoining rooms until they were forced to quit the House! [Laughter.]

It was rumored that he read part of it to friends, and they repeated in all the saloons and places of amusement in the city what he was going to say. The libels, the gross insults which we have heard to-day have been conned over, written with cool, deliberate malignity, repeated from night to night in order to catch the appropriate grace, and then he came here to spit forth that malignity upon men who differ from him—for that is their offense.

Mr. President, I ask what right has that Senator to come here and arraign three fourths of the body for a direliction [sic] of duty? Is there anything in the means by which he got here to give him a superiority over other gentlemen who came by the ordinary means? Is there anything to justify it in the fact that he came here with a deliberate avowal that he would never obey one clause of the Constitution of the United States, and yet put his hand upon the Holy Bible, in the presence of this body, and appealed to Almighty God to witness that he would be faithful to the Constitution with a pledge to perjure his soul by violating both that oath and the Constitution?

He came here with a pledge to perjure himself as the condition of eligibility to the place. Has he a right to arraign us because we have felt it to be our duty to be faithful to that Constitution which he disavows—to that oath which he assumes and then repudiates?

The Senate have not forgotten the debate on the fugitive slave law, when that Senator said, in reply to a question whether he was in favor of carrying into effect that clause of the Constitution for the rendition of fugitive slaves—"Is thy servant a dog that he should do this thing?" A dog—to do what you swore you would do! A dog—to be true to the Constitution of your country! A dog—to be true to your oath! A dog—unless you are a traitor. That was his position; and still he comes here and arraigns us for crime, and talks about "audacity!" Did mortal man ever witness such audacity in an avowed criminal? He comes here with a pledge to defy the Constitution of his country, and the wrath of God, by not obeying his oath, and then talks about audacity. . . .

I do not intend to-day to go into the discussion of the Kansas question, or of the regularity of the proceedings there. I have shown on a former occasion, conclusively, that the conduct of the leaders of the State movement there is an act of rebellion against the Constitution and laws of the country. What is the defense? The defense is that they are carrying out the principles of the Declaration of Independence; that they are doing what our fathers did in the Revolution; that they have a right to do what our fathers did; and, hence, inasmuch as our fathers were rebels against England, they have a right to be rebels against the United States of America. The argument would hold good, provided they prove that the American Constitution is as vile as the English constitution; provided they prove that the American Government is as oppressive as the British Government; but until they prove that this Government is so weak, so corrupt, so unjust, that it is better to destroy it than to live under it, they must abandon this revolutionary right under the Declaration of Independence. That they are aiming at revolution is no longer to be disguised. "Revolution" is becoming their watch-word. And why? Because disunion is the object. . . .

Now, sir, this dealing in general terms of insult; this talk about crime, treachery, and swindling; this indulgence in coarse, vulgar denunciation against three fourths of the body to which you belong, does not meet the points between us. You challenged me to this great issue, which you say you have made up between the Negro worshipers and the "slave power," as you call it. What you call the slave power is simply observance of the Constitution of the country, as our fathers made it. Let us have that fair issue between the parties, and let us discuss that, instead of dealing in denunciation against one another here. I wish the Senate to bear in mind that, in the many controversies in which I have been engaged since I have been a member of this body, I never had one in which I was not first assailed. I have always stood on the defensive. You arrange it on the opposite side of the House to set your hounds after me, and then complain when I cuff them over the head, and send them back yelping. I never made an assault on any Senator; I have only repelled attacks.

The attack of the Senator from Massachusetts now is not on me alone. Even the courteous and the accomplished Senator from South Carolina [MR. BUTLER.] could not be passed by in his absence.

MR. MASON: Advantage was taken of it.

MR. DOUGLAS: It is suggested that advantage is taken of his absence. I think that is a mistake. I think the speech was written and practiced, and the gestures fixed; and, if that part had been stricken out, the Senator would not have known how to repeat the speech. [Laughter.] All that tirade of abuse must be brought down on the head of the venerable, the courteous, and the distinguished Senator from South Carolina. I shall not defend that gentleman here. Every Senator who knows him loves him. The Senator from Massachusetts may take every charge made against him in his speech, and may verify by his oath, and by the oath of every one of his confederates, and there is not an honest man in this Chamber who will not repel it as a slander. Your oaths cannot make a Senator feel that it was not an outrage to assail that honorable gentleman in the terms in which he has been attacked. He, however, will be here in due time to speak for himself, and to act for himself, too. I know what will happen. The Senator from Massachusetts will go to him, whisper a secret apology in his ear, and ask him to accept that as satisfaction for a public outrage on his character! I know how the Senator from Massachusetts is in the habit of doing those things. I have had some experience of his skill in that respect.

The Senator has also made an assault on the late President of the Senate, General Atchison—a man of as kind a nature, of as genuine and true a heart, as ever animated a human soul. He is impulsive and generous, carrying his good qualities sometimes to an excess which induces him to say and do many things that would not meet my approval; but all who know him know him to be a gentleman and an honest man, true and loyal to the Constitution of his country. He is assailed here as a Catiline. After exhausting all the epithets in the English language, the Senator went off to the Latin, to see if he could not find more of them there to denounce this man, and he employed some which Cicero used towards Catiline.

Why these attacks on individuals by name, and two thirds of the Senate collectively? Is it the object to drive men here to dissolve social relations with political opponents? Is it to turn the Senate into a bear garden, where Senators cannot associate on terms which ought to prevail between gentlemen? These attacks are heaped upon me by man after man. When I repel them, it is intimated that I show some feeling on the subject. Sir, God grant that when I denounce an act of infamy I shall do it with feeling, and do it under the sudden impulses of feeling, instead of sitting up at night writing out my denunciation of a man whom I hate, copying it, having it printed, punctuating the proof-sheets, and repeating it before the glass, in order to give refinement to insult, which is only pardonable when it is the outburst of a just indignation. . . .

Senator Mason gave the most bitter response. His insults against Sumner were as strong as any in Sumner's speech. Mason's assessment of Sumner effectively summarized the feelings of most Southern members of Congress. His dismissal of Sumner as no gentleman and his questioning of Sumner's masculinity were widely echoed in public comments by other Southerners. His questions about the existence of Sumner's "slave power" probably reflect the frustrations of a Southern nationalist over divisions within the South. Far from being united, Mason knew white Southerners to be deeply split over how to best defend slavery and other regional interests. In the tradition of John C. Calhoun, Southern political leaders such as Mason were accustomed to viewing themselves as part of an embattled minority. To them, Sumner's notion that there was a "slave power" that controlled the nation seemed simply ludicrous.

Response from Democratic Senator James Mason, of Virginia[25]

MR. MASON: Mr. President, the necessities of our political position bring us into relations and associations upon this floor, which, in obedience to a common Government, we are forced to admit. They bring us into relations and associations, which, beyond the walls of this Chamber, we are enabled to avoid—associations here, whose presence elsewhere is dishonor, and the touch of whose hand would be a disgrace. They are the necessities of our political position: and yet, Mr. President, it is not easy to bear them. Representing our States here, under a Constitution which we came here to obey, we are constrained to listen, from day to day, from sources utterly irresponsible, to language to which no gentleman would subject himself elsewhere. I say it is difficult to bear. We bear it from respect to the obligations of the Constitution, and in obedience to the constitutional trust which we have undertaken to perform.

Sir, the Senator who here represents Massachusetts undertook to-day to assail the absent—to assail one honorable man, who honored this Chamber when he was a member of this body, but who is no longer a member, and to assail him when he was at the distance of some two thousand miles from his presence; and to assail him how? Assuming to be the Cicero of the occasion, to denounce him as a Catiline! Mr. President, the Senator who did it, while assailing, also, a man whom I am honored in calling my friend—the Senator from South Carolina—that Senator who assailed them both here on this floor, was base enough to declare the turpitude of his own ancestry and to avow it; ay, sir, declared the turpitude of his own ancestors and avowed it here. Now, Mr. President, let the accusation go forth, and let the self-drawn character of the accuser go with it. I am not here to vindicate those gentlemen. The Senator from South Carolina will return in good time to his place. He is now at home, where he has been for the last two weeks. I will say this, however, in the presence of the Senate, that when the Senator from Massachusetts dared, in this Chamber, and among those who know the Senator from South Carolina, to connect his name with untruth—for he did so—he presented himself here as one utterly incapable of knowing what truth is—utterly incapable of conceiving the perceptions of an honorable mind, when directed to the investigation of truth. He presented himself as the cunning artificer or forger, who knows no other use of truth than to give currency to falsehood; who uses the beaten gold to enable him to pass off the false coin; who distinguishes between that which is pure metal and that which is not so, only to enable him to deceive those who have trusted him here.

But, Mr. President, I did not intend to be betrayed into this debate. I have said that the necessity of political position alone brings me into relations with men upon this floor who elsewhere I cannot acknowledge as possessing manhood in any form. I am constrained to hear here depravity, vice in its most odious form uncoiled in this presence, exhibiting its loathsome deformities in accusation and vilification against the quarter of the country from which I come; and I must listen to it because it is a necessity of my position, under a common Government, to recognize as an equal, politically, one whom to see elsewhere is to shun and despise. I did not intend to be betrayed into this debate; but I submit to the necessity of my position. I am here now united with an honored band of patriots, from the North equally with the South, to try if we can [to] preserve and perpetuate those institutions which others are prepared to betray, and are seeking to destroy; and I will submit to the necessity of that position at least until the work is accomplished.

What I desired chiefly to do, Mr. President, was to bring before the American people, and more especially the people represented by the Senator from Massachusetts, what he calls the supremacy of the "slave power." That Senator is not alone in exhibiting this power to the quarter of the country from which he comes. The ribald sheets of a depraved press in unison with that Senator, use the same language which he has used on this floor within the last twenty-four hours, though by another name—they call it the "slaveocracy." The Senator from New York [MR. SEWARD] speaks of it as an "oligarchy." All these confederate Senators are loud in their denunciation of the "slave power." They declare that it exercises a supreme control over the affairs of this Government. They taunt Senators who come here from States where there are no slaves, with submitting to it. And yet they have never told you what it is—never. What, then, is the "slave power" which Senators denounce? It is not the wealth of the slaveholding States, for the Senator from Massachusetts himself, by an extravagance of speech, declared here yesterday, that, the productive industry of his own small State was greater than the whole cotton-growing labor of the South. . . .

It is not the wealth of the South, then, which constitutes the "slave power." Is it the numerical strength? No; for indisputably we are numerically in a minority. Is it in political power meted out by the Constitution to the States? No; for we are in a minority in the Senate where the States are represented: we are in a minority in the other branch where the people are represented numerically; and we are in a minority in the electoral college. . . .

Now, let the Senator survey the whole field of power to find whence the "slave power" comes; and when he admits, as he must admit, that it is not in wealth, or in numerical strength, or in the constitutional allotment of power, what is it? He says it exists; that it is supreme; that Presidents bend to it; that Senators yield to it; and his own acknowledgment of the existence of the power, shows that his *morale* feels it also. Let me ask him whence comes it? The picture is his; not mine. If there be any slave power exerting an influence upon the counsels of this country, it is that moral power diffused through the world, acknowledged everywhere, and to which kings and potentates bow—it is the moral power of truth; adherence to the obligations of honor, and the dispensation of those charities of life that ennoble the nature of man. That is the moral power which the Senator ascribes to the institution of slavery.

Now, Mr. President, if that be so, how ungrateful is that Senator and his State of Massachusetts. . . ? They have grown rich by means of this very confederacy. I say, then, the Senator is ungrateful. He ascribes to that slave power the controlling influence over this confederacy; and yet is not grateful, as he should be, for the beneficent rule (and at their own expense) of this very "slave power!"

Mr. President, the first criminal known to the world, in the complaint which instigated him to crime, declared only that the offering of his brother was more acceptable than his. It was the complaint of Cain against Abel, and he avenged it by putting that brother to death, and then went forth with the primeval curse upon his brow. In the fortunes of those who are enlisted with the Senator from Massachusetts against this confederation now, let them go, as Cain did, with the curse upon their brow of fraternal homicide, but with the still deeper guilt that they instigate others to shed blood when they shed none themselves.

Sumner's rebuttal reflected his passion for principle over personal relationships. Although seemingly surprised at Senator Cass's resentment over his account of Michigan history, Sumner's convictions would not allow him to retract anything. There is some irony in his challenging Douglas for offensive personalities in debate and then characterizing the Illinois Senator as a "noisome, squat, and nameless animal."

Sumner's Response[26]

MR. SUMNER: Mr. President, three Senators have spoken—one venerable with years, and with whom I have had associations of personal regard longer than with any person now within the sound of my voice—the Senator from Michigan. Another, the Senator from Illinois; and the third, the Senator from Virginia. The Senator from Michigan knows full well that nothing can fall from me which can have anything but kindness for him. He has said on this floor to- day that he listened with regret to my speech. I have never avowed on this floor how often, with my heart brimming full of friendship for him, I have listened with regret to what has fallen from his lips. I have never said that he stood here to utter sentiments which seemed beyond all question disloyal to the character of the fathers and to the true spirit of the Constitution; but this, with his permission, and in all kindness, I do now say to him.

That Senator proceeded very briefly and cursorily to criticise my statement of the Michigan case. Sir, my statement of that case was founded upon the actual documents. No word was mine: It was all from Jackson, from Grundy, from Buchanan, from Benton, from the Democratic leaders of that day. When the Senator criticised me, his shaft did not touch me, but fell upon them. I pass from the Senator from Michigan.

To the Senator from Illinois I should willingly leave the privilege of the common scold—the last word: but I will not leave to him, in any discussion with me, the last argument, or the last semblance of it. He has crowned the audacity of this debate by venturing in rise here and calumniate me. He has said that I came here, took an oath to support the Constitution, and yet determined not to support a particular clause in that Constitution. To that statement I give, to his face, the flattest denial. When it was made on a former occasion on this floor by the absent Senator from South Carolina, [MR. BUTLER,] I then repelled it. I will read from the debate of the 28th of June, 1854, as published in the *Globe*, to show what I said in response to that calumny when pressed at that hour. Here is what I said to the Senator from South Carolina. . . .

[Sumner then summarized his Reply to Assailants. See part one.]

After explaining at some length my understanding of the clause, I concluded on this point in these words:

"I desire to say that as I understand the Constitution, this clause does not impose upon me, as a senator or citizen, any obligation to take part, directly or indirectly, in the surrender of a fugitive slave."

Yet, in the face of all this, which occurred in open debate on the floor of the Senate, which is here in the records of the country, and has been extensively circulated, quoted, discussed, criticised, the Senator from Illinois, in the swiftness of his audacity, has presumed to arraign me. Perhaps I had better leave that Senator without a word more; but this is not the first, or the second, or the third, or the fourth time, that he has launched against me his personalities. Sir, if this be agreeable to him, I make no complaint: though, for the sake of truth and the amenities of debate, I could wish that he had directed his assaults upon my arguments; but, since he has presumed to touch me, he will not complain if I administer to him a word of advice.

Sir, this is the Senate of the United States, an important body, under the Constitution, with great powers. Its members are justly supposed, from age, to be above the intemperance of youth, and from character to be above the gusts of vulgarity. They are supposed to have something of wisdom and something of that candor which is the hand-maid of wisdom. Let the Senator bear these things in mind, and let him remember hereafter that the bowie-knife and bludgeon are not the proper emblems of senatorial debate. Let him remember that the swagger of Bob Acres and the ferocity of the Malay cannot add dignity to this body. The Senator has gone on to infuse into his speech the venom which has been sweltering for months—ay, for years; and he has alleged facts that are entirely without foundation, in order to heap upon me some personal obloquy. I will not go into the details which have flowed out so naturally from his tongue. I only brand them to his face as false. I say, also, to that Senator, and I wish him to bear it in mind, that no person with the upright form of man can be allowed—[Hesitation.]

MR. DOUGLAS: Say it.

MR. SUMNER: I will say it—no person with the upright form of man can be allowed, without violation of all decency, to switch out from his tongue the perpetual stench of offensive personality. Sir, that is not a proper weapon of debate, at least, on this floor. The noisome, squat, and nameless animal, to which I now refer, is not a proper model for an American Senator. Will the Senator from Illinois take notice ?

MR. DOUGLAS: I will; and therefore will not imitate you, sir.

MR. SUMNER: I did not hear the Senator.

MR. DOUGLAS: I said if that be the case I would certainly never imitate you in that capacity, recognizing the force of the illustration.

MR. SUMNER: Mr. President, again the Senator has switched his tongue, and again he fills the Senate with its offensive odor.

I pass from the Senator from Illinois. There was still another, the Senator from Virginia, who is now also in my eye. That Senator said nothing of argument, and, therefore, there is nothing of that for response. I simply say to him, that hard words are not argument; frowns not reasons; nor do scowls belong to the proper arsenal of parliamentary debate. The Senator has not forgotten that on a former occasion I did something to exhibit on this floor the plantation manners which he displayed. I will not do any more now.

MR. MASON: Manners of which that Senator is unconscious.

MR. DOUGLAS: I am not going to pursue this subject further. I will only say that a man who has been branded by me in the Senate, and convicted by the Senate of falsehood, cannot use language requiring reply, and therefore I have nothing more to say.

THE ATTACK: FIRSTHAND ACCOUNTS

Brooks attacked Sumner two days after the speech. He had attended the first day of Sumner's oration but it is not clear if he came back to hear the second day. He certainly knew of Sumner's concluding attacks on Butler from newspaper reports and conversations with other members of Congress. His first known description of the incident, written to his brother just after the attack, is both terse and forthright. It should be compared with his statement to the Senate and his resignation speech (both follow). The letter expresses a striking combination of violence, sentimentality, and fearlessness. His account in this letter of Sumner's response is especially revealing.

Most firsthand accounts gave the same general outline of what happened during the attack. It was in recollecting the details that witnesses showed their own sense of the event's meaning. Some emphasized the choice of weapon; others emphasized Sumner's defenselessness. With the significant exception of Brooks, eyewitnesses also emphasized the role of specific bystanders in aiding or preventing the assault. That Brooks's own version mentions the name of the man who had given him the cane but omits the role of fellow Congressman Lawrence Keitt in holding off his opponents is curious. Given Brooks's concern with reputation, his discussion of the uproar that followed the attack is less surprising.

Preston Brooks Describes the Incident to His Brother[27]

My dear Ham.

As you will learn by Telegraph that I have given Senator Sumner a caning and lest Mother should feel unnecessary alarm I write to give a detailed statement of the occurence [sic]. Sumner made a violent speech in which he insulted South Carolina and Judge Butler grossly. The Judge was and is absent and his friends all concurred in the opinion that the Judge would be compelled to flog him. This Butler is unable to do as Sumner is a very powerful man and weighs 30 pounds more than myself. Under the circumstances I felt it to be my duty to relieve Butler and avenge the insult to my State. I waited an hour and a half in the grounds on the day before yesterday for [Sumner] when he escaped me by taking a carriage. Did the same thing yesterday and with the same result. I then went to the Senate and waited until it adjourned. There were some ladies in the Hall and I had to wait a full hour until they left. I then went to [Sumner's] seat and said. "Mr. Sumner, I have read your speech with care and as much impartiality as was possible and I feel it my duty to tell you that you have libeled my State and slandered a relative who is aged and absent and I am come to punish you for it." At the concluding words I struck him with my cane and gave him about 30 first rate stripes with a gutta percha cane which had been given me a few months before by a friend from N. Carolina named Vick. Every lick went where I intended. For about the first five of six licks he offered to make fight but I plied him so rapidly that he did not touch me. Towards the last he bellowed like a calf. I wore my cane out completely but saved the Head which is gold. The fragments of the stick are begged for as *sacred relics*. Every Southern man is delighted and the Abolitionists are like a hive of disturbed bees. I expected to be attacked this morning but no one came near me. They are making all sorts of threats. It would not take much to have the throats of every Abolitionist cut. I have been arrested of course and there is now a resolution before the House the object of which is to result in my expulsion. This they cant do, it requiring two thirds to do it and they cant get a half. Every Southern man sustains me. The debate is now very animated on the subject. Dont be alarmed it will all work right. The only danger that I am in is from assassination, but this you must not intimate to Mother. Love to all. I am glad you have all paid our Brother James a visit.

Your affectionate brother

P. S. Brooks

Some indication of Preston Brooks's motives can be inferred from his brother's reply. Since to Southern elites Sumner was no gentleman, a duel would not have been proper. To challenge Sumner would have been to acknowledge him as an equal. Instead he gave Sumner a whipping. This was a punishment usually reserved for children, slaves, and other inferiors who were incapable of understanding logic and manners. The enthusiasm in this letter is typical of the tone taken by most of Preston Brooks's Southern correspondents. Brooks's attack on Sumner seems to have released a flood of pent-up resentments.

Albany, Georgia

May 30th, '56

My Dear Brother

Your kind letter reached me just in time to relieve me of much anxiety—for there were many reports which I could not well understand, among others that you were in jail. Of course I did not much believe this. You did *perfectly right*. I have not been more delighted for years & only wish I could have *participated* with you. If they fine you a thousand dollars, if I were you, I should regard it as money well invested.

I am more proud of you than ever! I believe I love you better! And if I can serve you either *by purse* or *otherwise*, call on me & you will find it's not empty boasting. All the circumstances singularly & collectively were glorious, rich beyond measure. Your address to him; the *weapon* used; the manner in which it was applied; & lastly but by far the most important the cause, render it to me one of the most enchanting little tragedies extant. I would not have made the slightest alteration *but one.* I might have substituted the cow-hide for the Gutta percha, but the difference is too small to complain.

I see most of the papers (all in fact I have seen) of Carolina sustain you. Jim Gardenier is delighted. A [Know-Nothing] Savannah paper calls it "reprehensible conduct of Mr. B.," But this place tho' K. N. as far as I can learn is delighted.

A gentleman named Hill related to the Edgefield H[ills] in speaking of it said"By G** I haven't had any thing to do me as much good in four years." I think I can give you the true sentiment of the South by a quotation from Gardenier's paper, viz. "While many may honestly differ as to the propriety of the place, there are few who will not admit that he *deserved* a good *gutta perchering* & he received it."

Old Capt. Robert when told I had a letter from you, begged me to read it for him in the presence of Col. Lawton Senator from this county. I read most of it & when I concluded, I said—"he is a Trump." He then proposed to the Capt. to have a public meeting for the purpose of adopting complimentary resolutions & sending them to you. They finally agreed to wait till the meeting of the Democratic convention next week, as a more suitable time. . .

We leave on Monday & will be in Augusta till Thursday, cant you drop me a line then? Your affectionate brother. LHB.

Brooks's second letter shows the same sensitivity to perceived slights he evidenced in his Mexican War correspondence. The importance of his reputation among friends, kinsmen, and constituents is palpable. The letter also shows his sensitivity to the political landscape in Washington. He accurately forecasts the attempt to censure him, its failure, and his resignation. His discussion of the Republican party shows how little he trusted their motives or acknowledged their credibility. Like most opponents of the Northern party he labeled them "Black Republicans." This served to underscore the supposed falseness of their political philosophy. The term also served to associate the Republicans with an ethnic minority that most white Northerners despised. Brooks's reaction to the letters he received is consistent with his belief that deeds rather than words were the true test of character. His supporters were clearly pushing him into a more aggressive stance that abandoned the moderation he advocated in 1853.

Washington D. C. 21st. June [1856]
My dear Ham.

Your letter of this morning was a great comfort to me, as it was the first information I had received from *home* for several weeks. You must pardon me for saying that under the circumstances in which I am situated you keep a curiously accurate account of the number of letters which have passed between us. The only intelligence I have had of Mother and yourself for upwards of three weeks is through the Newspapers of Augusta. Neither Col. Carroll[28] or Dunovant have written me a line, while entire strangers from nearly every State in the Union have expressed a word of kindness & sympathy. I don't distrust their affection but I do dispise [sic] their inertness and undemonstrativeness. I suppose you have seen in the papers every thing of interest here relative to myself. Sumner has not yet made his appearance—is lying up with a view to make political capital for the black Republican party. Wilson[29] declined my challenge and has been away all the time save one day. I am to be tried next week in the criminal court and expect to be fined a thousand Dollars. The week after the resolutions of Expulsion are the special order. These resolutions cant pass, but the vote will stand about 120 to 70 and this vote will be censure enough for me. I will resign and appeal to my own people. My plan is to rise when the vote is announced and in a few temperate remarks enter my protest against the proceedings and say that I throw off all responsibility to the House by resigning my Commission. It may be that the matter will stop at this point and it may be that the Black Republicans may persue [sic] me as a private citizen. They may send the Sergeant at Arms to bring me before the House to be reprimanded by Mr. Speaker Banks, and I will die before I submit my people to this indignity in the person of their representative. It is understood that I am to be bitterly denounced by their Speakers on the discussion of the resolutions. I shall not violate the proprieties of the House myself, but if this is done there will be an exciting time. My course will be to hear all they have to say and to hold the most respectable of the number to the strictest account. I cant fight every body who denounces me, for their name is legion, but I can again degrade the most prominent man of their party, by making a selection in the House and that is to degrade their party too. There is no telling when the affair is to end as the deepest feeling exists on both sides. You however must not think of coming here. I have as many friends as I want and never intend to permit a friend to be involved on my account. The responsibility of my position is painfully heavy, for I have lost my individuality in my representative capacity. I am regarded to a great extent as the exponent of the South against which Black Republicanism is war[r]ing in my person. I shall do my full duty in this position, nor shrink from any issue which involves a yielding of the constitutional rights or a taming of the lofty spirit of the people of the southern portion of the Confederacy. You need not apprehend any injury to myself. I always go armed and will use my weapons if attacked. The dogs may bite when I kick them but will never dare assail me, though I have fifty letters saying I shall be killed. I am grieved at Martha's loss and fear that anxiety has much to do with it. Give my tenderest love to Mother and Nelle and a kiss to your wife. I rarely think of you as a married man. If I resign, which I am certain to do and no effort is made to detain me here I will come directly home. Tell Scurry to take good care of Jack—he loves me more than any dog I ever had and I like him for that though I do not admit that he is without decided professional merit.

Your Brother P. S. Brooks

Brooks offered another version of the attack and its motivations in his 29 May letter to the Senate. His emphasis on technicalities of jurisdiction ("the Senate had adjourned for more than an hour") and his apology for creating an embarrassment is similar to his behavior in the South Carolina College incident of 1839. Brooks identified Sumner's reckless speech and rejection of the code of honor as the most provocative causes for the assault. As with his previous account of the attack his emphasis or omission of certain details is revealing.

Apology of Preston Brooks to the Senate[30]

House of Representatives, May 29, 1856

Sir: I have seen in the public journals, this morning the report of the committee of the Senate, to whom was referred a resolution of the Senate directing an inquiry into an assault made by me on the 22d instant on a Senator from Massachusetts.

It is with unfeigned regret I find in the report that what I had intended only as a redress of a personal wrong, had been construed into, or must necessarily be held as, a breach of privilege of the Senate.

Whilst making a full and explicit disclaimer of any such design or purpose, I ask leave to say that, for the occasion, considering myself only as a gentleman in society, and under no official restraint as a member of the House of Representatives, I did not advert to, or consider there was, any alternative or restraint imposed upon me by reason that the offense came from a member of the Senate.

I had read attentively and carefully the speech delivered in the Senate on the 19th and 20th instant by the Senator from Massachusetts, and found therein language which I regarded as unjustly reflecting not only upon the history and character of South Carolina, but also upon a friend and relative. To such language I thought I had a right to take exception under the circumstances, the Senator from South Carolina, who was affected by these remarks, being absent from the Senate and the city.

I had reason to believe that the Senator from Massachusetts did not acknowledge that personal responsibility for wrongs in personal deportment which would have saved me the painful necessity of the collision which I sought; and in my judgment, therefore, I had no alternative but to act as I did.

That the assault was made in the Senate Chamber was caused only by the fact that, after a careful search elsewhere, on the previous as well as on the same day, the offender could not be found outside the walls of the Senate Chamber, and the Senate had adjourned for more than an hour previous to the assault.

I submit the foregoing statement from the high respect I have for the Senate of the United States, and ask that it may be received as a full disclaimer of any design or purpose to infract its privileges or to offend its dignity. I cheerfully add that, should the facts as reported by the committee of the Senate be nevertheless necessarily considered as a conclusion of law, my earnest desire is to atone for it, as far as may be, by this unhesitating and unqualified apology.

Asking that you will oblige me by communicating this to the Senate as its presiding officer, I have the honor to remain, sir, with great respect, your obedient servant.

P. S. Brooks.

The House of Representatives organized a committee of inquiry the day after the assault. Under standard parliamentary procedure this committee was selected by the Speaker of the House. The speaker in this session was Nathaniel Banks of Massachusetts. The committee he appointed had three moderate Northerners and two Southern Democrats, none of whom had any special ties with Sumner.[31] The committee began taking testimony on the Monday following the assault. Sumner was one of the first witnesses. His description of the events shows how surprised he was by the actual attack. His recollection of the language used by Brooks and the roles played by specific bystanders compares interestingly with Brooks's account. Sumner's failure to arm himself or accept the protection of friends led some commentators to suspect his motives. They concluded that he had deliberately left himself unprotected in order to become a symbolic martyr for the antislavery cause.

Testimony of Charles Sumner[32]

Question: (by Mr. Campbell.) What do you know of the facts connected with the assault alleged to have been made upon you in the Senate chamber by Hon. Mr. Brooks, of South Carolina, on Thursday, May 22, 1856?

Answer: I attended the Senate as usual on Thursday, the 22nd of May. After some formal business, a message was received from the House of Representatives, announcing the death of a member of that body from Missouri. This was followed by a brief tribute to the deceased from Mr. Geyer, of Missouri, when, according to usage, and out of respect to the deceased, the Senate adjourned. Instead of leaving the chamber with the rest on the adjournment, I continued in my seat, occupied with my pen. While thus intent, in order to be in season for the mail, which was soon to close, I was approached by several persons who desired to speak with me; but I answered them promptly and briefly, excusing myself for the reason that I was much engaged. When the last of these left me, I drew my arm-chair close to my desk and with my legs under the desk continued writing. My attention at this time was so entirely withdrawn from all other objects, that, though there must have been many persons on the floor of the Senate, I saw nobody.

While thus intent, with my head bent over my writing, I was addressed by a person who had approached the front of my desk, so entirely unobserved that I was not aware of his presence until I heard my name pronounced. As I looked up, with pen in hand, I saw a tall man, whose countenance was not familiar, standing directly over me, and at the same moment, caught these words: "I have read your speech twice over carefully. It is a libel on South Carolina, and Mr. Butler, who is a relative of mine—." While these words were still passing from his lips, he commenced a succession of blows with a heavy cane on my bare head, by the first of which I was stunned so as to lose sight. I no longer saw my assailant nor any person or object in the room. What I did afterwards was done almost unconsciously, acting under the instinct of self-defence. With head already bent down, I rose from my seat, wrenching up my desk, which was screwed to the floor, and then pressed forward, while my assailant continued his blows. I have no other consciousness until I found myself ten feet forward, in front of my desk, lying on the floor of the Senate, with my bleeding head supported on the knee of a gentleman, whom I soon recognized, by voice and countenance, as Mr. Morgan, of New York. Other persons there were about me offering me friendly assistance; but I did not recognize any of them. Others there were at a distance, looking on and offering no assistance, of whom I recognized only Mr. Douglas, of Illinois, Mr. Toombs, of Georgia, and I thought also my assailant, standing between them.

I was helped from the floor and conducted into the lobby of the Senate, where I was placed on a sofa. Of those who helped me to this place I have no recollection. As I entered the lobby, I recognized Mr. Slidell, of Louisiana, who retreated; but I recognized no one else until sometime later, as I supposed, when I felt a friendly grasp of the hand, which seemed to come from Mr. Campbell, of Ohio. I have a vague impression that Mr. Bright, President of the Senate, spoke to me while I was lying on the floor of the Senate or in the lobby. . . .

Question: (by Mr. Campbell.) Did you at any time between the delivery of your speech referred to, and the time when you were attacked, receive any intimation in writing, or otherwise, that Mr. Brooks intended to attack you?

Answer: Never, directly or indirectly; nor had I the most remote suspicion of any attack, nor was I in any way prepared for an attack. I had no arms or means of defence of any kind. I was, in fact, entirely defenceless at the time, except so far as my natural strength went. In other words, I had no arms either about my person or in my desk. Nor did I ever wear arms in my life. I have always lived in a civilized community where wearing arms has not been considered necessary. When I had finished my speech on Tuesday, I think it was my colleague came to me and said; "I am going home with you to-day—several of us are going home with you." Said I: "None of that, Wilson." And, instead of waiting for him, or allowing him to accompany me home, I shot off just as I should any other day. While on my way from the Capitol I overtook Mr. Seward, with whom I had engaged to dine; we walked together as far as the omnibuses. He then proposed that we should take an omnibus, which I declined, stating that I must go to the printing office to look over proofs. I therefore walked alone, overtaking one or two persons on the way. . . .

Question: (by Mr. Pennington.) Have you ever defied or invited violence. . . ?

Answer: Never, at any time.

Question: State what was the condition of your clothing after this violence, when you were taken from the chamber.

Answer: I was in such a condition at the time that I was unaware of the blood on my clothes. I know little about it until after I reached my room, when I took my clothes off. The shirt around the neck and collar was soaked with blood. The waistcoat had many marks of blood upon it; also the trowsers. The broadcloth coat was covered with blood on the shoulders so thickly that the blood had soaked through the cloth even through the padding, and appeared on the inside; there was also a great deal of blood on the back of the coat and its sides.

Question: Were you aware of the intention of Mr. Brooks to strike or inflict a blow before the blow was felt?

Answer: I had not the remotest suspicion of it until I felt the blow on my head.

Question: (by Mr. Campbell.) Do you know how often you were struck?

Answer: I have not the most remote idea.

Question: How many wounds have you upon your head?

Answer: I have two principal wounds upon my head, and several bruises on my hands and arms. The doctor will describe them more particularly than I am able to.

Question: (by Mr. Cobb.) You stated that when Mr. Brooks approached you he remarked that he had read your speech, and it was a libel upon his State and upon his relative. I will ask you, if you had, prior to that assault, in any speech, made any personal allusions to

Mr. Brooks' relative—Mr. Butler—or to the State of South Carolina, to which Mr. Brooks applied this remark?

Answer: At the time my assailant addressed me I did not know who he was, least of all did I suppose him to be a relative of Mr. Butler. In a speech, recently made in the Senate, I have alluded to the State of South Carolina, and to Mr. Butler, but I have never said anything which was not in just response to his speeches according to parliamentary usage, nor anything which can be called a libel upon South Carolina or Mr. Butler.

Reporter James W. Simonton represented the New York *Times*, which was controlled at the time by moderate Republicans. His account of the incident was brief but showed a reporter's eye for detail. His version highlights the role of Brooks's fellow South Carolina Congressman Laurence Keitt in preventing interference with the attack. Keitt would be censured by the House for his behavior in the incident.[33]

Testimony of New York *Times* Reporter James W. Simonton[34]

James W. Simonton sworn.

Question: (by Mr. Campbell.) What do you know of the facts connected with the assault alleged to have been made upon Mr. Sumner in the Senate chamber by the Hon. Mr. Brooks of South Carolina, on Thursday, May 22, 1856?

Answer: I was standing in the Senate chamber near Mr. Clayton's seat, conversing with Mr. Morgan and Mr. Murray of the House, when I heard a blow. I exclaimed, "what is that?" and immediately started. One step brought me in view of the parties. My attention was directed at once to Mr. Sumner, with a view to notice his condition. I saw that he was just in the act of springing forward. As he came upon his feet I noticed him spin around, and then stagger backwards and sideways until he fell. Mr. Brooks was striking him with his cane, which then seemed to be broken off one-third of its length. I rushed up as rapidly as possible, with other gentlemen, and as I reached him, or near him, Mr. Keitt rushed in, running around Mr. Sumner and Mr. Brooks with his cane raised, crying "let them alone! Let them alone!" Threatening myself and others who had rushed into interfere. Mr. Brooks continued to strike until he was seized by Mr. Murray, and until Mr. Sumner, who had lodged partly against the desk, had fallen to the floor. He did not fall directly, but, after lodging for an instant upon, then slipped off from his desk, and fell upon the floor. I do not know of anything further.

Question: How often did Mr. Brooks strike?

Answer: With great rapidity; at least a dozen, and I should think twenty blows. Mr. Sumner, at the first moment when I looked at him, seemed to me to be unconscious.

Question: (by Mr. Pennington.) Do you know of any concert between Mr. Brooks and any other person, a member of Congress, to attack Mr. Sumner?

Answer: I do not know anything of my own knowledge. I noticed several persons who were there. I saw Mr. Keitt there. I have a distinct recollection of seeing several parties, perhaps not distinct enough to mention them. I saw several senators present immediately afterwards, but whether they were there at the time in the occurrence I could not say. My attention was directed especially to Mr. Sumner and to Mr. Keitt, who seemed to be acting in concert with Mr. Brooks. . . .

Question: State, if you can, what Mr. Keitt said or did from first to last?

Answer: I saw him as I was approaching the parties. I noticed him run in from the centre isle, and raise his cane. He used the words I have spoken; or rather my impression is that the precise expression was, "Let them alone, God damn you. . . ."

Question: Did he strike any blow?

Answer: I saw him strike no blow. He had his cane flourishing over his head.

Question: Was that the effect of excitement, or of a blow aimed at somebody?

Answer: I could not say that it was aimed at anybody. It might have been from excitement. He brandished his cane as I have described, and almost completed a circle around Mr. Sumner and Mr. Brooks.

Brooks discussed his plans with several associates before he made the attack. Congressman Henry A. Edmundson, of Virginia, encountered him twice in the time between the speech and the caning. Edmondson's testimony reveals Brooks's increasing agitation and frustration on the eve of the attack. It also shows that neither Edmondson nor the other Southerners made any effort to talk Brooks out of an encounter. Like Keitt, the Virginia Congressman would be censured for this failure. Edmundson's testimony gives the most thorough account we have of Brooks's actions and motives between the time of the speech and the time of the assault.[35]

Testimony of Democratic Rep. Henry A. Edmundson of Virginia[36]

Hon. Henry A. Edmondson sworn:

Question: (by Mr. Campbell.) What do you know of the facts connected with the assault alleged to have been made upon Mr. Sumner, in the Senate chamber, by the Hon. Mr. Brooks, of South Carolina, on the 22d of May, 1856? And state anything you may have heard Mr. Brooks say in relation thereto, previous to said assault.

Answer: I was not present when the alleged assault was made. The first intimation I had that Mr. Brooks had taken any offence at what Mr. Sumner said, was on going into the Senate chamber on the second day of the speech, when I heard a gentleman say that Mr. Brooks had taken exceptions to remarks made by Mr. Sumner, the day before, in relation to Judge Butler, and the State of South Carolina. The morning after Mr. Sumner closed his speech, while on my way to the House with some other gentlemen, I met Mr. Brooks at the foot of the first flight of steps approaching the Capitol. I accosted him, saying, "you are going the wrong way for the discharge of your duties." He asked me to walk with him. I did so. He then told me Mr. Sumner had been very insulting to his State, and that he had determined to punish them, unless he made an ample apology. We took a seat in the Capitol grounds, near the walk leading from the Avenue to the Capitol. He said to me, "I wish you merely to be present, and if a difficulty should occur, to take no part in it. Sumner may have friends with him, and I want a friend of mine to be with me to do me justice." I asked him what was his purpose? He replied it was to call upon Mr. Sumner for the insulting language used towards his State; and if he did not apologize, to punish him.

Question: About what time was this?

Answer: I met Mr. Brooks about ten minutes before the time for the meeting of the House on Wednesday morning. I remember to have heard Mr. Brooks say it was time for southern men to stop this coarse abuse used by the Abolitionists against the Southern people and States, and that he should not feel that he was representing his State properly if he permitted such things to be said; that he learned Mr. Sumner intended to do this thing days before he made his speech; that he did deliberately, and he thought he ought to punish him for it. That is all that occurs to my mind that has any relevancy to this matter. The next morning, when coming to the Capitol, about the time for the House to meet, I saw Mr. Brooks sitting in the gatehouse of the Capitol grounds at the entrance from Pennsylvania Avenue, alone. I supposed what his object was, and stopped in. I said, you are looking out. He said he was desirous of seeing Mr. Sumner; that he could not overlook the insult; that he had scarcely slept any the night before, thinking of it; and that it ought to be promptly resented. We sat there only a few moments, during which time I learned that his purpose was to meet Mr. Sumner before he got into the Senate chamber; that he could see from that position whither he should walk or ride; if he should be in a carriage, he (Mr. Brooks) intended to pass through the grounds and Capitol and meet him before he reached the Senate chamber. I stated to him, that would be an imprudent course; that I had no doubt Mr. Sumner was physically a stronger man than himself, and the exertion and fatigue of passing up so many flights of steps would render him unable to contend with Mr. Sumner, should a personal conflict take place. We walked then to the Capitol; our conversation, as we passed on, was in relation to other matters. When we arrived at the door entering into the rotundo he remarked that he was going into the Senate chamber, and went in that direction. I went into the House, where I found Mr. Lindley, of Missouri, was announcing the death of his colleague, Mr. Miller; he was followed by Mr. Marshall, of Kentucky, after which the House adjourned.

I then walked over to the Senate, and saw Mr. Brooks standing in the lobby on the opposite side of the main aisle from where Mr. Sumner was sitting. I seated myself, and heard Mr. Geyer announce the death of Mr. Miller in the Senate. The Senate then adjourned. When I noticed Mr. Brooks again he was occupying a seat in the Senate chamber. As I was passing near him, I asked him if he was a senator? He then said to me that he would stand this thing no longer; he would send to Mr. Sumner to retire from the chamber. He then got up, and went into the vestibule outside of the chamber with that view. I followed him, and said, that if he sent such a message, Mr. Sumner would probably send for him to come into the Senate chamber. He seemed to be busy at his desk directing documents, as I supposed; and he would effect nothing by this, he having previously said he did not desire to have an interview with Mr. Sumner while ladies were present, and I knew there still remained a lady occupying a seat in the lobby not far from where Mr. Sumner was sitting. This is all the conversation that I now remember to have had with Mr. Brooks that had any relevancy to this matter. We then stepped back into the Senate chamber. I immediately passed on through another door, near which I met a friend, (Senator Johnson,) to whom I propounded the question, if there would be any impropriety, should an altercation occur between Mr. Brooks and Mr. Sumner, of its taking place in the Senate chamber, the Senate having adjourned at the time? My recollection is, that I suggested, in the said conversation, there seemed to me no impropriety in calling on Mr. Sumner in the Senate, it having adjourned some time before, and there being few persons present; the insult was given there, and that might be looked upon as the proper place to resented; and further, that should a collision follow, both parties might prefer it to take place where it would be more private than it would probably be outside of the Capitol. Here the conversation terminated; and, as I turned away from this gentleman, heard a noise in the Senate chamber, with exclamations of "Oh! oh!" I went back as quickly as I could; but when I got into the Senate chamber the whole difficulty was over. I found Mr. Sumner in a reclining position, Mr. Morgan holding him by the arm, saying that he was very badly hurt, and a physician must be procured. There was some conversation between Mr. Brooks and Mr. Crittenden. In a short time it was suggested that Mr. Sumner had better go into the ante-room, and he was carried out in a leaning position.

I saw three pieces broken off the small end of the cane. My attention was called to them, by Mr. Brooks requesting me to procure the head of his cane. My recollection is that he said it was presented to him by some one from Philadelphia. I got a portion of the stick and gave it to Mr. Glossbrenner, Sergeant-at-Arms of the House, and have not seen it since.

Two weeks after the incident Senator Butler had an opportunity to offer his own public assessment of what had happened. The following excerpts are part of a speech given during the Senate's debate over the incident. The speech contains not only his own reactions but also an evaluation of the motives guiding Brooks and Sumner. As an interested party and as the only individual who knew both men personally, Butler had unique insights into their conflict. His rich psychological descriptions have strongly influenced how historians have interpreted the caning. Butler refers several times in his speech to a set of resolutions from the Massachusetts Legislature condemning the caning, which had been submitted directly to the president of the Senate and the speaker of the House rather than to the Massachusetts delegation, as was custom.

Speech of Hon. A. P. Butler, 12 June 1856[37]

MR. BUTLER: Mr. President, the occasion and the subject upon which I am about to address the Senate of the United States, at this time, have been brought about by events over which I have had no control, and could have had none—events which have grown out of the commencement of a controversy for which the Senator from Massachusetts (not now in his seat) [MR. SUMNER] should be held exclusively responsible to his country and his God. He has delivered a speech the most extraordinary that has ever had utterance in any deliberative body recognizing the sanctions of law and decency. When it was delivered I was not here; and if I had been present, what I should have done it would be perfectly idle for me now to say; because no one can substitute the deliberations of a subsequent period for such as might have influenced him at another time and under different circumstances. My impression now is that, if I had been present, I should have asked the Senator, before he finished some of the paragraphs personally applicable to myself, to pause; and if he had gone on, I would have demanded of him, the next morning, that he should review that speech, and retract or modify it, so as to bring it within the sphere of parliamentary propriety. If he had refused this, what I would have done I cannot say; yet I can say that I would not have submitted to it. But what mode of redress I should have resorted to, I cannot tell.

I wish I had been here. I would have at least assumed, as I ought to have done on my responsibility as a Senator, and on my responsibility as a representative of South Carolina, all the consequences, let them lead where they might; but instead of that, the speech has involved his own friends, and his own colleague. It has involved my friends. It has involved one of them to such an extent that, at this time, he has been obliged to put his fortune and his life at stake. And, sir, if the consequences which are likely to flow from that speech hereafter shall end in blood and violence that Senator should be prepared to repent in sackcloth and ashes.

Now, I pronounce a judgment on that speech which wilt be adopted by the public. I am as certain as I am speaking that it is now condemned by the public mind, and by posterity it will be consigned to infamy, for the mischievous consequences which have flowed from it already, and such as are likely yet to disturb the peace and repose of the country.

I said nothing, Mr. President, at any period of my life—much less did I say anything in the course of the debate to which the Senator from Massachusetts purports to have made a reply—that could have called for, much less have justified, the gross personal abuse, traduction, and calumny, to which he has resorted.

When I was at my little farm, enjoying myself quietly, and as I thought had taken refuge from the strifes and contentions of the Senate, and of politics, a message was brought to me that my kinsman had been involved in a difficulty on my account. It was so vague that I did not know how to account for it. I was far from any telegraphic communication. I did not wait five minutes before I left home to put myself within the reach of such information—and garbled even that was—as was accessible. I traveled four days continuously to Washington; and when I arrived I found the very subject under discussion which had given me so much anxiety, and it has been a source of the deepest concern to my feelings ever since I heard of it, on many accounts—on account of my country, and on account of the honor and the safety of my kinsman. When I arrived here, I found the subject under discussion. I went to the Senate worn down by travel; and I then gave notice that, when the resolutions from Massachusetts should be presented, I would speak to them, as coming from a Commonwealth whose history, and whose lessons of history, had inspired me with the very highest admiration—I would speak to them from a respect to a Commonwealth, whilst, perhaps, the Senator who had been the cause of their introduction ought not to deserve my notice, and would not have received it. Well, sir, days passed, and those resolutions were not presented. Now, they have been presented, and presented in a different way from any that I have ever known to be submitted from any Commonwealth before. They were not presented by one of its Senators, but were sent directly to the President of the Senate, and the Speaker of the House of Representatives. I waited for some time with the expectation that, when these resolutions should come, I would acquit myself of the painful task which circumstances had devolved upon me. They did not come until yesterday—more than two weeks after their adoption.

In the mean time—on Monday last—I gave notice that I would address the Senate to-day, under the confident belief, not that the present Senator [MR. WILSON] would be here—because I have nothing to do with him—but that the Senator who has been the aggressor, the criminal aggressor, in this matter, would be present; and if I give credence to the testimony of Dr. Boyle, I see no reason why he should not be present. For anything that appears in that testimony, if he had been an officer of the Army, and had not appeared the next day on the battle-field, he would have deserved to be cashiered.

Sir, I am at a loss to know why he has aimed his assaults at me individually, and at my State on more occasions than one; but I am willing to adopt the clew afforded by the Rev. Mr. Beecher;[38] and, as it is a clew upon the subject, I rely on it. I wish nothing of mine to go out that I do not intend to be entirely consistent with the convictions of my mind. I ask to have Mr. Beecher's remarks read. I adopt them, and they will acquit the Senator—or they will go very far to acquit him. The secretary read as follows:

"The only complaint which I have ever heard of Senator Sumner has been this: that he, by his shrinking and sensitive nature, was not fit for the 'rough and tumble' of politics in our day. He would have held himself back, and avoided giving the slightest offense, had it not been that he was reproved and goaded into it by, as I think, the injudicious criticism of friends."

MR. BUTLER: Sir, I believe it, and it will acquit his motives to some extent. Instead of making his speech here his own, as a Senator, under the obligations of the Constitution, and the highest sanctions which can influence the conduct of an honorable man—instead of making it the vehicle of high thoughts and noble emotions that would become a man and a Senator, it is obvious now that he has made that speech but the conduit—I will use a stronger expression—the fang, through which to express upon the public the compound poison of malignity and injustice. This *is* confirmed by his remarkable exordium; for, in many respects, this is the most extraordinary speech that has ever found its way in any book, or upon any occasion, ancient or modern. I have never before heard of proem or exordium by proclamation; and yet, before the delivery of his speech, by a telegraphic proclamation to Theodore Parker,[39] he uttered this remarkable sentence: "Whilst you are deliberating in your meeting I am about to pronounce the most thorough philippic that was ever heard in the Senate of the United States." This is in conformity with Mr. Parker's opinion. He was a flexible conformist invoking the spirit of Theodore Parker as his muse to sustain him in the strife for which, by his nature and his talents, he was not fit. Sir, it was the tribute and deference of a flexible conformist, willing to be a rhetorical fabricator to carry out the views and subserve the purposes of a man who, as I understand, is of an iron will and robust intellect; who loves controversy, and has abilities which more fit him, perhaps, for that, than for worshiping the lamb as the emblem of innocence, and as the prototype of that Christ whose doctrines he has professed. To conciliate Parker, the Senator must make war upon South Carolina and upon myself. . . .

While he has charged me with misstating history, law, and the Constitution, let me say that "he who lives in glass houses should not throw stones." I here say, and I pledge myself to it, that I will convict him, and shall demand of the Senate a verdict of guilty. . . .

[Mr. Butler concluded his speech the following day.]

I said yesterday that my friend, my representative, my relative, one who is associated with me by more ties than either of these—had taken redress in his own hands—had resorted to his own mode of redress. I said that there were considerations connected with the occasion which, though they could not justify him before a legal tribunal, would excuse any man of his character and position, representing such constituents as he represented, and bound in some measure to sympathize with the opinions of the section with which he is associated. It was impossible that he could separate himself from those conclusions which others might not appreciate, and some could not understand. But I say that gentleman dare not—I do not say I would have advised him—but in his estimation he could not go home and face such a constituency without incurring what is the worst of all judgments—the judgment of the country against a man who is placed as a sentinel to represent it. . . .

But, sir, before I approach the constitutional and legal view of these resolutions, I must acquit myself of the duty which I in some measure assumed yesterday evening, of presenting to the public the circumstances under which the fracas, as it is termed, or the assault, on the Senator from Massachusetts, occurred.

I said that my friend and relative was not in the Senate when the speech was being delivered, but he was summoned here, as I have learned from others. He was excited and stung by the street rumors and the street commentaries, and by the conversations in the parlors, where even ladies pronounced a judgment; and, sir, woman never fails to pronounce a judgment where honor is concerned, and it is always in favor of the redress of a wrong. I would trust to the instinct of woman upon subjects of this kind. He could not go into a parlor, or drawing-room, or to a dinner party, where he did not find an implied reproach that there was an unmanly submission to an insult to his State and his countrymen. Sir, it was hard for any man, much less for a man of his temperament, to bear this. . . .

What was my friend to do? Sue him? Indict him? If that was the mode in which he intended to take redress, he had better never go to South Carolina again. Was he to challenge him? That would have been an exhibition of chivalry having no meaning. Although he has been upon the field, both in open war and in a private affair, I should be very sorry to see any crisis requiring it again. A challenge would have been an advertisement to the world of his courage, when there was not a probability of its being tried. He would have made himself contemptible, and perhaps might have been committed to the penitentiary for sending a challenge.

Then, what course was left to him to pursue? Mr. Sumner had opportunities enough to make an apology. God knows I could not have resisted the admonitory criticism of the distinguished Senator from Michigan, perhaps the most imposing authority in the Senate. He paid no regard to him, and for a very good reason: his speech was written, and had gone out, and he could not contradict what he had sent forth to the public with malice aforethought.

Well, sir, what did Mr. Brooks do? It is said he sought Mr. Sumner in the Senate Chamber. It is the last place in which he wished to seek him. He would have met him in an open combat, on a fair field, and under a free sky, at any time. And when the Legislature of Massachusetts chooses to say that his conduct is cowardly, let her try him in any way she chooses. . . . [Applause.]

Sir, a man who occupies a place in the Senate, representing a great Commonwealth like Massachusetts, or representing any State, as one of her Senators, occupies a very high position, from which he can send forth to the public what may affect the character of almost any man, except General Washington, or some one upon whose character the verdict of history has been rendered. There is scarcely any man who can withstand the slander which may be pronounced from the Senate Chamber of the United States. For this reason I would never look, and I never have looked, beyond the public position of a member here, to go into his private and personal character. I would not do it, because by so doing I should do a wrong which I could not redress. Even a word escaping my tongue in this Chamber, as a Senator, might go far to injure a man where he could not correct it. We are in a position which requires high considerations for the regulation of our conduct. I agree thoroughly with General Jackson, that the slanderer who involves third persons in difficulty and danger, is an incendiary, against whom we should guard more than any one else, in a parliamentary point of view. . . . A single murder is horrible. It may take a single individual from society. But when I look at the mischievous influence of slander, I find that it pervades a whole community; makes war in society; sets family against family; individual against individual; section against section. It is the most cowardly mode in which a war can be conducted.

With the state of opinion to which I have alluded prevailing, what did Mr. Brooks do? Of course he did not undertake to challenge Mr. Sumner to a fist fight, or a stick fight, or any other kind of fight. He thought Mr. Sumner deserved a castigation, and he undertook to give it to him according to the old-fashioned notion, by caning him. I have not heard Mr. Brooks detail the circumstances. I have not conversed with him in regard to the matter; I take my information from the published testimony. Mr. Brooks, not finding him anywhere else, came to him while he was sitting in his seat here, after the Senate had adjourned. He came to him in front—different from the statement made to the Massachusetts Legislature. . . .

Instinct would have prompted most men to rise immediately. Mr. Sumner did rise. In the act of rising, Mr. Brooks struck him across the face—not, as has been represented, over his head, for that is not the truth, nor is it borne out by the testimony. On the second stroke the cane broke. It is the misfortune of Mr. Brooks to have incurred all the epithets which have been used in regard to an assassin-like and bludgeon attack, by the mere accident of having a foolish stick, which broke. It broke again; and it was not, as I understand, until it came very near the handle, that he inflicted blows which he would not have inflicted if he had an ordinary weapon of a kind which would have been a security against breaking. His design was to whip him; but the stick broke, and that has brought upon him these imputations. . . .

He approached that man with no other purpose than to disgrace him as far as he could; but the stick broke. After it broke he was reduced to a kind of necessity—a contingency not apprehended at all in the original inception of the purpose of making the assault. Notwithstanding all that has been said of his brutality, he is one of the best tempered fellows I ever knew—impetuous, no doubt, and quick in resentment, but he did not intend what has been assigned to him.

After all that has been said and done, on a *post bellum* examination, what is it? A fight in the Senate Chamber, resulting in two flesh wounds, which ought not to have detained him from the Senate. Being rather a handsome man, perhaps he would not like to expose himself by making his appearance for some time: but if he had been in the Army, there was no reason why he should not go to the field the next day; and he would deserve to be cashiered if he did not go. What does his physician say? He says that there were but two flesh wounds; that he never had a fever while under his care and attendance, and that he was ready to come into the Senate the next day, but for his advice; and his advice was, that he should not come into the Senate, because it would aggravate the excitement already too high. He did not recommend him not to go into the committee room to be examined on the ground that his wounds had enfeebled him, but for other considerations, because it might aggravate the excitement already prevailing to an extent which might lead to mischievous consequences.

This, then, is the mode of redress to which Mr. Brooks resorted. I do not say what I should have advised him to do, but perhaps it was fortunate that I was absent in one respect, for I certainly should not have submitted to that insult. Possibly it might not have been offered if I were present, though I do not know the fact, because I cannot say exactly what would be the course of one of those persons who have a way of fabricating speeches. Perhaps, being in his speech, he would have had to read it; but I think it possible that on the appeal which I would have made on my discretion, his friends might have induced him to reform it in some way so as to conform at least to the requirements of common decency in public opinion. If he had not done so, I do not know what would have been my course. . . .

This affair is said to be an evidence of southern violence and southern ruffianism. Some papers speak of the bowie-knife and the revolver of southern blackguards. Why, sir, the first fight which took place in Congress was between Matthew Lyon and Roger Griswold, from Connecticut. Our ancestors in those days looked upon a fight with very little of the importance which is now attached to it. They said it was so unimportant, that they were vexed that so much of the time of the House was occupied in considering it. . . .

If a civil action were brought by Mr. Sumner against Mr. Brooks for assault and battery, I pledge myself that, with all the resources he could bring to his command, he would be able to reduce the verdict to a penny damages. What would be the state of the pleadings? Mr. Brooks struck Mr. Sumner, would be the allegation. It would be admitted that he struck him, and inflicted two flesh wounds. Mr. Sumner would reply, "I am a Senator of the United States; and although the Senate was not in session, I was in that sacred temple, and my character is so sacred under the privileges of the Senate, that I am not to be assailed." What would Mr. Sumner's counsel rejoin? The rejoinder would be, "Sir, you had profaned and disgraced the seat you occupied, before you were struck."

Then the question would be, what is this privilege so much spoken of—freedom of debate? The court would examine the question, whether what was said was privileged within the rules of the Senate, or whether it was a libel. If it should be pronounced to be a libel, and I were the judge before whom an action were brought—if a man brought before me could show that another insulted his mother, or his father, or his sister, or himself, or his country, I would say to the man who inflicted the blow, "My duty is to fine you; you are not justified by the law; but it is my privilege to say that, whilst I will enforce the law and maintain its dignity, I shall fine you as small a sum as I possibly can within my discretion. . . ."

THE ASSAULT: LEGISLATIVE DEBATE

The first person to speak in the Senate after the assault was Henry Wilson, Sumner's fellow Republican Senator from Massachusetts. Wilson's remarks were brief but to the point. The symbolism he used of the "vacant chair" would be invoked by Republicans as long as Sumner's disabilities kept him from Washington. Wilson would be Sumner's most vocal defender in Congress and would even entertain the idea of fighting a duel with Brooks. His characterization of the attack as a violation of free speech would become characteristic of Northern responses to the incident.

Speech of Massachusetts
Senator Henry Wilson, 23 May 1856[40]

Mr. President, the seat of my colleague is vacant to-day. That seat is vacant to-day for the first time during five years of public service. Yesterday, after a touching tribute of respect to the memory of a deceased member of the House of Representatives, the Senate adjourned. My colleague remained in his seat, busily engaged in his public duties. While thus engaged, with pen in hand, and in a position which rendered him utterly incapable of protecting or defending himself, MR. PRESTON S. BROOKS, a member of the House of Representatives, approached his desk unobserved, and abruptly addressed him. Before he had time to utter a single word in reply, he received a stunning blow upon the head from a cane in the hands of MR. BROOKS, which made him blind and almost unconscious. Endeavoring, however, to protect himself, in rising from his chair his desk was overthrown; and while in that condition, he was beaten upon the floor of the Senate exhausted, unconscious, and covered with his own blood. He was taken from this Chamber to the ante-room, his wounds were dressed, and then by friends he was carried to his home and placed upon his bed. He is unable to be with us to-day to perform the duties that belong to him as a member of this body.

Sir, to assail a member of the Senate out of this Chamber, "for words spoken in debate," is a grave offense, not only against the rights of the Senator, but the constitutional privileges of this House. But, sir, to come into this Chamber and assault a member in his seat until he falls exhausted and senseless on this floor, is an offense requiring the prompt and decisive action of the Senate.

The Massachusetts legislature was in session when the caning occurred. Because Sumner's exchanges with South Carolinians had involved issues of state sovereignty these resolves from an official state entity are of special interest. It was not unusual for state legislatures to pass resolutions on a variety of issues and to pass copies along to their Federal representatives for submission to Congress. In this case, however, the legislature bypassed their representatives and sent their resolves to the President of the Senate and the Speaker of the House. Brooks and Butler both viewed this strategy as an unconstitutional affront to the independence of the Federal legislature. Their attention to the rules, restrictions, and qualifications of petition is consistent with longstanding Southern resistance against antislavery petitions dating back to the 1830s.[41]

Massachusetts Legislative Resolves Concerning the Recent Assault upon the Honorable Charles Sumner at Washington[42]

Resolved, By the Senate and House of Representatives of the Commonwealth of Massachusetts, that we have received with deep concern information of the recent violent assault committed in the Senate Chamber at Washington upon the person of the Honorable Charles Sumner, one of our Senators in Congress, by Preston S. Brooks, a member of the House of Representatives from South Carolina,—an assault which no provocation could justify, brutal and cowardly in itself, a gross breach of parliamentary privilege, a ruthless attack upon the liberty of speech, an outrage of the decencies of civilized life, and an indignity to the Commonwealth of Massachusetts.

Resolved, That the Legislature of Massachusetts, in the name of her free and enlightened people, demands for her representatives in the National Legislature entire Freedom of Speech, and will uphold them in the proper exercise of that essential right of American citizens.

Resolved, That we approve of Mr. Sumner's manliness and courage in his earnest and fearless declaration of free principles and his defence of human rights and free territory.

Resolved, That the Legislature of Massachusetts is imperatively called upon by the plainest dictates of duty, from a decent regard to the rights of her citizens, and respect for her character as a sovereign State, to demand, and the Legislature of Massachusetts hereby does demand, of the National Congress, a prompt and strict investigation into the recent assault upon Senator Sumner, and the expulsion by the House of Representatives of Mr. Brooks of South Carolina, and any other member concerned with him in said assault.

Resolved, That his Excellency the Governor be requested to transmit a copy of the foregoing resolves to the President of the Senate and Speaker of the House of Representatives, and to each of the Senators and Members of the House of Representatives from this Commonwealth, in the Congress of the United States.

Sumner's opponents were a majority in the Senate. The Senate's President *pro tem* was Jesse Bright, a Democrat from Indiana who owned slaves in Kentucky and whose Southern sympathies were so strong that he would be expelled from the Senate in 1862 for seeking to sell rifles to the Confederacy. Although Bright normally selected committee members the Senate decided to elect the investigative committee directly. In the vote that followed two border state Whigs and three Democrats but no Republicans won seats. After a week of hearings they reported a mild resolution condemning the assault as a breach of privilege but denying that the Senate had jurisdiction to punish Brooks for the offense. The Senate voted without debate to request that the House take up Brooks's punishment. As Brooks and his supporters knew, Republicans in that body did not have the two-thirds majority necessary to pass a censure resolution. Southern senators could vote to refer the resolutions without endangering Brooks. The House committee's final report reached the floor of Congress on 9 July. After several days of debate the House voted 121 to 95 in favor of expulsion, 23 votes short of the necessary two-thirds majority.[43]

Brooks resigned immediately after the vote. His focus on the precise details of jurisdiction is consistent with his other statements and suggests how much thought he had given the issue. Similarly, his explanation for why he chose not to challenge Sumner to a duel shows how carefully he considered his opponent's style. Brooks's invocation of Sumner's alleged refusal to uphold his oath to the Constitution gives especially interesting insights into Brooks's prior attitudes about his opponent. The speech also indicates how carefully he assessed the potential costs to himself. His reluctance to incur additional civil penalties contrasts with his repeatedly stated disregard for physical danger but fits with his preoccupation in other incidents with the letter of the law. The resignation's final paragraphs are a stunning display of masculine bravado.

Resignation Speech of Preston Brooks, 14 July 1856[44]

MR. SPEAKER: Until this moment I have felt that there was a propriety in my remaining silent, and in trusting my defense to friends who are abler and more learned than myself. I have heretofore felt that other and higher interests than any which affect me personally were involved in the proceedings of this case. The interests of my constituents, of this House, and of all, indeed, who are concerned in the Constitution itself, in my view, have been intimately and inseparably complicated. . . . I have been content, therefore, to meet personally and in silence all the consequences of these proceedings.

Some time since a Senator from Massachusetts allowed himself, in an elaborately prepared speech, to offer a gross insult to my State, and to a venerable friend, who is my State representative, and who was absent at the time.

Not content with that, he published to the world, and circulated extensively, this uncalled for libel on my State and my blood. Whatever insults my State insults me. Her history and character have commanded my pious veneration; and in her defence I hope I shall always be prepared, humbly and modestly, to perform the duty of a son. I should have forfeited my own self-respect, and perhaps the good opinion of my countrymen, if I had failed to resent such an injury by calling the offender in question to a personal account. It was a personal affair, and in taking redress into my own hands I meant no disrespect to the Senate of the United States or to this House. Nor, sir, did I design insult or disrespect to the State of Massachusetts. I was aware of the personal responsibilities I incurred, and was willing to meet them. I knew, too, that I was amenable to the laws of the country, which afford the same protection to all, whether they be members of Congress or private citizens. I did not, and do not now believe, that I could be properly punished, not only in a court of law, but here also, at the pleasure and discretion of the House. I did not then, and do not now, believe that the spirit of American freemen would tolerate slander in high places, and permit a member of Congress to publish and circulate a libel on another, and then call upon either House to protect him against the personal responsibilities which he had thus incurred.

But if I had committed a breach of privilege, it was the privilege of the Senate, and not of this House, which was violated. I was answerable *there*, and not *here*. They had no right, as it seems to me, to prosecute me in these Halls, nor have you the right in law or under the Constitution, as I respectfully submit, to take jurisdiction over offences committed against them. The Constitution does not justify them in making such a request, nor this House in granting it. If, unhappily, the day should ever come when sectional or party feeling should run so high as to control all other considerations of public duty or justice, how easy will it be to use such precedents for the excuse of arbitrary power, in either House, to expel members of the minority who may have rendered themselves obnoxious to the prevailing spirit in the House to which they belong. . . .

So far as public interests or constitutional rights are involved, I have now exhausted my means of defence. I may, then, be allowed to take a more personal view of the question at issue. The further prosecution of this subject, in the shape it has now assumed, may not only involve my friends, but the House itself, in agitations which might be unhappy in their consequences to the country. If these consequences could be confined to myself individually, I think I am prepared and ready to meet them, here or elsewhere; and when I use this language I mean what I say. But others must not suffer for me. I have felt more on account of my two friends who have been implicated, than for myself. . . .

Sir, I cannot, on my own account, assume the responsibility, in the face of the American people, of commencing a line of conduct which in my heart of hearts I believe would result in subverting the foundations of this Government, and in drenching this Hall in blood. No act of mine, and on my personal account, shall inaugurate revolution; but when you, Mr. Speaker, return to your own home, and hear the people of the great North—and they are a great people—speak of me as a bad man, you will do me the justice to say that a blow struck by me at this time would be followed by revolution and this I know. . . . [Applause and hisses in the gallery.]

At the same time, Mr. Speaker, I am not willing to see the Constitution wounded through me; nor will I submit voluntarily to a wrong if I can avoid it. I will not voluntarily give my name to countenance parliamentary misrule or constitutional aggression. If I am to be tried again for the matter now before us, I will choose my own tribunal. I will appeal from this House to my own constituents. If an expression of public opinion is to be invoked in my case, let my constituents and my fellow-citizens pronounce upon it. From that verdict I will not appeal. The temper of the times is not favorable for a calm and dispassionate judgment of the case; and if, by any act of mine, I can save the majority of this House from the consequences of a rash decision, the time may come when the good men who are pursuing me—and I believe there are such in the Opposition—will admit that I deserve their thanks for the deed. The ax that is uplifted to strike me may fall upon others, and fall upon them after they have parted with the shield of the Constitution to protect them.

For myself I have only to say that, if I cannot preserve my self-respect and constitutional rights, together with a seat in this body, I must renounce the last rather than the former.

I have no desire, sir, to continue an argument which my friends have exhausted. The determination of the majority is fixed, and it is in vain to resist it. I will make no appeal to a packed jury, but I protest against its inconsistencies and its usurpations. . . .

And in whose behalf is this extraordinary stretch of constitutional power invoked? Sir, I do not intend to violate any rule of this House, or of parliamentary courtesy, but it cannot be denied that he is, par excellence, the representative of a sovereignty which is at this instant in open statutory rebellion—not to a simple rule of a single House, but to the Constitution and laws of the United States of America. Massachusetts sits in judgment upon me without hearing, and presents me for a breach of privilege! Sir, is it not strange that it did not occur to that sage Legislature, that its demands upon the Congress of the United States, relative to a member, was a greater breach of privilege in them than that complained of the member himself? What right, sir, has the Legislature of Massachusetts to make any demands upon this House? She has not the right of even instructing the most insignificant member from the State, and has, by her resolutions, but given additional proof that she neither comprehends the theory of our Government nor is loyal to its authority. I have said, sir, that, if I have committed a breach of privilege, it was the privilege of the Senate. If I have in any particular violated the privileges or proprieties of this House, I am unconscious of it, and I challenge every member to specify a single disorderly or improper act. In my intercourse with its members I have endeavored to preserve a civil and respectful deportment; I have rendered prompt and implicit obedience to its constituted authorities; and I can truly say that which many who have recorded their votes against me cannot—and that is, that never once, in the three years that I have held a seat on this floor, have I been declared out of order. If before the transaction for which a majority have declared me to be deserving expulsion, I have offended any officer or member, or have been unkind even to employee, I regret and am ignorant of it.

And yet, sir, the vote which has just taken transmits me to posterity as a man unworthy, in the judgment of a majority of my peers, of a seat in this Hall. And for what? The member from New Jersey, [MR. PENNINGTON][45]—the prosecuting member—the thumb-paper member, [laughter]—the Falstaffian member, who, like his prototype, was born about four o'clock in the morning, and if he has not the bald head, is graced with the corporeal rotundity [great laughter] of his predecessor upon his advent into this sublunary world—he says it was for making a "murderous" assault with a "bludgeon;" and he, forsooth, would have this House and the country believe, with an intent to kill. . . . If I desired to kill the Senator, why did not I do it? You all admit that I had him in my power. Let me tell the member from New Jersey that it was expressly to avoid taking life that I used an ordinary cane, presented to me by a friend in Baltimore, nearly three months before its application to the "bare head" of the Massachusetts Senator. I went to work very deliberately, as I am charged and this is admitted and speculated somewhat as to whether I should employ a horsewhip or a cowhide; but knowing that the Senator was my superior in strength, it occurred to me that he might wrest it from my hand, and then—for I never attempt anything I do not perform—I might have been compelled to do that which I would have regretted the balance of my natural life. . . .

For this act, which the Senate, with a solitary exception of the distinguished gentlemen from Georgia, [MR. TOOMBS,] have pronounced me guilty of a breach of its privileges—for this act I am complained of by that body to this House. Your committee have declared, and this House has now concurred in the opinion, that my offense is to the Senate, and that no rule or order of this body have I violated.

Now, sir, let me ask why the Senate did not protect its own rights? The argument has been made here, that *ex necessitate*[46] this House must have the power to protect itself. If that principle be true in its application here, why has not the Senate the same powers of protection? But what right has this House to punish me for offenses committed out of its presence? Again, sir, I challenge comparison with any member, aged or young, pious or not, as to the propriety of my demeanor as a gentleman and a member. They tell me that my responsibility to this House is because of the general responsibility which attaches to every member. How far does your authority extend? Across the Potomac? To my own home? Why, sir, if I go to my home, and find that one of my slaves has behaved badly in my absence, and I direct him to be flogged, I may be charged with—to use the language which is familiar here "crime the blackest and most heinous;" and when I come back—and come back I will—may be punished myself for inflicting a chastisement which, by the common law and the constitutional laws of my country, I have the right to inflict upon my slave, who is my property. Where do you stop in this question of authority of the House over its members? As we understand it, there is sense in this authority controlling a member while the House is in session and restraining him from disturbing or embarrassing its proceedings. If the Government was constitutionally administered, every citizen would have a direct interest in this much. But if your authority goes into the Senate Chamber, and even when the Senate is not in session, why should it not go into the ante-rooms and down the steps of the Capitol? Why not pursue me into the Avenue—into the steamboat—to my plantation? I take the gentlemen who have labored for my expulsion on their own declaration. They are committed to it, and they cannot now evade it. They say that my responsibility is not because of any offense committed in the presence of or to this House, but because of the general and necessary authority which the House has over its members. Now, it seems to me that, if my responsibility to this House for an offense committed elsewhere is because of my membership, it is a logical conclusion, that my responsibility ceases when that relation is dissolved. Whether or not the authority of the Senate reaches me after my relations to this House have terminated, it is not for me now to inquire; but, in justice to myself, I take occasion to say to the country, that if the Senate take that view, I shall recognize its authority. Now, sir, let me inform the honorable members who have been pursuing me so fiercely, that my present attitude was long since foreseen, and that I am altogether prepared for any of its emergencies. I knew with whom I had to deal, and my resignation has been for more than ten days in the hands of the Governor of South Carolina, to take effect the very instant that I announce my resignation upon this floor. But, before I make the announcement, I desire to say a word or two in reference to what has been said of me in debate and elsewhere. I saw in some of the New York papers that a certain feminine gentleman from that State [MR. MORGAN] had applied to me the term "villain." Well, that was not a word "spoken in debate," and I only allude to it to advertise the indignant gentleman that I have seen the word and know that it was spoken in New York, and not here in debate. He need not be much alarmed; and, if he will "hold still" when I get hold of him I'll not hurt him much; and this is all that I can say about that matter here. . . .

I now desire the attention of my *quondam* friend from Massachusetts, [MR. COMINS.]. . . .[47] From his place in this House—in his representative character, and at the time armed to the teeth, and not with a rifle hypocritically and cowardly disguised as a walking cane, and carried in the hand of a poltroon and a puppy, but with the genuine articles—he quoted the language and endorsed the sentiment of Chevalier Webb, of poor Jonathan Gilley notoriety, as follows:

"looking at it solely as an insult to the country, a trampling upon the Constitution, and an outrage upon the sanctity of the Senate Chamber, it was an outrage which merited death upon the spot from any patriot present who was in a position to inflict the punishment."

Now, sir, I say to that gentleman that no man has the right to wear arms who does not dare to use them. In my country, the cock that crows and won't fight is despised by the hens, and even by the pullets, who know a thing or two instinctively. [Great laughter.] His chivalric spurs dwindle before the charges of the valorous gout, and his place is—out of sight. I feel, sir, that "the blood more stirs more to hunt the lion then to chase the hare;" but if my *quondam* friend has any ambition, under the directions of the Chevalier Webb, to play the "*patriot*," let him or *le preux* chevalier,[48] separately or together, or backed by the whole Black Republican crew, come take the life which they say is forfeited.

Now, Mr. Speaker, I have nearly finished what I intended to say. If my opponents, who have pursued me with unparalleled bitterness, are satisfied with the present condition of this affair, I am. I return my thanks to my friends, and especially to those who are from non-slave-owning States, who have magnanimously sustained me, and felt that it was a higher honor to themselves to be just in their judgment of a gentleman than to be a member of Congress for life. In taking my leave, I feel that it is proper that I should say that I believe that some of the votes that have been cast against me have been extorted by an outside pressure at home, and that their votes do not express the feelings or opinions of the members who gave them.

To such of these as have given their votes and made their speeches on the constitutional principles involved, and without indulging in personal vilification, I owe my respect. But, sir, they have written me down upon the history of the country as worthy of expulsion, and in no unkindness I must tell them that for all future time my self-respect requires that I shall pass them as strangers. And now, Mr. Speaker, I announce to you and to this House, that I am no longer a member of the Thirty-Fourth Congress.

[Mr. Brooks then walked out of the House of Representatives.]

NOTES

1. An overview of events in Kansas can be found in David M. Potter, *The Impending Crisis, 1848–1861* (New York, Harper & Row Publishers, 1976), 199–224, and Freehling, *Road to Disunion*, 536–565. Andrew Reeder was a native of Pennsylvania who was appointed territorial governor by President Pierce. He remained in office until removed by Pierce in mid-1855.

2. Sumner's attentions in the months before the speech are described in Donald, *Charles Sumner*, I, 278–281, and Michael D. Pierson, " 'All Southern Society Is Assailed by the Foulest Charges:' Charles Sumner's 'The Crime Against Kansas' and the 'Escalation of Republican Anti-slavery Rhetoric,' " *New England Quarterly* (December 1995), 531–557; and Pierce, *Memoir*, III, 425–440.

3. "Annual Message of the President," *Congressional Globe*, 34th Congress, 1st Session, Appendix, 4–6.

4. Charles Sumner to Salmon P. Chase, 26 February 1856, in Palmer, ed., *Selected Letters*, I, 447.

5. Charles Sumner to Gerrit Smith, 18 March 1856, *Ibid.*, 453.

6. On the widespread familiarity with these and related texts see Carl J. Richard, *The Founders and the Classics* (Cambridge, Mass: Belknap Press, 1995). The intellectual origins of the speech are best described in Pierson, "All Southern Society Is Assailed," and Donald, *Charles Sumner*, I, 282.

7. See speeches by Wilson (18 February), John P. Hale (28 February), Lyman Trumbull (14 March), Jacob Collamer (3 April), and Henry Seward (9 April) in *Congressional Globe*, 34th Congress, 1st Session, Appendix, pp. 89–407. Charles Sumner to Salmon P. Chase, 15 May 1856, in Palmer, ed., *Selected Letters*, I, 456.

8. The scene is eloquently described in Kevin Baker, "Capitol Punishment: When Mudslinging in Congress led to Actual Bloodshed" *American Heritage* (September 1999). Baker writes that the thermometer was over 90 degrees. Contemporary records show highs of 77 degrees Fahrenheit on Monday and 85 degrees the following day, with extremely high humidity both days. See National Oceanic and Atmospheric Administration, "Register of Meteorological Observations, District of Columbia," May 1856.

9. See, for example, his "True Grandeur of Nations" speech, earlier.

10. Text from U.S. House of Representatives, 34th Congress, 1st Session, "House Select Committee Report on the Assault upon Sen. Sumner," House Report 182, Appendix.

Classical translations derived from Gregory Crane, ed., "Perseus Digital Library" <http://www.perseus.tufts.edu/>.

11. "but something compounded of all these strifes, and was in itself more than war." From Florus, *Epitome*, II, 13.

12. "He is gone, he has departed, he has disappeared, he has rushed out." Cicero, *Second Oration Against Catiline*.

13. Shakespeare, *Macbeth*, Act III, Scene 1.

14. The St. Bartholomew's Day Massacre of 1572 was one of the most bloody moments of the French Wars of Religion. Thousands of Protestants were killed by their Catholic enemies, who justified their acts as a religious purification of the French state.

15. Ovid, *Metamorphoses*, Book 1 (tr. Garth and Dryden). The passage describes the plea of the nymph Daphne to be saved from the god Apollo, who has fallen in love with her ("aspiring to her bed," according to Ovid) and is chasing her through the wilderness. Her wish is granted and she is turned into a laurel tree.

16. Sumner's note: 3 *Elliot's Debates*, 107—Mr. Corbin.

17. For example, "the loose expectorations of his speech," and "he cannot open his mouth but out there flies a blunder."

18. Cicero, *First Oration Against Catiline*.

19. From James Russell Lowell's antislavery poem, "The Present Crisis," 1844.

20. Virgil, *Aeneid*. Book 6.

21. Sumner's note: Deut. 27:17.

22. Sumner's note: Ezekiel, 14:8

23. *Congressional Globe*, 34th Congress, 1st Session, 544 (20 May 1856).

24. *Ibid.*, 544–546.

25. *Ibid.*, 546–547.

26. *Ibid*, 547.

27. Letters in Brooks Family Papers, South Caroliniana Library.

28. Probably James Carroll, his brother-in-law.

29. Senator Henry Wilson of Massachusetts, who had been involved with a challenge to Brooks.

30. *Congressional Globe*, 34th Congress, 1st Session, 1347 (2 June 1856).

31. There were five committee members. Ohio Representative Lewis Davis Campbell (1811–1882), a former Whig elected to the 34th Congress on an American-Fusion ticket, would run as a Republican in the next election. Francis Elias Spinner (1802–1890) of Herkimer County, New York, was nominally a Democrat but would also run as a Republican in the next election. Alexander Cumming McWhorter Pennington (1810–1867) was a Whig Congressman from Newark, New Jersey. This was his final term. Georgia Rep. Howell Cobb was a Democrat and former Speaker who would become President Buchanan's Treasury Secretary and an active leader in the Immediatist secession movement. Alfred Greenwood (1811–1889), of Bentonville, Arkansas, was a Democrat.

32. "Alleged Assault on Senator Sumner," 34th Congress, 1st Session, House Report 182, pp. 23–27.

33. Laurence M. Keitt (1824–1864), Democratic Representative from Orangeburg, South Carolina.

34. "Alleged Assault on Senator Sumner," 57–58.
35. Henry A. Edmundson (1814–1890), was the Democratic Representative from Salem, Virginia, from 1849 to 1861.
36. *Ibid.*, 58–63.
37. *Congressional Globe*, 34th Congress, 1st Session, Appendix, 625–635 (14 July 1856).
38. Henry Ward Beecher was son of the noted American evangelist Lyman Beecher and brother of Harriet Beecher Stowe. He was the most prominent antislavery religious leader in the North, and frequently the target of negative commentary by Southern editorialists and theologians. Butler refers in this passage to a speech given by Beecher at the large Sumner indignation rally held in New York City a few days after the caning. The rally and Beecher's remarks were reported in the New York *Tribune*, 31 May 1856.
39. Theodore Parker was one of the leading Unitarian pastors in Massachusetts, an active abolitionist, and one of Sumner's most regular correspondents. The charge that Parker prodded Sumner into giving the speech is consistent with Butler's general view that Sumner was an otherwise sensitive, refined, and intelligent man who had been corrupted by abolitionism. It may be an artifact of Butler's earlier friendship with Sumner that he refused to accept that the Massachusetts Senator's antislavery passions were a genuine part of his character and personality.
40. *Congressional Globe*, 34th Congress, 1st Session, Appendix, 1279 (23 May 1856).
41. See, for example, Senator James Mason's response to petitions from the Massachusetts clergy in part one.
42. The complete text of the speech can be found in Sumner, ed., *Works of Sumner*, vol. V, 305.
43. For details on Jesse Bright see Kenneth M. Stampp, *Indiana Politics During the Civil War* (Bloomington: Indiana University Press, 1949), esp. 15–16, 97–98. The committee process is detailed in Donald, *Charles Sumner*, Part One, 298–299; and Pierce, ed., *Memoir*, III, 476–492. James Pearce and Henry Geyer were Whigs; Phillip Allen, Henry Dodge, and Lewis Cass were Democrats.
44. *Congressional Globe*, 34th Congress, 1st Session, Appendix, 831 (14 July 1856).
45. See part one.
46. From necessity, perforce.
47. Linus Bacon Comins (1817–1892) Know-Nothing/Republican Congressman from Roxbury, Massachusetts.
48. "The valiant knight." A phrase used to describe someone of exceptional virtue, courage, and social dignity. Brooks used the term sarcastically.

3
Coming to Terms with the Caning

Editorial Reactions

M ost people learned of the Sumner incident from their local newspapers. Their perceptions were guided by the structure of the newspaper industry in the mid-nineteenth century. By the 1850s, growing literacy and fascination with politics had produced a nation of newspaper readers. In the previous two decades publishers had slashed prices and multiplied production through steam presses and cheaper paper manufacturing techniques. Meanwhile, the creation of a national telegraph network by the early 1850s had allowed news information to be distributed in hours rather than weeks. Daily papers in New York and other major cities began reporting details of the Sumner assault less than a day after it occurred. Competition was vigorous. The largest cities had half a dozen or more major papers, and a surprisingly large number of small towns in the rest of the country had at least two rival weekly presses. Then as now, publishers recognized the value of controversy in boosting circulation. The drama of the Sumner incident gave editors an opportunity to rally their readers, attack the errors of their opponents, and illustrate how the American republic itself had been endangered by the recklessness of either Sumner or Brooks. Perceptions of the incident were guided by the fact that most antebellum newspapers were "party organs," associated with, and usually subsidized by, political organizations. Editors such as Horace Greeley of the New York *Tribune* and Thurlow Weed of the Albany, New York, *Evening Journal* exercised as much power over Republican party politics as did its senators and congressmen; the editors of papers such as the Boston *Post*, Detroit *Free Press* and New Hampshire *Patriot* were equally important to the Democracy. Because circulation and elections were both local, however, editors normally framed these party controversies in light of local concerns and local enemies, even when the issues were national.[1]

The Sumner incident shifted this pattern. Because its protagonists belonged to different regions, editors had more than normal difficulty recasting the events in local terms. Any editor who criticized the personal behavior of Brooks could scarcely avoid raising the issue of Southern character in general; likewise for those who attacked Sumner. These indictments of regional character in turn provoked defenses from editors in the other part of the country. The resulting Sumner editorials were unusually sectional. Yet editors could not entirely forsake their party obligations. Since Sumner was a Republican and Brooks was a Democrat, reactions also carried partisan overtones. If nothing else, rivals could accuse each other of stirring up the event for purely partisan advantage. Party and section thus intersected in unusual ways. With four national party organizations (Democrats, Whigs, Republicans, and Know-Nothings), and several geographic regions, the range of reactions became quite complex.

HOME TOWN RESPONSES: BOSTON

This range of reactions was found even in Sumner's hometown of Boston. While no paper openly defended the caning, opinion on Sumner's speech split along party lines. The Boston *Atlas*'s response was typical of Republican editorials across the country. It defended Sumner's speech as no worse than any made against Sumner by his opponents. As Sumner had done in the congressional debates the editors invoked the history of the American Revolution and other historic cases of civil disobedience as a justification for strong language. The paper also raised standard Republican party arguments about the existence of a "slave power conspiracy" to extend slavery nationwide. Their implication was that even Bostonians were no longer safe from the violence and corruption of the slave regime. The *Atlas*'s assertion that an unbridgeable cultural divide existed between the North and South would be closely echoed by the responses to the incident by papers in the South.

The Assault on Mr. Sumner

Boston *Atlas,* 23 May 1856

The outrage in the Senate, on Thursday last is without a parallel in the legislative history of the country. Nothing has heretofore seemed so bold, so bad, so alarming. There have been affrays, more or less serious, in the House, for the House is a popular, and therefore, a tumultuous body; there have been rencounters [sic] in the streets, for the streets are arenas in which any assassin may display his prowess; but never before has the sanctity of the Senate Chamber been violated; never before has an intruder ventured to carry into those privileged precincts his private hostilities; never before has a Senator been struck down in his seat, and stretched, by the hand of a lawless bully, prostrate, bleeding, and insensible upon the floor. The wrong is full of public importance; and we almost forget the private injury of Mr. Sumner in the broad temerity of the insult which has been offered to the country, to Massachusetts, to the Senate. This first act of violence may pass into a precedent; what a single creature has done today, a hundred, equally barbarous, may attempt tomorrow; until a band of alien censors may crowd the galleries, and the lobbies, and even the floor of the Senate, and by the persuasive arguments of the bludgeon, the bowie knife, and the revolver, effectually refute and silence any member who may dare to utter, with some thing of force and freedom, his personal convictions. The privileges which we have fondly supposed were conferred with the Senatorial dignity; the right to characterize public measures and public men, with no responsibility, save to God and to conscience; the freedom of debate, without which its forms are a mere mockery—these will all disappear; and in their place we shall have the government of a self-constituted and revolutionary tribunal, overawing the Senate, as the Jacobins of Paris overawed the National Assembly of France, as the soldiers of Cromwell intimidated the Parliament of Great Britain. Shall we have, did we say? We have it already. There is freedom of speech in Washington, but it is only for the champions of slavery. There is freedom of the press, but only of the press which extenuates or defends political wrongs. Twice already the South, failed in the arguments of reason, has resorted to the argument of folly. Driven from every position, constantly refuted in its reasoning, met and repulsed when it has resorted to invective, by an invective more vigorous than its own, at first astonished and then crazed by the changing and bolder tone of Northern man, the South has taken to expedients with which long use has made it familiar, and in which years of daily practice have given it a nefarious skill. Thank God, we know little of these resources in New England! We have our differences, but they are differences controlled by decency. We have our controversies, but we do not permit their warmth to betray us into brutality; we do not think it necessary to shoot, to slash, or to stun the man with whom we may differ upon political points. The controversial ethics of the South are of another character, and they find their most repulsive illustration in the event of Thursday.

The barbarian who assaulted Mr. Sumner, and who sought in the head of his bludgeon for an argument which he could not find in his own, complained that South Carolina have been insulted by the Senator from Massachusetts, and that his venerable uncle had been spoken of in disrespectful terms! If every State, the public policy of which is assailed in the Senate, had been entitled to send to Washington a physical champion, we should long ago have despatched thither our brauniest athlete. If every nephew, whose uncle provokes criticism by public acts, is to rush into the Senate, the champion of his kinsman, we shall have a nepotism established quite unauthorized by the Constitution! The South complains of hard words, of plain speech, of licentious language! Have its members then been accustomed to bridle their tongues, to control their tempers, to moderate their ire, to abstain from personalities? What indeed have we had from that quarter, save one long stream of vituperation, one endless rain of fish-wife rhetoric, one continuous blast of feverish denunciation and passionate threat? Let the world judge between us. We have borne and forborne. We have been patient until patience has become ignominious. There are wrongs which no man of spirit will suffer tamely; there are topics which it is impossible to discuss with coldness; there are injuries which must lend fire to language, and arouse the temper of the most stolid. Mr. Sumner's speech is before the country and it is for the country to decide whether it does or does not justify the violence with which it has been met. Our Senator comments freely upon the character of the Kansas bill, upon the apologies which have been made for it, in Congress, upon the readiness of the Administration to promote the schemes of its supporters, upon the unparalleled injuries which have been inflicted upon the unfortunate people of Kansas. Others have spoken upon the same topics with equal plainness, although not perhaps with equal ability. Mr. Sumner is singularly well sustained in all his positions, in his opinions of the bill, and in his estimate of Douglas and Butler, by the mind and heart, not only of his constituents, but of the whole North. The time had come for plain and unmistakable language, and it has been uttered. There are those who profess to believe that Northern rhetoric should always be emasculated, and that Northern members should always take care to speak humbly and with "bated breath." They complain with nervous fastidiousness that Mr. Sumner was provoking. So were Mr. Burke and Mr. Sheridan, when in immoderate language they exposed the wrongs of India and the crimes of Hastings; so was Patrick Henry, when he plead against the parsons; so was Tristram Burges, when he silenced Randolph of Roanoke; so was Mr. Webster, when, in the most remarkable oration of modern times, he launched the lightning of his overwhelming invective, while every fibre of his great frame was full of indignation and reproach. Smooth speeches will answer for smooth times; but there is a species of oratory, classic since the days of Demosthenes, employed without a scruple upon fit occasions, in all deliberative assemblies, perfectly well recognized, and sometimes absolutely necessary. Who will say that Kansas, and Atchison, and Douglas together, were not enough to inspire and justify a new Philippic?

But we care not what Mr. Sumner said, nor in what behalf he was pleading. We know him only as the Senator of Massachusetts; we remember only that the commonwealth has been outraged. Had the Senator of any other State been subjected to a like indignity, we might have found words in which to express our abhorrence of the crime; but now we can only say, that every constituent of Mr. Sumner ought to feel that the injury is his own, and that it is for him to expect redress. A high-minded Senate would vindicate its trampled dignity; a respectable House of Representatives would drive the wrong-doer from its benches; in a society unpolluted by barbarism, the assaulter of an unarmed man, would find himself the object of general contempt. We can hardly hope that such a retribution will visit the offender; but Massachusetts, in other and better times, would have had a right confidently to anticipate the expulsion of Preston Brooks from the House of Representatives. We leave it to others to decide how far it may be fit and proper for her officially to express her sense of this indignity. For our own part, we think she can rely upon the generosity and the justice of her sister states, that an outrage so indefensible will meet with a fitting rebuke from the people, if not from the representatives of the people. And if in this age of civilization, brute force is to control the government of the country, striking down our senators, silencing debate, and leaving us only the name of Freedom, there are remedies with which Massachusetts has found it necessary to meet similar exigencies in the past, which she will not hesitate to employ in the future.

Know-Nothing party responses in Massachusetts were conditioned by the long rivalry between Sumner and the state's Know-Nothing governor Henry J. Gardner. Since both parties appealed to essentially the same ex-Whig, Protestant and anti-slavery constituency, the party's papers had to condemn Brooks without drawing too much attention to Sumner himself. The reaction of the Boston *Bee*, which was the chief Know-Nothing paper in the city, was typical for its emphasis on Brooks and lack of commentary on either Sumner or his speech.

Attack on Mr. Sumner

Boston *Bee*, 23 May 1856
—By referring to our telegraphic column it will be seen that Hon Chas. Sumner, M. C., of this city, was ferociously and brutally assaulted in the National Senate Chamber yesterday, by a cowardly scoundrel named Brooks. An outrage so gross and villainous was never before committed within the walls of the Capitol. It is rendered additionally infamous and barbaric from the fact that fiendish bystanders prevented persons who were disposed from interfering. This bully Brooks who has disgraced the name of man, ought to be branded as a villain of the blackest dye, and then mercilessly kicked from one end of the continent to the other. The black mark of Cain will stand out on his brow to the last moment of his disgraced life.

There were still remnants of the old Whig party in Boston, represented in print by the Boston *Courier*. These "Old Line" Whigs had opposed Sumner during his entire public career, and the Whig response reflects this longstanding animosity. The paper's chief audience consisted of conservatives who were unmoved by threats of a "slave power" conspiracy. They tended to blame the abolitionists for aggressively seeking to overturn the social order and thus creating the sectional crisis. In contrast to the *Atlas* and other Republican papers, the *Courier*'s response seems to depict Brooks's behavior more as a case of personal misconduct than as the behavior characteristic of the entire South. The *Courier*'s editorial was widely reprinted in Southern newspapers as evidence of Northern opinion against Sumner and his speech.

Attack on Mr. Sumner

Boston *Courier*, 23 May 1856
The telegraph gives us an account of an unmanly personal attack by a Representative of South Carolina upon Senator Sumner of Massachusetts, while our Senator was sitting at his desk, after the body to which he was attached had adjourned. We do not know that we have the whole story of the incident, but the fact as mentioned is, that Mr. Sumner was writing at his desk, after the closing of the Senate

session, and was brutally assaulted by a South Carolina member of the House. There is no excuse for brutalism—there is no excuse for the man who assaults another at disadvantage anywhere, and the Senators of the United States will without doubt take care of their privileges and prerogatives.

But we have a word to say about the manner in which this Kansas debate has been carried on in the Senate. Members have shifted the time of the pronouncement of their speeches as it has suited their convenience. The speech of Mr. Sumner was exceedingly insulting towards some gentlemen who sit with him upon the Senate floor. It was not in consonance with the sort of arguments which people expect to hear from U.S. Senators upon a grave question. They do not want flowery adjectives or far-fetched allusions to, or illustrations from Greece and Rome, to give them an opinion as to how they shall act with regard to a practical question which is now before them. When Mr. Sumner compares Senator Butler of South Carolina and Senator Douglas of Illinois to Don Quixote and Sancho Panza, assimilating one to the character of a crazy man and the other to that of a fool, he takes a ground which Massachusetts, in her dignity and her ability, never presented before. In the great debate between Webster and Hayne, in which Massachusetts came out best, beyond all comparison, no such allusions were made. The Senator of Massachusetts of that day descended to no low blackguardism. In the strength of his faith and in the force of his ability he presented Massachusetts before the Senate of the United States in such a manner that men bowed down and worshipped her. "There," said he, "is Boston and Concord, and Lexington and Bunker Hill." "I employ no scavengers," said he again, in answer to the taunts of the Senator from South Carolina, who had produced against him the rakings and scrapings of all which political venom could bring out from the cesspool of party politics. Mr. Webster came out of that controversy with South Carolina with the admiration of every man in the country. The time has changed—a different man takes his place, with only the memory of an insulting speech and a broken head.

We offer no palliation for the brutal assault which was made upon Mr. Sumner by a Representative from South Carolina. It is a well understood axiom and rule of the United States Congress, that no member shall be allowed to be held responsible for words spoken in debate. The member from South Carolina transgressed every rule of honor which should animate or restrain one gentleman in his connections with another, in his ruffian assault upon Mr. Sumner. There is no chivalry in a brute. There is no manliness in a scoundrel. If Mr. Brooks is a nephew to Senator Butler, as it is said that he is, the Senator has only cause to regret that his blood runs through such ignoble veins.

The Boston *Post* was the chief Democratic paper in the city. It had a long history of attacking Sumner, and its constituency had been even more hostile than the Old Line Whigs to the antislavery movement. Nor did the paper have any particular obligations to Preston Brooks, who although a Democrat, had no constituency in the North. The paper was thus free to condemn both men for their fanaticism and violence. The *Post*, in common with many papers in the South, raised questions about the severity of Sumner's wounds and accused the Republicans of scheming to exaggerate the incident for partisan purposes.

Boston *Post,* 24 May 1856
The despatches from Washington yesterday afternoon were that "Mr. Sumner was better, and would be able to occupy his seat in a day or two." This shows that his wounds could not have been so very dangerous as has been represented. The hollow gutta percha cane which was broken over his head was evidently not a weapon to do murder with. It appears that the reason why Mr. Brooks took a seat in the senate chamber, and waited, was because there were several ladies present, whose nerves he did not wish to shock. One account says the only person who knew beforehand of the attack was Mr. Edmundson, a member from Virginia, and that Mr. Crittenden caught Mr. Brooks around the body and arms. Mr. Wilson, who it is said carries deadly weapons, rushed in after the fracas was over, and found that Mr. Sumner had been carried to the vice-President's room. He then helped to put his colleague into a carriage, and went with him to his lodgings.

The affair was disgraceful and we lament and condemn it; and not even the slander of an absent and aged relative or libel on his native state, affords sufficient apology to the assaulter. But surely the bitter tirade of personality, the wanton vituperation of high personal character, the absolute vulgarity of language, poured forth for two days by Charles Sumner ought not to be countenanced by those who would respect the dignity of the senate or the honor of the country.

The free soil politicians are prompt in their endeavors to make party capital out of this affair. It will be seen under our local head that there was a public meeting in this city on the subject last evening, composed, in part at least, of those who figured when Mr. Batchhelder[2] was killed while assisting in the defence of that temple of justice, the court house in this city, when assailed by an infuriate mob.

HOME TOWN RESPONSES: SOUTH CAROLINA

Reactions in South Carolina were decidedly sectional. The state was unique even in the South for the absence of a vigorous two party political system. Single party dominance was a legacy of John C. Calhoun, who had insisted upon local unity as the best means for defending the state against the abolitionists and "centralizers" who lurked beyond its borders.[3] Consequently, reactions to the incident in South Carolina were crafted with less concern for party rivalries within the state and more concern to the implications of the caning for the South as a whole. None of the state's papers defended Sumner, and only a handful questioned even the location Brooks had chosen for the attack. The Laurensville *Herald,* was an ardent Southern rights paper published in the rural western piedmont region of Brooks's district. The *Herald's* first Sumner editorial appears next. Its editor shared the belief expressed by many Republicans in the North that the incident was a watershed in the sectional conflict. His expectation that the incident would cause antislavery Northerners to moderate their opinions seems a little surprising given the number of anti-Brooks editorials and public meetings that had occurred in the North in the week before this piece was published; it is possible that full reporting of the Northern reaction had not reached Laurensville by May 30.

The Washington Difficulty

Laurensville, South Carolina, *Herald*, 30 May 1856

In consequence of the communications of our friends, the exciting news from Kansas, and the necessity of publishing the most authentic account of the difficulty between our noble Representative, Hon P. S. Brooks, and the notorious Charles Sumner, we find ourself so short of space in our columns, that we can only give our most hearty endorsement of the conduct of Mr. Brooks, and call upon his constituents in Laurens District to meet here on Monday to give him a testimonial of their determination to sustain him. Our Representatives have been heretofore quietly submitting to the vile calumnies and slanders that have of late years, at every opportunity, been heaped upon the South by our enemies, and we have often wondered at the calmness and discretion of Southern members, under such circumstances; but there is a point when forbearance ceases to be a virtue, and, from the following extract of Sumner's speech, which brought upon him the merited chastisement, it must be evident the fanatical fool had passed that boundary, and it was not in the nature of such a man as Preston S. Brooks to submit to it. Argument, reason, courtesy and conciliation had long since proved ineffectual to silence the wild calumniators.

The only means left untried has now been made use of by Mr. B, and we sincerely hope it will prove a salutary lesson to others who may have the temerity to provoke a like act.

The Edgefield *Advertiser* defended Brooks even more enthusiastically. The editor's glee that "an immense and greedy audience" saw the caning is striking. Presumably he hoped that these witnesses might start taking Southern rights more seriously. His praise for the caning incident indicates how far some Southern leaders were willing to go in defending the right of property in slaves. Paradoxically, despite publishing one of the most violently anti-Sumner editorials in the country the *Advertiser* retreated from sectionalism as war drew nearer. Alone among South Carolina newspapers it supported national Democratic candidate Stephen A. Douglas rather than Southern Rights candidate John C. Breckinridge in the 1860 presidential election.

Capt. Brooks' Castigation of Senator Sumner

Edgefield *Advertiser*, 28 May 1856.

"Hit him again."

Hon. P. S. Brooks took an admirable occasion the other day to give Mr. Senator Sumner, of Massachusetts, a handsome drubbing. As we learn the particulars, the affair was on this wise:

Mr. Sumner had just delivered himself of an elaborate abolition speech, which occupied the Senate a part of two successive days. The galleries were crowded during the time of its delivery with an immense and a greedy audience, made up in large part of Mr. Sumner's own abolition constituents, who had come on to hear their great man make his great speech. In the course of that speech, however, he "slung his slosh" so madly at large as to produce the denouement we now record.

Our Representative, Mr. Brooks, was among Mr. Senator Sumner's audience, on the second day; and it was on this day that Sumner emptied one of his vials of vile vituperation on the head of Senator Butler, who was then absent at home. As soon as the speech was done and the Senate had adjourned, Mr. Brooks advanced to Sumner and demanded some explanation or retraction of his abuse of Judge Butler; and upon Sumner's refusal to accede to the proposition, our member fell to work upon him with a cane he happened to have in hand at the moment. The beating is said by all the reporters to have been a thorough one. Some say he received fifty stripes; yet we very much doubt if the Captain cared to exceed the legal number of thirty-nine, usually applied to scamps. But the beauty and propriety of the proceeding consists, to no small extent, in the fact that it was accomplished while yet the galleries had not emptied themselves, and while many of Sumner's constituents were probably there to look upon the deed. For our own part, we feel that our Representative did exactly right; and we are sure his people will commend him highly for it. We have often heard of a word in good season, but this is *an act* in good season. By the way, the battle at Lawrence, Kansas, is said to have been fought only forty-eight hours before; and it may be that a passing breeze wafted the spirit of combat to the Capitol at Washington just in time for our member to catch it up and act out its promptings. Well, we have borne insult long enough, and now let the conflict come if it must.

VIOLENCE IN THE POLITICAL ARENA

One of the most aggressive Northern responses to the caning came from the Pittsburgh, Pennsylvania, *Gazette*, a zealously Republican paper. The *Gazette*'s editors viewed the incident as a significant turning point in the sectional conflict. They seemed enthusiastic that Northerners for the first time were refusing to cower under Southern threats. The paper's insistence that the leaders of the other section had descended into barbarism and therefore that the normal rules of civilized behavior should be suspended is strikingly similar to the statements in the South Carolina papers and to the comments by Virginia Senator James Mason that declared Sumner and his associates as not "possessing manhood in any form." The *Gazette*'s claim that even the Christian duty to "turn the other cheek" no longer applied is a further indication of how alienated Republicans had become from the "slave power." This dehumanization and de-Christianization of the opposition by both sides was one of the key factors that allowed armed conflict to erupt just five years later.

The Attack on Mr. Sumner

Pittsburgh, Pennsylvania, *Gazette*, 24 May 1856

The news of the cowardly attack on Mr. Sumner by a villainous South Carolinian, stirred up a deeper indignation among our citizens, yesterday, than we have ever before witnessed. It was an indignation that pervaded all classes and conditions of men. The assault was deliberately planned, being made in the presence and under the encouragement of a crowd of bullies, when Mr. Sumner was alone, unarmed and defenceless, and it was conducted so brutally—fifty blows being inflicted upon an unresisting victim, until the weapon of attack was used up, and not one hand raised among the bystanders to stay the fury of the perfidious wretch, that every feeling of human nature revolts at the exhibition. Barbarians and savages would not be guilty of such unmanliness; and even the vulgar blackguards who follow the business of bruisers and shoulder-hitters would have a far higher sense of fair play than was shown by these patterns of chivalry. A universal cry of "Shame!" would go up from the lips of the people, if, unfortunately, the people did not, in view of this and similar outrages, feel a bitter shamefacedness at their own degradation in having to submit to them.

It is time, now, to inaugurate a change. It can no longer be permitted that all the blows shall come from one side. If Southern men will resort to the fist to overawe and intimidate Northern men, blow must be given back for blow. Forbearance and kindly deportment are lost upon these Southern ruffians. It were as well to throw pearls before swine as turn one cheek to them when the other is smitten. Under the circumstances now prevailing, neither religion nor manhood requires submission to such outrages. Northern men must defend themselves; and if our present representatives will not fight, when attacked, let us find those who will. It is not enough, now, to have backbone; there must be strong right arms, and a determination to use them. The voters of the Free States, in vindication of their own manliness will, hereafter, in addition to inquiring of candidates, Will you vote so-and-so, have to enlarge the basis of interrogation, and demand an affirmative answer to the question, Will you fight? It has come to that, now, that Senators and Representatives cannot enjoy the right of free speech or free discussion, without being liable to brutal assaults; and they must, of necessity, arm themselves with sword-canes or revolvers. To think of enduring quietly such attacks as that upon MR. SUMNER, is craven and pusillanimous.— These cut-throat Southrons will never learn to respect Northern men until some one of their number has a rapier thrust through his ribs, or feels a bullet in his thorax. It is lamentable that such should be the case; but it is not in human nature to be trampled on.

The Charleston, South Carolina, *Mercury* was the most famous of the South's secessionist newspapers. Its columns were frequently quoted in other major newspapers as representing the extreme Southern Rights position on national issues. Even within South Carolina, however, it was a minority voice; each edition of the *Mercury* sold only about a fourth as many copies as did the relatively moderate Charleston *Courier*. As this editorial shows, its antagonism from the North had a long history, and its editor welcomed incidents such as the Sumner caning which would hasten separation between the North and South. Like the Pittsburgh *Gazette* it celebrated a definition of manhood that called for men to speak only those words they were willing to defend even to the point of fighting. Its implication that abolitionists had a "womanly" lack of courage was a sentiment widely shared in the South and another contributing factor in the movement to war.

The Right View of the Subject

Charleston, South Carolina, *Mercury*, 30 May 1856.
The Pittsburg *Gazette*, after indulging in the usual amount of howling and railing over Senator SUMNER'S recent castigation, comes at last to the following sensible view of the question. It sees that if aggression is to be the policy of the North, it is necessary to have the armed band, as well as the venomed tongue and malignant vote. We are surprised that the North has not opened its eyes to this fact long since. To suppose that war in Congress, and war in Kansas, could be successfully conducted to its issue by such champions as SUMNER in the one, and GREELEY and REEDER in the other, was a dream in which fanaticism alone could indulge, and which is likely to be dispelled by the recent developments. The South certainly has become generally convinced that it is by hard blows, and not by loud blustering and insulting denunciation, that the sectional quarrel is to be settled. We need not say that this has been our opinion for the last twenty years.

For the last year, the country has rung with the threats of Freesoil resistance in Kansas, and the Southern people have been told that if they ventured upon that territory, they would be welcomed with Sharpe's rifles and "bloody hands to hospitable graves." From the incessant and terrible noises made all through the North, we were almost led to believe that "death or victory," "liberty or death," would be the battle-cry of the Freesoil warriors in Kansas. But, mortifying to relate, while these shouts have been echoing through the press of the North, the men of Lawrence have been on their knees before Governor SHANNON, and the rampant correspondent of the Tribune, fleeing from that ill-fated city, like LOT'S wife from Sodom, turned, at a safe distance, to see only a cloud of smoke and dust rising over what he supposed to be its burning ruins. If he was not petrified on the spot, it was evident that it was the extremity of his fears that saved him from being converted into anything solid.

CHIVALRY AND DEGRADATION

Across the country, reactions to the incident shared a preoccupation with chivalry, cowardice, and degradation, though editors differed sharply over which of the two men had been most offensive and which standards of honor had been most grossly violated. Even in the South a number of papers portrayed the caning as a threat to conservative ethics of order and propriety. Its advocates drew upon a viewpoint long championed by the Whig party, an organization to which many editors had once belonged. These men condemned the event for undermining the stability and refinement Americans expected from their highest officials. Most importantly, the response by Brooks had been unchivalrous. Brooks had taken Sumner at a disadvantage, thereby undermining his claims of nobility. To these editors, Brooks's pretense of honor had become an excuse for violence and intimidation. The caning had given ammunition to the region's enemies. An example of this argument can be found in an editorial from the Louisville, Kentucky, *Journal.* This editorial was widely reprinted in Northern newspapers to show that not all Southerners supported the caning.

Louisville *Journal,* 28 May 1856
The assault of Brooks upon Sumner in the Senate Chamber has created a prodigious excitement throughout the North. The assault is deeply to be regretted, because in the first place it was a very great outrage in itself, and because in the second place it will, especially if not promptly and properly punished at Washington, greatly strengthen the anti-slavery and anti-Southern feeling in the Northern States and thus help the Black Republican party.

It may be said with truth that Sumner, in his speech against Butler, Douglas, and others, transcended the legitimate freedom of debate. He certainly did, but that was properly the Senate's business. It is monstrous that a member of the House of Representatives should beat a Senator upon the floor of the Senate for a speech made in the Senate and having no reference to the individual administering the punishment. Sumner's speech, violent and incendiary and disgraceful as it was, was certainly no worse in its personalities than the speeches of Douglas have habitually been; and then its personalities, shameful as they were, had at least the advantage of being expressed in a style of scholarship greatly in contrast with the slipshod billingsgate of the Illinois Senator.

We have no sympathy for Sumner. He has deported himself as a pestilent enemy of the peace and harmony of the country and no doubt deserved more punishment than he has received, yet every consideration of propriety and of the public good demands that Mr. Brooks shall be expelled from the House of Representatives. The Senate should deem his expulsion necessary to the maintenance of its dignity and its rights. And if the House should refuse to expel him, we think the Senate would be right in withdrawing from the members of the House the privileges they now enjoy upon the floor of the Senate.

We are not surprised to see that the people of South Carolina are holding meetings and passing resolutions in approbation of Mr. Brooks's conduct. They are a violent people, and we don't think they ever fail to approve an act of violence against what they hate—whether it be a man, a party, a law, or the Constitution of the United States. The U.S. Constitution ordains that a member of Congress shall not be called to account for words spoken in debate, and Mr. Brooks has sworn to support this very Constitution which he deliberately violated in the Capitol where the oath was taken, breaking his oath and violating the Constitution and perpetrating what looks like an act of gross cowardice, all at the same time, and yet the South Carolina Democracy resolve that for his conduct he is worthy of all praise. This only proves, that, bad as the representative may be, he is no worse than the State he represents.

We do not believe that Senator Butler approves the conduct of his nephew. Sumner's bitter attack upon Mr. Butler in that gentleman's absence was contemptible, and contempt would have been a very proper punishment to be meted out for it. The absurd and wicked resolutions which the South Carolina people are adopting will serve only to exasperate to a still greater degree the public sentiment of the North. But this is what the South Carolinians want. They rejoice in whatever seems likely to promote the dissolution of the Union. There were twice as many traitors in South Carolina in the days of the Revolution as in any other State in proportion to population, and we think that her soil as a general rule grows worse men now than it did then.

In Southern states with well-established two party systems, political leaders routinely accused their opposition of being "unsound" on the slavery issue. The Southern Whigs had been most successful in the established plantation districts and commercial cities of the region where the desire for order and predictability was strongest. They had delighted for years in charging the Democrats with recklessly inviting the attacks of Northern abolitionists. The Wilmington, North Carolina, *Herald*'s depiction of the assault by Brooks as an example of ill-mannered brawling and bullying reflected their disdain for a party whose main appeal was to the Southern back-country and Southern plain folk. The paper's reaction is simultaneously a claim for authentic rather than postured chivalry, a plea for a conservative rather than an aggressive defense of slavery, and a latent denunciation of the Democrats. Like the Louisville *Journal*, the *Herald* devoted more attention to Brooks than to Sumner.

Wilmington, North Carolina, *Herald*, 26 May 1856
The uppermost topic in the papers, North and South, now, is the recent chastisement of Senator Sumner, by Mr. Brooks, of South Carolina.—As was expected, the affair has been a perfect Godsend to the Abolitionists, and they evidently intend to make the most of it. In Massachusetts, especially, public opinion is at fever heat. The House of Representatives of that State have appointed a committee to report what action shall be taken in the matter. A large indignation meeting was held in Boston, another in Springfield, and we presume more will follow in quick succession. The affair has assumed a party aspect already. Freesoilism, languishing for an excitement, has received a sudden impetus, and Sumner will be glorified into the dignity of a persecuted patriot, if not a martyr in the cause of freedom.

What we have to say with regard to this affair shall be brief. We think Sumner deserved what he got, but we do not approve the conduct of Brooks. Sumner had not insulted him, and he was not called upon to resent an indignity offered to Senator Butler, even though the latter was his relative and absent. Again, he attacked Sumner under very reprehensible circumstances. He caned him in the Senate chamber, and took him, moreover, at an advantage—while sitting in his chair. The Senate Chamber is not the arena for exhibitions of this character. It is disgraceful that scenes of violence like these should be permitted to occur within it.—If Congress is to be levelled to a mere ring for bullying and fighting, we had best amend the Constitution and abolish the Congress. We should at least preserve more respectability at home and abroad.

Mr. Brooks should have sought a different time and place for his meeting with Sumner. But, to attack him in the Senate Chamber and chastise him, while the latter was unprepared and in a defenceless position, was unjustifiable. Granting that the provocation was sufficient, he has yet given a good handle for the Northern people to seize, in denunciation of his course, and deprived the South of the opportunity of justification.

FREEDOM OF SPEECH

The Sumner controversy was ultimately a debate over freedom of speech and its limits. As early as the supposed Denmark Vesey "conspiracy" of the 1820s where white Southerners claimed that slaves had been influenced to plan a revolt by congressional discussion of abolition, many political leaders had called for restrictions on debate. Forthright talk of abolition, they feared, would lead to a bloodbath in America such as had occurred during the Haitian revolution of the 1790s. From the 1830s forward these leaders had instigated a series of actions designed to prevent the "incitement" of slaves and the polarization of the nation over the slavery issue. These had included the seizure and burning of mail shipments alleged to contain abolitionist tracts, the passage of a "gag rule" banning the introduction of abolitionist petitions into the Federal Congress, and the lynching of several abolitionists, North and South, who had threatened to disturb the status quo.[4]

Each of these attempts at restriction had produced a backlash in support of free speech rights. As we have seen, Sumner's "Crime Against Kansas" speech belonged solidly to this tradition. For Republican editors the incident itself symbolically confirmed these warnings. The South, they argued, was determined not only to mistreat the slaves, but also take away the liberties of Northern whites. It was a contention with far broader appeal than the old abolitionist arguments about slavery's immorality *within* the South. The party's ability to convert the incident into an assault on basic rights gave them a significant edge over their Northern Know-Nothing rivals. The following editorial from the Albany *Evening Journal,* representing the William H. Seward wing of the Republican party, was a typical statement of their case.

The Ruffians in the Senate

Albany, New York, *Evening Journal,* 23 May 1856

South Carolina has its barbarians as well as ancient Gaul. The brutal soldiery of Brennus were the types of the ruffians of Slavery. Those first dishonored the Roman Senators with personal violence, and slaughtered them as they sat in their curule chairs. These have degraded the American Senate, and brutally applying force to repress freedom of debate upon the subject of Slavery, have murderously clubbed a Massachusetts Senator in his seat, till he was insensible. For the first time has the extreme discipline of the Plantation been introduced into the Senate of the United States. Is there not some Camilus to make it the last time, and to assure the dignity of that body, and the political freedom of the Nation?

No severity of language—no violence of debate,—could furnish any excuse for the assault of the ruffian Brooks upon Mr. Sumner. But in this case there is wanting altogether the usual apology of the provocation of unjustly severe and aggressive speech. Every man who has sat in the Senate Chamber and seen and heard Butler of South Carolina, during the discussion of any question touching Slavery, knows well that Mr. Sumner's picture of him in his great speech, is not exaggerated, but is toned down, and altogether moderate. The South Carolinian's manner, his speech, his appearance, excite in a Northern gentleman, mingled feelings of astonishment, anger, and disgust. Insolent, dictatorial and contemptuous—with the head of a half-breed and the voice and temper of an overseer—painfully discordant in his exhibition of young violence coursing through a trembling and bent form, and agitating whitened locks hanging over his maroon face as well as down his shoulders—the South Carolina Senator browbeats and flies at every opponent of Slavery Propagandism, and spits coarse abuse upon every measure of Freedom, and cracks his plantation whip at the greatest and best men in this nation. His customary demeanor in the American Senate, is the most humiliating spectacle in the city of Washington. The picture of him in Mr. Sumner's speech is but an outline sketch. A likeness would have excited astonishment in all, accustomed to think of Daniel Webster, William H. Seward, Silas Wright, John Bell, Lewis Cass, and Henry Clay in connection with this Senate of the United States.

But the assault upon Mr. Sumner was not on account of the injured vanity of the Southern Senator. It was the resentment of his speech. It was the answer to his argument against Slavery—an answer already fearfully common, and which threatens to be the *ultima ratio* of Southern logic throughout the Republic. The Editor of the *Tribune* was replied to with the rifle and the bowie-knife—the question of self-Government in the Western Territories the South proposes to debate with ball cartridges and bayonets. No. The logic of the Plantation, brute violence and might, has at last risen where it was inevitable it should rise to—the Senate of the United States. If we are not virtuous and firm, in the discharge of our duty to ourselves and the Republic, to strangle this serpent of Slavery Extension, it will fold us at every point in its grasp. State liberty can not long survive the extinguishment of Federal freedom. And is the Senate of the United States no longer free to the North?

Pro-Brooks editors responded by making a case for ordered liberty. Drawing on the political ideology of republicanism, they argued that a republic was only as healthy and virtuous as its citizenry. Not only had the abolitionists provoked slave insurrections, but through their beliefs and behavior they were attempting to destroy *every* natural social relationship in society. The Richmond *Enquirer* was at once a staunch defender of this traditional view and a firm believer that the national wing of the Democratic party was the best hope for preserving America. The editor's optimism about Northern political trends would be reversed in the incident's aftermath. This editorial was reprinted by several newspapers in both regions.

Liberty of Speech, of the Press, and Freedom of Religion

Richmond, Virginia, *Enquirer*, 3 June 1856

Liberty is only desirable so long as it is enjoyed without abuse. It is the highest evidence of the morality, piety, intelligence and general well-being of peoples and of individuals, that they require but little legal restraint. The continual enjoyment of national and individual liberty is the noblest of distinctions and greatest of blessings, because such continued enjoyment can only proceed from the habitual exercise of every virtue. But, whilst to such peoples and individuals, liberty is a good, it is an unmitigated evil to the vicious, who use their privileges to injure themselves, and to annoy and disturb society. Despotism of some sort is just as necessary for this latter class as for madmen, thieves and murderers.—The Northern Abolitionists do not let a day pass without showing to the world that they are as little fitted to be trusted with liberty as thieves with keys or children with firearms. Their daily abuse of liberty of speech and of the press, and of freedom of religion, are but the means which they habitually employ for greater mischief and crime. The disgusting proceedings of their men, women and negroes, in their infidel, agrarian and licentious conventions, the [illegible] and destructive doctrines emanating from their press, and their lecture rooms, and the unfeminine bearing of their women, would justify and require an immediate and despotic censorship, if it were possible to take away their liberties without invading those of other people. A community of Abolitionists could only be governed by a penitentiary system. They are as unfit for liberty as maniacs, criminals, or wild beasts. The worst aspect of their case, is, that they are endangering the liberties of the people. Just such conduct as theirs induced the despotism of Cromwell and the two Bonapartes, and of all other usurpers who have destroyed their country's liberty. All men prefer despotism to anarchy, the rule of a single man to the mad riot and misrule of infidels, criminals and agrarians.—These men complain that liberty of speech has been violated in the person of Mr. Sumner. This is but the beginning of the end. They will soon destroy all liberty of speech, if they employ it only to teach heresy, infidelity, licentiousness, and to stir up to deeds of violence. Better, far better, that man were without the gift of speech, than to use it as they do. Better that he could neither read or write, than have his head and heart perverted, by the foul and filthy stuff that oozes from the abolition press. Better, that his religion were prescribed by a priest and enforced by an inquisition, than that he should become an habitue of Greeley's philansteries, of Andrew's gorgeous saloons of Free Love, of Mormon dwellings, or of Oneida dens.[5] Better that the cut of his coat and the number of his buttons were fixed by statute and enforced by penalties, than that women should defy public opinion and parade the streets in unfeminine apparel. The liberties of America are safe so long as they are not abused. They are not worth preserving when abuse becomes general. If the noxious heresy of abolition and its kindred isms are not arrested; if a salutary reaction does not take place, ere long, even good men, religious men and patriots, would prefer the quiet of despotism, to the discord, licentiousness, the anarchy and the crime, which those men practice and invoke. Yet, we neither fear nor tremble for the future. These wretches are more noisy than numerous. The edifice of American liberty, the most glorious structure of freedom the world has ever seen, is not destined to be sapped and undermined by pismires, nor carried by the assaults of crazy lilliputians. These creatures will be soon driven from their places, and lashed into obscurity by an indignant people, whose confidence they have betrayed and abused.—All the elections at the North for the last twelve months, show that the storm is gathering that is to sweep these noxious insects from the hearts of men and the face of day.

Although the partisan papers of Richmond agreed on few other issues, they shared a revulsion for Sumner and his defenders. The Richmond *Whig* was unusual among Opposition papers for not using the incident to lash its local Democratic opponents. Its response to an "indignation meeting" held in New York a few days after the caning incorporated most of the arguments used by other pro-Brooks editorialists. Like the *Enquirer*, the *Whig*'s editor called into question the masculinity of Northern society. The paper also raised questions about the Northern attempt to convert the controversy from a narrow focus on slavery to the broad and conservative issue of free speech. The editorial implies that this was a deception devised by the Republicans for political gain.

The Progress of the Revolution

Richmond, Virginia, *Whig*, 4 June 1859
We desire that the Southern people should have the opportunity to see what sentiments are expressed with reference to them by their brethren of the North that they may be the better able to judge of the advantages and probabilities of our continuing a united people. . . . These gentlemen claim that members of Congress have the right, as members, to say anything they choose, with impunity, about anybody or anything. There is no limitation whatever to the exercise of the privilege. A M. C. [Member of Congress] may vilify and defame

individuals *ad libitum*—it is his constitutional right. The aggrieved party has no redress. Submission is his only alternative. This is a very convenient doctrine for foul-mouthed dastards; but it is one which has no sanction in reason, in justice, or the manly sense of resentment, which animates the bosom of a high-spirited people.

These gentlemen—we are willing to concede that they are what they claim to be—the foremost characters in New York, set up to be the arbiters of chivalry and true courage. By their discourses and conduct towards others, they furnish us with their idea of a man of honor and heroism. Three hundred miles from the scene of danger, and proclaiming to the world that they repudiate all personal responsibility for insults, they denounce Mr. Brooks as a coward, and stigmatize the whole population of the South as "ruffians," "assassins," "brutes," "murderers," "scoundrels," "cowards," &c. We confess our inability to appreciate the valor of this proceeding. Wherein its daring manhood consists we are unable to perceive. In all our reading of brave men and heroic nations, we have never encountered any who did not seem to consider that a willingness to incur some degree of personal risk was essential to the attribute of courage; and if we were to subject the wordy heroes of New York to those tests, we should say they were destitute of the first principle of honor and the least particle of generous manhood. To speak of feeling an insult as a wound would be to them an unintelligible jargon. Not one of them ever experienced the sensation implied in the phrase. They are dead to its effects—they are unconscious of its existence. That they possess the gross, brute courage of barbarians, or that which cowards derive from superior numbers, we doubt not. A Mr. Ruggles, one of the fiery orators, supplies a lively illustration of the fact. "Let us all go to Washington," he exclaimed. The valiant man had no idea of going alone. Mr. Morgan, a M C. from New York, also figured on the occasion. He took it upon himself to pronounce Mr. Brooks a "villain." We do not know that Mr. M. is a dastard—and we shall not, therefore, denounce him as one. But, if, when he returns to Washington, Mr. Brooks shall demand a retraction of the insult, or satisfaction for it, and he shall refuse the one or the other, it will be impossible for us to resist the conviction that he was describing himself when speaking of Mr. Brooks.

Mr. Calhoun and many other sagacious and profound thinkers have contended that the Northern people were incapable of preserving free institutions. With a population far from dense, compared with Europe, a resort to the military is no unfrequent occurrence among them, even at the present time. Their breed of noble men is well nigh extinct. . . . They, however, as represented by the elite of New York, claim to be the only fit people to uphold free Government, and manage the affairs of a Republic. The only evidence we have of their fitness, is their late and continued attempt to subvert the legal Government of Kansas by a mob of craven fanatics, who, after defying war, either sold or threw away their arms, and took to their heels, and their recent proposition, through the columns of the *Tribune*, to send a band of bullies to Washington to overawe Congress. . . .

The funniest part of the imposing exhibition was the failure of the effort to conceal its real character by keeping the avowed abolitionists muzzled and out of view. But old Beecher was on hand, and to the horror of the pretended conservatives, appropriately closed the proceedings.

EDITORIAL IMPLICATIONS

Because there were no opinion polls in the 1850s the impact of these editorials on public attitudes can only be inferred from anecdotal evidence. Both Sumner and Brooks paid close attention to the editorial commentaries, gathering them into scrapbooks as a record of the incident. Many others at the time viewed the editorial reactions as good indicators of the public's mood and were also alert to their effect in guiding opinion. The private correspondence of editors and political leaders shows an especially conscious and concerted effort to shape commentary about the Sumner incident.

The North's advantage in population and cities, and therefore in the number of newspapers, gave the region an edge in setting the terms of editorial debate. News of the incident generally appeared earlier and spurred a larger number of competing editorials in the North than in the South. Rival dailies in places like New York, Boston, and Chicago had thoroughly debated the incident before many of the Southern papers had given their first printed reports of the incident. This only worked to enhance the feeling of the South's political leaders that they were the victims of Northern aggression and that their side could never get a fair first hearing in the national press.

PUBLIC RALLIES AND RESOLUTIONS

One of the most important outgrowths of the confrontation was what came to be called "indignation meetings." These were public rallies to condemn the incident and to offer resolutions on behalf of either Sumner or Brooks. As was the case with newspaper editorials, Northerners had a decisive advantage in both the timing and the size of these rallies. For days after the incident Northerners attacked the South without rebuttal. This fact was not lost on Southerners, and it contributed greatly to the region's sense of being under siege.

Although neither the first nor the largest of the pro-Sumner indignation rallies, the meeting in Concord, Massachusetts, is interesting because Ralph Waldo Emerson gave the keynote address. Emerson reemphasized the principles of self-reliance that had been such a formative influence on Sumner's character. His celebration of Sumner's courage under intellectual attack has intriguing parallels with Brooks's ethic of disregard for physical danger. Both men became celebrated for their "manly" courage. Emerson shared Sumner's contempt for Southern culture and society. This confidence in the superiority of the North was a constant irritation to Southerners.

Ralph Waldo Emerson Speaks at the Concord Indignation Meeting[6]

Mr. Chairman,

I sympathize heartily with the spirit of the Resolutions. The events of the last few years and months and days have taught us the lesson of centuries. I do not see how a barbarous community and a civilized community can constitute one state. I think we must get rid of slavery, or we must get rid of freedom. Life has no parity of value in the free-state and in the slave-state. In one, it is adorned with education, with skilful labor, with arts, with long prospective interests, with sacred family ties, with honor and justice. In the other, life is a fever; man is an animal, given to pleasure, frivolous, irritable, spending his days on hunting and practising with deadly weapons to defend himself against his slaves, and against his companions brought up in the same idle and dangerous way.

Such people live for the moment, they have properly no future, and readily risk on every passion a life which is of small value to themselves or to others. Many years ago, when Mr. Webster was challenged in Washington to a duel by one of these madcaps, his friends came forward with prompt good sense, and said, such a thing was not to be thought of; Mr. Webster's life was the property of his friends and of the whole country, and was not to be risked on the turn of a vagabond's ball. Life and life are incommensurate. The whole State of South Carolina does not now offer any one or any number of persons who are to be weighed for a moment in the scale with such a person as the meanest of them all has now struck down.—The very conditions of the game must always be,—the worst life staked against the best. It is only the best whom they desire to kill. It is only when they cannot answer your reasons, that they wish to knock you down. If therefore Massachusetts could send to the Senate a better man than Mr. Sumner, his death would be only so much the more quick and certain.

Now as men's bodily strength or skill, with knives and guns, is not usually in proportion to their knowledge and mother wit, but oftener in the inverse ratio, it will only do to send foolish persons to Washington, if you wish them to be safe. The outrage at Washington is the more shocking from the singularly pure character of its victim. Mr. Sumner's position is exceptional in its honor. He had not taken his degrees in the caucus, and in hack politics. It is notorious, that, in the long time when his election was pending, he refused to take a single step to secure it. He would not so much as go up to the State House to shake hands with this or that person whose goodwill was reckoned important by his friends. He was elected. It was a homage to character and talent. In Congress, he did not rush into a party position. He sat long silent and studious. His friends, I remember, were told, that they would find Sumner a man of the world, like the rest: 'tis quite impossible to be at Washington, and not bend: he will bend as the rest have done. Well, he did not bend. He took his position and kept it. He meekly bore the cold shoulder from some of his New England colleagues, the hatred of his enemies, the pity of the indifferent, cheered by the love and respect of good men with whom he acted, and has stood for the North, a little in advance of all the North, and therefore without adequate support. He has never faltered in his maintenance of justice and freedom. He has gone beyond the large expectations of his friends in his increasing ability and his manlier tone.

I have heard that some of his political friends tax him with indolence or negligence in refusing to make electioneering speeches, or otherwise to bear his part in the labor which party organization requires. I say it to his honor. But more to his honor are the faults which his enemies lay to his charge. I think, sir, if Mr. Sumner had any vices, we should be likely to hear of them. They have fastened their eyes like microscopes, now for five years, on every act, word, manner, and movement to find a flaw, and with what result? His opponents accuse him neither of drunkenness, not debauchery, nor job, nor peculation, nor rapacity, nor personal aims of any kind; no, but with what? Why, beyond this charge which it is impossible was ever sincerely made, that he broke over the proprieties of debate, I find him accused of publishing his opinion of the Nebraska Conspiracy in a letter to the People of the United States with some discourtesy.

Then, that he is an abolitionist; as if every sane human being were not an abolitionist, or a believer that all men should be free. And the third crime he stands charged with, is, that his speeches were written before they were spoken; which of course must be true in Sumner's case, as it was true of Webster, of Adams, of Calhoun, of Burke, of Chatham, of Demosthenes, of every first-rate speaker that ever lived. It is the high compliment he pays to the intelligence of the Senate and of the country. When the same reproach was cast on the first orator of ancient times by some caviller of his day, he said, 'I should be ashamed to come with one unconsidered word before such an assembly.'

Mr. Chairman, when I think of these most small faults as the worst which party hatred could allege, I think I may borrow the language which Bishop Burnet applied to Sir Isaac Newton, and say, that Charles Sumner 'has the whitest soul I ever knew.'

Well, sir, this noble head, so comely and so wise, must be the target for a pair of bullies to beat with clubs! The murderer's brand shall stamp their foreheads wherever they may wander in the earth. But I wish, sir, that the high respects of this meeting shall be expressed to Mr. Sumner; that a copy of the Resolutions that have been read may be forwarded to him. I wish that he may know the shudder of terror which ran through all this community on the first tidings of this brutal attack. Let him know, that every man of worth in New England loves his virtues; that every mother thinks of him as the protector of families; that every friend of freedom thinks him *the* friend of freedom. And if our arms at this distance cannot defend him from assassins, we confide the defence of a life so precious, to all honorable men and true patriots, and to the Almighty Maker of men.

One of the first Southern rallies by Brooks's own constituents took place five days after the caning. Martin's Depot was in Edgefield county. The statement's plea for unity can be read as a response to the contentious factionalism of local politics in the years leading up to the incident. It underscores how important the caning incident was in helping South Carolinians overcome their political divisions as secession approached. The resolutions sought to defend slavery as a household matter not suited to the jurisdiction of civil government.

Resolutions of the Citizens of Martin's Depot, South Carolina, 27 May 1856[7]

Information has reached us that our immediate Representative Hon. P. S. Brooks saw proper to inflict a castigation on the Hon. Charles Sumner, Senator from Mass. for sentiments in debate highly offensive to South Carolina and a dastardly attack on Senator Butler who was absent from his seat. Be it therefore Resolved, That we a portion of the constituents of the Hon. P. S. Brooks highly *approve* of the chastisement inflicted on Charles Sumner and would say well done thou good and faithful servant. 2nd., That in the opinion of this meeting Southern Members have been insulted long enough by Northern Abolitionists.

3. If Northern Fanatics will persist in meddling with our private institutions we deem it expedient that Southern Members should reply to them by the use of the *Gutta Percha*.

4. That in as much as meetings are being held in Mass. and other places, North, denouncing Hon. P. S. Brooks and calling for his expulsion we would respectfully suggest that a meeting be held on sale day next that we may endorse the action of our Representative and his defiance to Northern abolitionists.

Students from more than a dozen Northern colleges held pro-Sumner rallies. Among these were students from Union College, which at the time was one of the nation's largest and most prestigious schools. The resolutions are representative of middle class northern views. Their emphasis on the attack as a denial of free speech shows how Northerners came to view Southern values and behavior as a threat to the rights and liberties of white people. The final resolution's concern with rule of law and America's reputation is similar to arguments Northerners would make to justify keeping South Carolina in the Union in 1861. Large numbers of Union College graduates would fight in the Union armies.

Resolutions of the Students of Union College, Schenectady, New York, 27 May 1856[8]

To the Hon. Charles Sumner:—
At a full meeting of the students of Union College held yesterday after noon & called for the purpose of giving some public expression with regard to the late out-

rage upon yourself the following resolutions were almost unanimously adopted. Per order of the meeting they are herewith transmitted to you.—

Whereas on Thursday the 22d of May the Hon. Charles Sumner was violently assaulted while in the discharge of his official duties by Preston S. Brooks, a representative in Congress from South Carolina whose declared purpose it was to inflict punishment upon Mr. Sumner for words spoken by him in senatorial debate therefore be it

Resolved, That we have heard with grief & indignation of this attack upon a Senator distinguished not less for his accomplishments as a scholar than his preeminence as an orator. And that we regard it as an effort to strike down the freedom of speech as well as an unprovoked & cowardly assault.—

Resolved, That as freemen we look upon this unprecedented outrage with horror; regarding it as a bold attempt to terrify the representatives of a free people in the exercise of their constitutional rights.

Resolved, That the attack is a disgrace to the national councils and a stain upon the American character which every lover of his country must deplore and which we trust Congress will take immediate measures to remove.

Union College
Schenectady N.Y. May 27/56

New England's leading abolitionists met for their annual May meeting less than a week after the attack. They had mixed reactions. Their debate over Sumner shows the movement's deep divisions about motives and strategy. Most delegates recognized the value of the incident as a symbol of slaveholder brutality. They were more ambivalent about Sumner himself. Abby Kelley Foster and her husband Stephen represented the radical wing. She had been one of the first women in American history to speak publicly to mixed audiences of both men and women. Her demand that women be fully included in the movement's leadership helped provoke abolition's "Great Schism" of 1840. The radicals, led by William Lloyd Garrison, demanded equality for women as well as slaves, and rejected the political system as irredeemably corrupt. Their moderate opponents steadfastly supported political abolitionism, first in the Liberty party and later as Free-Soilers and Republicans. In this debate over Sumner further strategic divisions among the radicals are visible. The accommodationism of Garrison and orator Wendell Phillips contrasts strikingly with the uncompromising perfectionism of the Fosters. That Republicans, despite their political compromises, might become politically effective enough to end slavery was an attraction that Garrison and Phillips found difficult to resist. Their debate with the Fosters underscores the limits of Sumner's popularity. It also offers an interesting parallel to the way in which the caning incident forced South Carolina's political activists into a choice between cooperation with the national Democratic party and the traditionally antiparty state rights positions espoused by the Calhounites.[9]

Proceedings of the New England Antislavery Convention Wednesday, 28 May and Thursday 29 May 1856[10]

Wednesday.

S. S. Foster had thought that, at such a crisis as the present, a new impulse would be given to the cause; but when he heard Mr. Phillips say on the platform yesterday, that the two words to be spoken now are, SUMNER and KANSAS, he had felt a great sinking of his soul. But who is this Charles Sumner, he asked, that this Society should espouse his quarrels with the slaveholders? He has long stood by and seen the rights of the millions of slaves stricken down, but what has he done? He has been striking hands with villains, and aiding them in their works of iniquity. This point Mr. Foster enlarged upon in his peculiar manner, amidst demonstrations of approving and disapproving feeling; many asking him questions upon the subject, and he answering them, much to the interest, if not to the conviction of the audience which had now got to be large. The mission of true anti-slavery is, he insisted, to separate the wheat from the chaff; but the danger now is, that we shall accept the chaff *as* wheat. He felt it, therefore, to be his first duty to make it everywhere realized that the Free Soil movement and the Kansas movement are unable to bring salvation to the country. No State in the Union, he said, had passed such barbarous laws against the black man as Kansas has passed. He contended earnestly, therefore, that the slave can be freed only over the ruins of the American Union; and the men at Washington who do not want to get caned for any free speech there, ought to leave the company of villains, and come home. . . .

Let Charles Sumner take the highest ground possible, and he would become the man of men; but as long as he should remain in the present position he could do little or nothing. Mr. F. closed his speech by offering the following resolution:—

Resolved, that the first and most important duty of this Convention, at the present time, is to convince the entire community that the anti-slavery of any and every political party which acknowledges allegiance and promises support to the Federal Government, is necessarily tainted and spurious; and the nearer its resemblance to the genuine, the more injurious it is to the cause of freedom, because the more likely to deceive and mislead the honest and true-hearted. . . .

Mr. Phillips, in some criticisms upon Mr. Foster's speech, said that he considered the Free Soil Party one of the greatest obstacles in the way of Liberty—not *the* greatest—but when a man sets his face in the right direction, he does one good act, and he would honor him, and thought we all should. Theodore Parker acknowledges the merits of Henry Ward Beecher fifty times where orthodox timidity dares return the complement once.

Abby Kelly Foster wanted to make a suggestion in reference to the honesty of some Free Soil leaders. Giddings and Wilson acknowledge, she said, our principles, but will not live by them. They may be politically honest, but they are not honest in a Christian sense.

Mr. Phillips said of Henry Ward Beecher, that he believed him honest in keeping with his present position; and though he did not come to us, it was enough to prove him an honest Anti-Slavery man that he was the object of pro-slavery hatred throughout the land. So of Mr. Giddings and Henry Wilson. . . .

S. S. Foster thought, in relation to Charles Sumner, that we must be impartial in the application of our rebukes to all parties, and that Mr. Sumner must not, therefore, be spared, standing as he does in union with slaveholders. He thought that all intelligent supporters of the Government are dishonest men, and ought to be rebuked and denounced. Henry Ward Beecher, he said, had received too much eulogy on this platform; he was too *pure* and *good* to stand on the platform with Mr. Garrison and Mr. Phillips, but he could sit in religious association with Presbyterian cradle plunderers! So of the other leading Free Soilers. . . .

Mr. Swazey, in speaking of Charles Sumner, said he had never been a great admirer of the distinguished Senator; but in regard to his recent services and present suffering, he gave him his hearty approval and admiration. He thought, however, that our Society ought to be cautious how it endorsed the leaders of the Republican Party, or the Party itself; approving them, indeed, for any good acts, and reproving them for any bad acts, but discriminatingly. . . .

Thursday.

Mrs. A. K. Foster said it was not her purpose or expectation, on leaving home, to speak at the Convention; but she wished to revive a discussion of yesterday, which did not seem to her to be clearly settled. The New England Convention, she said, was the place of all others to get at the truth, which is to be carried out into practical life. . . . As to the discussion of the Free Soil question, she hoped all personalities would be avoided; but, above all, it was important that our *uncompromising* position should be maintained. We love, she said, our Free Soil friends, and in various ways they manifest their friendship for us; but we owe them a *duty* to rebuke them, when they compromise the truth. She spoke most impressively of the disagreeableness of this duty, and of the sacrifices she and her husband often had to make in discharging it, but this was the special mission given to them from Heaven, and they must follow it faithfully. It was a most noble and Christian speech, worthy the glorious spirit of the woman, always illustrated, as it is, by her pure and martyr-like life.

Rev. Gardner Dean . . . thought it a poor time to criticise Charles Sumner, as some had criticized him on this platform. He spoke in eulogy of Mr. Sumner, and the Republican Party, as based on the Constitution of the United States, and urged a union of all anti-slavery parties.

Mr. Garrison urged the point that, unless we base our anti-slavery movement upon *principle*, we must go down—there is no other foundation to build upon. The South are united to the man on slavery; at the North all the great political and religious parties are on the same side—the Republican Party, as under the Constitution of the United States, is implicated in the support of slavery like the rest. But to succeed, there's an absolute necessity of abolitionists being uncompromising on the ground of 'no Union with Slaveholders. . . .'

Stephen S. Foster said that in rising to speak, he was conscious that he stood almost alone in the position he had taken in reference to the Free Soil party, and against the unmatched eloquence of Mr. Phillips and Mr. Garrison, and their well-earned influence. But he must be true to his own judgment and conscience. He thought the present to the true time to criticize Mr. Sumner, because he is, as never before, the idol of New England.

Mr. Garrison said Mr. Sumner was the product of our anti-slavery movement; and the question is, whether we have been making him a dangerous man.

Mr. Foster thought that Mr. Sumner is a dangerous man to the anti-slavery cause, and more dangerous at present than in any time before. He insisted, too, that if our movement had made Mr. Sumner a better man than he was ten years ago, it had thereby made him a greater obstacle to that movement. . . .

He said he had none but kind feelings towards Mr. Sumner, and he believed that Mr. S. had been the very best Abolitionist he could be under the Government. Still, it was his duty to criticize him, for in his present position he inevitably drew off even some of the tried-and-true of our Anti-Slavery platform. He went into a thorough exposition of Mr. Sumner's position, showing that he stood, with other supporters of the Union, on the necks of four millions of human beings—a thankless work to him, he said, but a necessary one to the cause. Mr. F. himself was not in favor of the Northern States withdrawing from the Southern; but he was in favor of uniting with the slaves, as Cassius M. Clay proposed, as against their masters. And let those who believe using the sword, use it, for such as those can do nothing without it.

Mr. Phillips replied, that according to Mr. Foster's philosophy, there could not be a good idea going around the world, unless it came from the Garrisonians. To be consistent with it, we ought to pray for the advent of Griers, and Jeffrieses, and Kanes, as a protection against good men not wholly right. But Mr. Phillips repudiated this whole philosophy as absurd; and denied also that he had endorsed the Republican Party or Mr. Sumner as an Abolitionist. Mr. Sumner's position in the U.S. Government, he himself had always criticized, as had Mr. Garrison; but he would be ever ready to render honor to every man for any good act—even to the slaveholding judge of Mississippi, who, amidst his long career of service to slavery, gave one manly and righteous decision for freedom. And of the nearer man come to the truth, the more he would honor them; believing that the better they are, the most useful they must be.

Mr. Foster complained that he had not been met by Mr. Phillips with fairness: but as it was suggested by Mr. Garrison and others that he had occupied much time in the discussion, he took his seat.

Sumner received a stronger endorsement from a meeting of the "Colored Citizens" of Boston. The officers of this group represented the city's African-American elite, including attorney Robert Morris, whom Sumner had assisted during the school desegregation cases of 1849–1850. Others, especially Leonard Grimes and Coffin Pitts, had been active in the Anthony Burns trial. There was even an historian, William C. Nell, who had just completed the first study of black contributions to the American Revolution. Each of them had been a slave or knew slaves. Most had seen slaveholders give beatings or had been attacked themselves. Like the Union College students they viewed the attack as an assault on free speech but linked this to the physical violence inflicted on slavery's victims.[11]

Resolutions of the Colored Citizens of Boston, 6 June 1856[12]

Hon. Charles Sumner
My Dear Sir
At a meeting of the colored citizens of Boston held in the twelfth Baptist Church Tuesday eve June 3d to express their indignation at the recent outrage committed upon you, in Washington, the following named persons were chosen as officers: President Deacon Coffin Pitts. Vice Presidents, Rev. L. A. Grimes, Robert Morris, Esq, Jno. Clark, Wm. Logan, Robert Johnson, Wm. C. Nell, Major Mindrucu, Rev. M. Freeman, Wm. Preston, Henry Randolph, H. T. Sidney. Secretaries. J. S. Rock, M. D., John Stephenson, Geo. L. Ruffin.

Dr. Rock then offered the following resolutions,

Resolved that the colored citizens of Boston, regard the recent brutal cowardly and murderous assault, in the Senate Chamber of the United States, upon our distinguished Senator, *Charles Sumner,* eminent alike for his statesmanship, eloquence and philanthropy, with feelings of mingled abhorrence and indignation.

Resolved that we tender to our advocate and friend, in the hour of his physical prostration and suffering, the warm sympathies of loving and grateful hearts, where every aspiration has been quickened by his long-continued disinterested services in our behalf.

Resolved that in this dastardly attempt to crush out Free Speech, we painfully recognise the abiding prevalence of that spirit of Injustice which has for two centuries upon this continent, ground our progenitors and ourselves under the iron hoof of slavery.

Resolved, that we hereby express to Mr. Sumner our entire confidence in him as a faithful friend to the slave.

The meeting was addressed by Robert Morris Esq., Rev. L. A. Grimes, Rev. Mr. Hall, Mr. Robt. Johnson and Dr. J. S. Rock after which the resolutions were unanimously adopted. Three cheers were then given for *Charles Sumner* and a resolution passed requesting the secretaries to furnish our Senator with a copy of the proceedings of the meeting. The Meeting adjourned at a late hour and enthusiastic cheers for Charles Sumner.

J. S. Rock, Secty.

The editorial reactions to meetings in South Carolina show the complexity of the state's social conditions. It is notable that A. C. Garlington, who had run against Brooks in the 1854 Congressional elections, played such an active role in the rally. Given the volatility of the state's political alliances in the 1850s such a shift was not unusual, but it underscores the incident's unifying effects. The editorialist's reference to "one of South Carolina's truest and most honored matrons" shows the complex role of elite women in antebellum Southern politics. Southern custom barred women from speaking in public. This particular matron remained nameless and could only express her political support for Brooks through male intermediaries. Yet the editorialist considered female support to be a powerful endorsement of Brooks's behavior. The *Carolinian*'s conclusion that slave support for Brooks was a "crowning glory" proved more controversial. It produced a heated response from the the editor of the *Mercury*, who retorted that political endorsements by any slave group "offends every sentiment of Carolina society." For the *Mercury*, anyone who degraded the status of whites or elevated slaves deserved condemnation, be it Charles Sumner or the editor of the *South Carolinian*.

Public Approval of Mr. Brooks

Columbia, South Carolina, *South Carolinian*, 27 May 1856

We were not mistaken in asserting, on Saturday last, that the Hon. Preston S. Brooks had not only the approval, but the hearty congratulations of the people of South Carolina for his summary chastisement of the abolitionist Sumner. Immediately upon the reception of the news on Saturday last, a most enthusiastic meeting was convened in the town of Newberry, at which Gen. Williams, the Intendant, presided. Complimentary resolutions were introduced by Gen. A. C. Garlington, and ardent speeches made by him, Col. S. Fair, Maj. Henry Sumner, and others. The meeting voted him a handsome gold-headed cane, which we saw yesterday, on its way to Washington, entrusted to the care of Hon. B. Simpson. At Anderson, the same evening, a meeting was called, and complimentary resolutions adopted. We heard one of Carolina's truest and most honored matrons from Mr. Brooks' district send a message to him by Maj. Simpson, saying "that the ladies of the South would send him hickory sticks, with which to chastise Abolitionists and Red Republicans whenever he wanted them."

Here in Columbia, a handsome sum, headed by the Governor of the State, has been subscribed, for the purpose of presenting Mr. Brooks with a splendid silver pitcher, goblet and stick, which will be conveyed to him in a few days by the hands of gentlemen delegated for that purpose. In Charleston similar testimonials have been ordered by the friends of Mr. Brooks.

And, to add the crowning glory to the good work, the slaves of Columbia have already a handsome subscription, and will present an appropriate token of their regard to him who has made the first practical issue for their preservation and protection in their rights and enjoyments as the happiest laborers on the face of the globe.

Meetings of approval and sanction will be held, not only in Mr. Brooks' district, but throughout the State at large, and a general and hearty response of approval will re-echo the words, "Well done," from Washington to the Rio Grande.

The largest rally for Brooks was a barbecue and ball held in early October near his home in Ninety Six, South Carolina. According to the Edgefield *Advertiser,* between five and eight thousand people attended the meeting. Some sense of the event's size can be determined from the newspaper's account, which reported that "four tables, each one hundred yards long were in readiness for the multitude generally, while three other tables in a different part of the grounds awaited the ladies, their attendants and the invited guests."[13] Planning for the meeting had begun in early September. Organizers sent invitations to many leading Southern politicians, including Jefferson Davis, James Mason, and Georgia's United States representative and former governor Howell Cobb. One of the most interesting responses to this invitation came from John McQueen, who was one of Brooks's fellow Congressmen from South Carolina. His assessment of the incident's implications is remarkable for its racial views, its assessment of the Republican party program, and its hostility to Massachusetts.

Letter from Congressman John McQueen[14]

Gentlemen:—I had the honor to receive your kind invitation to the Brooks 96 Dinner on the 3rd *proximo*, and would be greatly more than gratified, were it in my power to be present, as well to contribute my mite in doing honour to your distinguished Representative, as to form the acquaintance and enjoy the well-known hospitality of his generous constituents. . . . Well may you, however, thus do honour to your Representative, who has triumphantly sustained and vindicated your honour, with a head, a heart, and a hand, that should not only endear him to you and to his State, but to every Southron, whose impulses are true to the memory of his ancestors, and to the land that gave him birth.

When his State, and his venerable and distinguished relative, than whom no nobler spirit, or truer heart, ever adored the counsels of our once happy confederacy; were ruthlessly assailed with an assassin-like slander; the hands of a crazy and libelous fanatic, your Representative at the right time, in the right place, and in the right manner, administered to him my argument, the only kind in my judgement, that will now avail against impudent, arrogant and mad fanaticism, that regards no truth, no right, no justice, no honour, no law or compact; And when the fires of black fanatical fury and revenge were kindled against him at the hands of an unscrupulous majority, and the shaft of personal insult was feebly attempted to be hurled at him, he met it with a firmness and repelled it with a promptness that would do honour to a Roman, as they well entitle him to the admiration of every one who is at all endowed with true feelings of manliness; the duty could have fallen in no better hands.

We have arrived at a period in the affairs of this Republic as portentous as it is trying to the South, and those, even who do not wish to, may as well understand it. Abolition has loomed up with a progress and rapidity, recently, that those of us who were most apprehensive, were scarcely prepared to witness. It is now strong and arrogant enough to control the most numerous branch of Congress, to elect a speaker who would not decide whether we, or our Negroes are the superior race— to clot the wheels of the Federal Government, at will—to engage in open rebellion and war, and murder our friends for daring to claim equality in the Territories purchased with our money and our blood, and more than all, to nominate an ordinary Lieutenant of the army for President of the United States, without even desiring nor asking the co-operation of a single Southern State, with the determination to subdue the South below the condition of a province, to destroy her honour and rights, and ultimately, to reduce us to equality, with our slaves, and authorize them to claim (as now by Law in Massachusetts,) to associate in our families and marry our children. If they succeed in this election, I trust all will agree with me that the Union is dissolved and *ought to be dissolved*, for there can no longer be union of interest, of right, of property, of sentiment, of honour or equality, and the election of Freemont will proclaim it to the world. Should Buchanan be elected, the Union may survive for a time, and possibly be preserved, provided Democrats be Democrats and Statesmen, maintain their position and administer the Government according to their professions and the Constitution, and look, much less, to offices and plunder. In my judgment the year 1860, in any event, will settle the matter, and I think it our duty to await the result of the pending election—watch well the signs of the times, and be prepared to act as becomes men capable of, appreciating their rights and honour, and with the spirit to maintain them at any and every cost. If forced by the North into a Southern Confederacy, I have no gloomy apprehensions either for our honour, our happiness, or the institution of slavery. Indeed in view of the fate of the Roman Republic and the history of our own Government to the present moment, I am doubting more and more, that a Republic can well exist without the institution of slavery. A very large proportion of the North constitutes now but a mad fanatical rabble, with all the wicked isms of which man can conceive—repudiating God, the Bible, the law, marital rights or the constitution, and if it were not for the extraordinary extent of territory in which their wickedness may be diluted, and the conservatism of the South, they would ere this, have been consumed by the infernal fires of their own abominations. Truly may it be said of them, (with all proper honourable exceptions) "those whom God would destroy, he first makes mad," but I am admonished, I must close this already too protracted letter. Allow me to offer the following sentiment:

The South, the beloved South; she will never be reduced to the condition of Massachusetts as long as the example of Col. Brooks is in the memory of her sons.

PRIVATE LETTERS OF PRAISE, CONSOLATION, AND CONDEMNATION

Sumner received an outpouring of letters in the weeks following the incident. Nearly all were supportive. The first of these came from people in the North's urban areas. News of the attack had arrived in the major cities within a few hours. Later letters were also disproportionately from the North's most developed commercial market zones. Towns along the Erie canal, along the main highways from Boston to Washington, and at major shipping centers were strongly represented. Despite high concentrations of political activists he received few notes of sympathy from the major state capitals. With the exception of Illinois, almost no letters

FIGURE 3.1   Origins of Letters Sent to Senator Charles Sumner from Massachusetts

were sent from the North's rural areas. Even those agricultural areas that had historically supported Free-Soilers and Republicans were underrepresented.

Patterns within Massachusetts resembled national trends. The first letters came from Middlesex and Suffolk Counties (which included Boston), along with Franklin, Hampshire, and Hamden Counties in the Connecticut River valley. As in the rest of America, people in the state's agricultural areas responded little and late to the incident. It is curious that Sumner received so little support from Worcester. As the second largest city in Massachusetts and one of the state's strongest Free Soil districts Worcester might have been expected to generate an outpouring of letters after the attack. This was not the case. The impact of Know-Nothings and radical abolitionists who disliked Sumner may have been a factor that dampened public outcry.

Sumner received more mail from Boston than any other community. The following, one of the first letters written after the attack, shows the excitement that swept the city. The author was one of Sumner's most ardent supporters and in the future would become the first editor of the Boston *Commonwealth*, a pro-Sumner Republican newspaper. His term "Hunkers" is a derogatory label for Northerners who supported Southern political positions. His assessment of their response suggests the incident's political impact. This letter is typical of dozens of letters to Sumner, which invoked the incident as a sign of God's providential designs.

FIGURE 3.2   Origins of Letters Sent to Charles Sumner from Massachusetts

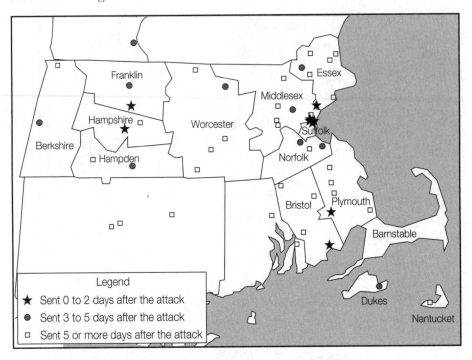

TABLE 3.1   Relationship Between Sumner Condolence Letters and Voting in Massachusetts

COUNTY	TOTAL VOTES	FREE SOIL VOTES	LETTERS TO SUMNER	LETTERS PER 10,000 VOTERS	LETTERS PER 1,000 FREESOIL VOTERS
Suffolk	14,502	470	47	32	100
Dukes	394	3	1	25	333
Nantucket	596	3	1	17	333
Middlesex	22,614	921	22	10	23
Plymouth	7,339	534	5	7	9
Bristol	9,141	535	4	4	8
Franklin	4,841	265	2	4	8
Hampshire	5,086	366	2	4	6
Norfolk	10,415	458	4	4	9
Essex	16,944	987	6	4	6
Hampden	7,035	44	2	3	46
Berkshire	7,114	176	2	3	11
Worcester	19,586	1,573	5	3	3
Barnstable	3,096	147	0	0	0

Source: *Tribune Almanac.*

Letter of James W. Stone to Charles Sumner[15]

Boston, 22 May 1856

My Dear Sumner,

Indignation at the brutal attack upon you is in every lip, and fills every heart. To many of those hitherto esteemed as unconvertible Hunkers, it seems to be the last feather that breaks the camel's back of their sympathy with slavery.

And thus from the wickednesses of our opponents does the Almighty One evolve food to our great cause.

Be of good cheer! The sympathy of the virtuous will ever accompany you.

There is a great desire for a public meeting to express the outraged feelings of all classes of our citizens.

I am an invalid, and can write no more, but command for any service

Your Friend Ever,

James W. Stone

Sumner received few letters from the South. About half of these came from expatriate Northerners or border state abolitionists expressing sympathy and outrage. The remainder came from Southern rights defenders who wrote to approve of Brooks's deed. This anonymous author's concern with how Sumner had damaged the South's reputation and their desire to correct such abuses through physical discipline is ideologically consistent with the views of Brooks and Butler. Its anger and resentment point to the challenges this worldview faced as Northern influence over American politics and culture grew.

Letter from "A Friend Indeed" to Charles Sumner, 22 May 1856[16]

Columbia, S. Ca. May 22 56

Respected Senator,

This is to inform you that I am very well pleased at the castigation you [received] recently at the hands of an honorable member from the Palmetto State. You have learnt from painful experience, that the forbearance of the South has limits which even *you* dare not impinge without impunity. Sir the insults you have heaped on the South are so many and so aggravated in kind, that if I had not a little charity in my heart, I could have wished Mr. Brooks had used other and more deadly weapons against you than a mere horsewhip or cowhide. We will not tolerate your insolence longer. If you infernal abolitionists don't mind your own business at home, and let ours alone, the People at the South, will take the matter in hand themselves, and go

in a mass to the Capital—tar and feather—horse-whip & expel every rascal of yours.
Beware in time & learn a useful lesson from what you have [received].
"A Friend indeed"

Excluding the northeast's urban areas Sumner received more letters from Illinois than
from any other state. Close proximity to Kansas and bitterly competitive politics sensi-
tized Illinoisians to the issues raised by the Sumner incident. This letter was typical of
many that Sumner received. It provides clues to the nature of the Republican party's
appeal to ordinary voters. The author of this letter described himself as a "mechanic,"
meaning someone from the working classes employed in a skilled trade such as car-
pentry or blacksmithing. It seems likely that someone from this background would
understand the brutality of labor subordination and would have a special appreciation
for individual autonomy. The writer's allusions to the American Revolution as a model
for action is interesting in light of his desire for courageous men in Congress.

W. Richardson to Charles Sumner, 24 May 1856[17]

Alton, Ill. May 24th 1856
My Dear Sir,
The blood boils in my veins as I read the telegraphic dispatch this morning of the
cowardly brutal assault on you in Senate by the *fiend* from South Carolina. I feel as
though no other provocation was needed to justify the North in shouldering the
musket & fighting the battles of the revolution over again & can hardly have
patience to sit still while I write these few lines.
    O, my God, my God, how much more must men suffer for *Freedom?* How much
more must men be insulted for speaking the *Truth?* How long will it be before people will learn that *men* are required for Legislators, Governors, & Presidents, instead
of miserable demogogs [sic]? What a spectacle does our country present to [the]
world at the present time. Professing to be *free* & independent, proclaiming to the
world that we believe in the principle that *all* men are born free & equal & at the
same time the President bending his influence & perhaps the troops of the
U. States to assist an ignorant, selfish, armed mob of Missourians in breaking down
the advocates of freedom in Kansas & driving them from the Territory, while Representatives in cool blood & in open day light walk up to men & stealthily assassin
like beat them to the earth with clubs, & for what? Merely because they have boldly
advocated the principles of the Constitution that all men are born free & equal.
Most truly did Mr. Banks speak when he said we wanted men in Congress who
would stand *Hell Fire.* O, that I had the ability & education to write, I would make
these rascals feel what I feel. I would make their very souls writhe with agony. I
would score them until they would wish to hide their heads in dirt for very shame.
After all it would be like teaching philosophy to hogs—they are brutes & can only
be met by brute force. There is none other way to fight the *Devil* but with *fire* & I
only wish he could have it to his heart's content. But my Dear Sir, when I com-

menced this letter I merely ment [sic] to say I am a poor mechanic yet I have a warm heart. I wish only for the welfare & happiness of my brother man & as your cause ever since I first heard of you has been so just, so magnanimous, so kind & so patriotic that I can't but frankly acknowledge that I love & admire you. You have my most cordial sympathy & I wish to God I could lend you any assistance. It is hardly reasonable to expect you to expose your life with such a despicable set of scamps. Still I hope the country will not, for the present at least be deprived of your services. I don't know if you will be able to read what I have written, or to make sense of it, if you do read it. It is written in much haste & under excitement. It is a frank expression of my feelings, & I hope you will not feel insulted by its coming from so humble a source. I am yours Most Truly,
W. Richardson

Slave-owners used the term "Cuffy" as a generic name for slaves. It implied not only an individual who was subordinate enough to be struck ("cuffed") by the master, but one who resisted often enough to require such "soft" violence as a means of subjugation. The term was phonetically similar to African names and slaves may have accepted it as means of preserving African traditions.[18] This anonymous letter, obviously written by a white person from Charleston, adopted a satirical "blackface" dialect similar to those used in minstrel shows. Like "A Friend Indeed," the writer of this letter evidences considerable concern about breakdowns in racial and social hierarchy. The allusion to a previous incident where Butler had saved Sumner from a horsewhipping is intriguing. It may refer to the events of May and June 1854.

"Cuffy" to Charles Sumner, 26 May 1856[19]

Dear Massa Sumner,
I cannot depress de feelings dat pervades dis poor niggers heart, when I did hear all dem Charleston people talking bout your beating. I hear dem say—sarbe him right—I hear dem say—he ought to been kill him, and what for—cause you tak de part of all poor niggers and try hard for git your self on quality with dem.
   You did wrong to sail de character of good kind old massa Butler, case you was under oboliations to him, as he sabed you from a hose whipping once, and I only wish he had been day de oder day, to pertect your poor head—I know he would as done it, aldo it was him you 'bused, case he would feel pitty for you, as praps you is a little light-headed.
   But Dear Massa I must blame you, blame you case you stand dere, take it cooly—only saying "I'm almost dead, almost dead—den why didn't you die, dis nigger would have come spressly to go to de funral, and would have wear a piece of crape two yards long on each arm for seventy-five days—You didn't do right— you ought to have jumped into de mutton of your ponnent, even if it was cartain def, for tho the Brook was a little miffled at de rope, still the chances are you would

have been git a more severe hammering and at de same time answered all the purposes for washing out some of your dirty language—Yes I say you ought to habe been jump in, Massa Sumner, as you was so anxious to vindicate de nigger's cause, but I guess jist at dat time your courage been fail you and you say: "I guess I done enough, I will lefe my colored Bredren for do de rest."

I hope all my Bredren did help to dress your scratches, dis nigger ought to hab been dere to take care of you & rub your head wid turpentine & vinegar, and if it aint too late send for him tho I see Mr Herald[20] says you are getting no better fast—

One of your belubbed Colored Bredren

Cuffy

Charleston, S.C. 26 May

Although Brooks reported receiving hundreds of letters supporting his actions, only those having some personal connection to him seem to have been preserved. The author provides a sense of the public mood in South Carolina. Like those South Carolinians who had written directly to Sumner, Jones took delight in what he thought was a deserved punishment. His mention of the "pecuniary" costs of the attack refers to the fines Brooks would be assessed in his criminal trial.

Seaborn Jones to Preston S. Brooks, 1 June 1856[21]

Dear Sir:

I have just seen the glorious news (by the *News*) of the severe castigation you have given Charles Sumner, & I hope you will pardon the liberty I take in returning you my humble thanks for what you have done. It is what the Rascal has wanted a long time, & he has only received a small portion of what he deserves if you had given him ten times as much not a lick would have been amis[s], upon his dam hide. Let them abolitionists crack their whips while there is a dollar in South Carolina. They will never hurt you in a pecuniary way and they can do nothing else. You have the good wishes of everyone I have heard speak on the subject and everyone is full of it. Nothing else talked of. I doubt if you have forgotten me and if you have I hope this note will recall me to your recollection when a boy you seemed to *take to me* as we say, in these parts . . .

One of the most unusual letters to Sumner came from young girl in Cambridge, Massachusetts, just across the river from Boston. Mary Rosamond Dana was the daughter of Richard Henry Dana, author of the famous sea narrative *Two Years Before the Mast*. At the time this was written he was a lawyer who actively supported abolitionism and the Republican party. Sumner was a family acquaintance. That children would be so stirred up by the incident suggests the breadth of its effect on the local community.

Mary Rosamond Dana to Charles Sumner, 1 June 1856[22]

Dear Mr. Sumner,

How do you do? I am very sorry that you were hurt and I hope you will get well.

Mr. Brooks is a very naughty man and if I had been there I would have torn his eyes out and so I would do now if I could. The School boys in Cambridge and Cambridge Port have each made an image of Mr. Brooks, laid it down on the ground and let the dogs and carriages run over him, and (in Cambridge Port) hung on the United States flag pole, and in Cambridge on the Washington elm, and I believe he is there now. He is dressed in black pantaloons, red vest, and black coat. He has got black hair. I don't know what it is made of, black eyes, and dark red whiskers and, I believe he is stuffed with Mr. Longfellow's hay for we saw the hay strewed all along his path. My Grandmother and Aunt are here, and we are having a real nice time. I wish you were having much a nice time as we. We shall be very happy to see you when you get well. I must now bid you Good bye.

From your friend,
Mary Rosamond Dana

Many of Sumner's correspondents expressed their sympathy by predicting that his "martyrdom" at the hands of the Slave Power would revitalize the Republican coalition. A striking example of such a conversion was the case of John D. Van Buren, son of former president Martin Van Buren. His father had been one of the country's foremost Democratic leaders until a quarrel with the party's Southern wing over the slavery issue. In 1848 Martin Van Buren had bolted the party and served as the Freesoiler's presidential candidate. The son had followed but both men had returned to the Democratic party in the early 1850s.

John Van Buren to Charles Sumner, 10 June 1856[23]

Newburgh, N.Y.
June 10, 1856
Dear Sir,

I hope you will not think me too intrusive for expressing under sanction of so slight an acquaintance, my warm sympathy with you since the late outrage. It has changed me from a decided pro-slavery man into as decided a supporter of the Republican or northern ticket, be the names on it what they may.

I thank you specially for the authentic report of your late speech, received to day.

Very Respectfully,
Your Obedient Servant,
Jno. D. Van Buren

Brooks's supporters universally agreed that Sumner was incapable of understanding rational argument. The following letter is representative of those who celebrated the attack as the logical response to a supposedly illogical man. The letter also offers evidence of the attack as a unifying agent in South Carolina politics.

W. F. Holmes to Preston Brooks, 27 May 1856[24]

Maybinton, [Newberry County, South Carolina], May 27th, 1856
Dear Col.,
    (That title does not sufficiently express the honor which you have gained by your noble conduct in castigating the foul mouthed senator from Massachusetts. You must have a more elevated one for the future.)
    I must apologize for troubling you with this communication at the present interesting crisis in your political history, but really I am so delighted with your cool, classical caning of Mr. Sumner that I cannot refrain. You have immortalised yourself in the opinions of your immediate constituency. With one tremendous bound you have cleared all the intermediate rounds, and alighted on the summit of Fame's ladder. Even your most bitter personal opponents, Moorman, Maybin *et ed gen omane genus* [men of the same ilk], men who so strenuously antagonised you in the Sullivan and Garlington contests, cry "long live Brooks, the heroic representative who dared to introduce his arguments thro' the hide of the abolition Senator from Massachusetts." I heard one of your whilom strenuous defamers say to day that he would vote for you to fill the distinguished post of President to a Southern Confederacy. That's right, address your arguments to the skin, to the physical sensibilities. The moral perceptions and the mental faculties of the freesoilers have been preached to long enough. Give it to them over the shoulders. We are proud to have you as our representative and hope you will ere long fill a more distinguished position. Accept my sincere congratulations.
    With the highest respect,
    I remain yours,
    W. F. Holmes

IMAGES OF THE CANING

Photography was so new in 1856 that no cameras were present to capture the caning on film. The only images we have of the encounter were developed by artists and wood engravers. These craftsmen based their representations on written news reports and stock images of the leading participants. One of the first to be published was the print designed by noted political cartoonist Henry Magee (see Figure 3.3). Copies of the print were advertised for sale in the *Liberator* and other

FIGURE 3.3   Henry Magee, "Southern Chivalry: Argument Versus Clubs"

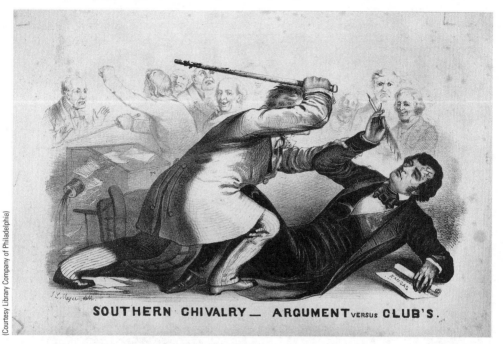

(Courtesy Library Company of Philadelphia)

SOUTHERN CHIVALRY — ARGUMENT versus CLUB'S.

newspapers. The print's details were intended to underscore the irony of the South's self-described chivalry. In the image Sumner's pen is juxtaposed against the canes of Brooks and Keitt, and the grimaces of Sumner and his friends contrast with the evident pleasure taken by Brooks's allies. Scholars have speculated that Magee drew Brooks's arm over his face because he did not know what the South Carolinian looked like. Because of its evocative imagery this print has been frequently reproduced in textbooks.[25]

America's first illustrated newspapers were published in the 1850s. Among the most widely circulated of these in 1856 was *Frank Leslie's Illustrated Weekly*. Unlike the New York *Tribune* and most of the nation's other print newspapers, *Leslie's* was officially non-partisan. Because it was published in New York and the bulk of its readers lived in the North, however, *Leslie's* usually favored the tastes of its region and clientele. The wood engraving, entitled, "The Assault in the Senate Chamber," appeared on the cover of the magazine's 7 June 1856 issue (see Figure 3.4). At the time it was probably the most widely viewed image of the attack. In contrast to Magee, this unknown artist relegated the incident itself to a small corner of the image. His decision to emphasize the details of the Senate chamber rather than the protagonists is intriguing. The resulting depiction was less overtly political than the Magee image but was still consistent with the Northern idea of the attack as a desecration of the nation's sacred temple of democracy. Artistically speaking, the image contains an eclectic combination of motifs from both the Classical and Romantic styles.

FIGURE 3.4   "The Assault in the Senate Chamber," from *Frank Leslie's Illustrated Weekly*

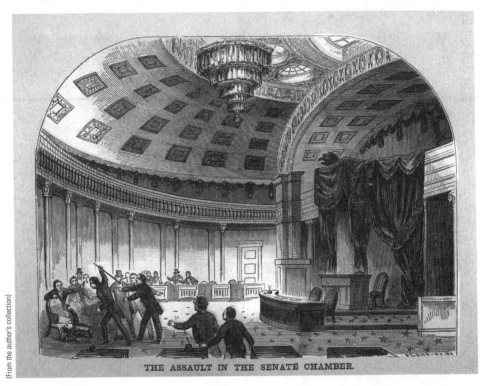

(From the author's collection)

THE ASSAULT IN THE SENATE CHAMBER.

The incident's political importance in the Fall 1856 elections is shown in the Republican party campaign print (see Figure 3.5). In the left background the artist depicted a notorious raid by pro-slavery forces on the Free Soil community of Lawrence, Kansas. Called the "sack of Lawrence," it had occurred just one day before the Sumner assault. Henceforth Republicans would consciously link "Bleeding Sumner" and "Bleeding Kansas" as twin outrages of the Slave Power. In the right side background a warship is depicted cannonading a coastal community on the Gulf of Mexico. This may refer either to an attempt by American adventurer William Walker to overthrow the government of Nicaragua in 1855, or to Democratic plans for the annexation of Cuba. The two figures chained to the flagpole are slaves. The artist's version of the Sumner assault is similar in posing and layout to the two earlier prints. This suggests the role of visual preconceptions in shaping how artists and the public responded to the event.

FIGURE 3.5   Republican Party Campaign Print, "The Democratic Platform Illustrated"

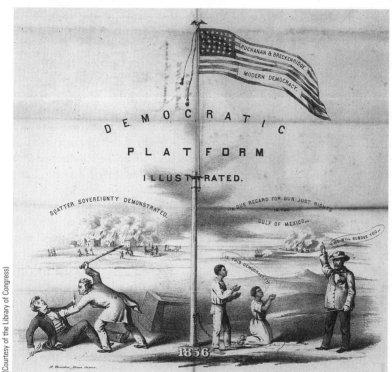

(Courtesy of the Library of Congress)

THE FATE OF PRESTON BROOKS

Brooks had become a celebrity and a target. In the Summer and Fall of 1856 he struggled to adapt to his new identity as an icon of sectionalism. Most immediately he faced not only Congressional censure but also criminal assault charges. He was arrested and summoned before district Judge Hollingsworth, who set him free on a five hundred-dollar bond for misdemeanor simple assault. To the great disappointment of the Republicans he had avoided the more serious felony charges of assault with a deadly weapon and assault with intent to kill. The case came to trial on July 7. Brooks's political associate James Orr joined with local attorney John Linton to serve as his defense team. District judge Thomas Crawford, a Pennsylvania Democrat who had been appointed to the court by James K. Polk, evidently agreed with the arguments made by Brooks. Judge Crawford ordered Brooks to pay a minimal fine of three hundred dollars. Brooks's supporters were delighted by the verdict, while Sumner's supporters viewed it as confirmation of the Slave Power's chokehold on the Federal judiciary.[26]

Trial Remarks by Preston Brooks[27]

May it please your Honor: May I be permitted to say a word? [Judge Crawford— Certainly]. I appear in person before this honorable Court simply to receive its judgment. I would have preferred that the person upon whom the assault was committed had been present to answer whether or not his speech which libeled my State and blood was printed before its delivery in the Senate. I feel confident that under oath he could not have denied this fact, which, with due deference to your Honor, I regard as material to my defense, insomuch as a libel in contrary to law, and to that extent would operate in extenuation of my offense. I would like to have inquired of him, in person, as to the degree of his personal injuries, and to have been informed in what way he could reconcile that part of his statement as to the words used by me when the assault was made, with the sentence which immediately succeeds this language in his testimony before the Investigating Committee, and which is as follows:

'While these words were passing from his (my) lips he commenced a succession of blows with a heavy cane on my bare head, by the first of which I was stunned so as to lose sight.'

It would have gratified me had he been compelled to answer under oath as to the violence of the first blow, which I aver, was but a tap, and intended to put him on his guard. But, Sir, he is conveniently and deliberately absent and on travel, notwithstanding but six days ago this case was postponed on account of his extreme indisposition and the materiality of his testimony; and yet, with all these disadvantages, I prefer to receive the judgment of the Court than to continue in suspense. It is not my purpose to address any evidence in defense. I have already accomplished more than half of the journey of life, and this is the first time that it has been my misfortune to be arraigned before any judicial tribunal as a breaker of any law of my country. I confess, Sir, and without shame, that my sensibilities are disturbed by my novel position, and I have but to express my profound regret that in discharging a duty imposed upon me by my own sense of right and the sentiment of the gallant people it is my pride and honor to represent, I am constrained as a consequence to approach you as a violator and not as a maker of the laws.

In extenuation of my offense, permit me to say that no extraordinary power of invention is requisite to imagine a variety of personal grievances, which the good of society and even public morality require to be redressed; and yet no adequate legal remedy may be had. So also are those cases which may fall under the condemnation of the letter of the law, and yet like considerations will restrain its penalties. The villain who perverts the best feelings of the better sex, and rewards unsuspecting devotion with ruin, may bid defiance to this honorable Court. But where a sister's dishonor is blotted out with blood of her destroyer, an intelligent and wholesome public opinion, embodied in an intelligent and virtuous jury, always has, and always will, control the law, and popular sentiment will applaud what the books may condemn. It is the glory of the law that it is founded in reason.

But can that reason be just which is not regardful of human feeling? Sir, no one knows better than yourself that such a reproach does not rest upon our jurisprudence; for, even the stern letter of the law touches with tenderness the husband who slays in the act the usurper of his bed. The child who kills in defense of its parent is excused by the law, which is ever regardful of the virtuous impulses of nature. By a parity of reasoning, patriotism is regarded by every nation upon earth as the cardinal political virtue. Songs are made to reward it, and to perpetuate the names of those who are its exemplar. And can it be expected—will it be required—that, with a heart to feel and an arm to strike, I shall patiently hear and ignobly submit while my political mother is covered with insult, and obloquy and dishonor? While her character is slandered, and her reputation libeled?

Sir, the substance which I have been gathering for my children may be squandered, my body may be consigned to the common jail, my life may be forfeited, but I will be true to the instincts of my nature—true to the home of my maturity, and to the mother that bore me. The first political reason which my ripening faculties fully comprehended and appreciated, was the high moral and social obligations of every citizen to bow himself to the majesty of the law. In obedience to the precepts of my youth, which are sanctioned by the experience and judgment of mature years, I submit my case to the discretion of the court with entire confidence; that while you, Sir, as a magistrate, perform your whole duty to the country and yourself, you will remember that in every regulated community public opinion distinguishes between crime and honorable resentment, and tolerates the refuge which men sometimes seek in the magnanimity of their judges.

DUELS

The threat of legal action did not keep Brooks from other controversies. On 27 May Massachusetts Senator Henry Wilson once again spoke in defense of Sumner. In the midst of saying that his colleague had been "stricken down by a brutal, murderous, and cowardly assault," he was interrupted by Senator Butler, who protested so angrily that his words were purged from the official proceedings. Threats against Wilson were so serious that his friends formed a bodyguard to escort him through town. When Brooks heard of this exchange he immediately challenged Wilson to a duel. Wilson refused to back down but declined to duel, saying that such encounters were "a lingering relic of a barbarous civilization, which the law of the country has branded a crime."[28]

Massachusetts Congressman Anson Burlingame had no such reservations. After giving a speech on 21 June denouncing the assault, he too received a challenge from Brooks, who accused him of "injurious and offensive" language. Fearing that Brooks would run afoul of Federal regulations against dueling in the capital city, his seconds proposed a meeting outside the District of Columbia. Burlingame's representative accepted the challenge, proposing that the two men meet near a hotel on the Canadian side of Niagara Falls. Brooks refused the offer, saying that an enraged Northern public would endanger his life during the trip. For accepting the challenge Burlingame was summoned before Judge Hollingsworth and ordered to post a five thousand dollar good behavior bond. Sumner reacted with disappointment. In a letter to his old Free Soil friend Joshua Giddings he wrote: "Alas! for Burlingame, he has deliberately discarded the standard of Northern civilization to adopt the standard of Southern barbarism."[29]

Brooks's choice to avoid confrontation made him the subject of ridicule in the North. The following poem, authored by New York *Evening Post* editor William Cullen Bryant, was widely reprinted in Northern newspapers.[30]

Brooks's Canada Song[31]

To Canada Brooks was asked to go;
To waste of powder a pound or so,
He sighed as he answered No, no, no,
They might take my life on the way, you know.
Those Jersey railroads I can't abide
'Tis a dangerous thing in the trains to ride.
Each brakeman carries a knife by his side;
They'd cut my throat, and they'd cut it wide
There are savages haunting New York Bay,
To murder strangers that pass that way;
The Quaker Garrison keeps them in pay,
And they kill at least a score a day.
Beyond New York, in every car,
They keep a supply of feathers and tar;
They daub it on with an iron bar
And I should be smothered ere I got far.
Those dreadful Yankees talk through the nose;
The sound is terrible, goodness knows;
And when I hear it, a shiver goes
From the crown of my head to the tips of my toes.
So, dearest Mr. Burlingame,
I'll stay at home, if 'tis all the same,
And I'll tell the world 'tis a burning shame
That we did not fight, and you are to blame.

Brooks received much more enthusiastic treatment from his own constituents. On 28 July there was a special election in his congressional district to fill the seat he had resigned. Brooks billed the election as a referendum on his behavior. In a campaign card published in newspapers throughout the district he pleaded for voters to re-elect him "with an unanimity which will thunder into the ears of fanaticism the terrors of the storm that is coming upon them."[32] He ran without opposition and remained in Washington, factors, which would normally depress turnout. The election provided a clear show of support, however. He received 7,922 votes, an almost 30 percent increase over his 1854 total. In October he ran again, this time in the regular congressional elections. By then the excitement had decreased, though still no opponent dared challenge Brooks at the ballot box. He received 4,093 votes in the regular election, or slightly more than half his July total.[33]

The drop in turnout paralleled Brooks's increasing ambivalence about being an icon of sectionalism. During the October campaign he had exclaimed "I have been a disunionist since the time I could think."[34] After his return to Washington, however, Brooks showed signs of moderation. In a December debate over the power of Congress to legislate in the territories he endorsed the notion of popular sovereignty for Kansas, though not during the territorial phase. Remarkably, he stated that he would not oppose the admission of Kansas as a free state, as long as its citizens had complied with the terms of the Nebraska bill. This he interpreted in the standard Southern way as meaning non-interference with slavery until the time of statehood. The following extract from the speech gives Brooks's description of his political evolution as a Congressman. It provides a good indication of his political attitudes and sense of duty in the wake of the incident. It also suggests how conditional Southern support for the Democratic party could be. Like Calhoun before him Brooks remained suspicious of party mechanisms and the compromises they required. Yet he recognized the power parties wielded. This put him in a difficult situation. South Carolina's governor and four of its six congressmen had opposed participating in the Democratic convention. Seeming too cooperative with Northerners of any variety might cause him to lose the political capital he had earned with the caning. The drop in turnout from July to October was a clear indication that voters could take away what they had given him. Even the strict state rights position he took on the admission of Kansas might be used against him by a savvy opponent.[35]

Remarks of Preston S. Brooks on Party Politics and Kansas[36]

Heretofore, and elsewhere, I have declared that I was not much of a national Democrat. Nor am I; yet I have affiliated with the Democratic party, and so long as our present Government continues I shall continue to cooperate with the party, by whatever name it may be called, which represents its principles. My connection with it, however, is not of so intimate a character as to make it responsible for my positions, or to embarrass me by any which it may take. I believe that most of its principles are the true principles of the Constitution, and I have the fullest confidence in the wisdom, patriotism, and orthodoxy of many of the party leaders at the North, and in the free States. Yet in the party, as such, I have neither the fullest reliance nor confidence, and I will give my reasons. When I first entered this Hall, I was an unqualified disunionist. I had been made so by the action of the General

Government in reference to the tariff, to the territory acquired from Mexico, and its whole legislation in regard to slaves. Shortly after the meeting of the Thirty-Third Congress, a bill was passed repealing the Missouri restriction line,[37] whereby the States of the South had been excluded, as inferiors, from the common domain. A change of sentiment immediately occurred within me, and my heart expanded with love for our whole country. I chided myself for having done injustice to the Democratic party, which, by repealing an odious restriction, had relieved my people from an insult which had burned them for many a long year. I reproached myself for distrusting the virtue of a people who, by an unprecedented majority, placed General Pierce in power over the greatest living military captain,[38] with all the prestige of military glory fresh upon him. I felt that I had wronged, in my appreciation of them, the Democratic members of Congress who had nobly redeemed their pledge of non-intervention made at Baltimore, and on the first occasion which presented itself, had applied the principle of non-intervention by removing the obstacle they encountered in Kansas and Nebraska—the line of intervention. They had been elected, as had the President, upon the Baltimore platform, the cardinal feature of which was non-intervention by Congress with the subject of slavery in the District of Columbia and the Territories. This was the distinct issue before northern and southern Democracy, and the people of both sections elected Democrats to Congress. Yet, sir, for faithfully doing that which they were commissioned to do, what was the consequence? Complaints of treachery and broken faith filled the air. A contract had been broken, with the terms of which one of the contracting parties had never complied; a common statute had been repealed, which, forsooth, was irrepealable and christened a compact between sections, when it was notorious that representatives from the different sections had indiscriminately voted—some for and some against. A sepulchral howl was wafted from Maine to Iowa, and our northern friends chased down with a hue and cry.

The act which repealed the Missouri restriction also provided territorial governments for Kansas and Nebraska, and further provided for their admission as States upon the terms and conditions heretofore stated. When the Thirty-Fourth Congress assembled, and I inspected the new material sent to succeed the Nebraska Democrats of the North—when I learned more of their principles and observed their efforts to extend them, my faith in northern Democracy began to lose some of its saving grace. I had observed the deluding influences of a secret political association, which mysteriously made dark lanterns of the thinking heads of men,[39] and endeavored to cajole myself into the belief that northern Democracy had been temporarily led astray by its bewilderments; but that, aided by the light of the Constitution, they would ultimately recover the true faith. I hoped for a reaction, and felt bound in honor and in gratitude to stand by such of our northern friends as had remained faithful to the principles of the Constitution, and who had stood to us in the hour of their adversity. Influenced by these and other like considerations, my friend of the mountain district in South Carolina [MR. ORR] and myself alone of our delegation, advocated the representation of our State in the Democratic Convention at Cincinnati;[40] and the people of our State, not because of our influence, but of their own free will and generous nature, which never fails to respond to acts of justice or magnanimity, met our Democratic friends in common council for the common good.

Brooks never got the chance to try these strategies. He remained in Washington while the congressional session dragged on through January 1857. On the 22d he told friends that he had developed a cough and sore throat. He stayed at his boardinghouse to rest and recuperate but never improved. After a five-day bout with the sickness he died on 27 January. Reports described the cause of death as croup or laryngitis. His body was laid in state in the capitol. Senate eulogies were delivered by Senators Josiah Evans of South Carolina, Robert M. T. Hunter of Virginia, and Robert Toombs of Georgia. Eulogists in the House included Lawrence Keitt, Mississippi representative John Quitman, who had served with Brooks in Mexico, and Ohio representative Lewis Campbell, who had been a member of the House investigating committee. The speakers avoided referring to the incident. Rather, they emphasized Brooks's amiability, courage, loyalty, and conviction. Only one person, representative John Savage of Tennessee, mentioned the attack, equating the deed to that of Brutus in assassinating Julius Caesar. Outraged by this analogy, the majority of the Republican congressmen left the House as soon as Savage stopped speaking. To prevent further controversy Senator Butler had Savage's remarks omitted from the published proceedings. Brooks's body was transported to Edgefield in mid-February. After an elaborate funeral his body was buried in the graveyard of the Episcopal church. Sumner was in Boston recuperating when Brooks died. He visited with Longfellow the day that the death was reported. Longfellow's journal described Sumner's mood. "His assailant Brooks has died suddenly at Washington. I do not think Sumner had any personal feeling against him. He looked upon him as a mere tool of the slaveholders, or, at all events, of the South Carolinians."[41]

Epitaph

Ever Able, Manly, Just And Heroic;
Illustrating true Patriotism
By his devotion to his Country;
The whole South unites
With his bereaved family
In deploring his untimely end.
"Earth has never pillowed
Upon her Bosom a truer Son.
Nor Heaven opened wide her Gates,
To receive a manlier spirit."

• • •

Preston S. Brooks will be Long, Long Remembered:
As one in whom the virtues loved to Dwell
Tho' sad to us, and dark this dispensation.
We know God's wisdom
Orders all things well.

FIGURE 3.6   Preston S. Brooks Gravesite, Edgefield, South Carolina

(Photo by the author)

The Brooks tombstone includes an eclectic blend of symbolism. (see Figure 3.6)
The tombstone's obelisk shape emerged as a favorite design for commemorating
heroes, especially after this geometric form was adopted for the Washington monument in the 1840s. For Egyptians the shape originally represented a shaft of light
connecting the Sun and the Earth, and thus the bridge between mortality and eter-
nity. Conquest of Egypt, both by ancient Romans and by French Emperor
Napoleon, led to the relocation of many obelisks to Europe and symbolically associated the obelisk with military triumph. The laurel wreaths on the tombstone's
base were a classical symbol of distinction. Both the endlessness of the circular
form and the laurel's evergreen leaves represented eternal victory over death. The
Brooks tombstone's consciously elaborate and impressive design exemplifies the
increasingly fashionable interest in mortality of the 1840s and 1850s. Victorian
Romanticism transformed the once forlorn graveyards of the dead into cemetery
gardens for the renewal of the living. Guided by lush landscaping, the hallowed
memories of the departed, and the lessons of tombstone epitaphs, cemetery visitors would be indoctrinated into the sublime mysteries of nature: life, death, and
rebirth. The result was what scholars have termed the "beautification of death."
American cemetery designs also embodied a complex intersection between
democracy and status. The 1850s represented a high point for ostentatious burials
by members of the elite. When these elaborate customs and rituals became widely

practiced by lower and middle classes after the Civil War, elites tended to adopt a much more restrained burial style. The Brooks tombstone provides a good example of the more imposing elite style.[42]

SUMNER'S ILLNESS: WAS HE SHAMMING?

Apart from the caning itself, nothing proved more controversial than discussions of how severely injured Sumner had been during the attack. Sumner's friends believed that the attack had severely wounded him. They concluded that Brooks was responsible for aggravated assault and perhaps even attempted murder. As long as Sumner remained absent from the Senate his vacant chair testified silently to slaveholder brutality. Brooks's defenders, however, argued that Sumner's wounds were minimal. It was their claim that he was shamming his injuries for political effect. A typical example of this charge was published a few days after the attack in the Richmond *Whig*.

Possuming

Richmond, Virginia, *Whig*, 31 May 1856
The daily and hourly reports from Washington concerning the condition of Sumner, are all very strange and funny, and lead us to believe that the Abolition wretch, with his Abolition physicians as accomplices in the trick, is playing possum. We hear one moment that he is "comfortable and doing well"—we hear the next, that his condition is "extremely critical," and that no one is allowed to see him; and then a few hours afterwards we are favored with a different story.

Now, for our part, we never have believed that Sumner was sufficiently hurt to make it necessary for him to take to his bed at all. Least of all do we believe that the well-deserved gutta-perching he received was of so severe a character as to detain him in confinement for more than a week. But we believe it is a miserable Abolition trick from beginning to end—resorted to keep alive and diffuse and strengthen the sympathy awakened for him among his confederates at the North. Nigger-worshipping fanatics of the male gender, and weak-minded women and silly children, are horribly affected at the thought of blood oozing out from a pin-scratch. And Sumner is wily politician enough to take advantage of this little fact.

We suggest that the Senate appoint a committee, consisting of one Southern man, to ascertain Sumner's actual condition. We think the bare sight of a hundredth part of a Southern man would impart to the possuming wretch strength enough to enable him to take up his bed and walk—yea, walk even to Boston.

Sumner's injuries were thoroughly investigated by the House committee during their late May hearings. They questioned Dr. Cornelius Boyle, who attended Sumner just after the attack, and Dr. Marshall Perry, who had arrived from Boston on 24 May to assist with Sumner's care. Dr. Boyle described himself as an "Old-line Whig" who had "nothing to do with any man's politics." He often treated members of Congress and had become acquainted with Brooks during the illness of another Congressman. Suspicious of this relationship, Republicans accused Boyle of offering bail for Brooks. Boyle emphatically denied the charge but was not able to remove Republican doubts that he had understated the severity of Sumner's injuries. The timing of his testimony contributed significantly to these doubts. Boyle gave the following account less than a week after the attack, at a point when Sumner was beginning to feel better. By the evening of the day Boyle had testified, however, Sumner's condition began to worsen as his wounds became inflamed and his fever climbed. Boyle himself was called to treat Sumner's largest wound, which he closed with a solution of gun-cotton and chloroform. Because his testimony had preceded the flare-up by several hours, however, those who saw Sumner over the next few days assumed that he had consciously minimized the severity of the Senator's wounds.[43]

Doctor Cornelius Boyle's Testimony (Tuesday 27 June)[44]

Question: State the condition in which you found [Senator Sumner], and the character of his wounds.

Answer: I found Mr. Sumner in the ante-room of the Senate bleeding very copiously, and with a great deal of blood upon his clothes. The blood went all over my shirt in dressing his wounds. His friends thought I ought not to dress his wounds there, but take him to his residence. I differed, and stated my reason, that if I dressed his wounds at once and at that place, they would heal by first intentions; and that if I did not, suppuration might take place. Mr. Campbell, I think, was present, and some others, and they agreed with me. I put four stitches—two into each wound; he then went to his room. I came there an hour afterwards. The blood stopped as soon as I drew the wounds together. He was doing very well.

Question: Describe the character of the wounds, and where they were.

Answer: They were both on the scalp. There were marks of three wounds on the scalp, but only two that I dressed. One was a very slight wound, that required no special attention. One was two and a quarter inches long, cut to the bone—cut under, as it were, and very ragged. This wound has healed up without any supperation at all. The other is not quite two inches long, and has healed up within about half an inch, and has supperated.

Question: Were they both cut to the bone?

Answer: They were. I have the probe now in my pocket, from which the blood has not been washed. [Instrument produced.] One was a cut to the depth of nearly an inch. It is only an eighth of an inch to the scalp, but it was cut in and down. I have mentioned the fact that one of the wounds was two and a quarter inches long, and the other about one sixteenth of an inch less than two inches.

Question: State on what part of the head the gashes were inflicted?

Answer: One wound was behind, on the left side of the head, and the other was rather in front, about two inches from the median line.

Question: Were there any other bruises or cuts upon his head?

Answer: There was one slight mark on the back of his head, but not severe enough to require dressing, and I have not paid any attention to it since. There were marks on the hands also, and a red mark down the face near the temple, which has disappeared, as though it was caused by a faint blow. . . .

Question: (by Mr. Cobb.) What is your opinion of these wounds, just as they are?

Answer: I look upon them simply as flesh wounds.

Question: What is your opinion in reference to the condition of Mr. Sumner? How long need he be confined on account of these wounds?

Answer: His wounds do not necessarily confine him one moment. He would have come to the Senate on Friday, if I had recommended it.

Question: Could he have come out with safety?

Answer: He could have come with safety, as far as the wounds were concerned. . . .

Question: State in this connexion, whether there were any other persons with him—I mean any physicians who advised that perhaps it might not be safe for him to go out.

Answer: I have seen no medical man with him but myself. There has been none there. There are a great many friends present, and they make Mr. Sumner out a great deal worse than he is. They say he has a fever. I have never discovered any. I have been his constant attendant, and I have never known his pulse at any moment higher than eighty-two. I yesterday corrected on article in the *Intelligencer,* stating that he had a fever, and the correction appears in to-day's paper. He has no fever to my knowledge. I have visited him twice a day. His brother said he ought not to come out, and cited a great many cases that had come under his observation in Paris, where death had taken place in six weeks from blows on the head. Senator Sumner of course took the advice of his brother and his friends, and I, of course, allowed them to do as they thought proper. Perhaps I ought to state my reason for objecting to his coming out on Friday. There was a good deal of excitement at that time, and I thought that, if Mr. Sumner did not go into the Senate for a day or two, the excitement might wear off. . . .

Question: Where you accidentally called to attend Mr. Sumner?

Answer: No, sir; Mr. Jones said he was coming for me. I met him in a carriage, and he said he was on his way to my office. I was then coming down the Avenue. I had not seen Mr. Sumner before that time. I've since called regularly.

Question: What are your political affinities?

Answer: I am an old-line Whig—if I have any politics. I was born in the city of Washington.

Question: Were you bail for Mr. Brooks?

Answer: I was not.

Question: (by Mr. Cobb.) Are you a regular practicing physician of the city; and if so, for how long have you practiced?

Answer: I've been practicing since 1844. I have been connected with hospitals and medicine since 1833.

Question: I ask whether in your practice your treatment depends upon the political opinions of your patients?

Answer: No, sir.

Question: Do you treat them with reference to their political opinions, or you judge more by the pulse?

Answer: I have nothing to do with any man's politics.

Dr. Perry testified the following day. His comments reflect the early stages of Sumner's medical relapse. Although careful to support Dr. Boyle's diagnosis and treatment, Dr. Perry did express subtle reservations about the use of collodion to close the largest wound. It is clear from the comments of Rep. Campbell that Dr. Boyle's treatment had already become controversial. Dr. Perry's discussion of the shock to Sumner's nervous system provides tantalizing hints about his patient's mental state. Some historians have suggested that the attack led Sumner to have a psychological breakdown similar to modern cases of post-traumatic stress disorder.[45]

Doctor Marshall Perry's Testimony (Wednesday, 28 June)[46]

Question: State, if you please, the character of his wounds, and the number.

Answer: I did not examine them very critically. I did examine the wounds on the back of his head. There were two cuts upon the back part; one upon the right of the median line, and one upon the left; the one upon the left was about two inches in length. Apparently, at the time, they were doing very well; I did not disturb pus. Upon the right side of the head was a pulpy feeling, which I disliked. The wound upon the left side had healed, or nearly so, when I first saw it; in the one on the right side there was perhaps an inch, or three-quarters of an inch, which had not adhered. He had some bruises about him—one upon the left hand, where the blood had settled under the skin; he also has a slight one upon the right hand. These were the only bruises I saw. I did not examine his body.

Question: Did you regard these wounds as endangering the life of Mr. Sumner?

Answer: I did not suppose, at the time, they would endanger his life, and I do not think now there is much danger. Up to yesterday he appeared very comfortable. Still, his nervous system has received such a shock that I told him he should be very careful, or reaction would come on. I did not consider, and I so told him, that he had then come to the crisis. Yesterday afternoon I saw him. He then had a very hot skin—was in a very excitable condition. His pulse was over ninety—quite full; a very different state of things from what he had had before. I told him then that reaction was coming on, and that he would be able to find out something by to-day. Last night he had a very uncomfortable night—great pain in the back of his head, especially. The glands on the back of his neck were beginning to swell. He was quite feverish through the night. This morning they sent for me and I met his physician. I did not consider myself as his physician, and therefore did not prescribe. I met his physician: we saw that suppuration had taken place in the wound on the right side of his head. The wound had nearly closed over. The physician had the night before applied collodion, which prevented the escape of pus. His head was hot; his pulse one hundred and four. We opened in the wound, and there was about a tablespoonful of pus discharged, which had gathered under the scalp. Of course he was very much relieved from the extreme suffering he had had during the night. What the results of the state of things will be it is impossible for me to say; but I think he is not out of danger. I think now the case is at the critical period. . . .

Question: State whether you regard the treatment of his physician as proper. [Mr. Campbell here stated that he asked his question at Dr. Boyle's request.]

Answer: I have not seen anything that was not perfectly proper. I think that fever now is the result of local inflammation. The collodion closed over the wound, and prevented any discharge of pus. I have seen nothing myself which I do not regard perfectly professional. I had not seen Dr. Boyle until this morning. I did not consider the case as one in which I was called upon to interfere professionally. I was here merely as a personal friend of Mr. Sumner, and did not come as his physician. When I met Dr. Boyle this morning, and heard his reasons for acting, I came to the conclusion that everything in the management of the case was entirely professional. . . .

Question: (by Mr. Pennington.) from the first moment you saw Mr. Sumner, has he been in a condition that you, as his physician, would recommend him to go out?

Answer: He has been in that condition that I told him, and told his brother, it would not be safe to go through the excitement of any exposure of any kind. I consider it very important that he should be kept quiet.

Question: From your knowledge of the wounds inflicted, has there been any time when it would have been prudent and proper for him to leave his lodgings?

Answer: No, sir.

By the end of the day on 28 June, Sumner was in increased pain and his fever had risen dangerously. Sumner's brother George, who had rushed to Washington as soon as he heard about the attack, took charge of medical care. Reacting to doubts about the effectiveness of Dr. Boyle's collodion treatments and suspecting that Boyle's friendship with Brooks had caused him to understate Sumner's injuries, George Sumner removed Boyle from the case. With help from Dr. Perry he selected a new team of doctors. By Friday Sumner's fever had broken and the inflammations had subsided.

Although he told his friends he wanted to return to the Senate as soon as possible, Sumner would spend the summer an invalid. His doctors screened visitors and kept him confined to his room for several weeks after the attack. In mid-June they suggested that he move out of the unhealthy environment of Washington. He was invited to stay at the Blair home in Silver Spring, Maryland, where he remained for three weeks. On 6 July he left for Philadelphia. Critics noted that Sumner had conveniently departed the city just one day before the Brooks trial. In a letter to the prosecuting attorney he said that he had "no desire to take any part in this proceeding."[47] By mid-July he had gone to Cape May, New Jersey, a seaside resort popular among the era's elites.

In a letter to his old friend and famed reformer Samuel Gridley Howe, Sumner gave an assessment of his condition. The document shows his anxious mental state and his lingering physical disabilities. It also shows his close attention to the political situation in Massachusetts. Sumner's senatorial term was due to end in 1857. The legislature chosen by voters in the fall elections would be responsible for re-appointing him or selecting a replacement. His physical condition was therefore as much of a political issue within Massachusetts as it was in the national arena.

Charles Sumner Reports on His Recuperation, 22 July 1856[48]

My strength is not re-established; but I ride on horseback, converse, read, write letters, and hope soon to be in working condition, though I fear that a perfect prudence would keep me from all public effort for some months to come. I feel as if composed of gristle instead of bone, and am very soon wearied by walking, which induces a pressure on the brain, so also has any attempt with the mind. But I believe these things are passing away. I strive by alternations of rest and exercise to solidify my system. More than three mouths have thus been blotted from all public activity, at a moment when more than ever in my life I was able to wield influence and do good. This has been hard to bear. They write to me of a public reception on my return home. I am sorry; I am against it. Gladly would I slip into Massachusetts, run about for a few days, and then, if able, commence our campaign. The war of liberation is begun.

Sumner spent late July and early August at Cape May, New Jersey. In late August his doctors recommended that he move to the mountains, and he relocated for several weeks to Cresson, Pennsylvania, in the Alleghenies. In early September he went to Philadelphia for a while, but he did not feel strong enough for the excitements of either Washington or Boston.

As his external wounds began to heal, rumors continued to circulate that Sumner was shirking his duty for political effect. The attack and the debate over his injuries even became a political issue in the Indiana state elections of October 1856. For years the Hoosier state had been a stronghold for the Democratic party. Jesse Bright, the state's senior senator, was a staunchly pro-southern Pierce loyalist who even kept slaves on a Kentucky plantation, and the state's other senator, John Pettit, had been the first person to attack Sumner for "violating his oath to the Constitution." Bitter factional disputes over the Nebraska bill had weakened the Democrats, however, while emboldening their Whig, Know-Nothing, and Free Soil opponents to form a fusion coalition. A state that had been solidly Democratic now became one of the nation's crucial partisan battlegrounds. As the elections approached, events in Indiana underscored the importance of the Sumner attack as an issue *within* the North as well as between Northerners and Southerners. In Indianapolis, Republicans put on a parade with floats dramatizing the assault on Sumner and the horrors of Kansas. Democrats responded by charging that Sumner's claims of continued disability were merely Republican propaganda. To counteract these accusations Massachusetts Senator Henry Wilson secured the following letters from Sumner's physicians.[49]

The Libels on Senator Sumner; Testimony of His Physicians

New York *Tribune*, 6 October 1856
To the editor of the N. Y. *Tribune*.

Sir: journals and orators devoted to the cause of Mr. Buchanan, have seen fit for partizan purposes, and in extenuation of an indefensible act, to charge a gross fraud upon my colleague, the Hon. Charles Sumner, by asserting that the injuries arising from the assault which left him insensible on the floor of the Senate Chamber on the 22d May last were so trivial that he could at any moment have resumed his public duties, from which it is alleged he has unnecessarily withdrawn.

This attempt to arrest the disgust awakened by the most shameful act in the legislative history of the world, and this calumny upon an absent man, have more especially been employed in Indiana. . . . Meanness and falsehood naturally consort with brutality and cowardice; and it is by a resort to such agencies, that the friends of Mr. Buchanan seek to sustain his failing cause.

That in characterizing this calumny upon my colleague, I do not use too strong language, let the testimony of his physicians show. . . .

I am, Sir, faithfully yours,
Henry Wilson.
Oct. 4, 1856.

• • •

Boston, Oct 2, 1856

Hon. Henry Wilson - Sir: I first visited Mr. Sumner on Monday, 25th May, three days after the assault upon him by Mr. Brooks, and saw him constantly to the 29th May, when Dr. Lindsly became his regular physician.

For three days of this time he was in a critical situation from the external injuries, and I remained in Washington in order to attend upon him. My fears on leaving him were that, besides the external injuries, his brain had received a shock from which it might not recover for months, and I felt it my duty to caution him strongly against all exertion until it was fully restored from the effects of the shock.

I pressed this upon him because he expressed a determination to resume his duties at once, which according to my opinion, he could not do without the risk of losing his life.

Very respectfully, &c.,
Marshall S. Perry

• • •

Washington, Sept. 23, 1856

Hon. Henry Wilson—Dear Sir: In reply to your inquiry, I state that I was the regular medical attendent of Mr. Sumner, from May 29 to the time of his leaving Washington, at the beginning of July.

During this whole period he was suffering from the effects of the injuries received in the Senate Chamber on the 23d of May. Much of this time he was confined to his bed; and at no part of the time was he able to resume his public duties. His constant wish, expressed repeatedly to me, was that he might be speedily restored, so as to take his seat again in the Senate, from which, as I am informed, he had never before been absent for a single day.

Mr. Sumner left hereby my advice, in order to enjoy the advantage of a change of air, either at the seashore or on the mountains. I inclined in favor of the latter, and recommended Schooley's mountain in New Jersey.

In the event of his great weakness continuing on his going to Philadelphia, I urged him to consult an eminent physician there, and be governed by his advice.

I remain, faithfully yours,
Harvey Linsley, III

• • •

Philadelphia, Oct. 2, 1856.

Hon. Henry Wilson—Sir: in reply to your inquiries, I begin by stating that my intercourse with Mr. Sumner has been wholly of a professional and social nature, as, personally, I should derive no satisfaction from the success of those political principles to which he is committed.

I never saw Mr. Sumner before the 9th of July, when, upon his arrival in Philadelphia, he came under my professional care. Since then, down to the present moment, he has acted entirely in compliance with my advice, given to promote his restoration to health at the earliest period. I have insisted upon his seclusion, much in opposition to his own earnest desires, and the repeated calls of some of his political friends, convinced that his early recovery depended upon his entire abstraction from all excitement.

I make the statement in justice to Mr. Sumner, in order to repel the unfounded rumors of his complicity with party tactics in thus withdrawing himself. What he has thus done, he has done absolutely under my professional direction, and in the discharge of my duty I could not have given any other advice.

When Mr. Sumner came under my care he was exceedingly feeble, with a morbid irritability of the nervous system, with sleeplessness, and inability to make any exertion, mental or physical; also without apparent recuperative power. His condition awakened my solicitude, as it was difficult to determine whether he labored under functional or organic injury of the brain. It was evident that the injuries he had originally received on the floor of the Senate had been aggravated by the peculiar condition of his nervous system at the time, a condition induced by severe mental exertion, and nervous tension from the loss of sleep for several consecutive nights, but also by the peculiar susceptibility of his temperament, which is highly nervous. I enjoined absolute repose, and, especially, withdrawal from all public duties, and advised mountain air, preferring Cresson, on the Alleghanies, to Schooley's mountain, as higher and more retired.

Mr. Sumner has returned from Cresson improved, though still an invalid, and he is now under my constant care. His restoration to health at an early day depends entirely upon his complete abstraction, except within prescribed limits, from mental or physical exertion.

Very respectfully, your obedient servant,
Casper Wister.

Against Dr. Wister's advice, Sumner returned to Boston in late October to help with the Republican campaign. Being at home brought no respite from his pains. A few days before the election he attempted to deliver a speech at a welcome rally given in his honor. Although he had written out a long address he was only able to read a few sentences before abandoning the effort. The sweeping victory by Massachusetts Republicans in the elections that followed provided little relief, but it did guarantee Sumner's reappointment to the Senate. Although encouraged by the results, Sumner grew increasingly frustrated that his disabilities would stop him from returning to Washington. "My chief sorrow," he wrote to abolitionist poet John Greenleaf Whittier, "has been that I have been shut out from the field of action. . . . I long to speak and liberate my soul."[50] Sumner considered resigning from the Senate but received strong opposition from his friends. The symbolism of his absence, they contended, spoke as effectively against the brutality of the slave power as could any of his speeches. Future Massachusetts governor John A. Andrew succinctly stated the point: "sit in your seat if you can. If you can't, let it be *vacant.*"[51]

Sumner took their advice, remaining away from Washington until late February. When he did resume his seat it was just for a single day, to sustain a schedule of tariff reductions supported by Massachusetts wool manufacturers. The effort provoked a relapse so severe that he nearly passed out in his Senate seat. His doctor ordered him to cease working, and after being sworn in for a second term on 4 March he initiated plans for a recuperative vacation to Europe. By the end of the month he was in Paris. He continued his travels through the summer, stopping in England, Scotland, Belgium, Holland, Switzerland, and Italy. Europe's intellectual and political leaders embraced him. He dined with William Thackeray, had meetings with William Gladstone, Lord Aberdeen, Lord Palmerston, and Lord Russell, and visited Alexis de Tocqueville at his country estate. He did not return to Boston until mid-November 1857. When the United States Senate reconvened in December Sumner was in his seat but unable to participate in the crucial debate over the admission of Kansas. Another relapse in April 1858 increased his anxiety. In a letter to Wendell Phillips he wrote "I must regain my health, or cease to cumber the earth. That vacant chair must be filled." Once again he went to Europe, issuing the following letter to his constituents as an explanation of his course. Sumner issued the letter exactly two years to the day after the attack.[52]

Sumner's Letter to the People of Massachusetts, 22 May 1858[53]

Two years have now passed, since, when in the enjoyment of perfect health, I was suddenly made an invalid. Throughout this protracted period, amidst various vicissitudes of convalescence, I seemed to be slowly regaining the health that had been taken from me, until I was encouraged to believe myself on the verge of perfect recovery.

But injuries so grave as those originally received are not readily repaired; and a recent relapse painfully admonishes me, that, although enjoying many of the conditions of prosperous convalescence, I am not yet beyond the necessity of caution. This has been confirmed by the physicians in Boston and Philadelphia most familiar with my case, who, in concurrence with counsels previously given by medical authorities in Europe, have enjoined travel as best calculated to promote restoration. Anxious to spare no effort for this end, so long deferred, I to-day sail for France.

To the generous people of Massachusetts, who have honored me with an important trust, and cheered me by so much sympathy, I wish to express the thanks which now palpitate in my bosom, while I say to them all collectively, as I would say to a friend, Farewell!

These valedictory words would be imperfect, if I did not seize this occasion to declare, what I have often said less publicly, that, had I foreseen originally the duration of my disability, I should at once have resigned my seat in the Senate, making way for a servant more fortunate in the precious advantages of health. I did not do so, because, like other invalids, I lived in the belief that I was soon to be well, and was reluctant to renounce the opportunity of again exposing the hideous barbarism of Slavery, now more than ever transfused into the National Government, infecting its whole policy and degrading its whole character. Besides, I was often assured, and encouraged to feel, that to every sincere lover of civilization my vacant chair was a perpetual speech.

The 1858 trip to Europe and the medical treatments Sumner received while abroad sparked a new round of controversy. The New York *Tribune*, the New York *Times*, and other Republican newspapers carried full reports on his case. These were intended to counteract efforts by Sumner's critics to lampoon the "vacant chair" as yet another political trick. The accounts spared no detail of Sumner's suffering under what amounted to a second martyrdom.[54]

The treatments also offer a window into the state of medical science in the mid-nineteenth century. At the time when Sumner received these remedies, many medical treatments we take for granted were still in early development. General anesthesia using ether and chloroform, for example, had been introduced less than a dozen years before. Louis Pasteur's innovative work on the role of germs in fermentation had just been announced, and it would be several years before he would develop "Pasteurization" of food products. It would be in this same year of 1858 that Rudolf Virchow's revolutionary work on cell pathology would reach print, finally discrediting the notion that imbalances in what classical scholars had called the "four humours" were responsible for pain and disease. Other scientific breakthroughs relevant to Sumner's case would come too late for him. It was not until 1865 that the first scientific studies documenting the role of bacteria in causing infections would become widely known. Had doctors Boyle and Perry been aware of the importance of achieving sterility in Sumner's initial wounds, his whole recuperation process would have undoubtedly been different. The person who treated Sumner in Paris was Dr. Charles Edward Brown-Séquard, a native of France who had lived in the United States and who had been on the faculty at the Medical College of Virginia until his antislavery opinions had rendered him unwelcome. Brown-Séquard would go on to be a pioneering neurologist and physiologist, but few of his innovations played any role in Sumner's healing.[55]

The State of Mr. Sumner's Health

New York *Tribune*, 9 July 1858
FROM Our Own Correspondent.
PARIS, June 23, 1858.
On coming abroad this time [Senator Sumner] was counting mainly on the curative influences of travel, exercise in the open air, and absence of that excitement on home affairs which he could not escape in America. At Paris he met Dr. Geo. Hayward, the eminent Boston surgeon, who, in view of his present condition, at once urged "active treatment"—that is, the application of a system of counter-irritants in order to reach the malady in the cerebral system and in the spine. With the sanction of Dr. H, Mr. Sumner then put himself in the hands of Dr. Brown-Sequard, the celebrated physiologist, so well known in England and America. . . , whose "specialty" as a practicing physician is diseases of the spine and nervous system. Dr. Brown-Sequard's careful and acute investigation of the case resulted in a diagnosis which, if yours were a medical instead of a general journal, I should be inexcusable for not giving in detail from the memorandum before me. Suffice it for the lay reader to say: the brain itself is ascertained to be free of any serious remaining injury, but the effects of the original commotion there are still manifest in an effusion of liquid about the brain and in a slight degree of congestion, chiefly if not only confined to the membrane around the brain; it was also found that the spine was suffering in two places from the effect of what is called *contre-coup*. . . . Dr. Brown-Sequard agrees with Dr. Hayward as to the necessity of an active treatment, doubting very much whether any degree of care or lapse of time, unless the morbid condition of the system be directly acted upon, would not always leave the patient exposed to a relapse. He proceeded, therefore, at once to apply fire to the back of the neck and along the spine. Now, fire is fire, and the quality of it is to burn, as surely as the "property of rain is to wet." And here I cannot do better than to quote entire a note I have just received from M. Sequard: "I think you will like to be able to say that I have told you that I have applied six *moxas* to Senator Sumner's neck and back, and that he has borne these *exceedingly* painful applications with the greatest courage and patience. You know that a moxa is a burning of the skin with inflamed agaric *(amadou)*, cotton-wool or some other very combustible substance—I had never seen a man bearing with such a fortitude as Mr. Sumner has shown, the extremely violent pain of this kind of burning" So you see the *morale* is sound. . . .

Mr. Sumner's general health has *almost* entirely rallied from the original shock. This is due to what the English physicians last year called "the wonderful recuperative energies of his constitution," and to what Dr. Sequard names "a remarkable power of resistance to injury." It is this, in alliance with his untouched vigor of will, that has enabled Mr. S. to throw off or resist so much of the effects of his original injuries, and now enables him to bear the moxa without the chloroform which Dr. Sequard recommended, and without the wincing which the Doctor expected. The present severe treatment, which Dr. S. is not yet ready to relinquish, may be followed, in the course of the Summer, by certain internal remedies and by baths.

The Charleston, South Carolina, *Courier*, called into question every aspect of these reports. Less notorious outside of South Carolina than the Charleston *Mercury*, the *Courier* was the city's moderate voice. Its Northern-born editor usually steered the paper toward the city's business interests rather than politics. That he felt compelled to attack Sumner more than two years after the caning is another interesting benchmark of the incident's role in forging Southern unity against an apparently deceptive and duplicitous North. That Northerners in general were untrustworthy and disingenuous became one of the persistent attitudes even among moderate Southerners as secession approached.[56]

The Latest Bulletin

Charleston *Courier*, 8 September 1858

It is evident that Charles Sumner has determined to get well as soon as the public mind shall be sufficiently impressed with the notion that he has been injured at all. No one conversant with the facts of the case and the nature of the cane used in the reply to Sumner's Rhodomantade of slang and slander garnished by plagiarism, will believe that anything more than chagrin and moral discomfiture have ailed him. Unfortunately, however, for Sumner—who was previously considered a gentleman—the ready letter writers who abound in Washington, give the cue to a story of bloody bones and broken heads, and Sumner himself, in the first shock of disappointment and uncertainty, assented to the story. The physician first in attendance was too honest and independent to become an accomplice in the game—hence his discharge and hence the mystery and privacy that have attended Sumner's movements.

Hence, also, the remarkable fact, that although the free-dirt papers have, at regular intervals, issued carefully detailed and seemingly official reports of the state of Sumner's bodily health, no American physician has a fixed his authority to any of these bulletins.

The opinions and treatment of Dr. Brown-Sequard—who is not a practicing physician, in our American usage of the term—are only known also through the reports of anonymous and irresponsible correspondents.

The positive testimony in the case is almost conclusive to the belief—honestly and reluctantly entertained by many—that Sumner has been malingering, or "playing 'Possum.' "

There has been no *testimony*, and not even responsible and avowed assertion, on the other side.

Twelve months ago Sumner skulked away to England, and his few surviving friends hoped that he would there find a good pretext for letting go his sham sickness, and consenting to become well.

The creature, however, could not deny himself the pleasure of parading his simulated sores and sorrows, and the first public act or appearance of the malingering refugee was at a dinner of the Benchers of the Inner Temple.[57] We were regaled with reports of this entertainment, coupled with the startling announcement that no American gentleman had been invited to such an entertainment. If the grave Benchers are not in the habit of inviting American *gentleman*, there was no exception in Sumner's case.

After other feasting and parading of this sort, Sumner returned, but the tone of the public mind and of the public journals was not prepared to admit that a man—or a biped in breeches—leaving America in the condition represented by Sumner could be cured by Thames water and Bencher's festivals.

It was soon found that to get well then, and after such therapeutic appliances, as a senatorial salary and a pleasure excursion, would be to confess the sham too openly.

Hence the second trip to Europe under a different cue and management—hence the "terrible tractoration" so eloquently detailed by reporters and correspondents, who, of course, are chosen friends of Dr. Brown-Sequard—hence the resort, not to a physician in practice and of repute for therapeutic success, but to a medical inquirer, whose pre-eminent and sole distinction is in a special and limited province of physiology. . .

IMPLICATIONS

That the friendship between Charles Sumner and A. P. Butler would degenerate into one of the nation's most shocking incidents demonstrates the corrosive power of the slavery issue in antebellum society. The two men had much in common. Their joy in the refinements of art and literature set them apart as members of an intellectual elite. More importantly, their shared desire to see the legacy of the American Revolution preserved and extended led them to agree on the Law as the elemental basis of the American polity. Their insistence that equality was essential to the democratic process differed only when it came to the decisive question of who would be allowed to participate. Under the influence of Romanticism, both men concurred that integrity of character and authenticity of motive were decisive to political virtue. Others could tolerate the disorderliness of partisan politics and accept the soothing ambiguities of things like popular sovereignty; neither Sumner nor Butler had lasting use for this kind of *realpolitik* expediency. Treating the law as a temporary working arrangement, after all, would undermine its enduring and even transcendental role as the bulwark of American liberties. Unfortunately for their relationship, Butler believed that the right to hold slave property was an essential part of the Constitution and the laws, while Sumner viewed slavery as a violation of the very equality both men cherished so strongly.

All things considered, Sumner found Senator Butler to be personally less troubling than those Northern Democrats, especially president Franklin Pierce and Stephen A. Douglas, who seemed willing to set aside their principles in order to appease what Sumner called the "slave power." In his "Crime Against Kansas" speech he mentions these two Northern Democrats over a hundred times, while referring to Butler less than twenty times. That a senator would craft speeches as much to undermine a competing party in his home-state as to address the immediate issues under debate was hardly extraordinary; it is intriguing to view Sumner's oration as an early campaign speech for the state elections of 1856. An alliance between Massachusetts Democrats and Know-Nothings could have put Sumner out of the Senate just as surely as the Coalition between Democrats and Free-Soilers had installed him to power. Thus Sumner had more at stake in the contest against his Northern Democratic rivals than against any particular Southerner. Because Douglas was a Northern Democrat but did not have a direct constituency in Massachusetts he was an especially attractive target for Sumner's wrath. It is not surprising that their personal conflict emerged well before Sumner's break with Butler.

For Preston Brooks the issues were even more complex. He was keenly aware of the debate over slavery and had a sharply pessimistic vision of abolition's consequences. Likewise, his sensitivity to the evolving partisan factionalism in Edgefield County, in South Carolina, and in America as a whole contributed to his behavior at the time of the attack. Above all, Brooks was influenced by his concern over reputation. Public statements by Brooks and his supporters were pervaded by fears of "degradation." Sumner's "Crime Against Kansas" speech described as immoral the very things Brooks cared most about. The impact of Kansas on South Carolina's economy would be relatively slight; the impact of saying that no slaveholding Southerner had moral worth enough to enter Kansas was devastating. Worse, Sumner piled on accusations that a member of Brooks's family was a liar and a cripple. Such a reduction in status was more than he could bear. It is revealing that he illustrated the seriousness of the circumstances by resorting to sexual and familial analogies. When Brooks characterized Sumner's attacks on South Carolina as the moral equivalent of rape he spoke of the most primal and vulnerable relationships in human society. For Brooks, both the speech and his response were thus tied to basic notions of masculine duty, honor, control, and rank.[58]

The uproar that followed provided full confirmation of the South's decline from power and respect. As the abolitionists were fond of pointing out, Southerners had dominated Congress, the presidency, and the Supreme Court since the nation's founding. The Sumner incident, however, became an important symbol of the transformations in favor of the North. Northern dominance of the post-attack debate in newspapers and rallies, along with an anti-Brooks expulsion vote by nearly two-thirds of all congressmen showed conclusively that Southern elites were facing a status revolution that they could neither channel nor contain. Moreover, Northerners like Sumner sought to minimize Southern contributions to the nation's history. The result was polarization. Before 1856, the fire-eaters had struggled to make their message resonate with the mass of Southern voters. Brooks himself had found more success associating with national Democrats than with Calhounite secessionists. Afterwards, however, the secessionists had little difficulty in persuading their audiences that the North cared little for them or their region.

In the North, too, the incident increased sectional polarization, although always in the context of partisan rivalries. Sumner's own opposition to slavery came from the abstractions of political philosophy, literature, and theology, none of which had much appeal to ordinary citizens. The attack transformed Sumner's ethereal warnings about the Slave Power into something concrete, immediate, personal, and local. Now every Northerner could visualize the dangers, and everyone could see how the "slave power" threatened white liberties as well as black. The incident was especially crucial in shifting momentum away from the Know-Nothings to Sumner's Republican coalition. By 1857, Massachusetts Know-Nothing governor Henry Gardner was able to attract less than half of his pre-assault vote, and Republicans gained control of the legislature, the governor's office, and the state's congressional delegation. From now on the Republican party would be a permanent institution in American politics.[59]

Sumner himself would return to his full senatorial duties in December 1859. When South Carolina left the Union in December 1860 he expressed the hope that secession would eventually lead to emancipation but feared that violence would ensue. "Much as I desire the extinction of Slavery," he wrote an acquaintance in England, "I do not wish to see it go down in blood."[60] Almost as soon as Lincoln took over the presidency Sumner began pushing him to declare emancipation. Sumner contributed significantly to laws banning slavery in the District of Columbia, to the emancipation proclamation, and eventually to the reconstruction amendments guaranteeing civil rights and suffrage protections for the former slaves. At the time of his death in March 1874 he was pushing for a bill outlawing racial discrimination in public accommodations. The bill would become the Civil Rights Act of 1875. Passionate and inflexible to the end, Sumner left an indelible mark on American history.

NOTES

1. On the late antebellum newspaper industry and its relationship to the political parties see William E. Huntzicker, *The Popular Press, 1833–1865* (Westport, Conn: Greenwood Press, 1993), e.p. 35–48, and Culver H. Smith, *The Press, Polotics, and Patronage: The American Government's Use of Newspapers, 1789–1875* (Athens: University of Georgia Press, 1977), 192–219.

2. James Batchelder was one of the guards who had the duty of keeping Anthony Burns from escaping or being set free by abolitionists during the so-called "Anthony Burns riots" of May 1854. He was killed during an unsuccessful rescue attempt. See Von Frank, *Trials of Anthony Burns*, esp. 92–96.

3. For Calhoun and the failure of South Carolina to develop a formal two party system, see William F. Freehling, *The Road to Disunions Secessionists at Bay* 1776–1854 (New York and Oxford: Oxford University Press, 1990) esp. 271–86.

4. Recent scholarship has suggested that the Vesey "conspiracy" may never have happened, and that whites connected with the trial may have deliberately altered

evidence to suggest that Congressional debates over Missouri had been its cause. See Michael P. Johnson, "Denmark Vesey and His Co-Conspirators," *William and Mary Quarterly* (October 2001), 915–976. Public reaction against the abolitionists and the demand by Southern political leaders for restrictions on free expression has received much recent attention from scholars. See Leonard L. Richards, *The Slave Power: The Free North and Southern Domination, 1780–1860* (Baton Rouge: Louisiana State University Press, 2000); William Lee Miller, *Arguing About Slavery: The Great Battle in the United States Congress* (New York: A. A. Knopf, 1996); Freehling, *Road to Disunion;* and Michael Kent Curtis, *Free Speech, "the People's Darling Privilege:" Struggles for Freedom of Expression in American History* (Durham, N.C.: Duke University Press, 2000).

5. The editor here refers to several of the most famous and controversial utopian social ideas of the mid-nineteenth century. Further information is available in Michael Fellman, *The Unbounded Frame: Freedom and Community in Nineteenth Century American Utopianism* (New Haven: Greenwood Publishing Group, 1973), and Hal D. Sears, *The Sex Radicals: Free Love in High Victorian America* (Lawrence, Kansas: University Press of Kansas, 1977). The editor's view that Northern civilization had become corrupted by these innovations was widespread among Southern intellectuals. See Jan C. Dawson, "The Puritan and the Cavalier: The South's Perception of Contrasting Traditions," *Journal of Southern History* XLIV (November 1978), 597–614.

6. Text from *The Liberator,* 6 June 1856.

7. "Resolutions of the Citizens of Martin's Depot, South Carolina," in Sumner Papers.

8. "Resolutions of the Students of Union College, Schenectady, New York," in *Ibid.*

9. See James Brewer Stewart, *Holy Warriors: The Abolitionists and American Slavery* (2d. ed., New York: Hill and Wang, 1996), and Dorothy Sterling, *Ahead of Her Time: Abby Kelley and the Politics of Antislavery* (New York: W. W. Norton & Company, Inc., 1991).

10. Text from *The Liberator,* 6 June 1856.

11. Adelaide M. Cromwell, *The Other Brahmins: Boston's Black Upper Class, 1750–1950* (Fayetteville: The University of Arkansas Press, 1994); Donald M. Jacobs, ed., *Courage and Conscience: Black and White Abolitionists in Boston* (Bloomington: Indiana University Press, 1993); and Albert J. Von Frank, *The Trials of Anthony Burns: Freedom and Slavery in Emerson's Boston* (Cambridge and London: Harvard University Press, 1998).

12. "Resolutions of the Colored Citizens of Boston," in Sumner Papers.

13. Edgefield *Advertiser,* 8 October 1856.

14. *Ibid.,* 15 October 1856.

15. James W. Stone to Charles Sumner, 22 May 1856, Sumner Papers.

16. "A Friend Indeed" to Charles Sumner, 22 May 1856, Sumner Papers.

17. W. Richardson to Charles Sumner, 24 May 1856, Sumner Papers.

18. On the complex meanings of the name Cuffy, see Freehling, *Road to Disunion,* 66–78.

19. "Cuffy" to Charles Sumner, 26 May 1856, Sumner Papers.

20. Probably a reference to the New York *Herald,* which at the time was the nation's most widely circulated paper.

21. Seaborn Jones to Preston S. Brooks, 1 June 1856, Brooks Family Papers, South Caroliniana Library.

22. Mary Rosamond Dana to Charles Sumner, 1 June 1856, Sumner Papers.

23. John D. Van Buren to Charles Sumner, 10 June 1856, Sumner Papers.

24. W. F. Holmes to Preston Brooks, 27 May 1856, Brooks Family Papers, South Caroliniana Library.

25. For a full discussion of these prints from an archival and artistic perspective see David Tatham, "Pictorial Responses to the Caning of Senator Sumner," in *American Printmaking Before 1876: Fact, Fiction, and Fantasy* (Washington: Library of Congress, 1975), 11–19.

26. Reports of the case are in the New York *Tribune*, 10 July 1856, and the *National Era*, 17 July 1856. See also *Pierce*, ed., *Memoir*, III, 487–488.

27. Washington *Star*, 9 July 1856, quoted in New York *Tribune*, 10 July 1856.

28. Wilson's speech and the recorder's summary of Butler's response are in *Congressional Globe*, 34th Congress, 1st Session, 1306; Henry Wilson to Preston Brooks, 29 May 1856, quoted in Montgomery, Alabama, *Advertiser*.

29. Charles Sumner to Joshua R. Giddings, 22 July 1856, in Palmer, ed., *Letters*.

30. Brooks's challenges are described in the New York *Tribune*, 30 May 1856 and 28 July 1856.

31. New York *Evening Post*, quoted in the New York *Tribune*, 28 July 1856.

32. "A Card," in Abbeville *Press and Banner*, 23 July 1856.

33. Vote totals are from the *Tribune Almanac for 1855*; *Congressional Quarterly Guide to U.S. Elections*, 2d ed.; and J. Dubin, ed., *U. S. Congressional Elections, 1788–1997: The Official Results*.

34. Charleston *Courier*, 7 October 1856, quoted in Mathis, "Preston Smith Brooks."

35. For a full treatment of factions within the Democratic party and the role of the territorial slavery issue in dividing it see Roy H. Nichols, *The Disruption of American Democracy:* (New York: The Free Press, 1967), esp. 25–28, 65–67.

36. *Congressional Globe*, 34th Congress, 3d session, Appendix, 108–111 (17 December 1856).

37. Brooks referred here to the Nebraska bill.

38. The "greatest military captain" he referred to here was Mexican war hero Winfield Scott, who had also been the Whig presidential candidate in 1852.

39. The lantern was one of the symbols of the Know-Nothings.

40. The national Democratic convention of 1856 was held in Cincinnati, Ohio.

41. Details of Brooks's illness and funeral are in "Hon. Preston S. Brooks," *Southern Quarterly Review* II (February 1857), 365–370; Edgefield *Advertiser*, 11 February 1857; *Congressional Globe*, 34th Congress, 3d session, 501–502 (29 January 1857); and Pierce, ed., *Memoir*, III, 521–524.

42. For tombstone symbolism and the transformation of American cemeteries see Blanche Linden-Ward, *Silent City on a Hill: Landscapes of Memory and Boston's Mount Auburn Cemetery* (Columbus: Ohio University Press, 1989); Stanley French, "The Cemetery as a Cultural Institution: The Establishment of Mount Auburn and the 'Rural Cemetery' Movement" *American Quarterly* (1974), 37–59, Aubrey Cannon, "The Historical Dimension in Mortuary Expressions of Status and Sentiment" *Current Anthropology* IV (August–October 1989), 437–458; and Barbara J. Little, et al., "Mortuary Display and Status in a Nineteenth Century Anglo-American Cemetery in Manassas, Virginia," *American Antiquity* LVII (1992), 397–418.

43. Accounts of Sumner's illness and treatments are in Pierce, ed., *Memoir*, III, 484–488, and Laura A. White, "Was Charles Sumner Shamming, 1856–1859?" *New England Quarterly* (September 1960), 291–324.

44. "Alleged Assault on Senator Sumner," 34th Congress, 1st Session, House Report 182, pp. 50–54.

45. See especially Donald, *Charles Sumner*, Part I: 336.

46. "Alleged Assault on Senator Sumner," 68–70.

47. Charles Sumner to Attorney of the District of Columbia Phillip Barton Key, 4 July 1856, in Palmer, ed., *Selected Letters*, I, 462.

48. Charles Sumner to Samuel Gridley Howe, quoted in Pierce, ed., *Memoir*, III, 507.

49. For Sumner's recuperation, see White, "Was Charles Sumner Shamming?" and Pierce, ed., *Memoirs*, 503–509. Indiana political leaders and the 1856 elections are described in Emma Lou Thornbrough, *Indiana in the Civl War Era, 1850–1880* (Indianapolis: Indiana Historical Society, 1965).

50. Charles Sumner to John Greenleaf Whittier, 20 December 1856, quoted in Pierce, *Memoir*, III, 514–515.

51. John A. Andrew to Charles Sumner, 18 December 1856, quoted in *Ibid.*, III, 518.

52. Charles Sumner to Wendell Phillips, 20 April 1858, in Palmer, ed., *Selected Letters*, I, 501.

53. Text from Pierce, ed., *Works*, IV, 406–407.

54. On derisive comments about the "vacant chair" and Sumner's medical martyrdom, see White, "Was Charles Sumner Shamming?" 312–316.

55. On the primitive but evolving state of medical science in the 1850s see Roy Porter, *The Greatest Benefit to Mankind: A Medical History of Humanity* (New York: W. W. Norton, 1997), esp. 330–333, 365–372, 431–435. On Séquard's biography and Virginia experience, see White, "Was Charles Sumner Shamming?"

56. On perceptions of Northern duplicity and its connections to fears of slave duplicity, see Freehling, *Road to Disunion.*

57. The Inner Temple was one of the main English legal organizations.

58. See especially Gradin, "Losing Control."

59. See Baum, *Civil War Party System*, 38–41, and Geinapp, *Origins of the Republican Party*, 439–448.

60. Charles Sumner to the Duchess of Argyll, 14 December 1860, in Palmer, ed., *Letters*, II, 38.

Abolition and Abolitionists, 9, 10, 28, 29, 31, 38, 39,
    40, 43, 48, 52, 53, 60, 62, 86, 117, 132, 140, 169,
    172, 173, 176, 178, 179, 182, 184, 185, 186, 194,
    205, 218
Abolition Vigilance Committee of Boston, 61
Adams, President John, 57, 64, 65, 73, 80, 102
Adams, President John Quincy, 177
Adams, Samuel, 64, 73, 80
American Revolution, 11, 13, 15, 23, 24, 29, 57–69,
    73–75, 77–78, 83–85, 108, 112, 118, 125, 158,
    169, 182, 190, 217
Appeal of the Independent Democrats, 34–39
Arms, Right to Bear, 113–114
Atchison, Sen. David, 96, 102, 105, 126, 160

Badger, Sen. George, 77
Banks, Rep. Nathaniel, 61, 134, 135, 190
Batchelder, James, 61, 62, 163
Beecher, Henry Ward, 143, 174, 180, 181
Bell, Sen. John, 171
Border Ruffians, 1, 94, 103, 105, 107
Boston Peace Society, 12
Boston, City of, 10, 11, 50, 63, 64, 73, 79, 83, 84, 158,
    169, 186, 187
Boyle, Dr. Cornelius, 143, 206, 208, 209, 214
    House Testimony of, 206
Bright, Sen. Jesse, 137, 148, 210
Brooks, Caroline Means, 27
Brooks, Hamilton, 131, 133
Brooks, Martha Means, 27, 134
Brooks, Mary Carroll, 24, 131
Brooks, Rep. Preston S.,
    Apology to Senate, 135
    Approval Meetings, 175, 178, 184, 185, 200
    Attends S.C. College, 24
    Attacks Sumner, 136, 137, 139, 141, 144, 145,
        161, 162
    Becomes Congressman, 28
    Challenges Burlingame to Duel, 199, 200
    Death of, 203
    Duel with Wigfall, 27
    Describes Caning, 131, 133, 134, 135, 151, 152
    Early History, 18, 23–27
    Expulsion from House, 132, 134, 148, 149, 151,
        152, 154, 160, 168, 178, 218
    Letters to, 192, 194
    Picture of, 24

    Remarks on Party Politics and Kansas, 201
    Remarks at Trial, 198
    Resignation Speech, 149
    Speech on Nebraska and Kansas, 28
    Tombstone and Epitaph, 203, 204, 205
    Trial, 197, 209
Brooks, Whitfield, 24, 27
Brooks's Canada Song, 200
Brown-Séquard, Dr. Charles Edward, 214, 215,
    216, 217
Bryant, William Cullen, 200
Buchanan, President James, 115, 123, 129, 186, 211
Bunker Hill, Battle of, 15, 64, 83, 112, 162
Burke, Edmund, 75, 160, 177
Burlingame, Rep. Anson, 199, 200
Burns, Anthony, 60, 62, 63, 108, 109, 182
Burr, Aaron, 102
Burt, Rep. Armistead, 28
Butler, Sen. Andrew Pickens
    Breaks Friendship with Sumner, 48, 63, 65, 67
    Early History, 18–23
    Elected to Senate, 24
    Final Nebraska Bill Speech in Response to
        Sumner, 77
    Friendship with Sumner, 33, 217
    Insulted by Sumner, 99, 117
    Nebraska Bill Speech in Reply to Sumner, 65
    Picture of, 23
    Speech on Caning Incident, 141
    Speech on the Nebraska Bill, 48

Caesar, Julius, 203
Calhoun, Sen. John C., 4, 9, 24, 127, 163, 174,
    177, 201
Campbell, Rep. Lewis D., 137, 138, 139, 203,
    208, 209
Caning
    House Majority Report, 1, 2, 4
    House Minority Report, 4
    Images of, 1, 194–197
    Reactions to, 1, 7, 9, 121, 133, 147, 157–197,
        218, 219
Cape May, New Jersey, 210
Carlyle, Thomas, 12, 17
Cass, Sen. Lewis, 106, 121, 122, 129, 171
    Response to Sumner's Kansas Speech, 122
Catiline, 96, 102, 103, 104, 105, 126, 127

Cato, 52

Channing, William Ellery, 12

Chase, Sen. Salmon P., 34, 36, 37, 38, 41, 48, 54, 61, 68, 95, 96

Cicero, 96, 126, 127

Clay, Cassius M., 182

Clay, Sen. Clement C., Jr., 50, 68, 76
  Speech Attacking Sumner, 68

Clay, Sen. Henry, 171

Clergymen of New England, Petition by, 56, 57, 58, 59, 60

Cobb, Rep. Howell, 4, 137, 185, 207

Collamer, Sen. Jacob, 96, 106

Colored Citizens of Boston, Resolutions of, 183

Comins, Rep. Linus Bacon, 153

Compromise of 1850, 16, 39, 43, 54

Cooper, Thomas, 25

Cornwallis, Gen. George, 15

Crawford, Judge Thomas, 197, 198

Creole (Slave Ship and Court Case), 12, 42

Cresson, Pennsylvania, 210, 212

Crittenden, Sen. John J., 141, 163

Cromwell, Oliver, 172

Dana, Mary Rosamond, 192, 193

Dana, Richard Henry, 192

Dante, 96

Danton, Georges, 100

Davis, Sen. Jefferson, 20, 33, 185

De Witt, Rep. Alexander, 37

Dean, Rev. Gardner, 181

Declaration of Independence, 42, 43, 44, 46, 57, 64, 78, 116, 117, 125

Democratic Party, 4, 8, 13, 16, 24, 27, 33, 34, 38, 40, 41, 54, 56, 59, 69, 85, 86, 95, 96, 100, 101, 108, 111, 113, 115, 121, 122, 124, 129, 133, 136, 139, 148, 157, 158, 162, 164, 169, 172, 173, 179, 186, 193, 196, 201, 202, 210, 217, 218

Demosthenes, 96, 160, 177

Dixon, Sen. Archibald, 34

Douglas, Sen. Stephen A., 1, 4, 33–42, 54, 55, 95–99, 100, 101, 108, 110, 111, 114, 116, 117, 121, 123, 126, 129, 130, 131, 136, 160, 162, 164, 168, 217, 218
  Insulted by Sumner, 118, 119
  Response to Sumner's Kansas Speech, 123

Duels and Dueling, 23, 26, 27, 28, 132, 134, 149, 176, 199

Edgefield County, South Carolina, 18, 19, 20, 21, 22, 23, 24, 26, 27, 133, 177, 184, 203, 218

Edmundson, Rep. Henry A., 2, 3, 5, 139, 163
  House Testimony, 139

Elections
  1824 (S.C.), 24
  1848 (Federal), 121
  1850 (Mass.), 87
  1851 (Mass.), 87
  1852 (Mass.), 87
  1853 (Mass.), 87
  1853 (S.C.), 28
  1854 (Kansas), 95
  1854 (Mass.), 84, 85, 86, 87
  1854 (S.C.), 183
  1855 (Kansas), 95, 105, 109
  1855 (Mass.), 87, 95
  1856 (Federal), 121
  1856 (Indiana), 210
  1856 (Mass.), 213
  1856 (S.C. Special Election), 200, 201
  1856 (S.C.), 186
  1857 (Mass.), 219
  1860 (Federal), 164

Emerson, Ralph Waldo, 17, 22, 175
  Speech at Concord Indignation Meeting, 176

Erie Canal, 186

Evans, Sen. Josiah, 203

Everett, Sen. Edward, 50, 52, 56, 63, 74

Fillmore, President Millard, 17

Fisk University, 18

Foster, Abby Kelley, 179, 180, 181

Foster, Stephen, 179, 180, 181, 182

Franklin, Benjamin, 101, 118

Freesoil Party, 8, 16, 29, 30, 34, 39, 84, 86, 105, 167, 179, 187, 193, 196, 200, 210, 218

French Revolution, 49

Fugitive Slave Act (1850), 16, 17, 33, 56, 57, 60, 62, 63, 65, 66, 67, 68, 71, 75, 81, 82, 85, 107, 109, 119, 125

Fugitive Slaves, 12, 20, 21, 29, 50, 60, 61, 67, 72, 76, 84, 95
  Return of, 19, 61, 64, 66, 67, 68, 70, 71, 72, 83, 125, 130

Gardenier, James, 133

Gardner, Gov. Henry J., 86, 87, 161, 219

Garlington, A. C., 183, 184, 194

Garrison, William Lloyd, 12, 179, 181, 182, 200

Gender and Language of Masculinity and Femininity, 17, 21, 23, 31, 48, 53, 62, 72, 97, 99, 117, 124, 127, 144, 149, 161, 167, 172, 173, 174, 175, 183, 184, 185, 198, 205, 218

George III, King of England, 63, 85, 113, 116

Geyer, Sen. Henry, 3, 111, 136, 140

Giddings, Rep. Joshua, 34, 37, 61, 62, 180, 181, 200

Goethe, Johann Wolfgang von, 17

Greeley, Horace, 157, 167, 173
Greenwood, Rep. Alfred, 4
Grimes, Leonard, 182, 183
Griswold, Rep. Roger, 146

Habeas Corpus, Right of, 63, 75, 119
Haiti, Revolution in, 170
Hancock, John, 64, 65, 73, 80
Harvard University, 11, 14
Hayne, Sen. Robert Y., 162
Hayward, Dr. George, 215
Henry, Patrick, 160
History, as Political Weapon, 9, 42, 51, 58, 64, 65, 66, 69,
    72, 75, 77, 79, 80, 84, 95, 108, 118, 142, 143, 158
Hoar, Sen. Samuel, 27, 73, 81
Holmes, W. F., 194
Honor, Chivalry and Degradation, Rhetoric of, 1, 23,
    25–27, 28, 29, 33, 55, 62, 68–70, 99, 100, 103,
    119–125, 127–128, 131–135, 144–150, 153, 162,
    163, 165–169, 174, 178, 181–185, 189, 195,
    198–202, 211, 218
House of Representatives
  Privileges of, 4, 5, 150
Howe, Samuel Gridley, 12, 209
Hunter, Sen. Robert M. T., 203

Illinois, State of, 41, 99, 100, 116, 130, 136, 162,
    186, 190
Indiana, State of, 148, 211
Insult, as Caning's Cause, 4, 100, 123, 131, 132, 135,
    137, 139, 140, 141, 143, 144, 146, 149, 159, 162,
    163, 165, 170, 171, 174, 178, 185, 199, 202, 216
Insurrection, Fear of Slave, 52, 170, 172

Jackson, President Andrew, 69, 71, 115, 122, 129, 145
Jefferson, President Thomas, 70, 101, 102, 104, 119
Johnson, Hon. William F., 73
Johnson, Robert, 183
Johnson, Sen. Robert W., 140
Jones, Seaborn, 192
Jones, Sen. James Chamberlain, 64
Juvenal, 48, 52

Kansas
  Petition for Statehood, 95, 114, 115, 116, 160
  Territory and State, 34, 53, 54, 87, 94, 95, 96, 97,
    98, 99, 100, 101, 102, 103, 104, 105, 107, 108,
    109, 111, 112, 113, 114, 115, 116, 117, 118, 119,
    120, 121, 122, 125, 162, 164, 167, 174, 180, 190,
    202, 210, 213
Keitt, Rep. Laurence, 5, 131, 138, 139, 195, 203
Know-Nothing (American) Party, 8, 41, 84, 85, 86,
    87, 133, 158, 161, 170, 187, 210, 218, 219

Laurens County, South Carolina, 164
Lawrence, Kansas, 103, 104, 118, 131, 165,
    167, 196
Letters to Sumner, Map of Origins, 186, 187
Lexington and Concord, Battles of, 64, 65, 162
Lieber, Francis, 25
Lincoln, President Abraham, 9, 20, 219
Linsley, Dr. Harvey, III, 211, 212
Longfellow, Henry Wadsworth, 12, 17, 193, 203
Lowell, James Russell, 96
Lyon, Rep. Matthew, 146

Madison, President James, 46
Magee, Henry, 194, 195
Mail Riots, Charleston, 72
Mallory, Sen. Stephen F., 76
Mann, Horace, 12
Marathon, Battle of, 15, 80
Marshall, Rep. Alexander K., 140
Martineau, Harriet, 12
Martin's Depot, Resolutions of the Citizens of, 178
Martyrdom, Caning as, 136, 169, 193, 214
Mason, Sen. James, 33, 44, 58, 67, 68, 69, 70, 71, 72,
    75, 76, 117, 126, 127, 129, 130, 131, 165, 185
  Debates Sumner over Northern Religion, 59
  Insulted by Sumner, 119
  Response to Sumner's Kansas Speech, 127
  Speech in Reply to Sumner, 67
Massachusetts Legislature, Resolutions of, 141, 142,
    147, 148, 151
Massachusetts, Commonwealth of, 9, 16, 48, 51, 52,
    62, 64, 66, 71, 73, 74, 77, 79, 80, 81, 82, 83, 84,
    85, 86, 87, 96, 112, 118, 122, 123, 128, 129, 144,
    147, 148, 149, 153, 159, 162, 164, 176, 185, 186,
    187, 199, 210, 213, 218
McDuffie, Gen. George, 26
McQueen, Rep. John, 185
Medical Care, 207, 208, 209, 214, 215
  Boyle, Dr. Cornelius, 143, 206, 208, 209, 214
  Brown-Séquard, Dr. Charles-Edward, 214, 215,
    216, 217
  Hayward, Dr. George, 215
  Linsley, Dr. Harvey, III, 211, 212
  Perry, Dr. Marshall S., 206, 208, 209, 211, 214
  Wister, Dr. Casper, 212, 213
Metternich, Klemmens von, 12
Mexican War, 13, 14, 16, 27
Michigan, Admission to Statehood, 115, 116,
    122, 129
Miller, Rep. John Gaines, 3, 136, 140
Milton, John (English author), 96
Missouri Compromise, 9, 34, 35, 38, 39, 40, 44, 45,
    49, 50, 54, 56, 94, 101

Morgan, Rep. Henry, 136, 138, 141, 153, 174
Morris, Robert, 17, 182, 183

Native Americans, Removal from Kansas
  Territory, 94
Nativism and Anti-Catholicism, 8, 28, 29, 41, 85,
  97, 111
Nebraska Bill, 28, 29, 33, 36, 43, 48, 54, 56, 57, 60,
  62, 73, 100, 101, 102, 116, 123, 124, 202, 210
Nell, William C., 182, 183
New England Antislavery Convention, Proceedings
  of, 180
New England Antislavery Society, 12
New England Emigrant Aid Association, 94, 95,
  110, 111
Newspapers, 28, 157, 158, 161, 163, 165
  Albany *Evening Journal*, 170, 171
  Albany, New York, *Evening Journal*, 157
  Boston *Atlas*, 158
  Boston *Bee*, 161
  Boston *Commonwealth*, 187
  Boston *Courier*, 161
  Boston *Post*, 162, 163
  Charleston *Courier*, 167, 216
  Charleston *Mercury*, 166, 184, 216
  Columbia *South Carolinian*, 184
  Detroit *Free Press*, 157
  Edgefield *Advertiser*, 20, 21, 164
  Frank Leslie's Illustrated Weekly, 195
  Laurensville *Herald*, 163, 164
  Liberator, 194
  Louisville *Journal*, 168, 169
  New Hampshire *Patriot*, 157
  New York *Evening Post*, 38, 200
  New York *Times*, 38, 138
  New York *Tribune*, 38, 157, 211, 215
  Pittsburgh *Gazette*, 41, 165, 166, 167
  Richmond *Enquirer*, 172
  Richmond *Whig*, 173, 205
  Washington *Evening Star*, 60
  Wilmington, North Carolina, *Herald*, 169

Orr, Rep. James F., 27, 197, 202
Otis, James, 64

Palmerston, Henry John Temple, Lord, 213
Palmetto Regiment, 27
Parker, Rev. Theodore, 60, 143, 180
Pennington, Rep. Alexander Cumming McWhorter,
  137, 138, 151, 209
Perry, Dr. Marshall S., 206, 208, 209, 211, 214
  House Testimony of, 208
Petition, Right of, 59, 65, 76, 77, 119, 170
Pettit, Sen. John, 43, 69, 210

Phillips, Wendell, 60, 179, 180, 181, 182, 213
Pickens, Andrew, 23
Pickens, Francis, 20, 21, 22, 28
Pierce, President Franklin M., 1, 27, 56, 60, 85, 95,
  96, 101, 103, 107, 109, 113, 116, 202, 210, 217
Pinckney, Charles, 11, 76
Pitts, Coffin, 182, 183
Platte County Self Defense Association, 94
Polk, President James K., 13, 197
Popular Sovereignty, 28, 29, 36, 101, 102, 107, 108,
  121, 201, 217
Prigg v. Pennsylvania, 81
Proslavery Argument, 25, 28, 30, 32, 41, 48, 119

Quitman, Rep. John, 203
Quixote, Don, 99, 100, 162

Race and Racial Hierarchies, 20, 22, 29, 30, 31, 40,
  49, 50, 53, 74, 78, 80, 86, 95, 118, 125, 185, 186,
  191, 192
Railroads, 8, 11, 94, 200
Reeder, Gov. Andrew, 95, 109, 167
Religion and Religious Organizations, 8, 10, 11, 20,
  22, 25, 30, 36, 37, 52, 56–60, 64, 85, 97, 104,
  108, 117, 121, 161, 165, 172, 180–181, 183,
  200, 203
Republican Party, 8, 9, 17, 34, 41, 84, 85, 86, 87, 95,
  96, 99, 133, 134, 138, 148, 153, 157, 158, 161,
  162, 163, 165, 168, 170, 173, 179, 181, 182, 184,
  185, 187, 190, 192, 193, 196, 197, 203, 206, 210,
  213, 214, 219
Rock, J. S., 183
Rockwell, Sen. Julius, 63, 86
Russell, Lord John, 12, 213
Rutledge, John, 76
Ryan, Henry, WPA Narrative, 19

Salamis, Battle of, 80
Savage, Rep. John, 203
Senate
  Picture of, 195
  Privileges of, 5, 6, 134, 135, 147, 150, 159, 162, 173
Seward, Sen. William Henry, 41, 48, 78, 96, 114, 116,
  122, 137, 170, 171
Shakespeare, William, 32, 96, 111
Shannon, Gov. Wilson, 167
Sidney, Algernon, 183
Simms, William Gilmore, 23
Simonton, James, 138
  House Testimony of, 138
Sims, Thomas (Fugitive Slave Case), 17
Slave Power Conspiracy, 37, 58, 85, 95, 96, 97, 98,
  100, 108, 109, 114, 117, 120, 125, 127, 128, 129,
  158, 161, 165, 171, 196, 197, 213, 218, 219

Slavery

Conditions of, 13, 20, 21, 22, 29, 30, 31, 35, 37, 53, 70, 78, 121, 180, 183

In Edgefield, 18, 19, 20

Fear of Insurrection, 52, 75

In Kansas Territory, 94, 95, 103

In Massachusetts, 50, 51, 65, 73, 75, 77, 78, 80, 84

Political Aspects, 19, 29, 30, 31, 32, 33, 34, 35, 39, 46, 54, 58, 83, 85, 98, 99, 101, 102, 105, 106, 107, 119, 173, 177, 193, 201

Slidell, Sen. John, 137

Smith, Rep. Gerrit, 37

South Carolina College, 23, 24, 26, 134

Report on Brooks Expulsion, 26

South Carolina, State of, 4, 7, 19, 26, 28, 69, 72, 73, 74, 75, 76, 77, 78, 79, 80, 81, 84, 99, 100, 117, 118, 119, 127, 131, 135, 136, 138, 139, 144, 148, 159, 161, 162, 163, 167, 169, 176, 178, 179, 183, 184, 192, 218

Speech, Freedom of, 4, 5, 41, 60, 74, 106, 107, 128, 147, 148, 159, 166, 170, 172, 173, 178, 179, 180, 182, 183

de Stael, Anne Louise Germaine Necker, Madame, 17

Stamp Act, 58, 63, 64, 65, 72, 80, 83, 84

State Rights, 63, 73, 179, 201

Story, Chief Justice Joseph, 11

Stowe, Harriet Beecher, 56

Stuart, Sen. Charles Edward, 47, 79, 82

Sumner, Charles P., 11

Sumner, George, 209

Sumner, Job, 11

Sumner, Relief Jacob, 11

Sumner, Sen. Charles S.

Attacked by Brooks, 131, 132

Breaks Friendship with Butler, 65, 66, 67

Crime Against Kansas Speech, 1, 28, 63, 67, 68, 69, 94, 96, 97, 100, 108, 112, 113, 114, 116, 117, 170, 218

Criticized by Abolitionists, 179–181

Describes Caning, 136

Early History, 10–13

Election to Senate, 17, 55, 86, 176

Final Protest Against the Nebraska Bill, 56

Friendship with Butler, 33, 217

House Testimony, 136

Indignation Meetings, 175

Injuries and Recuperation, 143, 198, 205–217

Insults Butler, 117, 142, 163, 169, 218

Insults Butler and Douglas, 99

Insults Douglas, 129, 130

Landmark of Freedom Speech, 42

Letter to the People of Massachusetts, 213

Letters to, 189, 190, 191, 193

Map of Letter Origins, 186, 187

Picture of, 10

Reaction to Death of Brooks, 203

Reports on his Recuperation, 210

Response to Kansas Speech Responses, 129

Returns to Senate, 219

Speech on Petition to Repeal the Fugitive Slave Act, 63

Speech in Reply to Assailants and Oath to Support the Constitution, 70

True Grandeur of Nations Speech, 13

Telegraph, 8, 82, 103, 157, 161

Territories, Debate Over, 9, 28, 29, 34, 36, 37, 40, 42, 94, 95, 101, 114, 201

Territories, Debate Over Slavery in, 9, 18

Thackeray, William Makepeace, 213

Thermopylae, Battle of, 80

Thornwell, James Henley, 25

Tocqueville, Alexis de, 213

Toombs, Sen. Robert, 136, 152, 203

Transcendentalists and Transcendentalism, 17, 175

Trumbull, Sen. Lyman, 96

Tyler, President John, 12

Union College, Student Resolutions, 178

United States Constitution, 4, 5, 6, 7, 9, 15, 30, 33, 36, 39, 40, 46, 63, 64, 66, 67, 68, 71, 73, 74, 76, 79, 81, 83, 84, 98, 99, 106, 110, 114, 115, 116, 119, 121, 125, 126, 127, 128, 130, 143, 149, 150, 151, 153, 159, 169, 170, 181, 186, 201, 217

Sumner's Oath to Uphold, 62, 67, 68, 69, 70, 71, 72, 83, 97, 125, 126, 129, 149, 210

Ursuline Convent Riot, 85

Vacant Chair, 146, 205, 213, 214

Van Buren, John, 193

Van Buren, President Martin, 12

Virgil (Roman author), 96

Waddell, Moses, Academy of, 23, 24

Wade, Rep. Edward, 37

Wade, Sen. Benjamin F., 48

Walker, William, 196

Warren, Joseph, 64, 80

Washington, Booker T., 20

Washington, Gen. George, 9, 15, 47, 62, 101, 119, 121, 144

Webster, Sen. Daniel, 12, 16, 17, 160, 162, 171, 176, 177

Weed, Thurlow, 157

Whig Party, 8, 16, 33, 34, 38, 40, 41, 56, 84, 85, 86,
    124, 148, 158, 161, 162, 168, 169, 205, 206,
    207, 210
  Conscience Whigs, 16
  Cotton Whigs, 16, 17
Whittier, John Greenleaf, 17, 213
Wigfall, Sen. Louis T., 26, 27
Wilberforce, Samuel, 48
Wilson, Gov. John Lyde, 23

Wilson, Sen. Henry, 86, 96, 137, 142, 146, 163, 180,
    181, 199, 210, 211, 212
  Speech on Caning Incident, 147
Winthrop, Rep. Robert, 16
Wister, Dr. Casper, 212, 213
Worcester, Massachusetts, Reactions to Caning, 187
Wordsworth, William, 12
WPA ex-Slave Narratives, 18, 19
Wright, Sen. Silas, 171